Buffalo Bill's
British Wild West

ALAN GALLOP

The
History
Press

This book is dedicated to my family and to
Major John M. Burke,
first of the really great P.R. men,
who blazed a trail I found easy to follow . . .

First published 2001
This edition first published 2009

The History Press
The Mill, Brimscombe Port
Stroud, Gloucestershire, GL5 2QG
www.thehistorypress.co.uk

British Library Cataloguing in Publication Data.
A catalogue record for this book is available from the British Library.

ISBN 978 0 7524 5060 5

Typesetting and origination by The History Press
Printed in Great Britain

CONTENTS

Buffalo Bill (seated centre) and his cowboys, photographed by James E. Hunt in the London Olympia arena in 1903. Front row (left to right): Jonnie Franz, Billie Burns, Joe Esquivel, Buffalo Bill, Tony Esquivel, Fred Burns, Ed Phillips, William McCloud. Second row: Thad Sewder, Tom Webb, Ed Dollard, Vill Merrill, Robert Mason, Billie Craver, Burt Schenek, Andrew Bellknap. Third row (back row): Silas Crompton, Clarence Baker, Tom Isabell and Harry Brennan. (Denver Public Library)

PREFACE TO
YET ANOTHER BOOK ABOUT
BUFFALO BILL

I may walk it, or 'bus it, or hansom it: still
I am faced with the features of Buffalo Bill.
Every hoarding is plastered, from East-end to West,
With his hat, coat, and countenance, lovelocks and vest.

Ode to Buffalo Bill, *The Globe*, 1887

More books have probably been written about Colonel William F. Cody – 'Buffalo Bill' – than about Sir Winston Churchill, Princess Diana and President John F. Kennedy put together. There are hundreds of them if autobiographies, biographies, personal reminiscences, 'dime' novels, story and comic books produced in America and Britain between 1869 and 1959 are taken into account. So why the need for another?

Factual books about Cody's life usually focus on Buffalo Bill's Wild West, his brilliant recreation of life and scenes from America's vanishing frontier, which played to millions of people in America and Europe for over 30 years. Apart from an occasional chapter or short reference, however, little detailed mention is made of Cody's four tours of Victorian and Edwardian Britain with his company of cowboys, Indians,* western girls and 'rough riders of the world'. The story of his adventures with Kings, Queens, commoners and the not-so-common in an alien country deserves to be told in depth, with the American section of his life taking second place for once.

Amazingly, many of today's Americans have never heard of Buffalo Bill. British people – and until recently I was one of them – believe Cody to be a fictional character from television, cinema or comics; someone like Clark Kent, Sherlock Holmes, James Bond or a person whose life was given the Hollywood treatment and re-written for entertainment (which has certainly been the scenario in Cody's case, thanks to the way his own life was chronicled in print and on the silver screen).

I bumped into Buffalo Bill by accident in a public telephone booth at London's Earls Court. After dialling a number and waiting for an answer, I looked above the call booth, searching for nothing in particular. My eyes fell on a metal wall plaque

* Native Americans.

carrying an engraving of a man with a goatee beard, long hair and wearing a large hat. Before the number was answered, I had a chance to read:

'Buffalo Bill's Wild West opened at Earls Court, May 9 1887 – the first appearance of the Wild West outside of the American continent coincided with Queen Victoria's Golden Jubilee . . .' The ringing stopped and the call was answered – but by now I was intrigued and told the person at the end of the line that I would call back later. I replaced the receiver and read the rest of the plaque:

'. . . the show was so well received it remained for over 300 performances – two of them "command performances" for Queen Victoria.'

The plaque went on to explain the origins of the show in North Platte, Nebraska in 1882 and how Cody had become 'a symbol of the most glamorous and colourful era in US history. He literally created and shipped a sample of the "old west" to centres of population around the world, giving millions of Americans and Europeans an opportunity to view at first hand a part of American history that had captured the popular imagination.'

The information on the plaque was enough to send me away wanting to know more and *Buffalo Bill's British Wild West* is the result of that research. Few books by or about Cody are currently in print in Britain and the United States. Newspaper archives, however, are full of eyewitness accounts of how he came, saw, and conquered England, Wales and Scotland during the time of Queen Victoria, King Edward VII and the great days of the old British Empire. To gather material for this book I have referred to over 800 different British, Welsh and Scottish newspapers and magazines from those periods and examined numerous personal letters, journals, private papers and official documents in private and public collections on both sides of the Atlantic. As a result, much of the story told in this book about Buffalo Bill and the people he came into contact with appears in print for the first time.

For readers 'new' to Buffalo Bill – and I expect that to be many – I have included sections about his life in America, before, between and after the British tours. To appreciate Cody the man, his private and public persona, his successes and failures, it is necessary to fill the gaps between in order to bring him back to life once again on the following pages.

Finally, some terms and sources used in the book. In describing the Native Americans who travelled across Europe and America with Buffalo Bill, I have frequently resorted to use of the traditional 'Indians', although I am of course aware that, particularly in the United States, this term nowadays tends to give some offence. This is not my intention; however, I was keen to preserve the historical flavour of the book. I have quoted liberally, too, from contemporary letters and newspaper articles whose patronising tone at the time was quite breathtaking. Readers need not take offence from this, but merely marvel that such attitudes could ever have prevailed in 'liberal' Western society. The spelling and grammar of these too have been kept as 'native' as my editor would allow, demonstrating that progress has also been made in the field of education over the past 100 years or so.

ACKNOWLEDGEMENTS

A great many people provided me with assistance in gathering material for *Buffalo Bill's British Wild West* and I am grateful to them all, especially:

Victor Bryant, Archivist at Earls Court–Olympia, who was my first port of call for research and who set me off on Cody's British train; Gail Cameron, assistant curator for Later London History and Collections at the Museum of London; Andrew Kirk at the Theatre Museum; Mr Michael Bayley of Maidenhead, Berkshire, Mr Jim Carey of Slough, Berkshire, and Mr Roger Partridge of Surbiton, Surrey, who generously shared their family Cody memorabilia with me; Mr Bryan Mickleburgh, a talented artist and western historian of Hadley, Essex for allowing me to examine and reproduce documents about *The Buffalo Bill Line*; Pamela Clark at the Royal Archives Collection Trust at Windsor Castle for providing me with material from Queen Victoria's private journals; Hugh Alexander at the Public Records Office Image Library, Kew; Mr Nate Salsbury of New Bern, North Carolina, for information about his grandfather; Eleanor M. Gehres and Kathy Swan at the Denver Public Library (Western History/Genealogy Department); Julie Logan and the Darke County Historical Society at the Garst Museum, Greenville, Ohio, and Bess Edwards, President of the Annie Oakley Foundation, Greenville, Ohio, for material on Annie Oakley; Susan Brady at the Beinecke Rare Book and Manuscript Library, Yale University for material on Nate Salsbury; Steve Friesen at the Buffalo Bill Museum at Lookout Mountain, Denver, Colorado for material on Johnnie Baker; Sam Maddra of Glasgow University and Maire Noonan of the Art Gallery Museum, Kelvingrove, for material on Glasgow's 'ghost dance' shirt; Robert Hale Ltd for allowing me to reproduce an excerpt from Godfrey James's book *London – the Western Reaches* (1950); my enthusiastic editors at Sutton Publishing, Jane Crompton and Paul Ingrams, whose ideas about style and design have contributed a great deal to 'the look' of the book; Barry J. Hughes for his enthusiasm, total support and belief in this book and last – but not least – the fantastic, always helpful and enthusiastic staff at the British Library's Newspaper Library at Colindale, London NW9, without whom . . .

Overture

A VERY BRITISH AFFAIR

Well, Eighty-Seven at last then is here,
The Year of Rejoicing, the Jubilee Year!
Omens of peace, may they find full fulfilling!
With loyal good will every bosom is thrilling.
Everyone hopes an irradiant Gloria
May shine on the Fiftieth Year of Victoria.

Punch, January 1887

Britain was full of expectation during the early months of 1887. Her Majesty Victoria, Queen of Great Britain and Ireland and Empress of India had been on the throne for half a century – most of that time spent out of the public spotlight in mourning for her husband and consort, Prince Albert of Saxe-Coburg and Gotha, who died of typhoid in 1861, aged 42.

Mounting pressure from politicians, the press and public had forced the 68- year-old monarch to take a more public role in life again, something she reluctantly agreed to do on the occasion of her Golden Jubilee in 1887.

It was decreed that the entire year marking one of the greatest reigns in history would be one of celebration, climaxing in festivities and public holidays. It would include street parades through London, with Victoria herself in a carriage as its centrepiece – the first time she would be seen by so many subjects for over 25 years. There would be a Thanksgiving Service at Westminster Abbey, picnics, parties, grand balls, sporting and artistic events plus an extended holiday weekend during the month of June offering a chance for some fun.

Most of Europe's crowned heads, along with Presidents, Prime Ministers and potentates from large and small nations, planned to be in London for the Jubilee. Half of Europe's crowned heads already claimed connections with Queen Victoria through marriage, so the presence of Kings, Kaisers, Emperors, Queens, Princes, Princesses, Marquises, Grand Dukes and their equally Grand Duchesses was assured. A visit to London in June 1887 would demonstrate their close ties with Britain and allegiance to the most powerful nation on earth.

Victoria's Jubilee was to be a very British affair. Foreigners were welcome to attend, witness, and marvel – but only from a distance. The event was a celebration of everything British; industrial power, artistic achievements, military victories and Imperial domination. It was an opportunity for the rest of the world to pay homage to the lady who had been dubbed 'the widow of Windsor' and who sat at the head of an Empire of tens of millions, most of whom would never see the plump little woman in black sitting on her golden throne.

But there was an exception. Without seeking anyone's official permission, the United States of America announced its intention to send a large delegation to the festivities. Britain's 'American cousins' planned to celebrate the Jubilee in a unique way, giving tens of thousands of Britons flocking to London for the event a special transatlantic treat.

Supported by a large body of influential politicians and businessmen (including Lord Randolph Churchill and his American-born wife, Jennie), the event was to be a showplace for America's own achievements, inventions and resources. It was designed to demonstrate that the Yankees were every bit as good – perhaps better and even more advanced – than the British.

London was told to prepare itself for 'a six-months long celebration of America and its achievements . . .'

What the Americans planned for London was a unique 'American Exhibition' right in the heart of Britain's capital, showing off everything that they claimed to lead the world with at the time. It was set to rival Prince Albert's own Great Exhibition of 1851, held in Hyde Park.

The American Exhibition was to be more than a trade fair presented by enterprising sellers for potential buyers. Entertainment, attractions, music, fine arts, food, drink and fun would also surround what the *Illustrated London News* predicted would be 'a complete collection of the productions of the soil, and of the mines and the manufactures of the United States, than has ever yet been shown in England at any international exhibition.' London was told to prepare itself for 'a six-months long celebration of America and its achievements, transplanted three thousand miles from the New World into the heart of an old one.'

News about the American Exhibition was enthusiastically received. The *Illustrated London News* reported:

. . . it is an idea worthy of that thorough-going and enterprising people. We frankly and gladly allow that there is a natural and sentimental view of the design, which will go far to obtain for it a hearty welcome in England. The progress of the United States, now the largest community of the English race on the face of the earth, though not in political union with Great Britain, yet intimately connected with us by social sympathies, by a common language and literature, by ancestral traditions and many centuries of a common history, by much remaining similarity of civil institutions, laws, morals, and manners, by the same forms of religion, by the same attachment to the principles of order and freedom, and by the mutual interchange of benefits in a vast commerce and in the materials and sustenance of their staple industries, is a proper subject of congratulation . . . And we take it kindly of the great kindred people of the United States, that they now send such a magnificent representation to the Fatherland, determined to take some part in celebrating the Jubilee of Her Majesty the Queen.

The publication stated that the idea for an American Exhibition had been three years in the making, and: 'after much thought and toil and the expenditure of many thousands of pounds, at length it assumed a definite shape . . . And Londoners and visitors from the country will be able to enjoy the results, in what promises to be one of the greatest, most original, and most instructive of similar Exhibitions.'

Advance information published in other British newspapers also revealed that the sole imported Jubilee event would include something called:

Buffalo Bill's Wild West Exhibition . . . The preparations for this unique entertainment have been very extensive; they were made under the supervision of Major J.M. Burke, general manager of the Wild West. This remarkable exhibition has created a furore in America, and the reason is easy to understand. It is not a circus, nor indeed is it acting at all in a theatrical sense; but an exact reproduction of daily scenes in frontier life, as experienced and enacted by the very people who now form the Wild West Company . . . It could only be possible for such a remarkable undertaking to be carried out by a remarkable man; and the Hon. W.F. Cody, known as 'Buffalo Bill,' guide, scout, hunter, trapper, Indian fighter and legislator is a remarkable man. He is a perfect horseman, an unerring shot, a man of magnificent presence and physique, ignorant of the meaning of fear or fatigue; his life is a history of hairbreadth escapes, and deeds of daring, generosity, and self-sacrifice, which compare very favourably with the chivalric actions of romance, and he has not been inappropriately designated the 'Bayard of the Plains'.

The British would take the American hero to their hearts for the next 17 years

This and other articles provided British newspaper readers with their first encounter with the name of Colonel William Frederick Cody – 'Buffalo Bill' – although readers of cheaply produced 'dime' novels published in America and exported to Britain needed no introduction. The British would take the American hero to their hearts for the next 17 years and remember him fondly for generations afterwards. Cody was already a household name in America, a dime novel superstar, heroic actor playing himself in theatricals about fighting savage Indians, a frontiersman, army scout and buffalo hunter.

Now he was coming to London in the role which had made him so famous at home, as a showman reproducing life in America's untamed west for folks living in the civilised east who had never seen genuine Indians or hard-living cowboys, ridden a stagecoach, witnessed sharpshooters in action or thrilled as a bronco buster hung on for life to the back of a wild mustang. Throughout the late Victorian and Edwardian era, he would imspire *Punch* cartoons, a souvenir industry and possibly some of the worst poetry ever written.

John Robinson Whitley, President of the American Exhibition, said that Buffalo Bill was: 'every bit as much a genuine product of American soil as Edison's telephones and Pullman's railway cars.'

But who exactly was William Frederick Cody and was the excitement surrounding him really worth all the fuss?

'Yours Truly – W.F. Cody – Buffalo Bill.' (Pencil portrait by H.S. Hopwood for *Black & White* magazine, 16 December 1887)

ENTER BUFFALO BILL

Strike the tent! The sun has risen,
Not a vapour streaks the dawn,
And the frosted prairie brightens
To the eastward, far and wan.
Prime afresh the trusty rifle,
Sharpen well the hunting spear,
For the frozen earth is trembling,
And the noise of hoofs I hear.

'Buffalo Hunting Song'
from *More Adventures with Buffalo Bill*

THE GENUINE ARTICLE – WILLIAM F. CODY'S BIRTH AND BOYHOOD –
A HOSTILE INDIAN ENCOUNTER – BOY WONDER OF THE PONY EXPRESS –
'A DISSOLUTE AND RECKLESS LIFE' – STAGECOACH DRIVER – MISS LOUISA
FREDERICI – HEADING WEST WITH 'WILD BILL' HICKOCK – GEORGE
ARMSTRONG CUSTER – ROME IS (ALMOST) BUILT IN A DAY – BUFFALO
HUNTING FOR THE KANSAS PACIFIC RAILROAD – CHIEF OF SCOUTS – THE
BUFFALO BILL 'LOOK'

The man known to millions as 'Buffalo Bill' was a genuine western article. He was named William Frederick Cody and born near the Mississippi in LeClair, Scott County, Iowa, on 26 February 1846 to Isaac and Mary Ann Cody. Will, as he was known to his pioneering parents, was the couple's fourth child. Four more followed. The first six years of his life were spent on his parents' farm, 'Napsinekee Place' – an American Indian name.

When Will was seven, the family moved to LeClair itself before Isaac took them across the plains to the unsettled territory of Kansas, where Congress had allowed permanent settlement in Indian territory. They travelled in horse-drawn prairie schooner wagons and a carriage. The family claimed land in the Salt Creek Valley, near Fort Leavenworth, where young Will saw 'vast numbers of white-covered wagons' pushing on even further west towards Utah and California.

Isaac traded with Kickapoo Indians, helped survey new towns and encouraged abolitionist settlers to move to Kansas to start new lives. His outspoken anti-slavery sentiments made him an enemy of pro-slavery vigilantes. While addressing a public meeting at a Kansas general store in 1854, he was wounded in the lung during a knife attack by a pro-slavery fanatic.

The Cody home became a refuge for freedom-loving emigrants, who filled up the family house and pitched their tents in its garden. In 1857, a severe outbreak of measles and scarlet fever killed four guests. In a bid to help, Isaac ran from one tent to another in freezing rain, doing what he could to assist the sick. He caught a severe chill which, combined with after-effects from earlier injuries, eventually killed him.

Mary Ann was now left alone to raise seven children – older brother Samuel having died after a riding accident at the age of 12 in 1852. At age 11, Will became head of the Cody household and its main breadwinner. Young Will learned to ride farm horses and by age eight he owned two ponies – 'Dolly' and 'Prince' – which his father had bought during an expedition in which the young child had his first experience camping out, sleeping under the stars and meeting native Indians who came into camp to trade furs for clothing, tobacco and sugar.

Many years later in his first autobiography, Will wrote: 'All of these incidents were full of excitement and romance to my youthful mind . . . and which no doubt had a great influence on shaping my course in future years. My love of hunting and scouting, and life on the plains generally, was the result of my early surroundings.' By this time, Will's education had consisted of primitive schooling, which had taught him the basics of writing and reading, but little else. By age 11, his formal education was over for good when it fell to him to support his family by getting a job.

Mary Ann persuaded the overland freighting firm of Russell, Majors and Waddell to give her son work as a messenger carrying dispatches from the Leavenworth office to the fort three miles away. Spotting his potential and ability to handle a horse, Will's employers gave him more important duties to perform, paying the boy a grown man's wages 'because he can ride a pony just as well as any man can'. He was paid $40 each month to herd cattle following wagons rolling west.

Will had his first encounter with hostile Indians before he was age 12 and claimed to have killed one in a moonlight attack on his wagon train. He could now handle a gun like a marksman. Two years later he was the 'boy wonder' of the Pony Express, an elite band of daring horsemen who sped mail between Missouri and California in ten days. Will's first route was a 45-mile stretch from Julesburg, where he would ride 15 miles non-stop before exchanging his horse for a fresh one and riding onwards to the next relay station.

'He can ride a pony just as well as any man can.'

Two months later, he was assigned a 116-mile run between Red Buttes on the North Platte to the Three Crossings of the Sweetwater River in Nebraska – dangerous Indian country. One day Will rode into Three Crossings to find his relief rider had been killed in a drunken fight. As no replacement was available, he climbed back into the saddle, rode a further 76 miles to the Pony Express station at Rocky Ridge where he passed on westbound mail and received eastbound shipments to take back to Red Buttes. The round trip was 384 miles, achieved in 21 hours and 30 minutes – the longest Pony Express journey ever made by one rider before the new telegraph service brought the operation to an abrupt halt in 1861 after less than two years.

Will had now become Bill – or Billy – to his friends, who included the famous scouts Jim Bridger and Kit Carson and fellow Pony Express rider James Butler (later 'Wild Bill') Hickock. He remained Will to his family, to whom he returned in 1861 when his mother became ill. She died of consumption shortly afterwards. Will and sister Julia were at her side.

The two oldest Cody children were given the task of bringing up the remaining siblings, aided by Al Goodman whom Julia had married shortly before her mother's death. Julia and Al became guardians of the remaining children, although for the rest of Will's life, Julia became his 'mother-sister', and they remained in touch, even when separated by thousands of miles.

In his own words, Will now 'entered upon a dissolute and reckless life – to my shame be it said – and associated with gamblers, drunkards, and bad characters generally . . . and was becoming a hard case.'

Will had promised his mother that he would never join the United States Army while she was alive, but within days of her death and 'under the influence of bad whisky, I awoke to find myself a soldier with the Seventh Kansas. I did not remember how or when I had enlisted, but I saw I was in for it, and that it would not do for me to endeavour to back out.'

His 18-month spell as a soldier during the closing months of the Civil War was not distinguished, despite claims that he served as a spy gathering intelligence for the Union cause and 'skirmishing around the country with the rest of the army' as a private soldier.

 Once out of uniform in 1865, 19-year-old Bill Cody became a stagecoach driver on a route between Kearney and Plum Creek. He had also: 'Made up my mind to capture the heart of Miss Louisa Frederici, whom I greatly admired and in whose charming society I spent many a pleasant hour. . . . Her lovely face, her gentle disposition and her graceful manners won my admiration and love; and I was not slow in declaring my sentiments to her.'

Bill met Louisa – Lulu – while working as a hospital orderly in St Louis earlier in the year. The daughter of an immigrant from Europe, Lulu had been educated by nuns and had become a fine dressmaker. Her background and temperament were very different from the 20-year-old former cattle drover, Pony Express rider, and self-confessed 'hard case' now knocking on her parents' door in St Louis!

The couple were married in March 1866 after Bill had obtained written permission from Julia and Al Goodman and given Lulu an assurance that he would quit the plains and settle into a quiet life. He later reflected: 'From that time to this I have always thought that I have made a most fortunate choice for a life partner'. There would be later times when Buffalo Bill Cody would feel differently about the lady who had just become Mrs Cody.

Lulu and Bill's marriage was not made in heaven – as the new bride was soon to discover when, an hour after their wedding, they left St Louis by steamboat to live at Julia and Al Goodman's ranch upriver in Salt Creek Valley, Kansas. This would be Lulu's first taste of country life, and she made it clear that she did not care for it.

'Under the influence of bad whisky, I awoke to find myself a soldier with the Seventh Kansas.'

Bill and Lulu rented a large house, which they turned into a hotel, called the Golden Rule. Reasoning behind the name was never clear, but Bill considered himself a good landlord who knew how to run a hotel, even if his own golden rule was to throw drinking parties for friends every night, dishing out free whisky and rarely charging money for rooms.

His sister Helen wrote later: 'Will radiated hospitality, and his reputation as a lover of his fellow man got so widely abroad that travellers without money and without price would go miles out of their way to put up at his tavern. Socially he was an irreproachable landlord; financially his shortcomings were deplorable.'

The newly-weds gave up the hotel business after six months. 'It proved too tame employment for me,' claimed Bill. 'And again I sighed for the freedom of the plains. Believing that I could make more money out West on the frontier than I could at Salt Creek Valley, I sold out the Golden Rule and started alone for Saline, Kansas, which was then the end of the track of the Kansas Pacific Railway, which was at that time being built across the plains.'

Bill kissed newly pregnant Lulu goodbye and headed west. Lulu stayed with other Cody family members before returning to her parents in St Louis, her first separation from Bill, who for the rest of his life never spent more than six months at a time at home with his wife.

An early photograph of Louisa Frederici Cody, William F. Cody's 23-year-old wife, taken around the time of their marriage in St Louis in 1866. (The American Collection)

On the way out west, Bill ran into old friend 'Wild Bill' Hickock, who was scouting for the government. He told Bill that more scouts were needed to help the US Army police the Arapaho, Cheyenne, Sioux and Comanche Indians who were resisting attempts to drive a railway track across their territory and onwards towards the Pacific. Bill followed Hickock to Fort Ellsworth, 'where I had no difficulty in obtaining employment'.

That winter Bill scouted the Great Plains for the army and the following spring had his first encounter with the army's most celebrated, courageous, impulsive and vain army officer – General George Armstrong Custer, who at age 23 was the Union army's youngest general and famed for his daring raids behind Confederate army lines.

Custer needed a guide to escort him and ten others across 65 miles of prairie to Fort Larned and Bill Cody was given the job. The journey was made successfully and Custer offered the young scout more work whenever he wanted it. They became firm friends, although it would be some time before Bill could take up Custer's offer. Hunting work for the railway, snaking its way across mountains and prairies at the rate of two miles a day, beckoned.

On the journey to the Kansas Pacific railhead, Bill learned of new towns springing up like mushrooms along the railway route. A man called William Rose told the young scout about a town he was thinking of laying out in a prime location to the west of Big Creek, near Fort Hays. The railroad company planned to lay tracks on its route towards California and build a depot complete with locomotive sheds, repair workshops and creating jobs for hundreds of labourers. Rose invited Bill to become a partner in the enterprise and: 'Thinking it would be a grand thing to be half-owner of a town, I at once accepted his proposition.' Once it was completed and populated, Cody and Rose planned to open a saloon and general store, make a mountain of money and enjoy an easy life.

'We gave the new town the old and historical name of Rome', wrote Bill, 'and as a "starter" donated lots to anyone who would build on them, but reserved corner lots and others which were best located for ourselves.'

Bill sent for Lulu and shortly after arriving from St Louis, she gave birth to a daughter they called Arta. The Cody family lived in hastily built quarters at the rear of the Cody & Rose general store, which was taking shape just as hastily as the town itself.

James Butler Hickock (1837–76) – later known as 'Wild Bill' – stagecoach driver, Pony Express rider, lawman and an early friend of William F. Cody. (Gregg White Collection)

The ancient city of Rome was not built in a day, but the new frontier railway depot town with the same name 'sprang up as if by magic, and in less than one month we had two hundred frame and log houses, three or four stores, several saloons and one good hotel. Rose and I already considered ourselves millionaires and thought we had the world by the tail', recalled Bill.

And so they had – until the Kansas Pacific Railroad got to hear about it. Angry at not being invited to become partners in the scheme, the railroad management announced they would build their own depot town, Hays City, a mile away from Rome. 'A ruinous stampede from our place was the result', remembered Bill. 'People who had built in Rome came to the conclusion that they had built in the wrong place; they began pulling down their buildings and moving them over to Hays City, and in less than three days our flourishing city had dwindled down to the little store that Rose and I built. . . . Three days before, we had considered ourselves millionaires; on that morning we looked around and saw that we were reduced to the ragged edge of poverty. . . . Thus ends the brief history of the "Rise, Decline and Fall" of modern Rome.'

Lulu – pregnant again – and baby Arta were packed off back to St Louis while Bill reluctantly put his idea of becoming a millionaire on hold for the time being. Many more new business ideas and 'get-rich-quick schemes' would follow in later years. Some would be wildly successful. Others were glorious failures. But for the time being he reverted to his original plan of working as a hunter of fresh meat to feed an army of 1,200 track layers, graders, section hands and engineers slowly pushing the railway line west. Every day, construction gangs needed to be fed huge quantities of cheap, fresh meat and the vast buffalo herds roaming the plains over which the railway crossed provided the diet. The only problem was the 'very troublesome' Indians who made it difficult for railwaymen to get the quantities of meat required day after day.

Bill was hired for $500 per month to hunt and kill not less than 12 buffalo each day. Only the hindquarters and rump were to be brought back to camp. Because of the close proximity of Indian camps, this was considered dangerous work and buffalo hunters were expected to ride five to ten miles away from the railway track to locate herds. Only one other man driving a wagon could go along on the daily hunt for meat.

'It was at this time that the very appropriate name of "Buffalo Bill" was conferred upon me by the road-hands. It has stuck to me ever since, and I have never been ashamed of it,' Bill later wrote about this period in his life.

During his employment as a hunter for the railroad company – a period of less than eighteen months – Bill claimed to have shot 4,280 buffalo – 69 in one afternoon. He said that the best way of bringing the massive animals down was to ride his horse, Brigham, to the right front of a herd, shoot down the leaders with his 50-calibre Springfield rifle (nicknamed Lucretia Borgia), and crowd their followers to the left until they began to run in a circle, when he would kill all the animals required.

George Armstrong Custer (1839–76), the most famous soldier in the history of the American West and the army's youngest-ever Major General, travelled with Buffalo Bill on early hunting safaris with sportsmen and rich 'toffs' from the east. (Gregg White Collection)

While the railroad companies were laying tracks between Nebraska and the Pacific, anything between 40 and 60 million buffalo roamed the plains of the United States and Canada. Indians depended on the herds for their existence, not just for food and clothing but also for hides to build their tepees, sinews for threads, horns and bones for tools and buffalo dung for fuel. The railway was responsible for buffalo destruction on a massive scale, bringing the species close to extinction, using it as a source of food for labourers and later as a means of transporting hunters and eastern-based sportsmen out west to kill them for the heads and hides. The railway also became an economical way of shipping hides east for fashionable fur hats and coats, horns for buttons and bones to manufacture fertiliser.

By the time Buffalo Bill's Wild West was thrilling Victorian London audiences, herds had been reduced to a fraction of what they had once been. With the passing of the buffalo went the nomadic way of life of the Plains Indians who were reduced to dependence on government handouts on their reservations.

In later years Buffalo Bill himself was horrified by the destruction of the animal he had helped to wipe out in such vast numbers, unaware at the time that his contribution to their mass slaughter would almost remove the buffalo from the face of the earth. With the creation of his Wild West entertainment, Bill later became a buffalo preserver and by 1890 his herd – described in his show programme as 'this monarch of the plains' – was the third largest in captivity; a herd of 'healthy specimens of this hardy bovine in connection with their instructive exhibition . . . interesting as the last of their kind'.

In 1868, a violent Indian war erupted on the Kansas plains and Bill was summoned by General Philip Sheridan to come to Hays City where he was appointed an army scout, later becoming Chief of Scouts to the Fifth Cavalry. He would eventually take part in 16 different Indian fights, be mentioned in numerous army dispatches for skill and bravery and take on the appearance of what has since become the 'Buffalo Bill look' – a buckskin suit trimmed with fringes and beads at the seams, broad-brimmed hat, shoulder-length hair, goatee beard and handlebar moustache.

Often Bill would also wear a crimson coloured shirt under the jacket, leather moccasins or knee-length leather boots with spurs and a huge belt with a massive buckle around his waist. As a civilian employed by the army, he could wear anything he wished. He later claimed that his famous clothing and appearance were practical for army work on the plains and in the mountains.

In May 1887 he told a reporter in London from *Tit-Bits* magazine:

> It is the general impression of people in the east that the long hair, wide brimmed hats, huge spurs, fringed leggings and other striking accessories in a cowboy's outfit, are worn simply for show and effect; but that impression is wrong. It was not a desire for picturesqueness that led to our 'make up' as it is today, although that effect has followed. Questions of necessity were the first considerations that prompted the adoption of our particular dress, from the big, cruel looking spurs to our hair like Samson's before he was shorn. All these appurtenances may be ornamental, but their usefulness is many times greater than their ornateness.
>
> Take for instance the cowboy's big-rimmed hat. The fact that it has been worn without change for half a century shows that use dictated its origin and use . . . to turn wild cattle and horses in the direction you desire them to go, when the sun is scorching hot and there is a blister in every puff of wind, this great hat is much cooler than straw; when the wind is blowing the sand like hot shot in our faces we should suffer greatly but for the protection afforded our eyes by the big rimmed hat. When the mud is flying from the heels of stampeding cattle, or the terrible rain-storms of the plains are pelting upon us, these hats are the best friends we have.

As to why Bill wore his light brown hair down to his shoulders, he explained:

> Our business is in the open, rain or shine, and in many changes of climate, and we have found from experience that the greatest protection for our eyes and ears is long hair. Old miners and prospectors know this well. Hunters, scouts, trailers and guides let their hair grow as a rule. Those who have been prejudiced against it have suffered the consequences of sore eyes, pains in the head and loud ringing in the ears. The peculiar result of exposure without the protection of long hair is loss of hearing in one ear, caused by one or the other ear being exposed more when the plainsman is lying on the ground. Healthy hearing and eyesight are of the greatest importance to

'When the mud is flying or the terrible rainstorms are pelting upon us, these hats are the best friends we have.'

a scout, hunter or herdsman. . . . Having found that the growth and wearing of long hair not only preserves but strengthens our sight, and makes our hearing more acute, we let nature have her way in the matter, and profit by it.

While Bill's explanation about his appearance might have been true, few others at the time also wore tailor-made buckskins, crimson shirts, fancy belts and spent so much time on their personal grooming and appearance. Perhaps his friends 'Wild Bill' Hickock and General George Armstrong Custer influenced him. By the time Bill had been promoted to Chief of Scouts, Hickock was equally famous for his long flowing locks, buckskin clothing and a stylish way of wearing six-guns with handles pointing forward in the gunbelt. Custer's hair also fell to his shoulders in ringlets. He was permitted to wear a uniform of his own design which included a velveteen jacket, trousers decorated in gold lace, a red kerchief around his neck and his hat positioned at a jaunty angle on his head.

Bill's early clothing was custom-made for him by Lulu on all-too-infrequent visits home to see his wife and baby. Later versions of the Cody costume, however, were commissioned from top eastern tailors for his appearances with the Wild West show.

Thanks to daring deeds on the prairie, striking appearance and unconventional clothing, Bill was starting to be noticed and talked about and by 1869 he was on the eve of becoming a national celebrity.

DIME NOVEL HERO, ACTOR AND 'THE FIRST SCALP FOR CUSTER'

Nature's proud she made this man,
This man Bill;
For it's always been his plan
To help others when he can –
Kindly Bill!
During all these hard-time years
He's been drying orphans' tears

And relieving widows' cares,
Has this Bill.
Often lightened hearts of lead,
Smiling Bill!
With your kind words and your bread
Both the soul and mouth you've fed,
Generous Bill!

An anonymous poem, sent to Buffalo Bill in 1886

NED BUNTLINE AND 'THE KING OF THE BORDER MEN' – DIME NOVEL HERO
– BUFFALO HUNTING WITH 'THE TOFFS' – GRAND DUKE ALEXEI – 'PAHASKA'
– A VISIT TO NEW YORK – AN ACTOR'S LIFE – INTRODUCING MAJOR JOHN
M. BURKE – 'WILD BILL' BECOMES AN ACTOR – DEATH OF KIT CARSON CODY
– 'THE FIRST SCALP FOR CUSTER'

Bill claimed that he was first introduced to 'Ned Buntline, the novelist' by Major William Brown who told him that the storyteller – whose name was new to Bill – would be joining them on a scouting expedition into Indian territory.

Edward Zane Carroll Judson, who wrote blood and thunder stories under the pen name of 'Ned Buntline', had run away to sea at the age of ten and much later wrote about his experiences. As a young man he published the *Western Literary Journal* and *Ned Buntline's Own*, full of adventure stories for easterners who could not read enough about life in the west. By 1849, Buntline had become America's highest paid writer. With an annual income of £20,000, he earned more than Mark Twain and Walt Whitman. Now Buntline was taking a westbound train seeking inspiration for new stories for his eastern readers to devour.

Buntline was hoping for co-operation from Major Frank North, who had found fame following an episode later known as the Battle of Summit Springs. On the expedition, Bill had guided Major North and the Fifth Cavalry to a position from which soldiers could encircle and surprise Chief Tall Bull's murderous Cheyenne warriors who had been terrorising settlers on the Kansas Plains. Two white women were being kept hostage at the Indian settlement. Major North won the credit, ably assisted by Bill who is said to have killed Tall Bull and captured his grey horse – also called Tall Bull – which he was allowed to keep and enter in local races.

Major North had no interest in talking to Buntline, and pointed across the parade ground to a wagon, under which a young man was sleeping off a hangover. The young man was 23-year-old Bill Cody, also known locally as Buffalo Bill. Buntline dragged him out, sat him in a chair, sobered him up and got him to talk about his exploits as a Pony Express rider, stagecoach driver, frontiersman and army scout.

On the following day's expedition, Buntline heard more about Bill's colourful life in the 'wild west' – which, with a few embellishments to heighten dramatic interest, became the first instalment of the serial story *Buffalo Bill, the King of the Border Men* in the 20 December 1869 edition of the *New York Weekly*.

When a copy eventually found its way back to Bill at Fort McPherson, Kansas, the star of the story was delighted and flattered by Buntline's account of his life on the frontier. 'Well, dog my cats!' he is said to have remarked – an expression he used during the rest of his life whenever surprised or delighted.

At the same time as thousands of others were heading west to claim a piece of land offered by the Homestead Act of 1862, Lulu and baby Arta took a train from

'Dime novel' adventure books by Ned Buntline and Colonel Prentiss Ingraham (pictured) helped shape the early legend of Buffalo Bill – one featuring his adventures as a young scout and buffalo hunter and the second as an Indian fighter on the western plains. (The American Collection)

St Louis to join Bill at the fort. The army had agreed to build a house for their Chief of Scouts and very own storybook hero. Lulu was heavily pregnant with their second child and gave birth to a son while Bill was away scouting with the Fifth Cavalry, which was having more real-life adventures with Indians on the plains. Bill was also in demand as a leader of hunting parties made up of rich easterners and European tourists wanting to see the west, bag a buffalo head to hang from their drawing room walls and catch sight of a savage Indian or two.

It was weeks before Bill returned to the fort to meet his new son. No name had been given to the child and Bill suggested Elmo Judson, in honour of Ned Buntline whose Buffalo Bill stories had now reached frontier readers, making Cody just as famous in his own back yard as he was in eastern cities. Officers and fellow scouts at the Fort objected to the name and it was agreed that the child be named Kit Carson Cody in honour of Bill's famous frontier friend.

Major North had no interest in talking to Buntline, and pointed across the parade ground to a wagon, under which a young man was sleeping off a hangover.

In later years, Buffalo Bill became the central character in hundreds of dime novels, the nineteenth century equivalent of today's comic book heroes or characters in popular fiction. Following Buntline's success with his serial story, others followed. Bill's fame as a living fighter of real Indians and hunter of huge bison on the western plains created demand for more exciting tales. When Bill later appeared in person in plays about his exploits and his Wild West entertainment attracted millions of excited spectators, Buffalo Bill's name was as well known in America as a top film star would be today. The public could not get enough of him.

Other writers took over where Buntline had left off. Colonel Prentiss Ingraham, later a publicist for the Buffalo Bill organisation, was responsible for over 200 dime novels with titles such as: *Buffalo Bill, the Buckskin King, or Wild Nell, the Amazon of the West*; *Buffalo Bill's Buckskin Braves, or The Card Queen's Last Game*; *Buffalo Bill's Sweepstake, or The Wipe-out at Last Chance* and *Buffalo Bill's Sure-Shots or Buck Dawson's Big Draw*.

Buntline was surprisingly slow to capitalise on his own success. It would be some while before he wrote more serials about America's popular frontier hero, but he eventually made a mint of money from converting his original story into a Buffalo Bill play for the theatre. He later collected his printed serials together and turned them into novels, wrote new ones and republished old stories right up until his death in the 1920s.

Although Bill had become a western storybook hero, the Cody family bills still had to be paid and there is no evidence that he received any fee for talking to Buntline and allowing his name to be used in stories. To supplement his income from scouting, Bill agreed to lead hunting parties on behalf of the military, made up of rich 'toffs' travelling out on new railway routes looking for wild west adventure – sportsmen, curiosity seekers and aristocratic tourists wanting to experience the thrill of the chase and shoot buffalo and wild game on the plains.

Friendly Indians were recruited to take part in expeditions and add 'local colour' to the frontier experience. They were called on to perform traditional songs and dances around the campfire for the amusement of the amateur huntsmen, and were well paid for their trouble. Bill also used the services of another white scout from

Fort McPherson, John Nelson, who had married the daughter of an Oglala Sioux Chief. Nelson had been given the Indian name Cha-Sha-Cha-Opoyeo (or Red-Willow-Fill-the-Pipe). In later years Nelson, his squaw wife and their half-breed family, travelled across the great waters to be part of Buffalo Bill's Wild West in England.

Hunting parties provided Bill with the extra income he needed to support his family, which had grown again with the birth of a second daughter called Ora Maude. As the Buffalo Bill legend began to grow, rich and influential easterners began asking for him by name. Hunting parties included the English Earl of Dunraven, James Gordon Bennett of the *New York Herald*, Charles L. Wilson of the *Chicago Evening Journal* plus wealthy eastern and mid-western sportsmen, business tycoons and Russia's Grand Duke Alexei. They all called on the army to give them a chance to hunt buffalo on frontier safaris with the famous Buffalo Bill as their guide.

Up to 16 supply wagons travelled with the hunting parties, one full of ice to make sure the champagne and vintage wines remained cold.

The sporting 'toffs' also paid for the privilege of going out on army scouting patrols and living the life of a frontier soldier – only their overnight accommo-dation and catering arrangements were worlds apart from the meagre rations and crowded tents experienced by the average trooper. Up to 16 supply wagons travelled with hunting parties, one full of ice to make sure the champagne and vintage wines remained cold. Another was crammed full of starched white linen, bone china, silver tableware and cut glass for multi-course dinners prepared by imported French chefs and served by waiters in evening dress. Life out west for a rich toff was often hard indeed. . . .

Bill soon discovered how to enjoy a champagne lifestyle. He acquired a taste for fine wines, rich food and influential company. All that were asked in return was plenty of dead buffalo for sportsmen to claim as their own at the end of the day. One party bagged over 600 buffalo and 200 elk – blazing a 194-mile-long trail of empty champagne bottles behind them.

The army agreed to host the frontier safaris to generate goodwill and favourable publicity for servicemen and officers stationed hundreds of miles away from civilisation. Newspaper stories about the hard life of a frontier soldier encouraged Washington politicians to appreciate how tough life in the west really was.

Stories about western hunting parties were eagerly followed in the east through dispatches cabled to newspaper offices in New York and Chicago. Thanks to these stories, people learned more about life on the plains 'guided by the renowned and far-famed Buffalo Bill'. His reputation and legend among influential easterners was starting to soar.

Some 'toffs' were good shots who managed to bring down buffalo with one or two shells. Others were not so skilled with weapons, including Grand Duke Alexei, fourth child of Russia's Tsar Alexander II, who was visiting America on a goodwill tour in 1872. After arriving in the United States with a Russian naval fleet as his escort, Alexei was given VIP treatment in New York and Washington.

The young Grand Duke then announced that instead of returning home to St Petersburg, he wanted to travel west and participate in the first 'Royal Buffalo Hunt' ever to take place in the United States – with Buffalo Bill as his guide.

Bill's old friend General Philip Sheridan was given the task of making sure the Grand Duke's every need was catered for. He instructed Bill to mobilise the army and create 'Camp Alexei', a comfortable base for the hunt. Bill was also told to track down Spotted Tail, a Sioux Chief, and persuade him to send 100 Indians to put on a show for the Russian guest. Sheridan wanted the royal buffalo safari to be a spectacular entertainment – no expense was to be spared.

Chief Spotted Tail, not involved in hostilities with white men at that particular time, said he would be pleased to join 'Pahaska' (the name the Sioux had given Bill – it means 'long hair') and welcome another 'great Chief from across the water'. Meanwhile, at Red Willow Creek, 40 miles away from the fort, troops were busy constructing 'Camp Alexei', complete with elaborate tents with wooden floors, carpets, pot-bellied heating stoves and fine furnishings shipped in by train from Chicago.

The special train carrying Alexei and a host of US Army top brass – including Custer and Sheridan – arrived at the camp to be met by a welcome party headed by Bill, Chief Spotted Tail, 100 Indian braves and a company of uniformed cavalry. The entire caravan immediately took off for the camp where a grand dinner was laid on and a fireside war dance cabaret was provided by the Sioux.

Next morning, protocol dictated that the first buffalo of the day be brought down by the Grand Duke, who chose to use a revolver. However, it soon became clear that Alexei was unable to hit a barn door from inside with the doors closed, let alone a giant buffalo. Bill had loaned Alexei one of his own horses – Buckskin Joe – and once the Russian had wildly emptied his pistol without success, rode up alongside the Grand Duke and passed him another fully loaded weapon. Again, Alexei missed every shot.

Bill takes up the story:

Seeing that the animals were bound to make their escape without his killing one of them, unless he had a better weapon, I rode up to him and gave him my old reliable Lucretia and told him to urge his horse close to the buffaloes, and I would then give him the word when to shoot. At the same time, I gave old Buckskin Joe a blow with my whip, and with a few jumps, the horse carried the Grand Duke to within about ten feet of a big buffalo bull. 'Now is your time,' said I. He fired and down went the buffalo. The Grand Duke stopped his horse, dropped his gun on the ground, and commenced waving his hat. Very soon the corks began to fly from the champagne bottles in honour of the Grand Duke Alexei, who had killed the first buffalo.

Grand Duke Alexei of Russia. (Private collection)

Thanks to rich 'toffs' and the Grand Duke Alexei, Buffalo Bill had begun producing his first Wild West shows.

Later that day Alexei killed a buffalo cow with his pistol and more champagne was opened. 'I was in hopes that he would kill five or six more if a basket of champagne was to be opened every time he dropped one,' noted Bill.

Thanks to Bill's skill and patience – and some gentle urging from Custer and Sheridan – Alexei managed to drop a further six buffalo by the time the five-day-long safari ended. Alexei was allowed to hunt with Spotted Tail's braves, seeing at first hand how they used a bow, arrow and lance to kill their prey. The Russian was thrilled with himself and sent a mountain of buffalo hides and trophy heads back to St Petersburg to display in his grand palace.

Before leaving, Alexei summoned Bill to his private carriage, where he presented his new American frontier-friend with some generous gifts – a large patchwork robe made from 57 different rare Siberian furs, a Russian fur coat and hat. Alexei also commissioned a pair of diamond-studded buffalo cufflinks and a tiepin to be specially made, which was sent to Bill as a farewell gift. Thanks to rich 'toffs' and the Grand Duke Alexei from Russia, Buffalo Bill had begun producing his first Wild West shows.

It was time for Buffalo Bill to be seen in person in the east and, in February 1872, he took 30 days' leave of absence to accept an invitation from a New York newspaper to visit the city. The army gave their Chief of Scouts free railway passes, the newspaper's editor cabled $500 for expenses and Bill was off to see the great city for himself, wearing the handsome fur coat given to him by Alexei.

He travelled via Chicago, where some hunting friends took him to a number of 'swell dinners' and a grand ball where he: 'Became so embarrassed it was more difficult for me to face the throng of beautiful ladies, than it would have been to confront a hundred hostile Indians. This was my first trip to the east and I was not accustomed to being stared at.'

In New York, Bill stayed at the Union Club, where the newspaper's editor and his influential friends gave their frontier guest a welcome reception and freedom to roam around the city on the Hudson: 'Everything being new and startling, convinced me that as yet I have seen but a small portion of the world.'

Bill received so many invitations and letters from well-wishers wanting to show him a good time in New York that he accepted everything, disappointing many by failing to show up. Some invitations stipulated that he should attend in his buckskins, so keen were the eastern hosts and hostesses to see 'the real Buffalo Bill'.

One of the people Bill wanted to seek out in New York was Ned Buntline, who lived in a stylish town house. Buntline had dramatised one of his Buffalo Bill stories, *Buffalo Bill, the King of the Border Men* and wanted to take his hero to a performance at the Bowery Theatre, where the actor J.B. Studley was playing the role of Bill.

Bill and Buntline watched the play from a private box. 'I was curious to see how I would look when represented by someone else,' remembered Bill, who was surprised to see the theatre full, with standing room only.

On learning that the genuine article was present in person in the theatre, the audience 'gave several cheers between acts, and I was called on to come out on to the stage and make a speech' [*and meet the actor playing the title role*]. 'I finally consented, and the next moment I found myself standing behind the footlights for the first time in my life. I looked up, then down, then on each side, and everywhere I saw a sea of human faces, and thousands of eyes all staring at me.'

Bill attempted to make a speech: 'And a few words escaped me, but what they were I could not for the life of me tell, nor could anyone else in the house. . . . I confess that I felt very much embarrassed – never more so in my life – and I knew not what to say . . . and, bowing to the audience, I beat a hasty retreat.'

Bill fled from the theatre pursued by the manager who called to the retreating figure in buckskins that he would pay him $500 a week to play the role of 'Buffalo Bill'. Bill kept running, shouting back that he was no actor and was afraid of crowds. The play continued to be a success in New York and later toured other cities across the country.

Bill Cody continued to have a grand time in New York and sent a cable to the army asking for his leave to be extended by another ten days. The army agreed, and Bill continued having fun, seeing more plays with Buntline and talking to reporters about life out west.

No sooner was Bill back on a train to Fort McPherson, than Buntline had picked up his pen again to produce another serial for the *New York Weekly* – *Buffalo Bill's Best Shot, or The Heart of Spotted Tail*, featuring a guest appearance by Grand Duke Alexei. *Buffalo Bill's Last Victory, or Dove Eye, the Lodge Queen* followed shortly afterwards.

On the journey home, Bill stopped off in Omaha to visit friends and got gloriously drunk. He was rushed back to the station to catch his connection but left his luggage behind. He arrived at the fort still soused from the champagne his friends had loaded on board, wearing his famous Russian coat and a stovepipe hat.

He immediately got back into the job of scouting and Indian fighting and his efforts were rewarded in May 1872 when he was awarded the Medal of Honor for skill and bravery in the service of the army.

Letters began to arrive at the fort from Ned Buntline urging Bill to return to New York to capitalize on his popularity and 'earn some real money' appearing in new plays he planned to write for his friend. Officers at the fort, who disliked Buntline, urged him to ignore the offers, but Ned's claim that 'there's money in it' persuaded Bill to forget his fear of appearing in public. He would try it. If it failed, he could always return to frontier life.

Bill resigned his post as Chief of Scouts and was paid off. Lulu and the children were packed off to her parents in St Louis while he carried on east to meet Buntline and fellow scout, Texas Jack Omohundro, who also wanted to get-rich-quick from acting.

Bill claims that when he arrived for a first reading of the play that was to become *The Scouts of the Prairie*, it was clear that Buntline had not yet written a word of it. Bill and Texas Jack were assured that now they had arrived he would

Bill fled from the theatre pursued by the manager who called to the retreating figure in buckskins that he would pay him $500 a week to play the role of 'Buffalo Bill'.

sit down and get on with it. Buntline is said to have gone out, bought pens, ink and paper, engaged all the hotel clerks as secretaries and dashed off the play in four hours.

As well as roles for Bill and Texas Jack, Buntline also wrote a part for himself. Ten Sioux and Pawnee Indians – played by 'genuine Indian Chiefs', according to advance publicity – were, in fact, out-of-work actors found walking the streets of Chicago. They would be dressed in full Indian costume and covered in war paint, so nobody would be the wiser. An exotic dancer of Italian origin, called Guiseppina Morlacchi, was hired to play the role of Dove Eye, an Indian princess.

The production was thrown together in a few days and opened at Nixon's Amphitheatre, Chicago, on 18 December 1872 to dismal reviews. 'Incongruous drama . . . execrable acting', wrote one critic. 'So wonderful in its feebleness that no ordinary intellect can comprehend it,' said another. But it was a bold, brassy and noisy story in which Buffalo Bill, Texas Jack and Ned Buntline leapt around the stage saving Miss Morlacchi from the clutches of hostile Indians, spinning lassos, shooting bandits and killing savages who died amid blood-curdling screams. By the time the curtain dropped, the brave scouts of the prairie had won the day and lived to fight another Indian war. Despite bad notices, *The Scouts of the Prairie* was a huge hit, grossing thousands of dollars everywhere it played – and generated $2,800 at the box office on the first night.

Whenever Bill or Texas Jack – or both – forgot Buntline's carefully crafted dialogue, they simply improvised until one of them managed to steer the plot back on course. The audience loved it. It was Buffalo Bill they had come to see and he could have been reciting nursery rhymes for all they cared.

In Chicago, *The Scouts of the Prairie* played to 2,500 people every night. On tour 'house full' notices were posted outside theatres and although Bill never became

Buffalo Bill moves in for the kill – hunting fresh meat for track layers and engineers on the Kansas Pacific railway. Bill claims to have shot 4,280 buffalo in the 18 months he worked for the company – 69 in a single afternoon. Later Bill admitted to being horrified by the destruction of the animal he had helped wipe out in such vast numbers, unaware that his contribution to their mass slaughter would almost remove the buffalo from the face of the earth. (The American Collection)

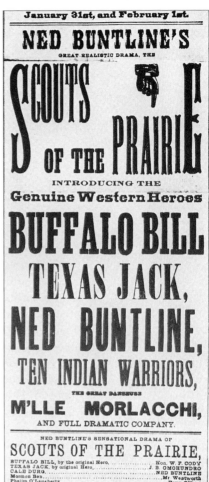

a great actor, his nervousness eventually disappeared and his voice and stage presence got better as the run progressed. His acting period helped develop his skills as one of the world's greatest showmen. And while they did not know it at the time, Buffalo Bill Cody, Texas Jack and Ned Buntline together invented a new type of entertainment which would still exist over a century later – the western.

 Lulu was curious about the actor's life her husband was living away from home, and attended a performance of the play when it came to DeBar's Opera House in St Louis. Bill spotted her in the third row and is reported to have leaned over the footlights and said to her: 'Oh, Mamma, I'm a bad actor,' to the delight of the packed audience. 'Honest, Mamma, does this look as awful out there as it feels up here?' he asked. The crowd lapped it up and urged Lulu to join him on stage. As she squirmed with embarrassment in her seat, Bill called: 'You can't be any worse scared than I am.

A poster for Ned Buntline's 'great realistic drama' *Scouts of the Prairie* starring 'genuine western heroes' (pictured left to right) Buntline himself, Buffalo Bill and Texas Jack Omohundro. (The American Collection)

Come on up.' Lulu sat frozen in the stalls as the audience around her laughed. 'Now you can understand how hard your poor old husband (*he was only 26 at the time*) has to work to make a living,' muttered Bill as he got back into the plot of Buntline's play.

Box-office cash tills rang as the play moved from theatre to theatre. Buntline earned handsome royalties from his 'masterpiece', as well as fees for mounting the production, promoting it and appearing as one of its stars. Texas Jack earned himself a wife when he married Miss Morlacchi the leading lady and Bill earned more money than he had ever been paid for hunting buffalo on the frontier.

The production arrived in New York in 1873 where one reviewer noted: 'It is so wonderfully bad it is almost good.' Nevertheless, the public loved it – or to be precise, they loved Buffalo Bill and his part in the enterprise. A critic praised Bill's 'lithe, springy step, realism, uncultured voice and utter absence of stage art'.

By the end of the season, both Bill and Texas Jack had gained confidence and become something resembling real actors, projecting their own personalities into the roles and learning how to handle audiences.

Bill dispensed with Buntline's services for the next season. The reason is unclear. Certainly, Ned was earning more money than the other stars. He was also full of talk, bragging about how they would tour America with the production, appearing under canvas, use real horses, play longer seasons in one place and take the show to London.

Buntline took his dismissal in his stride, sat down and 'dashed off' a new melodrama for an actor called Dashing Charlie, produced it, toured with it and lost a fortune. He retired from the theatre to concentrate on writing more serials and dime novels. He wrote one more pot-boiler about his old friend, *Buffalo Bill's First Trail, or Will Cody the Pony Express Rider* and spent the rest of his life publishing and re-publishing his stories about cowboys, Indians, lawmen and bandits living life on the disappearing frontier in a place called the 'wild west'.

Taking Buntline's place as Bill's theatrical promoter was another man destined to play an enormous role in the life of Buffalo Bill – Major John M. Burke. Also known as 'Arizona John', Burke was a former soldier, Indian fighter, stock company actor, manager of a touring acrobatic troupe, small town newspaperman, publicist and all-round organiser who would help shape the legend of William F. Cody over the next three decades. Friends said that Burke had 'nothing but brass and wind as his stock in trade' – coupled with enormous popularity in every newspaper, railway and theatrical office on both sides of the Atlantic.

It is not known how or where Burke acquired the rank of Major or his 'Arizona John' nickname. Born in New York and orphaned at the age of two months, Burke was brought up by an uncle in Washington and left home to enlist in the army at a relatively young age. The rank of Major was not awarded during his army days, so he almost certainly conferred it on himself while working in a variety of jobs in order to command better wages and status. Burke, a small, rotund figure with long hair and mutton-chop whiskers, could talk the hind legs off of a donkey – so if anyone challenged his rank, he would have talked up a convincing tale as to how he rose through the ranks to become a Major. The origin of his 'Arizona John' name

The production arrived in New York in 1873 where one reviewer noted: 'It is so wonderfully bad it is almost good.'

also remains a mystery, but the long scar across one side of his face was probably obtained in an early army skirmish with hostile Indians in the American north-west – earning him a second nickname to close friends who addressed him as 'old scarface.'

Burke was greatly impressed by Bill and years later he reflected on their first meeting by recalling: 'I have met a god . . . in my life. I came upon him just at sunset one night, out on the Missouri, and the reflection of the light from the river was shining up straight into his face and lighting it up like some kind of an aura. He was on horseback, and I thought then that he was the handsomest, straightest, finest man that I had ever seen in my life. I still think so.' Bill and Burke remained loyal friends and business partners for the next four decades.

With Major Burke's assistance, Bill formed a new theatrical company, known as The Buffalo Bill Combination, to tour in a new play by Frank G. Maeder called *The Scouts of the Plains* – a title dangerously close to Buntline's *The Scouts of the Prairie*. Major Burke was hired to publicise and later manage the show, which would star Miss Morlacchi herself in the role of Dove Eye the Indian Princess alongside an assorted bunch of players taking all the other roles, plus Bill and Texas Jack as themselves.

Major Burke had no convincing explanation for his military title, but must rank as one of the greatest PR men in history. (Earls Court/Olympia Archive)

For the next eight years the play toured for eight months of the year, leaving Bill free to return to Lulu and the children at their new home in Rochester, New York, and travel west to guide smart hunting parties. Major Burke's skill as a promoter guaranteed plenty of newspaper coverage, which was converted into full houses for the play.

'Wild Bill' Hickock joined the troupe for a season, but hated the life of an actor and 'playing the fool'. In exasperation at one performance, Hickock threw his pistol at a calcium spotlight, smashing it to pieces. He demanded real whisky in his glass instead of the apple juice normally used in theatrical performances and played fight scenes for real, beating-up half his fellow actors. He got into fights off-stage, too, smashing chairs over the heads of roughnecks daring to challenge him to a fight. They usually lost.

The rest of the company hated Hickock, especially those playing Indian roles who complained bitterly that 'Wild Bill' held his pistol so close to them when he fired his blanks that their skin was scorched with powder burns. Hickock quit the show in Rochester, New York, telling a stagehand: 'Tell that long-haired son-of-a-bitch I have no more use for him or his damned show business.' He was paid off with a £1000 bonus and everyone was pleased to see the back of 'Wild Bill' Hickock.

While Bill was waiting in the wings to go on stage in Springfield, Massachusetts, in April 1876, he was handed a telegram from Lulu telling him that his five-year-old son, Kit Carson Cody, was seriously ill with scarlet fever. Bill played the first act, leaving his understudy, the versatile Major Burke, to appear in the rest of the play while he rushed to catch a late train to Rochester. A friend met Bill at the station and rushed him to the family home. There he found Lulu and the girls also ill with fever. Bill wrote:

'We did everything in our power to save him, but it was to no avail.'

> I found my little boy unable to speak but he seemed to recognise me and putting his little arms around my neck he tried to kiss me. We did everything in our power to save him, but it was to no avail. The Lord claimed his own, and that evening at six o'clock, my beloved little Kit died in my arms. We laid him to rest in the beautiful cemetery at Mount Hope amid sorrow and tears.

Lulu and the girls recovered and as soon as they were well enough to be left, Bill closed his theatrical season early and headed out west 'because I was anxious to take part in the Sioux war, which was then breaking out'.

Bill had received letters from army top brass inviting him back to help them force the Sioux back on to their reservations in the Black Hills. The Indians were on the warpath after the government had gone back on its word on another treaty. Washington had pledged that South Dakota's sacred Black Hills would always be reserved for the Indians. However, stories about huge quantities of gold in the hills created a stampede of get-rich-quick prospectors and the Indians were pushed into resistance. Chiefs Sitting Bull and Crazy Horse called their warriors together in a mighty show of resistance under Sitting Bull's leadership.

The 7th US Cavalry wanted Bill as their guide and Chief of Scouts. Anxious for change after years on the road with his theatrical troupe, and feeling a need to come to terms with little Kit's death, Bill paid off his actors, put his scenery and costumes into storage, turned his back on the applause and took a train to Cheyenne to join General Crook.

Shortly after his arrival came news that General George Armstrong Custer, the daring and dashing leader of the 7th US Cavalry, had been defeated and killed by Sioux Indians at the Little Big Horn along with five regiments. Eight hundred Cheyenne warriors were now moving to join Chief Sitting Bull's forces in the Big Horn area. Custer had been a good friend to Bill. They had ridden on many missions and hunted buffalo together on the plains. Bill was devastated by news of his friend's violent death on the Little Big Horn battlefield.

A few days after news of Custer's death reached the fort, Bill was scouting with an army patrol at a place known as War Bonnet Creek. He was wearing one of his famous stage costumes, a brilliant Mexican vaquero outfit of black velvet slashed with scarlet and trimmed with silver buttons and lace. On his head, he wore a large plumed sombrero – hardly the authentic outfit of a scout of the plains, but the everyday clothing army friends now expected him to wear. A large party of Indians was seen heading in their direction. A group of them broke off and rode towards two soldiers riding towards Bill's group with dispatches. Not wanting the Indians to know how many soldiers were in the area, Bill suggested they wait until the last possible moment before he and a handful of others galloped in their direction and cut them off from the main Indian party coming over the hill.

Bill and 15 men dashed towards the Indians. He later wrote: 'A running fight lasted several minutes, during which we drove the enemy some little distance and killed three of their number. The rest of them rode off towards the main body, which had come into plain sight and halted upon seeing the skirmish that was going on.'

What followed became another important chapter in the legend of Buffalo Bill:

One of the Indians, who was handsomely decorated with all the ornaments usually worn by a war Chief when engaged in a fight, sang out to me in his own tongue: 'I know you Pa-he-haska (long hair). If you want to fight, come ahead and fight me'.

The Chief was riding his horse back and forth in front of his men, as if to banter me, and I concluded to accept the challenge. I galloped towards him for fifty yards and he advanced towards me about the same distance, both of us riding at full speed. And then, when we were only thirty yards apart, I raised my rifle and fired; his horse fell to the ground having been killed by my bullet.

Almost at the same time my own horse went down, he having stepped into a hole. The fall did not hurt me much, and I instantly sprang to my feet. The Indian had also recovered himself, and we were now both on foot, and now not more than twenty paces apart. We fired at each other simultaneously. My usual luck did not desert me on this occasion, for his bullet missed me, while mine struck him in the breast. He reeled and fell, but before he had fairly touched the ground, I was upon him knife in hand, and had driven the keen-edged weapon up to its hilt in his heart. Jerking his war bonnet off, I scientifically scalped him in about five seconds.

The rest of the Indians now charged down the hill towards Bill and the scouts and the army hurried to the rescue. 'As the soldiers came up I swung the Indian chief's top-knot and bonnet in the air and shouted: "The first scalp for Custer!"'

The entire regiment then charged the Indians who galloped off yelping at the tops of their voices. Later Bill learned that the Indian chief he had killed was called 'Hay-o-wei' or Yellow Hand, the son of Cut-Nose, a leading Cheyenne chief.

Bill decided to send Yellow Hand's scalp and war bonnet back to Lulu in Rochester. She recalled that when the lid of the packing crate was opened,

War Bonnet Creek 1876: Yellow Hand lies dead at Bill's feet. 'As the soldiers came up I swung the Indian chief's top-knot and bonnet in the air and shouted: "The first scalp for Custer!"' (Illustration from a Buffalo Bill's Wild West British programme)

'a terrific odour reached my nostrils. . . . I reeled slightly – then reached for the contents. Then I fainted. For I had brought from that box the raw, red scalp of an Indian.'

The scalp and war bonnet – which still exist – would later tour with Bill when he returned to the theatre and with his Wild West Show.

News of the duel with Yellow Hand found its way into a prairie newspaper, which wired the story on to eastern newspapers. Six days after the confrontation, Buffalo Bill fans in the east read the latest instalment about their western hero – only this time the exploit was real and there were plenty of witnesses on hand to prove it.

'The first scalp for Custer' episode would live on in adventure stories, Buffalo Bill's Wild West, theatrical dramas and later still in television and film re-creations.

There was more hunting and scouting to be done out on the plains, but: 'There being little prospect of any more fighting, I determined to go East as soon as possible to organise a new Dramatic Combination and have a new drama written for me, based upon the Sioux war.'

The play was *The Red Right Hand, or Buffalo Bill's First Scalp for Custer*, a five-act play 'without head or tail, and it made no difference which act we commenced the performance. . . . It afforded us, however, ample opportunity to give a noisy, rattling, gunpowder entertainment, and to present a succession of scenes in the late Indian war, all of which seemed to give general satisfaction.'

The play went on tour in eastern and mid-western states, and was advertised by displaying Yellow Hand's scalp and war bonnet in shop windows near theatres. The famous trophy was eventually withdrawn after local clergy and the squeamish objected to seeing such a gruesome item in public.

'There being little prospect of any more fighting, I determined to go East . . .'

Bill's theatrical earnings were sent home to Lulu each month, with instructions to find a suitable property where the family could settle down. He was already part owner of a cattle ranch on the south fork of the Dismal River and was eager to invest in more property in the west. In his first autobiography, which ends in February 1878, Bill informs his readers about a new ranch he had just bought in North Platte, Nebraska, where Lulu had given birth to another daughter, Irma Louise. The estate, known as Scout's Rest Ranch, later included a fine Victorian-style house, huge barns and outbuildings for cattle and horses. It eventually reached 4,000 acres and became one of Nebraska's finest ranches.

He concluded his book with the passage: 'My wife, tired of travelling, proceeded to North Platte, Nebraska, where, on our farm adjoining the town, she personally superintended the erection of a comfortable family residence, and had it all completed when I returned there early in May. In this house we are now living, and we hope to make it our home for many years to come . . . and thus ends the account of my career as far as it has gone.'

It appears from these closing words that Bill was planning to wind down a little. He had already lived the life of ten men and planned to work at: 'Making a better acquaintance of my family, for my long and continued absence from home made me a comparative stranger under my own roof-tree'. If the need arose, he could return to the stage, acting the part of himself in more melodramas. He had been asked to take a new play, *The Knight of the Plains, or Buffalo Bill's Best Trail*, by Prentiss Ingraham, to London. And there was always good money to be earned from a little light scouting and leading wealthy hunting parties over the plains, which could be easily combined with the life of a part-time rancher in Nebraska.

But Buffalo Bill Cody was far from ready to tie up his horse, take off his spurs and step out of the limelight. His adventures were only just beginning.

THE WILD WEST, THE PARTNERS & 'LITTLE SURE SHOT'

Who killed the bison, chased the bull,
Around his neck the lasso pull?
Who'll draw a million souls to see
The strange things from Amerikie?
Why, Buffalo Bill's crowd.

Topical Times, 1887

THE BIRTH OF THE WILD WEST – NATE SALSBURY – THE OLD GLORY BLOW-OUT
– THE DEADWOOD STAGECOACH – BUCK TAYLOR 'KING OF THE COWBOYS' –
'AMERICA'S NATIONAL ENTERTAINMENT' – JOHNNY BAKER 'THE COWBOY KID'
– MARRIAGE UNDER STRAIN – ENTER ANNIE OAKLEY – SITTING BULL JOINS
THE SHOW – TAKING NEW YORK BY STORM – ENGLAND BECKONS

The idea of mounting a massive outdoor pageant, a significant American entertainment that would celebrate the art of western horsemanship, had been in Bill's mind for some time. It would be too large to present in theatres, featuring genuine cowboys from the frontier, Indians from the plains and buffalo from the prairie. The event would recreate some of Bill's famous deeds from fact – and fiction – in genuine surroundings and play to large family audiences in open-air stadiums.

A pint-sized American actor, vaudevillean and theatrical impresario born in Freeport, Illinois, on exactly the same day as Bill and called Nathan – 'Nate' – Salsbury was of a similar mind. A man full of bright ideas and with plenty of experience running big theatrical events, Salsbury had made his fortune touring America 'in everything from Hamlet downwards' and with his vaudeville company, The Troubadours.

Salsbury invested his profits in a large cattle ranch in Montana. While the ranch and its wide-open spaces, cowboys and wranglers gave the easterner a taste for western life and traditions, Salsbury remained a city slicker at heart, never exchanging his tailored suits for chaps and spurs. But in his spare moments, Salsbury dreamed of creating a huge public exposition featuring skilled horsemen, marksmen and friendly Indians, who would re-enact western life for city dwellers such as himself in eastern arenas.

Salsbury met Bill for the first time in 1882 while they were both playing in New York. Over lunch at a Brooklyn restaurant, the two men shared their ideas and agreed to mount a western pageant and take it to Europe where – in Salsbury's words – 'it would be very interesting to the public at large, especially if the production could be made educational for the rising generation, instructive to better classes, and amusing to all'. In an interview with the British newspaper *Topical Times*, he added: 'Strange to say, when we first organised it, we intended to come to England at once, because we thought at this time that it would be a greater novelty here than anywhere else.'

Salsbury knew that the Wild West dime novel had found its way across the Atlantic and it made sense that a western-style entertainment featuring the famous Buffalo Bill should follow it over the ocean.

The following summer Salsbury sailed to England and 'looked the ground over'. He came to the conclusion that it would cost too much money to 'do the thing right'; and on his return, told Bill that he had insufficient funds at that time to invest in the project – but did expect to raise cash the following season with The Troubadours. The two men agreed to meet again a year later and revisit the project.

Nate Salsbury, actor, comedian, impresario and Vice President of Buffalo Bill's Wild West. From a Buffalo Bill Wild West British programme.

But Bill was impatient to try out the idea and the show, which later became Buffalo Bill's Wild West, made its debut as a Fourth of July entertainment in Bill's new hometown of North Platte, Nebraska. The venue was the Isaac Dillon Racetrack and the event was given the name of The Old Glory Blow Out. Local businesses were asked to donate prizes for shooting, riding and bronco busting. Five thousand handbills were printed inviting people to come forward and participate. Bill expected around one hundred responses. He received one thousand.

And so the Wild West show was born on the western frontier itself, a rip-roaring, one-day entertainment staged in primitive outdoor conditions in front of thousands of people, some of whom travelled 150 miles to be there. The event was a spectacular success. It bore little resemblance to Bill's later Wild West entertainment, and the only fees available for those taking part were the prizes on offer. But The Old Glory Blow Out included a demonstration by Bill on how to round up and kill buffalo, using a small private herd owned by a local rancher and blank ammunition. It also featured horse races, cash prizes for lassoing

Texas longhorns and riding a buffalo. There were sharp-shooting displays and demonstrations by visiting cowboys of how to break in wild ponies.

As soon as the Fourth of July show was over, Bill began making plans to recreate the entertainment on a grander scale, taking it to other mid-western cities. He sent Salsbury a telegram stating that he planned to stage the event on American soil. He asked the showman if he was still interested in becoming involved, taking a third share with William Carver – known as 'Doc' Carver – a famous rifle shot and plainsman. Salsbury was horrified to hear of Bill's association with Carver, a man known as the 'Spirit Gun of the West' and whom he had once described as 'a fakir in show business – a man who went west on a piano stool'. He told Bill he wanted no part of the enterprise.

Carver claims that the touring Wild West show idea was all his own. He later recalled that Bill came to see him one day complaining about his actor's life and pining for the wide-open spaces. Carver outlined his plans for an open-air show and Bill is reported to have said: 'Doc, I want to get out of doors. This inside business is killing me off. If you will take me in with you, I will never touch another drop of whisky as long as I live! But I have no money.'

'I will take care of that,' Carver claims to have told Bill. 'I will furnish the money for everything to get us started, and you can pay me back if we have a success, out of our profits.' And with that Cody and Carver signed an agreement and went ahead and hired cowboys, Indians, trick riders and marksmen to join the enterprise. They bought bucking horses, mules, buffalo, elk and wagons.

Bill also bought a stagecoach – one that had been abandoned after being attacked by Indians. Six horses once pulled the famous Deadwood stagecoach between Deadwood and Cheyenne, via Fort Laramie, Rawhide Buttes and War Bonnet Creek, where Bill had won the duel with Yellow Hand seven years before. It was built to transport 21 people, including a driver and two men beside him, 12 passengers inside and a further six on top. Drivers were chosen for their coolness, courage and skill. One of them had been 19-year-old Billy Cody in his first job after leaving the army. On hearing that the old Deadwood stagecoach was lying battered, travel-stained and neglected out on the prairie, Bill rescued it to use in the show.

Talent signed up to appear included Captain Adam Bogardus 'Champion Pigeon Shot of America' and the man who invented the famous trap-shoot designed to propel clay pigeons and glass balls into the air. Bill's old army friend Major Frank North got top billing. He would lead a re-creation of the Battle of Summit Springs, in which Indians would play the part of Chief Tall Bull and his murderous Cheyenne braves, surrounded, overthrown and defeated by Bill and Major North, with a little help from the army.

Leading the cowboys was William Levi Taylor, known as 'Buck', at 6 ft 5 ins the tallest member of the company. Buck worked at Bill's ranch, where his party piece was to throw a steer by its horns or tail and tie it up single-handed. He could also tame the most evil-tempered wild horses, and pluck a handkerchief from the ground while leaning out of his saddle, galloping past at full speed – talents which would make him a Wild West star in both America and England.

Salsbury knew that the Wild West dime novel had found its way across the Atlantic and it made sense that a western-style entertainment featuring the famous Buffalo Bill should follow it over the ocean.

A cornet-playing friend of Bill's, William Sweeney, also joined the company with a small band of other brass musicians. Together they created Buffalo Bill's Cowboy Band, who would play marches, overtures, light classical pieces and popular tunes to accompany the show for the next 30 years.

Behind-the-scenes staff included the redoubtable Major John M. Burke as general manager and press agent, and Jule Keen, a character actor in one of Bill's theatrical companies and now promoted to treasurer of the Wild West enterprise.

Someone else who begged to be taken on the Wild West adventure was a 12-year-old boy called Johnny (also known as Johnnie) Baker, who would have been about the same age as Bill's late son, Kit Carson Cody. Johnny's family had settled in North Platte, where he used to follow 'the Colonel' around town like a pet puppy, offering to hold Bill's horse. Bill gave him odd jobs at his ranch and taught him to shoot. He became known as 'Buffalo Bill's boy' and was virtually adopted by Bill in later years. In return, Johnny stayed with Bill for the rest of the great showman's life, graduating from behind-the-scenes helper to Wild West sharpshooting star, eventually becoming arena director of the entire enterprise.

'The best open air show ever seen. The real sight of the whole thing is Buffalo Bill, an extraordinary figure who sits on a horse as if he were born in the saddle.'

The Wild West played afternoon engagements at fairgrounds and other borrowed sites. It visited Omaha, Council Bluffs, Springfield, Boston and Newport where the local newspaper acclaimed it as 'the best open air show ever seen'. It added: 'The real sight of the whole thing is Buffalo Bill, an extraordinary figure who sits on a horse as if he were born in the saddle. His feats of shooting are perfectly wonderful.'

Such notices did not please 'Doc' Carver, billed as 'the world's championship marksman'. Carver had an evil temper and one day, when he missed a shot, smashed his rifle over his horse's head and punched an assistant.

Nate Salsbury caught up with the show when it came to Coney Island, New York, and was far from impressed. While many scenes and situations were well played, he felt the entire operation lacked discipline and good stage management. But the entertainment included scenes which were to remain part of the Wild West format for years, including the 'Capture of the Deadwood Mail Coach by the Indians, which will be rescued by Buffalo Bill and his Attendant Cowboys', and 'Cowboy Fun – picking objects from the ground, roping wild horses, riding the buckers', and races between Indians on foot and others mounted on bareback horses.

Later that year, when both the Wild West and Salsbury's Troubadours played Chicago at the same time, Bill knocked on Salsbury's dressing room door and asked to see him. He stated that if Salsbury did not come at once and take control of the show he was going to walk away from it. Although the season was far from a failure, Bill and Carver had only broken even, having spent a small fortune on advertising and renting suitable sites. They needed help – and they needed it now.

 Bill was summoned back to North Platte by the illness of his youngest daughter, Orra Maude, who died shortly after his arrival. The family was now reduced to two children, Arta now aged 17 and baby Irma. Lulu had moved from Scout's Rest Ranch to live in a home provided by

Bill in another part of town. His sister Julia Goodman and her husband Al were brought in to run the ranch.

Relations between Bill and Lulu were strained. The trouble began back in 1877 when his theatrical troupe closed their Denver season. Lulu came out to join Bill for the last days of the tour and waited in a hotel room while her husband went to another to pay four actresses and some actors their final pay packets. Everyone was in an end-of-season holiday mood and drinking beer before going their separate ways. Bill took his leave, and as he moved towards the door the ladies rushed up, surrounded and kissed him goodbye, amid much laughter and high-spirited noise.

Carver claimed that Bill was often so drunk that his gun had to be hidden away in case he shot someone – or himself.

All of this was overheard by Lulu listening through paper-thin walls in an adjoining room. She accused Bill of having affairs with showgirls – which he strenuously denied, claiming he was simply saying goodbye to his company.

Bill later learned that money he had sent home to Lulu with instructions to buy property had been spent in her name only – his own name failed to appear in any legal deeds. In a letter to his sister Julia in September 1883, he revealed that he had petitioned 'that woman' (Lulu) for divorce. 'She has tried to ruin me financially this summer,' he wrote. 'Oh I could tell you lots of funny things how she has tried to bust up the horse ranch and buy more property . . . in her name.' A divorce hearing was set for the following January, but various failed attempts to bring about a reconciliation between the couple delayed their day in court until 1905.

Doc Carver was also proving to be a problem. Carver wanted to tour the Wild West throughout the winter months, but Bill wanted time off to concentrate on his up-coming divorce case. They disagreed on other matters, too. Carver claimed that Bill was often so drunk that his gun had to be hidden away in case he shot someone – or himself. He also told anyone prepared to listen that Bill still owed him $29,000.

Back in Omaha the two men sat down and decided to divide their assets with the toss of a coin. One of the things Bill managed to hold on to was the Deadwood stagecoach.

While Carver went south with his half of the show, Bill, Salsbury and Bogardus pooled their resources to create a new enterprise which they called 'Buffalo Bill's Wild West – America's National Entertainment'. Although Salsbury became the organisation's business brain and Vice-President, credited in show programmes as the man 'in charge of the Amusement Department', he continued to appear with the Troubadours for the time being. Bill, Bogardus and Major North were the stars of the show. Although an accomplished actor, singer and comedian, Salsbury never appeared in the show itself, always remaining behind the scenes, carefully planning and refining the programme, supervising the proceedings and selecting cities where it would play.

The new entertainment opened in St Louis in the spring of 1884 and Salsbury paid a visit a few days before the first performance to see how his property was shaping up. He found Bill in a drunken state, surrounded by a bunch of cronies all getting equally drunk at his expense. Salsbury – a life-long abstainer – turned on his heel and left, later writing Bill a strong letter that he suggested his star read in a sober moment. The letter produced a remorseful response from Bill who replied:

Your very sensible and truly rightful letter has just been read and it has been the means of showing me just where I stand. And I solemnly promise you that after this you will never see me under the influence of liquor. I may have to take two or three drinks today to brace up on; that will be all as long as we are partners. I appreciate all you have done. Your judgement and business is good and from this day on I will do my work to the letter. This drinking surely ends today and your pard will be himself, and on deck all the time.

While Bill reduced his drinking, it would be years before he had control of his alcohol consumption. But he had learned his lesson. If the Wild West was to be a success, Bill needed Salsbury's complete support. For the rest of his 'pard's' life he worked hard and tried never to let him down again. Sometimes he failed.

Major Frank North, Buck Taylor, Johnnie Baker and most of the original cowboys stayed with Bill, along with Major Burke and Jule Keen. 'Squaw man' John Nelson, who had ridden with Bill on hunting parties for eastern sportsmen and had acted in some of Bill's melodramas, later joined them. Nelson's Sioux wife and their five half-breed children came along too. Before joining the Wild West, Nelson had lived a colourful life. In 1847 he had guided the American 'Moses' – Brigham Young – and his caravan of Mormon 'Children of Israel' across 1,500 miles of prairie and desert to their new promised land in the valley of Utah's Great Salt Lake.

Nelson would become one of the Wild West's Indian interpreters, wagon drivers – and tellers of tall stories. He liked to tell the tale of how he had once thrown his gunbelt down, setting off a pistol which fired a bullet through his left

Buffalo Bill's Wild West company pictured in Philadelphia in 1884. Bill sits at the centre, with a clean-shaven Nate Salsbury to his right and sharpshooter Adam Bogardus and his four marksmen sons to his left. Behind Bill and Salsbury is Johnnie Baker and seated in front of Bill is 'squaw man' John Nelson, his Indian wife and some of their children. (Photograph by William Phillippi & Brothers, courtesy of Denver Public Library) hand, up into his mouth removing several teeth, onwards through his upper jaw into the nostril, finally lodging itself inside his skull. Nelson claimed that the bullet stayed there for two and a half years before dropping out one day after he had sneezed. He claimed that the bullet worn around his neck as a lucky charm was the one which had been fired into his head.

Fred Matthews, an expert driver, was hired to manipulate the ribbons of the old Deadwood Stage, and former Pony Express rider Seth Hathaway was recruited to recreate some of his real-life exploits on the prairie.

The re-born show played to over 41,000 people in one night in Chicago, but the first of many accidents hit the Wild West when it arrived in Hertford, Connecticut, where Major North was thrown from his horse and trampled underfoot. He remained hospitalised for several months, briefly rejoined the show, left again early in 1885 and died shortly afterwards.

A steamboat was hired to take the show from one location to another. It collided with another vessel in mid-river and sank with all the show's wagons, props, guns, ammunition, equipment and costumes, plus buffalo, donkeys and elk. No lives were lost and the horses and the Deadwood stagecoach were saved. But the Wild West had professional engagements to fulfil in New Orleans and no money to replace their sunken equipment.

Bill sent an urgent cable to Salsbury, who was in Denver waiting to go on stage with the Troubadours and sing a comic song when it was delivered. He quickly tore open the telegram and read: 'Outfit at the bottom of the river. What do you advise?'

Salsbury asked the orchestra leader to play the opening bars of his song again in order to give him time to think. Then he penned a reply to Bill and handed it

Meet the family: 'Squaw man' John Nelson (centre) had ridden with Bill on hunting parties for eastern sportsmen and acted in some of his melodramas, married a Sioux princess, and was given the Indian name Cha-Sha-Cha-Opoyeo (or Red-Willow-Fill-the-Pipe). In later years Nelson fathered five children who all travelled to London with the Wild West. (Denver Public Library)

to the waiting telegram boy: 'Go to New Orleans, reorganise and open your date.' He then strode on stage and continued with the show.

A week later Bill had rounded up herds of elk and buffalo, bought new wagons and equipment and opened the show in New Orleans on time.

By the end of the season, the entertainment was £60,000 in the red, but Salsbury had planned another tour for the following season and was certain that financial losses would turn into profits.

Meanwhile performers from other touring shows and circuses began to look in on 'America's National Entertainment' hoping they might adapt their acts into a Wild West setting and land a job. In New Orleans, a pint-sized girl from Woodland, Darke County, Ohio, turned up at the showground asking to see the boss. She was under 5 ft tall, weighed less than 100 pounds and at age 25 looked ten years younger. Her name was Phoebe Ann Mosey, known to a few as Mrs Annie Butler but soon to be known to millions as Miss Annie Oakley.

Annie and her husband Frank performed a shooting double-act called Butler & Oakley with the Sells Brothers' Circus, also playing in New Orleans that week. They had heard that Wild West marksman Captain Adam Bogardus planned to quit the enterprise and enquired if they might be considered as a substitute act?

Bill and Salsbury had no further funds to pay for a new act, but Frank Butler suggested a three-day trial and it was agreed that they would make their debut in Louisville a few days later. Annie remembered: 'I went right in and did my best in front of 17,000 people, and was engaged in 15 minutes.'

Afterwards Bill introduced her to the company with the words: 'This little Missie here is Miss Annie Oakley. She's to be the only white woman with our show. And I want you boys to welcome and protect her.'

Annie remembered: 'My husband and I were introduced as one of them – the first white woman to stand and travel with what society then might have thought impossible. Every head bowed. I felt something like a wild gooseberry sticking in my throat as the friendly, rough hands covered mine, one at a time as they passed by with a "How! and *Waste*!" meaning "all is good". A crowned queen was never treated by her courtiers with more reverence than I by those whole-souled Western boys.'

Frank Butler decided that Annie would be the star while he would be her assistant. He developed a unique act for his wife, which nobody who saw it ever forgot. Dexter Fellows, recruited by Major Burke as a press agent, recalled: 'Her entrance was always a very pretty one. She never walked. She tripped in, bowing, waving, and wafting kisses. Her first few shots brought forth a few screams of fright from the women, but they were soon lost in round after round of applause. It was she who set the audience at ease and prepared it for the continuous crack of firearms which followed.'

The Wild West featured its new shooting star early in the show, billed as 'Miss Annie Oakley, Celebrated Shot, who will illustrate her dexterity in the use of Fire-Arms.'

To perform her act, Annie positioned herself in the centre of the arena where Frank had laid out pistols and rifles on a small table. Frank released clay pigeons

Salsbury was in Denver waiting to go on stage when it was delivered. He quickly tore open the telegram and read: 'Outfit at the bottom of the river. What do you advise?'

BUFFALO BILL'S WILD WEST·
CONGRESS, ROUGH RIDERS OF THE WORLD.

MISS ANNIE OAKLEY,
THE PEERLESS LADY WING-SHOT.

Miss Annie Oakley (1860–1926) 'the peerless lady wing-shot' – the stage name of Phoebe Ann Mosey – who joined the Wild West with husband Frank Butler in 1885 and became a success on both sides of the Atlantic. (Denver Public Library)

from one of Bogardus' trap-shoots, first singly, then in pairs, then in triplets and finally four at a time. She shot them all to pieces, firing from either her left or right arm. Annie could also place a rifle over her shoulder, turn around and, using a mirror in one hand to sight the target – a playing card – fire directly through its centre.

Under Frank's shrewd tutelage, Annie handled firearms with the authority and adroitness of an Indian fighter. She could break glass balls while riding horseback, clip the ashes from a lighted cigar held between Frank's lips and shoot coins held between his thumb and forefinger. She could draw heart-shaped designs with bullets on a target.

In the Wild West's early days, programme notes rarely named individual performers apart from Buffalo Bill himself. But after signing Annie Oakley and Frank Butler to the show, Salsbury went out and spent several thousand dollars on show posters featuring 'Miss Annie Oakley, the Peerless Lady Wing-Shot'. The large, coloured posters showed Annie wearing a smart, tailored costume with a pleated skirt with ribbons stitched along the hem below the knees and a dozen or more medals pinned to her tunic. She wore a western-style hat with a six-pointed star attached to its rim. In her gloved hand she held one of her famous rifles. Smaller pictures either side showed Annie in action, shooting glass balls thrown into the air by Frank and clay pigeons propelled by a trap-shoot. A full page in the show's programme was also devoted to her, along with a photograph – something denied to practically every other cast member.

Annie was a crowd-pleaser and an asset to the Wild West enterprise and both Bill and Salsbury acknowledged the fact. Her marriage to Frank – like Bill's to Lulu – was never publicised or even mentioned in Major Burke's publicity material. Bill and Salsbury wanted the world to accept Miss Annie Oakley as a tiny girl from the backwoods who could outshoot any man with a gun, and while she toured with the Wild West for the best part of 14 years, few people outside the Cody–Salsbury organisation ever knew she was a married lady.

Before joining the Wild West, Annie had appeared at the Olympic Theatre, St Paul, Minnesota, where the famous Sioux leader Tatanka Iyotake – better known as Chief Sitting Bull – was paraded before a curious audience eager to pay and see the man held responsible for Custer's death a few years before. Sitting Bull was so impressed with Annie's shooting that he asked to be introduced. He called her 'Watanya Cicilia' or 'Little Sure Shot'. He exchanged photographs with her and adopted her into the Sioux tribe as his daughter.

Major Burke told Sitting Bull that if he joined the Wild West he would be reunited with 'Little Sure Shot'. So it was that the great Chief went into show business with Buffalo Bill's Wild West.

Major Burke was never one to miss an opportunity. He tried to sign Sitting Bull for the Wild West, but the old chief refused. Technically, was a prisoner of war, and only permitted to be seen in public because the authorities were unsure what to do with him. Sitting Bull had been shown little consideration on an earlier tour, where he had been spat upon and shouted at by the audience. He was reluctant to be paraded before the public again.

Showing him the photograph of Annie Oakley in his tepee, Major Burke told Sitting Bull that if he joined the Wild West he would be reunited with 'Little Sure Shot' and see her every day. So it was that the great Chief Sitting Bull went into show business with Buffalo Bill's Wild West. He signed on to appear for four months at $50 a week. He was given two weeks' advance pay and promised a $125 bonus at the end of the season. He was allowed to sell his photograph, charge for his autograph and keep the profits. A small group of Sioux warriors travelled with him and were all promised travelling expenses back to the Standing Rock reservation after the tour was completed.

The public flocked to see the country's number one villain, who was required to do nothing more than trot around the arena on his horse, wearing full war bonnet and

Sitting Bull (Tatanka Iyotake), Chief of the Hunkpapa group of the Teton Sioux, who refused to obey US government orders to gather his people together on the reservation while 'palefaces' moved on to tribal lands searching for gold. Following the Battle of Little Big Horn, he was kept a virtual prisoner on the reservation, but freed in 1885 to tour for a season with Buffalo Bill – who he called *Pahaska* ('Long Hair') – and the Wild West. (Gregg White Collection)

traditional clothing. As his horse slowly moved around the showground, the audience hissed and booed. Sitting Bull rose above it all by simply ignoring the jeers.

Buffalo Bill and Sitting Bull got along like a prairie fire. The old Chief agreed to be photographed with *Pahaska* ('Long Hair') when the show arrived in Montreal and the picture appeared in show programmes and on postcards with the caption

'Foes in '76 – Friends in '85'. The most famous Indian of them all also liked meeting people, and ended up giving some of his earnings to those he considered poor and needy. Sitting Bull could not understand how poverty existed in a white man's rich society.

At the close of his single season in show business, Sitting Bull was sent home with a gift from Bill of a large white sombrero – size eight. When someone attempted to try it on, the old Chief angrily snatched it back, saying: 'My friend Long Hair gave me this hat. I value it highly, for the hand that placed it upon my head had a friendly feeling for me.' He was also given a grey horse he had admired, which had performed tricks in the Wild West arena.

The 1885 season was seen by over one million people during its first five months and brought in a profit of $100,000. The following year it played for an extended six-month season on Staten Island, New York, where during one July week, nearly 200,000 people took the ferry across to experience the Wild West. The *New York Dispatch* reported:

> The attendance of visitors to this extraordinary exhibition of the realism of life on the frontier seems to increase with each day's performances. The grandstands are packed long before the hour of commencement and the throng, elsewhere on the ground is, in its size, a spectacle of crowded humanity worthy of remembrance. There has never been in or near this city any attraction, which has had 'rain or shine', such an uninterrupted succession of immense and consistently increasing audiences, and it can be truthfully added, no attraction more deserving of patronage.

Sitting Bull had great regard for Bill. Here they pose together in full ceremonial dress for a studio shot taken on a visit to Canada (The American Collection)

Notable visitors to Staten Island included P.T. Barnum – a rival showman, and admirer of Buffalo Bill – and inventor Thomas Edison, curious to know how performances taking place after dark were illuminated. To light up the acts, Bill used a combination of lamps, gas flares and bonfires.

England's leading actor, Henry Irving – later the first British player to be knighted – also boarded the ferry to see the Wild West on a day off from appearing in his popular play *The Bells* in a Broadway theatre. After the show, he invited Bill and Salsbury to supper and encouraged the partners to reconsider transplanting the entire enterprise to England, where he was certain it would be a success.

Others also urged the partners to export the show across the Atlantic. In his second autobiography Bill recalls:

> Several leading gentlemen of the United States conceived the idea of holding an American Exhibition in the heart of London and to this end a company was organised

An early poster for Buffalo Bill's Wild West. (Denver Public Library)

that pushed the project to a successful issue, aided as they were by several prominent residents of the English capital. When the enterprise had progressed so far as to give flattering promise of an opening at the time fixed upon, a proposition was made to Mr Salsbury and myself by the president and directors of the company, to take our show to London and play the season of six months as an adjunct to the American Exhibition, the proposition being a percentage of the gate receipts.

Bill stated that the approach was given 'mature consideration' and as soon as the partners had transferred the Wild West to Madison Square Garden for the 1886/7 winter season, they dispatched Major Burke to London to scout out the foreign territory on their behalf. Burke was told to visit a site called Earls Court in the city's West Brompton and Kensington district. It was there that the American Exhibition was to be built on a large, triangular piece of waste ground owned by a group of private railway companies, which had once been a cabbage field and was now being used as a tip for London's refuse.

The Major must have been alarmed with what he found at Earls Court; a giant pile of stinking refuse, made higher every day by visits from dozens of horse-drawn dust carts and rubbish tippers. Crawling all over it were dozens of poverty-stricken Londoners, hoping to scavenge something worth dragging away to sell for a few pennies. But Major Burke kept calm as John Robinson Whitley, director-general of the American Exhibition, explained his vision to his new American friend while conducting him around the edge of the site.

After showing Burke the 23-acre plot where the American Exhibition would be presented, he pointed to an adjoining site covering several more acres where Wild West performances might be given if the Major's boss agreed to participate. It would be connected to the American Exhibition by a series of bridges crossing railway lines running parallel to rows of houses dominating the Earls Court landscape. He told the Major that, while the site was some distance from London's main theatres and music halls, it was close to four railway stations, making it easy for people living in London and the surrounding district to reach the site. Whitley also assured Major Burke that once the site had been cleared, modern sanitary and drainage facilities would be installed allowing the Wild West company to reside there comfortably for the duration of the event.

Whitley was secretly relying on the Wild West coming to London. In recent weeks, several leading exhibitors had withdrawn and he needed a major attraction to draw the public to Earls Court. He knew that if people could be persuaded to come and see cowboys and Indians, they might stay to learn about America's art and industrial miracles. Whitley also spotted a valuable asset in Major Burke, who he knew managed to generate more daily newspaper column inches for Buffalo Bill in America than President Grover Cleveland's staff produced in a month. Newspaper coverage for the Wild West in England would also be crowd-pulling publicity for the American Exhibition.

The portly Major Burke, with his long, dark, curly hair, mutton-chop whiskers, large scar on his right cheek and liking for gaudy waistcoats, had a friendly yet persuasive manner. After leaving Whitley, the Major travelled around London

The American Exhibition was to be built on a large, triangular piece of waste ground which had once been a cabbage field and was now being used as a tip for London's refuse.

Director John Robinson Whitley was secretly relying on the Wild West show to draw crowds to the American Exhibition. (*Illustrated London News*)

knocking on the doors of London's newspaper editors asking their opinion of the proposed American Exhibition. He found them generally enthusiastic about the scheme, which they considered might be amusing, instructive, diverting and a change from the pomp and ceremony surrounding official Jubilee events.

Burke told the newsmen something about his boss back home in America and promised to get in touch again should they decide to sail the Atlantic and introduce British audiences to the Wild West. Secretly, Major Burke could hardly contain his excitement. He immediately saw the possibilities of presenting the show in a country preparing itself for a long celebration and desperately in need of spectacularly original and affordable entertainment for the masses. He could not get back to New York quickly enough to give his report to Bill and Salsbury.

Meanwhile, back at Madison Square Garden, the Wild West received another distinguished visitor. America's best-loved author, Mark Twain, was so impressed with 'America's National Entertainment' that he returned the next evening, after which he wrote Bill a personal letter:

I have seen your Wild West Show two days in succession and have enjoyed it thoroughly. It brought vividly back the breezy, wild life of the Great Plains, and the Rocky Mountains, and stirred me like a war cry. Down to its smallest detail, the show is genuine, cowboys, vaqueros, Indians, stagecoach, costumes and all; it is wholly free from sham and insincerity and the effects produced upon me by its spectacles are identical with those wrought upon me a long time ago by the same spectacles on the frontier. Your Pony Express man was as tremendous and of interest to me as he was 23 years ago, when he used to come whizzing by from over the desert with his war news, and your bucking horses were even painfully real to me, as I rode one of these outrages once for nearly a quarter of a minute. It is often said on the other side of the water that none of the exhibitions we send to England are purely and distinctly American. If you will take the Wild West show over there, you can remove that reproach.

Everyone eagerly awaited Major Burke's return. Bill's nephew Ed Goodman – son of sister Julia and husband Al, now managing Scout's Rest Ranch – was employed by his uncle to sell programmes to Wild West audiences. In a letter to his mother dated 22 November 1886, he wrote: 'Mr John M. Burke arrived from London today and report that everything booming over there and think they can make big money.'

As soon as the New York season closed, Bill and Salsbury set about enlarging the organisation and making preparations to take the Wild West to England, investing $165,000 of their own money in the enterprise.

On Thursday March 31 1887, a company of over 200 men, women and children assembled on the New York harbour quayside ready to board the 4,700-ton chartered steamship *State of Nebraska* bound for London. They included 83 saloon passengers, 38 steerage passengers and 97 Indians, squaws and children including babes in arms.

Leading the company up the gangplank was Buffalo Bill Cody, age 42. Following closely behind was Nate Salsbury, also 42 and Rachel, his 21-year-old bride whom he had married in New York just a few days earlier.* Next up the gangplank ran Annie Oakley and Frank Butler, Lillian Smith 'the teenage sharpshooter', with her new husband, Joe Kidd, a cowboy in the company, Buck Taylor the 'King of the Cowboys', Johnnie Baker the 'Cowboy Kid', 100 other cowboys – including Master Bennie Irving, age 5 – William Sweeney with fifteen members of his celebrated Cowboy Band plus their instruments and 'squaw man' John Nelson, his Sioux Indian wife and small tribe of children.

Below decks the crew were busy loading 200 animals including 180 horses, 18 buffalo, ten American mules, four donkeys, ten elk, five wild Texan steers, two deer and enough feed for the two-week long voyage. Over 60 tents, 300 saddles, hundreds of guns and an arsenal of ammunition, twelve covered wagons plus the old Deadwood stagecoach had already been stowed in the hold.

That morning over 10,000 New Yorkers, a flotilla of steamboats, tugs and yachts, turned out to wave them goodbye. In England, triumph awaited them.

'It is often said on the other side of the water that none of the exhibitions we sent to England are purely and distinctly American. If you will take the Wild West show over there, you can remove that reproach.'

---

* Rachel had been a 'character performer' in the Troubadours company, but had now quit the stage to become the full-time Mrs Salsbury.

EASTWARD HO!

Midst cheering tremendous,
O'er valley and hill –
A marvel stupendous
Of courage and skill –
He's quickly advancing,
With singing and dancing
That Centaur Heroic called 'Buffalo Bill.'

Punch, 1887

A ROUGH ATLANTIC CROSSING – MAJOR BURKE GETS A MOVE ON – WELCOME
TO ENGLAND BUFFALO BILL – THE JOURNEY INTO LONDON

A mixed tribe of Indians – Sioux, Cheyenne, Kyowa, Pawnee and Arapaho
– squatted on the quayside in a circle and chanted prayers to their gods
for a safe journey on their expedition across the great waters. At the centre
stood a tall, proud man draped in a blanket. His name was Ogila-sa, or Chief
Red Shirt – 'a redoubtable warrior and second only in influence to Sitting Bull
himself', wrote Cody. He was billed in the Wild West programme as 'Chief of the
Sioux nation'.

Sitting Bull had been given the opportunity to travel to England with the
Wild West, and the Bureau of Indian Affairs was happy to see him go, knowing
that while he was with Bill he was in safe hands and out of trouble. The old Chief
declined the invitation. He had had his taste of show business and one experience
was enough. He preferred to remain at home, but offered his young second-in-
command – Red Shirt – as an alternative.

Red Shirt, like other Indians on the voyage, had never left his reservation in
South Dakota before joining the Wild West. Bill convinced the Bureau of Indian
Affairs that allowing Indians to join the company at home and abroad was good
for everyone – good for the Indians who would be paid fair wages, given board and
lodgings plus equal status with the rest of the company, and good for the Bureau
because it removed potential troublemakers from their care.

Before joining the Wild West, Red Shirt was told by Sitting Bull to end an
uprising among his people, in which a pretender was attempting to usurp the old
chief. Red Shirt and two followers invaded the pretender's camp, killed its leader
and restored peace to the tribe. By recruiting Red Shirt into the company, Bill

Members of Buffalo Bill's Wild West on the deck of the steam-ship *State of Nebraska* before sailing from New York to London, 31 March 1887. Buffalo Bill stands in front holding ropes with Buck Taylor 'King of the Cowboys' at his left and some of the 200 cowboys, Indians, squaws, children and Mexicans about to make the long, rough Atlantic crossing to England. (Photographed by Merritt & Von Wagner and reproduced courtesy of the Library of Congress, Washington DC)

knew it would be easy to capitalise on his influence and attract braves from other tribes.

But the Indians on the quayside that morning were reluctant to climb the gangplank. They included Little Bull, Cut Meat, Black Elk and Poor Dog who were all certain that as soon as they lost sight of land, death awaited them. They had been told that crossing the big water to a strange land would be beneficial to their tribes. Now they weren't so sure.

Captain Braes of the *State of Nebraska* sent word that he was ready to depart. 'Squaw man' John Nelson and 'Bronco Bill' Irving – cowboy and Indian interpreter – went down to reason with them. 'At the last moment it required all our arts of persuasion to induce them to go on board,' wrote Bill.

Red Shirt explained that his braves believed that, as soon as the ship set sail: 'They would be seized by a strange malady that would first prostrate the victim and then slowly consume his flesh, day after day, until at last the skin itself would drop from his bones, leaving nothing but the skeleton and this even could never find burial.'

Reluctantly they boarded what Black Elk called the big fire boat – 'so big that when I first saw, I could hardly believe it; and when it set forth a noise, I was frightened'. As the ship pulled from the pier, Bill heard 'such cheers . . . as I never before heard, while our cowboy band played 'The Girl I Left Behind Me' in a manner that suggested more reality than empty statement in the familiar air.'

The company waved hats in the air while the Indians performed a war dance on the upper deck. Some waved red and yellow blankets until the crowds faded in

. . . the Indians on the quayside that morning were reluctant to climb the gangplank. They were all certain that as soon as they lost sight of land, death awaited them.

Ogila-sa – or Chief Red Shirt – who was billed in the Wild West publicity material as 'Chief of the Sioux nation'. (Denver Public Library)

the distance and the *State of Nebraska* headed towards the open Atlantic. Bill recalled:

> A certain feeling of pride came over me when I thought of the good ship on whose deck I stood, and that her cargo consisted of early pioneers, rude rough riders from that section, and the wild horses of the same district, buffalo, deer, elk and antelope – the king game of the prairie – together with over 100 representatives of that same foe that had been

compelled to submit to a conquering civilisation and were now accompanying me in friendship, loyalty and peace five thousand miles from their homes, braving the dangers of the unknown sea . . . all of us combined in an exhibition intended to prove to the centre of the old world civilisation that the vast region of the United States was finally and effectively settled by the English-speaking race.

The following day subjected passengers and their four-legged cargo to a full Atlantic swell, and:

. . . the Indians began to grow weary and their stomachs, like my own, became both treacherous and rebellious. Their fears were now so greatly intensified that even Red Shirt, the bravest of his people, looked anxiously towards the hereafter, and began to feel his flesh to see it were really diminishing. The seal of hopelessness stamped upon the faces of the Indians aroused my pity, and though sick as a cow with hollow-horn myself, I used my utmost endeavours to cheer them up and relieve their forebodings. But for two days nearly the whole company was too sick for any other active service than feeding the fishes, in which I am not proud to say that I performed more than my ordinary share.

Annie Oakley and Frank Butler were the only passengers who managed to keep their food down and for the first two days had the ship to themselves. By day three, the waters were calmer – and so were the stomachs of passengers on board the *State of Nebraska*. Bill and Salsbury called the company together in the main saloon, 'and gave them a Sunday address, as did Red Shirt, who was recovered from his anxiety about the future'.

To keep the company occupied, an on-board entertainment was arranged every afternoon, in which Salsbury revived comic songs and vaudeville routines from the Troubadours 'to the intense delight of all on board'. Everyone now witnessed Salsbury in an entirely new light. Up to this point, they had known him as the boss, the arena director, a strict teetotaller, small in stature, fashionably dressed with a small cigar never far away from his bearded face. Cavorting before them now was a funny music hall artiste, a mime and a mimic, a face-puller, singer of comic songs, deliverer of humorous recitations performing in a fashion equally hilarious to cowboys, Indians and Mexicans. The Indians made him an honorary Chief, re-naming him 'Little Big Man'.

On the seventh day of the voyage, 'a storm came up that raged so fiercely that for a time the ship had to lay to, and during which our stock suffered greatly, but we gave them such good care, and had such excellent luck as well, that none of our animals, save one horse, died on the trip.'

Annie Oakley recalled:

En-route to London we encountered terrific storms that smashed our propeller. We drifted helpless in the trough of the sea for 48 hours. For ten hours I was wrapped in an oilskin, head protected by a sou'wester, and sat strapped to the Captain's deck.

For 48 hours the old grizzled Scotch Captain never left the deck. Double watches were at every post. Before I left the bridge word came up, 'all ready' and the boat

Cavorting before them now was a funny music hall artiste, a mime and a mimic, a face-puller, singer of comic songs, deliverer of humorous recitations. The Indians made him an honorary Chief, re-naming him 'Little Big Man'.

made a dangerous turn and headed towards London. We had drifted 264 miles out of our course. Not a passenger, except my husband and myself, knew that we had been in danger of losing our lives.

While the *State of Nebraska* was pitching and tossing in mid-Atlantic, in West Kensington 1,200 men were working shifts around the clock building American Exhibition pavilions and a giant Wild West stadium. By March 1887, the ground plan and buildings had begun to take shape, hidden from passing Londoners by giant wooden screens to keep out noise and intruders.

But by the time Major Burke arrived back in London in advance of the company, work was way behind schedule and newspapers voiced doubts that everything would be ready for opening day on 9 May. Heavy snow fell on London that March, interrupting building work and construction of drainage trenches for several days. An extra 800 men were hired to reinforce construction teams, but as the opening loomed, it was certain that parts of Earls Court would be incomplete.

Construction of the main exhibition building – 1,140 ft long and 120 ft wide – was weeks behind schedule. Builders were having difficulty erecting a galvanised iron roof, fitting large panes of glass to a special framework made from railway lines, also used as roof columns.

The wooden floor was being divided into four 'avenues' – Washington, Franklin, Lincoln and Cleveland – and at right angles to these were a number of 'streets' numbered American-style, '1st' to '10th'.

At the building's north end, 'Machinery in Motion' would be exhibited, the centrepiece being a 300 horsepower Wheelock engine supplied with steam by a battery of Babcock and Wilcox boilers, and 600 horsepower electric lighting would illuminate the building. Articles in various stages of manufacture would be on show 'because making something is always attractive to people', claimed exhibition publicity material. Agricultural machinery, collections of canned goods, jewellery, watches and clocks, false teeth 'and an endless variety of novel and curious products of American ingenuity and invention' would be displayed.

The dining saloon – 240 ft long and 90 ft wide – was located next to a main entrance near Earls Court station. The press voiced an opinion, still commonly held today, that exhibition catering was generally of a low quality. One publication stated: 'The refreshment department is generally the pitfall of the executive of such shows, and we trust in this instance the public will not be handed over to the untender mercies of those gigantic purveyors of expensive dyspepsia sometimes known as refreshment contractors, to be ill fed and overcharged without remedy or redress.'

Adjoining the dining saloon was the Fine Art Gallery – 160 ft long, 80 ft wide and 'of fireproof construction' – where 1,000 paintings loaned by American museums and private collections would be exhibited. 'This will be the most complete collection that has ever been assembled,' claimed a publicity brochure. 'Eight different rooms will exhibit wholly national art from the United States.'

By the time Major Burke arrived back in London in advance of the company, work was way behind schedule and newspapers voiced doubts that everything would be ready for opening day.

Land occupied by the American Exhibition was owned by London's private railway companies, who ensured that four local stations – West Brompton, West Kensington, Addison Road and Earls Court '& the American Exhibition Station' – were ready to handle the throng of sightseers expected to pass through turnstiles on their way to the event. Platforms were extended, ticket offices enlarged and extra staff hired. Tickets were placed on sale from every railway station in England to one of the four stations.

Major Burke, however, was horrified by what he discovered at the Wild West site, an island cut off from the rest of the exhibition by a triangle of railway tracks, the half-finished wooden amphitheatre sitting in a sea of mud, grim and uninviting against London's grey skyline.

Assurances were given that although construction was late, everything would be finished on time, including the Wild West's amphitheatre with covered seating and boxes for 20,000 spectators and standing room for 10,000, with open-air standing room for a further 10,000 people. There would be a circular arena measuring a third of a mile in circumference, corrals, stables and barns for animals – even a specially constructed hill made from gravel and rock and landscaped with native American trees and plants. This would screen the specially built Wild West camp from the rest of the site, allowing Indians to live in native tepees and the rest of the company in tents containing all the comforts of home. Another area for washrooms, toilets and a huge field kitchen where three daily meals would be prepared for the company and served in large dining tents had also to be completed.

The site would be surrounded by 12 acres of ornamental gardens and pleasure grounds laid out in pathways, flower gardens and a shrubbery featuring species of native American plants expected to survive the vagaries of London's unpredictable summer climate. Musical pavilions would be built and Mr Dan Godfrey and the band of the Grenadier Guards were engaged to give twice-daily concerts. The *Illustrated London News* reported:

> A great variety of amusements will be provided, including a diorama of the Harbour of New York, designed by M. Bartholdi, creator of the colossal Statue of Liberty, a model of the switch back railway, roller toboggans and other appliances and entertaining spectacles. In the evening, the Exhibition will be lighted by two hundred and fifty electric lights, each of two thousand actual candlepower, and nine huge searchlights, each of ten thousand actual candlepower. It is wonderful to think of this picturesque and fairy-like park and buildings, created by magical quickness on a piece of wasteland. And what will it be to see it at night, illuminated by lights equal to half a million candles!

Assurances were given that although construction was late, everything would be finished on time.

Before anything could be lit, however, it first had to be completed and Major Burke took on the responsibility of personally overseeing construction work on the Wild West site. In between twice-daily site visits, on which he goaded builders into working faster in return for free Wild West family passes, Burke kept his word and revisited newspaper contacts established on his previous London visit.

Burke was a master at planting press articles. Public relations consultants, press agents, promoters and spin-doctors were unheard of in England in 1887. Major

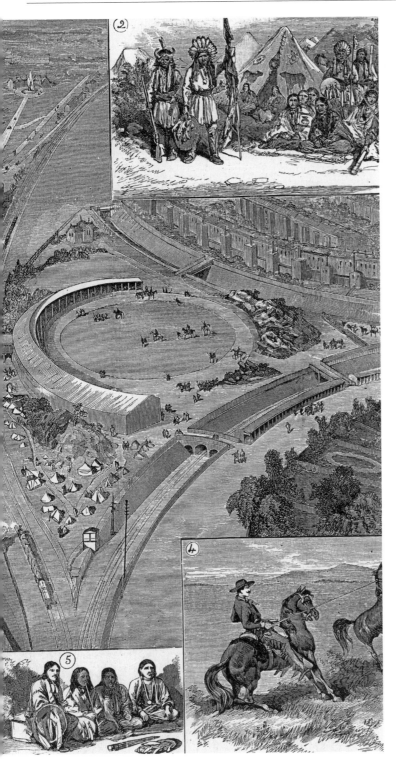

An artist's view of 'The American Exhibition, Earls Court, West Brompton and West Kensington' from the 16 April 1887 edition of *Illustrated London News*. When the artist produced the picture with so few people on site, he obviously underestimated how many paying customers would visit Earls Court, which attracted over two million people during Queen Victoria's Golden Jubilee year. The long building with the decorated façade opposite the wooden Wild West arena housed the American Exhibition. Inset drawings show: 1. cowboys taming wild steers; 2. Indians and their squaws prepare to sail to England; 4. rounding up wild mustangs; 5. Indians share a traditional pipe. (Earls Court/Olympia Archives)

THE MAJOR.

The portly figure of Major Burke attracted the cartoonist's eye. (*Illustrated Sporting & Dramatic News*)

Burke was probably Victorian London's first encounter with what became known later as 'the PR man'. They admired his brash American business methods and ability to come up with fresh and exciting stories about Buffalo Bill and the Wild West every day; everything from a small tit-bit of information which would make a paragraph or two to a front page lead story, already prepared for a newspaper 'incognito' by the pen of Major John M. Burke.

The following is an example of a story 'planted' by Major Burke in the *Daily News* while Buffalo Bill's company was still being tossed about on the high seas. Burke had twice crossed the Atlantic himself, and knew that some of the company – especially the Indians – would suffer from seasickness. Little did he know the full extent of the Wild West's troubles on the Atlantic when he wrote:

There is considerable speculation about the Red Indians composing Buffalo Bill's troupe. On the presumption that Nature never intended that interesting race for the functions of the mariner, it is thought possible that strange things may result from the voyage. Will the brave warriors exchanging the wigwam for the forecastle perish miserably from sickness? Will they rise with a whoop of vengeance, flourishing the tomahawk as they hold onto the weather shrouds, and scalp Jack Tar for putting the indignity upon them?

These are the questions propounded in joke. Seriously, however, the voyage is calculated to upset the Indians, take the heart out of the horses, and demoralise the buffaloes; and it has, in consequence, been arranged that they shall all have a good spell of rest before they are all called upon to career around the splendid circular track which is laid out overlooked by a substantial amphitheatre that will, sitting and standing, accommodate 40,000 spectators. . . . The steamship in which Buffalo Bill and his strange and numerous Wild West company voyage hither, the *State of Nebraska*, is now about four days out and under ordinary circumstances the trip would last about 12 days. After a good deal of negotiation, permission has been given to land the livestock in one of the London docks, and the vessel is therefore coming direct to the Thames having been chartered expressly for the exhibition.

The topical magazine, *Punch*, prepared its readers for Bill's arrival with a special poem called 'The Coming Centaur' (the first verse of which heads this chapter) based on Major Burke's lyrical descriptions of his boss:

> Soon he'll cross the Atlantic,
> In quest of new game,
> With horses half frantic
> And riders the same:
> A novel sensation
> He'll make in this nation –
> So cheers half a hundred for Buffalo Bill!

With horsemanship daring
Our sight will be blest;
All the town will be staring
At sports of the West.
His American cowboys
Will kick up a row boys,
Such as London will witness with rapturous Zest.
This Centaur Heroic
Would gladden a Stole.
So droll is his humour, so curious his skill.
We'll get something sunny
And fresh for our money –
Hip! hip! hip! hooray! Then, for Buffalo Bill.

Thanks to Major Burke's powers of persuasion, by the time the *State of Nebraska* sighted the British coastline, construction work on the Wild West site was nearing completion, Londoners had read countless newspaper stories – and poems – about Buffalo Bill, his exploits, his cowboys and Indians. Huge full-coloured posters advertising the event were everywhere. They featured Bill's portrait surrounded by Wild West scenes. It must have been difficult to have lived in London in the spring of 1887 and not known that Buffalo Bill Cody was coming to town.

It must have been difficult to have lived in London and not known that Buffalo Bill Cody was coming to town.

As the *State of Nebraska* ploughed through stormy waters towards London, *Punch* joked: 'At present we don't know much about "Buffalo Bill", but one thing is certain, that the Buffalo Bill-poster is doing its work uncommonly well.'

In a poetic mood, *The Globe* too wrote a special ode to Buffalo Bill on the eve of his arrival:

I may walk it, or 'bus it, or hansom it: still
I am faced by the features of Buffalo Bill.
Every hoarding is plastered, from East-end to West,
With his hat, coat, and countenance, lovelocks and
    vest.
Plunge in City or fly suburbwards – go where I will,
Bill and Bill's 'Billy-ruffians' appear on the bill.
But this pictured ubiquity's perfectly 'nil,'
To the actual crop-up of Buffalo Bill.
When my infants perambulate Sydenham Hill,
They get fits through the red-skins of Buffalo Bill.
And – an elderly man – I am scared in my walks
By their blankets, paint, feathers, clubs, scalps,
    tomahawks.
If I dine, I am dining with Cowboys and Sioux,
With a squaw near me feeding her copper papoose.
If for moral improvement I seek the Pavil-
ion, I rub shoulders there with some Buffalo Bill.

In my youth I was partial, it must be confessed,
To my Cooper, my Mayne Reid, and all the Wild West.
Quantum suff!* I am grizzling; a little will fill,
When the article's 'Injuns' and Buffalo Bill.

* 'Enough is enough!'

'At last as we cast anchor off Gravesend a tugboat approaching attracted the entire company on deck,' wrote Bill, thinking it contained Major Burke and a welcoming party. It turned out to be a government boat full of customs and quarantine officials wanting to inspect everything and everyone on the *State of Nebraska*.

The Major had arranged for the company's ammunition to be unloaded separately and stored in an arsenal. Supplies would be drawn daily. The animals were inspected and permits granted allowing them to be unloaded at the Royal Albert Docks, where they would be quarantined for a few days before being transferred to the Wild West camp. The rest of the company would also disembark at the Royal Albert, where chartered trains would be waiting to transfer the American passengers to their new home for the next six months.

Suddenly all thoughts of seasickness disappeared as word spread that the reception committee had arrived.

Before the ship turned into the Thames, Bill leaned on the railings to watch other craft of all sizes plying backwards and forwards on one of Europe's busiest waterways. Dozens of yachts, tugboats, barges and pleasure craft had turned out to meet the *State of Nebraska* and welcome Buffalo Bill's Wild West to England. 'I thought of the magnitude of the enterprise I was engaged in and wondered what its results would be,' Bill mused as he waved to his floating welcome party.

Another tug interrupted his train of thought. A starry banner flew from its mast and scores of handkerchiefs waved in the breeze. As the tug drew near, the strains of the 'Star Spangled Banner' could be heard, played by a band on the dock. William Sweeney's Cowboy Band immediately responded with 'Yankee Doodle' and suddenly all thoughts of seasickness and travel fatigue among the American passengers disappeared as word spread from bow to stern that the reception committee had arrived.

Heading the welcoming party was Major Burke with Lord Ronald Gower, a director of the American Exhibition, and other members of the organising committee, 'who made us feel at last that our sea voyage was ended'.

The tugboat landed Bill and the officials at Gravesend where a large group had gathered on shore to greet them. Major Burke had obviously been working hard. A 'Buffalo Bill Special' train waited to transport the VIPs to London and an hour later they pulled into Victoria Station. Bill noted that the railway tracks were level with rooftops and chimneys of thousands of homes, and:

. . . was a novel sight as we scurried along through what seemed to be an endless sea of habitation, and I have scarcely yet found where Gravesend finishes and London commences, so dense is the population of the suburbs of the 'boss village' of the British Isles, and so numerous the small towns through which we passed. The impression created by the grand Victoria station, by the underground railroad, the strange sights and busy scenes of the West End, the hustle and the bustle of a first evening view of mighty London, would alone make a chapter.

Bill's first impression of Victorian London's teeming streets was 'sufficiently lively and noisy to have alarmed all the dogs in every Indian village in the Platte country, from the Missouri river to the headwaters of the Platte, in its most primitive days.'

To reach the Wild West camp at Earls Court, the VIPs took a short journey on the new underground railway, which Bill found 'somewhat dark and sulphurous'. They left at West Kensington where Bill got his first view of the huge site where the American Exhibition and Wild West were still taking shape on the far side of a small bridge across the railway lines.

Entering the headquarters of the exhibition we found a bounteous repast set and a generous welcome accorded us. The heartiness of my reception, combined with the natural sense of relief after such a journey and the general indications of success, proved a happy relaxation of the nervous strain to which I had been subjected for several weeks. Speeches, toasts and well wishes . . . accompanied the spirited and spirituous celebration of the occasion. My genial hosts' capacity for the liquid refreshments would have made me envy them in the 90s, and led me to suspect that there might be accomplishments in England in which even western pioneers are excelled.

After welcome speeches 'and a tranquillising smoke' it was time to visit the Wild West camp where hundreds of labourers were still working on the arena, illuminated by naphtha flares and bonfires. Stables and corrals were almost completed and would be ready when the animals arrived in a few days' time. 'Everything so far impressed me favourably and I began to feel that if we did not command success we would, with our advantages of location, surroundings and novelty and realism, at least deserve it.'

As darkness fell on West London, Bill suddenly became aware that workmen had put down their tools to gaze at the famous Buffalo Bill now in their midst. 'The interest evinced by the British workmen in my presence detracting somewhat from their attention to business, caused us to retire after a brief inspection.'

It was now time for Bill to be introduced to 'that world-famed vehicle', the horse-drawn London hansom cab:

'My genial hosts' capacity for the liquid refreshments led me to suspect that there might be accomplishments in England in which even western pioneers are excelled.'

In one of them I was whirled through the West End, past the famous Hyde Park, through Piccadilly, around Leicester and Trafalgar Squares, to that central resort and theatrical hub of this vast community, the Strand. This narrow street, in its relation to the great city, reminded me of one of the contracted passes in the Rockies to which traffic had been naturally attracted, and usage had made a necessity. The density of its foot traffic, the thronging herd of omnibuses, the twisting, wriggling, shouting, whip-cracking cabbies, seemed like Broadway squeezed narrower, and I realised

Buffalo Bill wearing fringed buckskins, kid leather gauntlets and boots and a large felt hat. The picture was taken at the studios of society photographers Elliot & Fry at 55 Baker Street, London, and used as publicity material. It was also mass-produced as a postcard and offered for sale at Wild West showgrounds. Queen Victoria requested a similar photograph following the second of two Royal Command performances in 1887 and 1892 and a copy is included in the Royal Archive at Windsor Castle. (Michael Bailey Collection)

at once the utility and necessity of the two-wheeled curio in which I was whirled through the bewildering mingle of Strand traffic.

With but one or two hub-bumps, we were soon landed at the magnificent Hotel Metropole in Northumberland Avenue, where I met many American gentlemen from different cities, who recognised me on sight and gave me hearty greetings. I retired early, determined to re-trace my steps to Gravesend at daylight and ascend the Thames on board the *Nebraska*, as my great anxiety was the successful embarkation.

On his first night in London, Bill slept like a bear in a cave in his giant bed at the Hotel Metropole.

'THE YANKEERIES', 'BUFFALO BILLERIES' & 'THE SCALPERIES'

We hear that the Cowboys are wonders,
And do what rough riders dare,
So wherever the 'pitch' is in London
Its wild horses will drag us there.
O, fancy the scene of excitement!
O, fancy five acres of thrill,
The cowboys and Injuns and horses,
And the far-famed Buffalo Bill!

The Referee, 1887

ARRIVAL AT THE PORT OF LONDON – MAKING CAMP AT EARLS COURT – A SMALL WESTERN TOWN IN WEST LONDON – HENRY IRVING GREETS THE COWBOYS – '15 GOOD REASONS TO VISIT BUFFALO BILL'S WILD WEST' – ED GOODMAN WRITES HOME – INDIANS OUT AND ABOUT – MAILBAGS FULL OF INVITATIONS – MR GLADSTONE COMES TO CALL – GENTLEMEN OF THE PRESS – THE PRINCE AND PRINCESS OF WALES – ANNIE'S ROYAL BLUNDER – A GRANDSTAND SEAT ON OPENING DAY – A SENSATIONAL PRESS

Bill claimed that 'representatives of the leading journals' travelled on the welcome tugboat to Gravesend, but Major Burke had politely asked the press to stay away as he knew the American passengers would be tired and not at their best. Newspapers would be invited to meet the company a few days later and have access to them whenever they wished after that time. But this was not good enough for some journals, which, by now – thanks to Major Burke – could not get enough copy about Buffalo Bill.

The following demonstrates the lengths – and dangers – a reporter would go to to 'scoop' rivals over a century ago. The *Globe* sent its representative to Gravesend with strict instructions to board the *State of Nebraska* to get the first British interview with Buffalo Bill. The correspondent takes up the story:

> It was with anticipation all agog that I set out on my visit of reception. Nor was I altogether satisfied with my prospects of success. My information was of the slightest. The courteous staff at Earls Court who, one would of thought, would have known most about the arrival, were singularly ill-informed on this point, and all that they were enabled to tell me was that Mr Cody would treat me with the greatest courtesy

if I found him either at Gravesend or the Albert Docks. As no time, or indeed date, was mentioned, this information did not teach me very much, and I therefore threw myself on the mercy of Messrs Adamson and Donaldson, London agents of the State Line, to which the *Nebraska* belongs, for information and facilities about the arriving show. The firm in Leadenhall Street, with most exceptional good nature, put me 'au courant' with all that was going on, nay, more than this, they supplied me with some very valuable letters of introduction; and thus equipped I set out to Gravesend to bid the Redskins welcome to the shores of Albion.

At the Kentish Port I met with all the usual adventures. One person informed me that the *Nebraska* would not arrive until today; another that she was lying off the town; and yet another that she had departed for London some hours ago. After some difficulty I discovered that the vessel in question was lying-to off the Powder Magazine, two miles down river, and that she would shortly make for the Albert Docks, without staying at Gravesend at all. I had come down to board the *Nebraska*, and board her I must; therefore it was I placed myself in the hands of an enterprising waterman who, for a consideration – not much more than double the legal fare – undertook to put me on board the *Nebraska* by hook or by crook. That man kept his contract; but it was by crook. I will not describe the agonies of that passage across the bosom of the Thames. I will not detail my feelings on discovering that the little cockleshell in which I had 'put to sea' was right across the bows of the *Nebraska* advancing at some eight knots an hour; nor will I explain how, by some miraculous movement of the rudder, the Leviathan avoided the impending collision and shaved us by a couple of feet, while my waterman seized a chain, and placing my devoted feet on the bottom tread of a rope ladder, bade me good day and left me dangling some four feet above the rushing tide. How I swarmed up that ladder, I must refuse to divulge. Suffice it that in a more or less battered condition I found myself standing on deck in the middle of one of the quaintest scenes I have ever beheld. Around me stood . . . 100 individuals, all strangers to me. Their faces were decidedly foreign, and their clothes indescribably romantic. About one half of these had red faces, and their costume consisted principally of a blanket. The rest were of various shades, from pure white to dusky brown. They were mostly handsome, and of big stature; several were upwards of 6 ft in height. Such was my first glimpse of Buffalo Bill's Wild West Show.

Having recovered somewhat from my shaking, I proceeded to make my way to the bridge, there to present a letter of introduction to the Captain. I have no wish to be personal, but I should like to place on record my regret that I only made Captain Braes' acquaintance at the end of the voyage, for had I done so at its commencement I should inevitably have spent a very pleasant time in most delightful company. Having presented my credentials, I enquired for the Hon. W.F. Cody, better known to fame as Buffalo Bill. To my regret, I learned that the 'boss', as most of the passengers termed him, had gone ashore from the Powder Magazine, but I succeeded in finding Mr Nate Salsbury, his associate, who put me in charge of his henchman, Mr Irvine, rejoicing in the pseudonym of 'Bronco William', for the purpose of being introduced to the company, and making the round of the ship.

The living freight on board the *State of Nebraska* is probably as curious, and certainly as mixed, a company as was ever sent afloat . . . the whites include, firstly, the 'bosses' or chiefs; secondly, cowboys; thirdly, Mexicans, to say nothing of lady artists of whom more hereafter. The Indians are divided into Sioux, Cheyenne

'I will not detail my feelings on discovering that the little cockleshell in which I had "put to sea" was right across the bows of the Nebraska advancing at some eight knots an hour . . .'

(pronounced Shien), Pawnees and Raphoes.* Several of these gentry are accompanied by their squaws . . . there are eight children on board, besides several young people of both sexes. It is, however, unnecessary for me to dilate upon the appearance of the passengers on board the *Nebraska*, since it must be well known to every reader of modern literature. The scene on board the *State of Nebraska* might have been taken out of Fenimore Cooper. There stood the Redskins, mute and immovable. There in dignified silence they stood dressed in paint and blankets. Haughty in mien, graceful in manner, picturesque in dress, the Red Indians of the Wild West Show and the 'Last of the Mohicans' are one and the same. To minutely detail the manner of these interesting visitors would be but to forestall the pleasure of a visit to Earls Court. I will, therefore, content myself with describing the brief interview I enjoyed with 'Ogalisha' or Red Shirt, a handsome redskin of about 36, the acknowledged chief of the Indians on board. This gentleman's appearance is very much in his favour. He does not paint to the same extent that some of his comrades indulge in. He is satisfied with a single streak of vermilion down each side of his face, extending from the eyebrow to the chin. His costume consists of moccasins in pretty bead work, trousers once, apparently, 'a world too wide' and subsequently tacked all the way down, forming a compromise between a pair of inexpressible and a divided skirt, and a blanket, while his forehead is girdled with a silk handkerchief.

In response to a question put to him Ogalisha replies, 'I never saw the ocean or a boat before, but I enjoyed the trip very much. I look forward with pleasure to seeing this country. I should like to make friends among the natives over here.' This he enunciated in truly regal fashion. Having finished, he inclined his head, and I could well-nigh imagine the rest – 'I have spoken, go thy way'. The whole action of the man tallied with what we read, the only difference being that we are accustomed to associate this language with the backwoods, while the above took place on the Thames. It would be easy to dilate for hours on the picturesque outlines of these people as seen on board – the men squatting on the deck or playing cards in the smoking cabin; the women leaning against the boiler house for the sake of warmth, some nursing their little ones on their backs, while others wander to and fro smoking cigarettes.

I have not, however, said anything of the white element in the Wild West Show, and this is even more remarkable than the red. I have little fear of contradiction when I state that the passengers on board the *State of Nebraska* include some of the finest specimens of humanity ever brought to this country. An Englishman's notions of a cowboy are likely to be very considerably wide of the mark. I own that, for my part, I had thought that the word cowboy was a synonym for all that was rough and uncultured in the semi-civilised portions of the Great Republic. On the contrary, the American cowboy is an individual of striking manners, good education and elegant appearance, and a jolly good fellow to boot. I yesterday made the acquaintance of several of these gentlemen and a pleasanter set of men or better company it would be difficult to meet. Nay more, I predict that the gentlemen who come under this appellation are destined to play considerable havoc with hearts in this country, and feel certain that more than one romantic young damsel will fall head over ears in love with one or more cowboys on her first visit to Earls Court. The average cowboy is above average height, well built, compact, and handsome. He has a dashing sort of way, a happy sort of knack of 'palling up' with those who take his fancy, and he can

'The American cowboy is an individual of striking manners, good education and elegant appearance, and a jolly good fellow to boot.'

* Arapahos

give vent to the most extraordinary war-whoop that ever went from mortal throat. It is to Tom Duffey, an excellent specimen of this very enviable race, that most of my limited acquaintance with the fraternity is due, and if any reader doubts my word he need only glance at Buck Taylor, the cowboy chief, height six feet four inches, or Dick Dolmson, his comrade, six feet three inches, and he will surely be satisfied. If another and a duskier style of manly beauty be desired I need only to refer to Antonius Esquivel, the chief of the Mexicans; or to Andres Rozzals, the steer rider; while among the whites, Billy Bullock, height six feet; Billy Pough, Cherokee Bill and Jim Mitchell can hold their own against all comers.

But I have neglected the ladies! 'Tis true, but only as a bonne bouche, to keep them till last. I must excuse myself from describing them; their appearance is beyond description. I will therefore content myself with mentioning that Miss Emma Lake, the champion lady rider in the United States, Mrs Gregory Duffy, the famous rough rider, Miss Annie Oakley, the crack lady shot, and Señora Pancheo Ageure, the celebrated lady rider, are all among the passengers on board the *Nebraska*.

Early next morning Bill rushed back to Gravesend to sail into the city with the rest of his company under bright blue skies; and, 'with flags flying we entered amid a perfect ovation the great Port of London.'

With each horseman looking after his own mount, the cargo of passengers and animals was quickly discharged. British officials and stevedores on the wharf were amazed by the speed of the operation. The *Daily News* was on the quayside to witness the scene: 'Out of the holds fore and aft were swung at rapid intervals either bales of cargo, or horseboxes containing buffalo, horses or other livestock. The whirr of the steam winch, the shouts of the men engaged in landing cargo, and the miscellaneous bustle around were exciting enough to the spectators railed off from the wharf.'

The reporter noted that the Indians stood in the sunshine leaning over the rail silently watching the activity below.

Nothing disturbed their placidity now that the voyage was over, any more than on the voyage . . . It is rumoured that they did not think much of the scenery. The English, however, who looked at them yesterday thought a good deal of their picturesqueness. As they topped the larboard rail, ablaze with the scarlet and blue of their blankets, they were exceedingly striking. So were the scouts and the cowboys in their wide-brimmed hats, high boots and comely stature. But on the *Nebraska*'s decks, one came to closer quarters with the Indians. The eye welcomed it; the nose knew it; though the unencumbered stalls of the livestock had not a little – perhaps everything – to do with the last mentioned item.

Looking upon the chiefs, braves and squaws, one could not help recalling the delightful sensations of youth – the first acquaintance with the Last of the Mohicans, the Great Spirit, Firewater, Laughing Water and the dark Huron warrior. Here were their counterparts – moccasins, feathers, beaver skins, beads and a fine show of war paint; ugly faces made uglier by rude art; dignified countenances which retained a stamp of high-breeding through ochre and vermilion. . . . Not a glance was wasted upon a stranger. All that came to the Indians was taken for granted; an archbishop in all its finery would have fallen short of their mark. . . . The buffaloes seemed to us in need of a source of pick-me-ups; and the horses had not, to all outward appearance, much buck left in them. A few days rest, feeding and exercise at Earls Court will no doubt put them all right again, and it is really proof of good management that the voyage had been so successfully made.

Special trains from Galleon's station were diverted on to tracks running alongside the wharf to transport the company directly to Earls Court. On arrival, everything was quickly unloaded, 'Old Glory' run up the flagpole to the strains of the 'Star Spangled Banner' played by the Cowboy Band and, by mid-afternoon, a canvas city of tepees and box-sided tents had been erected next to the Wild West amphitheatre.

Crowds gathered to watch the operation from the street, hanging from upstairs windows and clinging to chimney pots on the rooftops of nearby 'third floor front' houses. In appreciation of their interest, the band played 'God Save the Queen' to roars of approval from the spectators. Wrote Bill:

Crowds gathered to watch the operation from the street, hanging from upstairs windows and clinging to chimney pots. The band played 'God Save the Queen' to roars of approval from the spectators.

Thus the Wild West and Bill Cody of Nebraska USA were at home in camp in London. The dining tents not being yet up, our first meal was taken in full view of our kindly and curious visitors. The meal was finished by 7 o'clock and by 9 o'clock the tired occupants of the camp, Indians, Mexicans, cowboys, scouts, men, women and children were peacefully and snugly reposing after a long and arduous voyage.

Although a large and luxurious tent was erected for Bill – known as the 'Pahaska Tepee' or 'Long Hair's Lodge' – there was to be no camp bed under canvas for the star of the show. London's smartest hotel, the two-year-old Hotel Metropole in Northumberland Avenue between Victoria Embankment, Charing Cross and The Strand, was to be his home for the first weeks of the engagement. This was one of London's most fashionable addresses, a perfect base for a prominent overseas visitor, providing easy access to all parts of the city – and its many temptations.

A thousand and one jobs still had to be completed before the official opening of the American Exhibition and Wild West show three weeks later. Bill visited the showground early each morning to supervise completion of the arena, check that his Wild West family was comfortable in their strange new inner-city surroundings and rehearse the show.

The public had been promised a chance to wander through the Wild West camp, view horses and buffalo used in the show, gaze at Indians in their tepees and meet the cowboy stars. Some Indians needed persuasion to allow strangers near their tepees. Red Shirt intervened and some finally agreed to sit outside with squaws and papooses to be stared at by a curious British public, who would be allowed to peep inside the flap of a wigwam for a glimpse into their primitive private lives.

Earls Court quickly became a small western town, with tents pitched on the artificial hill and alongside pathways winding through the camp towards the large mess tent. There was even a Medicine Tent, a 'sweat house' – an Indian version of a sauna – where Red Shirt and his braves could relax in a steam-filled tepee, created by heating stones over which water was poured. At one time, *'inikagapi'* or 'taking a sweat' only took place as a ritual purification before battle. At Earls Court it would be used as a place to relax and unwind between performing 14 weekly shows to excited British audiences.

The self-sufficient American community also included blacksmiths, cooks, cleaners, trainers plus scores of others working behind the scenes, caring for animals, selling tickets, programmes, refreshments, keeping accounts, directing crowds and churning out endless publicity stories for newspapers desperate for anything new about Buffalo Bill's Wild West.

Two British doctors were engaged to ensure that everyone in the Wild West camp remained healthy. Dr Maitland Coffin was appointed medical officer to the Wild West while Dr J.B.W. Bidlack was engaged as medical director to the American Exhibition. Both doctors were charged with making sure that the entire Earls Court site remained in a hygienic condition at all times and conducted daily inspection visits to every tent in camp. The doctors insisted that all beds had to be turned out for ventilation at 7.30 each morning.

The Wild West camp also included a team of purchasing agents. Their job was to order 6000 lbs of fresh meat every day from London's Smithfield Market.

The Wild West camp also included a team of purchasing agents reporting to Treasurer Jule Keen. Their job was to order 6000 lbs of fresh meat every day from London's Smithfield Market, vegetables and fruit from Covent Garden, fish from Billingsgate and tinned goods from general stores. They ordered tons of flour for the Wild West's cooks to bake bread, large drums of coffee, gallons of milk, sacks of coal to fuel ovens in the mess tent and the blacksmith's forge, wagons full of straw and animal feed plus other produce to keep the two-legged and four-legged cast well-fed and healthy. The purchasing agents were keenly sought out by London traders and Keen demanded that they bargain for the best prices and insist that fresh goods be delivered daily to Earls Court, including Sundays.

In addition to William Sweeney's 15-piece Cowboy Band, who would also play in their off-duty hours for the amusement of the company, the Wild West brought along its own sheriff, Con Groner – billed 'the sheriff of the Platte, the nemesis of the lawless'. Groner had been sheriff of Lincoln County, Nebraska, where it was said he had an encounter with the outlaw Jesse James, captured 50 murderers and scores of assorted horse thieves and cattle rustlers. As well as keeping the peace, enforcing law and order at the Wild West camp, Groner also appeared in the show – in the role of a frontier sheriff.

There were daily interruptions to rehearsals, mostly from visiting dignitaries, stage and society personalities and curious VIPs anxious to use their influence to gain a sneak preview of what the *Daily News* called 'The Yankeeries', *Punch* described as the 'Buffalo Billeries' and many a London wag nicknamed 'The Scalperies'.

First on the scene was England's 'royal couple' of the theatre, actor-manager Henry Irving with his leading lady from the Lyceum Theatre company, Ellen Terry. Irving had visited the Wild West

Buffalo Bill's Wild West company at Earls Court London in 1887. Bill sits on the ground at centre, with Nate Salsbury (wearing a top hat) to his right. Standing behind Bill is the show's youngest performer, five-year-old Master Bennie Irving, and champion lady sharpshooter Lillian 'Young California' Smith. Major John Burke – jacketless and wearing a Stetson hat – sprawls leisurely across a blanket at Bill's left, with Annie Oakley (holding rifle) and Wild West Treasurer, Jule Keen, behind. Buck Taylor stands head and

shoulders behind Mr Keen while Chief Red Shirt – 'a redoubtable warrior and second only in influence to Sitting Bull himself' – proudly stands over Indian squaws in the front row. Members of The Cowboy Band with their instruments stand on the hill behind Bill with 'squaw man' John Nelson. Johnnie Baker sits near the top of the hill, below Sergeant Bates (in uniform), as usual holding the American flag. (Photograph by Elliot & Fry, reproduced by kind permission of the Michael Del Castello Collection of the American West)

Jule Keen – 'The Dutchman' – started his show business career as a character actor with Buffalo Bill's touring theatre company and later became Treasurer of the Wild West organisation.

on Staten Island and encouraged Bill and Salsbury to bring it to London. In an interview with the *Era* newspaper, Irving had predicted 'when the show comes to London, it will take the town by storm'. Bill later recalled: 'Sir Henry [*who was knighted for his services to the theatre in 1895*] was among the first to offer his kindly offices and lent us a strength of public, professional, personal and social influence that to me was almost invaluable.'

Miss Terry kissed all the Indian papooses that came her way and accepted an eagle's feather from Red Shirt, while Bill and Irving sat together in the 'Pahaska Tepee' smoking cigars and discussing the merits of which brands were best – American or British.

Members of Parliament, United States Embassy officials, Lord and Lady Randolph Churchill, Lord Ronald Gower, 'and hundreds of other Lords, Knights and ladies of high degree, besides a host of distinguished American residents of London, visited our camp and stables before the regular day of opening to give expressions of friendship, goodwill and encouragement', recalled Bill.

Excitement about 'The Yankeeries' was at fever pitch. The *Anglo-American Times* reported: 'The time of opening is approaching, activity is observable in all directions. Among the attractive signs of coming entertainment being the large coloured pictures of Buffalo Bill and the Wild West, so striking displayed on hoardings in London. Already people feel they are about to have a show distinguished – if by naught else – for novelty, and suspect that before many weeks are over, "The Yankeeries" will be in the fashion.'

While Bill and Salsbury broke off from rehearsals to receive more guests, Major Burke continued his rounds of newspaper offices, using his marketing skills to ensure that every London journalist had a good story to write about 'the Boss'. Before leaving each editorial office, he left behind what today's PR people call a 'press pack' – an information kit containing background material, biographies and stories reporters could use freely.

One of the enclosures is worth repeating here. Called '15 Good Reasons to Visit Buffalo Bill's Wild West' it put forward a strong argument why everyone should give up an afternoon or evening to visit Earls Court (if, by this time, anyone needed further persuasion):

1.   Over 1 million people have set you the example.
2.   Because it is a living picture of life on the frontier.
3.   It is an opportunity afforded your family but once in a lifetime.
4.   See how cowboys, Indians and Mexicans live.
5.   You will see buffalo, elk, wild horses and a multitude of curiosities.
6.   You will see an Indian village transplanted from the plains.
7.   You will see the most wonderful riders the world can produce.
8.   You will see the greatest marksmen in America.
9.   You will see Indian warfare depicted in true colours.
10. You will see the attack on the Deadwood stagecoach.
11. You will see a method of capturing wild horses and cattle.
12. You will see a buffalo hunt in all its realistic detail.
13. You will see your neighbours there in full force.
14. You will see Buffalo Bill (Hon. W.F. Cody)!
15. You will see an exhibition which has been witnessed and endorsed by President Arthur and his cabinet, General Sheridan and staff, Generals Cook, Miles, Sherman, Carr, etc. and tens of thousands of well informed people in every walk of life.

How could the British public possibly stay away from the 'Buffalo Billeries'?

 Bill's nephew Ed Goodman travelled to London with the Wild West to work as a programme seller for a few shillings a week. In a letter to parents Julia and Al Goodman, dated 'London, England Apr. 22 1887'.

Ed shares his impressions of London, the British, the weather, 'Uncle Will' and behind-the-scenes activities at Earls Court. Spelling and punctuation are all Ed's:

My dear Ma and Pa.
London is so much different from N.Y. and the people are so much different. . . . They are all alike to me. I can not see any difference in them. The working class of people are the slowest people I ever saw. I believe one good American man can do as much work as 4 English men. No wonder they do not get a good salary. They do not earn what they get. The money is so much different, but I know it as well as American money now and it will be as easy to make change here as it was in America. Uncle Will has not learnt it yet, he cannot get on to the way of saying it.

There must be 3000 people working on the grounds preparing to open, which is May 9, Monday. Everything is so old & out of style. The ladies at the Theatre ware low neck and short sleeve dresses & lace & white dresses and part there hair in the middle and comb it strait back. You would almost kill yourself a laughing to see some things here. Americans are very few over here, more so than English are in America and what few things there are not much importance, at least what I have saw. Clothing and some things are very cheap while others are dearer. There clothing is not as good as ours I think. They have things here for cheapness and do not look at the quality. Tobacco is about 4 times as much as in America. That is where I will save money as I do not use it. Everyone here drinks! But I don't have to if they do. I and Mr Canfield and Mr Parker (one of the main men) are tenting together in a 12 x 14 wall tent.

We have about 35 small tents 7 mediums and 4 or 5 large tent and about 12 or 15 Indian tepese. So you can see we have a large Co. including about 90 or 95 Indians and there is about 250 head of stock including Horses, cattle Buffaloes Elks deers & others such as Burroes mules and oxen. We have a grand stand that will seat about 50,000 people more or less and I think I can sell abot that many books on the season I hope so anyway so I can pay Uncle Will what I owe him. Uncle Will is looking good & getting fat I think. . . . We have more performers than we had at Staten Is. Or people that take part in the preformance. There are 12 ladies in the company. More cowboys and more mexicans.

We have some terrible fogs here you cannot see across the streets at times and they last 3 & 4 days. We also have terrible rains so they say. . . . Uncle Will is all right and looking good only when he is on the war path about something that goes rong and then everyone has to watch out and me too if I happen to be about at the time. Lord Mayor was out to see him yesterday and they gave him a little of the proformance, and thot it was great. He is bound to make big money the opening day is $5 or 1 pound admission and they expect 20,000 people and if they come that will be $100,000 How is that? Wait and see if they come.

While finishing touches were put to the site, the cowboys, Indians, Mexicans and rough riders from the Wild West company began to be seen out and about on London's streets – and Major Burke made sure that no move went unreported in the press.

On 25 April about forty Indians with an interpreter were taken to the morning service at the Congregational Chapel, West Kensington where – reported the *Pall Mall Gazette*: 'They were accommodated with seats in the transept. During the service they sang the hymn "Nearer My God To Thee" in their own tongue. These remarkable looking men in their picturesque costumes, bedecked with paint and feathers, presented the most striking picture. The minister of the church, Revd Alfred Norris, prayed that God, the Father of all, would vouchsafe a blessing on His children thus assembled to offer their common worship in His temple.'

The following day Red Shirt and a party of Indians were spotted at Westminster Abbey where the *Pall Mall Gazette* reported: 'The Indians joined reverently in the service, and were afterwards conducted around the building. They were more impressed with the Abbey than by anything they have yet seen. They were particularly anxious to know why England's Kings and Queens were buried, and Red Shirt, the notorious Sioux Chief, thought it could only be

'Uncle Will is all right and looking good only when he is on the war path about something that goes rong and then everyone has to watch out and me too if I happen to be about at the time.'

because they could there-by be certain of going to the happy hunting grounds. The Indians were also much impressed with a visit to the Tower, so much so that they want to go again.'

Henry Irving invited Bill, Salsbury, Buck Taylor, Red Shirt, Annie Oakley and Frank Butler plus half of the company to the Lyceum Theatre off The Strand to see Ellen Terry and himself perform in *Faust*. The Indians occupied front row seats, where they watched the play eating sugarplums while Bill, Salsbury and the cowboys sat in boxes.

After taking his curtain call at the close of the performance, Irving called his American friends on stage to share the limelight with Miss Terry and himself. This was probably the only time the famous Victorian players would share their stage with an Indian wearing an eagle feathered war bonnet, a cowboy in riding chaps and boots and a pint-sized lady sharpshooter. The audience loved it. Major Burke told the newspapers later that Red Shirt had likened Irving's production '*to a great dream.*'

Other outings included a river trip up the Thames to Hampton Court Palace, a visit to London's best-known music hall, The Palladium; to performances of *The Beggar's Opera* and *The Butler* at Toole's Theatre. There was also a railway journey to Windsor Castle, St George's Chapel 'and other places of interest . . . and a large number of spectators assembled on the platform of the railway station to witness their arrival,' reported the *Evening News*. Another newspaper stated that: 'Some Indians have even been encountered walking in the neighbourhood of the scene of their future performances.'

Thanks to Henry Irving, Bill was also becoming the social lion of London. The gossip column of *The Referee* reported:

Illustrated Sporting & Dramatic News comment on Bill's role as the new social lion of London society, 14 May 1887.

Buffalo Bill is already winning golden opinions of all sorts and conditions of men. Mr Irving has personally conducted him through clubland, and the 'magnificent man' with his wonderful hair, is the centre of eager little crowds wherever he goes. Sitting in a comfortable armchair in the smoking room of a club, he gives off true stories of adventure in the Wild West which beat fiction in a canter. The company becomes so engrossed that it breaks up at the very last possible moment.

Another tit-bit of gossip from the same paper stated: 'I am told, but I don't vouch for the truth of the statement, that Buffalo Bill has received a round robin, signed by the wives of the married members of the Garrick Club, asking him not to tell any stories after midnight, as the husbands have lately taken to coming home at four and five, and when remonstrated with they all say, "I'm very sorry, my dear, but I couldn't tear myself away. Buffalo Bill was so interesting."'

Mailbags full of invitations arrived daily at the Cody suite at the Hotel Metropole. Everyone wanted Buffalo

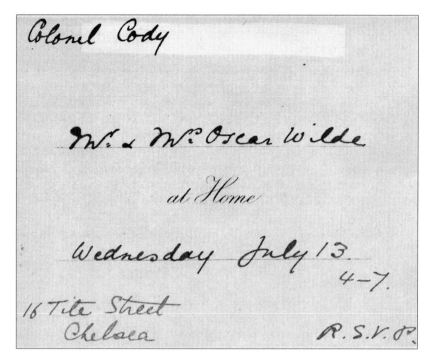

Colonel Cody

Mr & Mrs Oscar Wilde

at Home

Wednesday July 13.

4–7.

16 Tite Street Chelsea

R.S.V.P

Buffalo Bill's invitation to visit Mr and Mrs Oscar Wilde 'at home'. (Buffalo Bill Museum and Grave, Lookout Mountain, Golden, Colorado)

Bill to lunch, tea, dinner, and supper. He was invited to soirées, Grand Balls, civic functions, recitals, garden parties, matinées, dedications, sporting events and 'midnight doings'. He was made an honorary member of London's best gentlemen's clubs and 'many of them were distinctly distinguishing'. Bill told Salsbury that: 'In such cases as mine one should have as many lives as a stack of black cats, all working at once to keep the pace that was set for Buffalo Bill.'

At Salsbury's insistence, most daytime invitations were politely declined, a notable exception being lunch at the Mansion House with the Lord Mayor of London and a soirée at the home of Mr and Mrs Oscar Wilde at number 16 Tite Street, Chelsea. The Wild West had still to open and daylight hours were spent with his business partner making sure everything was ready for the premiere performance. Salsbury did not want his star becoming overtired and cautioned Bill to pace himself through the days leading up to the grand opening and avoid late night visits to gentleman's clubs. He told him there would be plenty of time for a social life once the show had opened.

Reflecting on this hectic time, Bill later recalled: 'To make the situation more exacting, as to my personal work, the hundred or so Indians with us from the Pine Ridge Agency were all new to the show and were of the wild variety; besides, we had a hundred new ponies from the plains of Texas that had never been bridled or saddled, much less shot over, and all these had to be brought into at least Wild West discipline, and largely under my personal supervision.'

Bill found social invitations hard to resist, especially those held late in the evening when he was able to escape from Earls Court for a few hours of fun with 'toffs' and influential new friends. One such invitation came from the Reform Club, where Bill was introduced for the first time to Edward, Prince of Wales, oldest son of Queen Victoria and heir to the British throne. At some stage during the evening, Bill plucked up the courage to invite Edward to visit the Wild West. Edward said he would love to attend, but Bill thought nothing further of the matter, appreciating that by accepting the Prince was almost certainly appearing polite in front of others.

Just over a week before the London opening, The Rt Hon William Gladstone, MP, the great Liberal reformer and former Prime Minister, announced that he wanted to visit 'The Yankeeries' with Mrs Gladstone. Gladstone had already served three terms as Prime Minister and a fourth would follow five years later. The press still followed every public movement made by the politician they referred to as the 'GOM' (Grand Old Man).

The Cowboy Band played 'Yankee Doodle' as the elder statesman and his party arrived at Earls Court to be met by a welcoming committee. The former premier quickly toured the American Exhibition before being escorted by Nate Salsbury to the Wild West site to be greeted by a large cheering crowd of cowboys and Indians – probably the strangest welcoming party ever to greet the 'GOM'. The *Daily News* reported: 'The Indians flocked out, greeting the ex-premier with cries of "Ugh, ugh," and readily shaking hands with him.'

Mailbags full of invitations arrived daily at the Cody suite at the Hotel Metropole. Everyone wanted Buffalo Bill to lunch, tea, dinner, and supper.

AT THE BILLERIES.

" Red Shirt," Chief of the Seeyou-at-West-Kensington Indians, receives a visit from " Grand Old White Collar," *alias* "Strong Will," Chief of the Opper Sishun Hinderuns.

Punch takes a satirical swipe at former British Prime Minister Gladstone's visit to Red Shirt's tepee at the Wild West camp, 7 May 1887.

Gladstone then entered the 'Pahaska Tepee', where the old politician admired some of Bill's trophies, including a ceremonial sword presented by US Army officers before his departure for England. The *Evening News* commented: 'The manly frankness of this splendid specimen of American backwoodsman highly interested Mr Gladstone and he remained in conversation with him for some time.'

The *Daily News* reported that 'the savage' Red Shirt was next to be introduced. Bill told the Indian chief that Mr Gladstone was England's 'Great White Chief'.

Red Shirt, possibly jealous of a Chief greater than himself, took in Mr Gladstone's measurement with a quick glance, drew his blanket closely around him and exhibited a stolid reserve when questioned. Presently he melted in response to his interpreter and answered more freely. Mr Gladstone asked him what he thought of the English climate, and Red Shirt, taking a minute or two to consider, said that he had not much to complain of in that respect so far. 'Well', said Mr Gladstone, 'do you see those similarities between Englishmen and Americans which might be expected to exist between kinsman and brothers?' This time Red Shirt answered without loss of a moment that he 'didn't know so much about their being kinsmen and brothers,' a reply which created a burst of laughter.

The item which pleased Gladstone most was a fight between cowboys and bucking horses.

The *Evening Standard* noted that during the laughter, 'the Indian stood like a marble statue'. The rival *Evening News* reported: 'Red Shirt's bright appearance and intelligent face won much admiration from the distinguished party, and Mr Gladstone was amused with some of his replies to questions put to him. The Right Hon. Gentleman could scarcely realise that this Indian was one of the most troublesome men in the United States, and had probably scalped more white men than any other Redskin now alive.'

Gladstone's party climbed into the new grandstand to see a shortened 'rehearsal edition' of the Wild West especially adapted by Nate Salsbury for the occasion. Along with a reporter from the *Daily News*, they saw 'Indians in their full war paint riding their speedy ponies dashing into the arena yelling their war cries. The whole body then forming into line with Buffalo Bill at their head galloped in line to the front of the grand stand, the scene being exceedingly picturesque. Some instances of skill were shown. An Indian at full gallop was hotly pursued by Buffalo Bill who threw a lasso over the man's shoulders, bringing him up immediately. Buck Taylor "the Cowboy King" who stands 6 ft 4 ins high, repeatedly picked small articles off the ground while riding at a hard gallop.'

The item which pleased Gladstone most was a fight between cowboys and bucking horses. 'Mr Gladstone watched the scene with evident enjoyment, cheering sometimes the horse and sometimes the rider and at the close repeatedly declared that his mind could never have conceived anything so interesting and amusing.'

Bill said later that Gladstone – not famous for his ability to laugh or relax in public – 'enjoyed himself like a veritable schoolboy'.

A luncheon in honour of the 'GOM' was held in John Whitley's office. A portrait of Gladstone was hung at one end of the room, another of George

Washington at the opposite end and one of Buffalo Bill on a side wall. At lunch, the former premier was seated next to Bill and politician and frontiersman spent the entire meal in animated conversation.

There was a toast to Gladstone and in reply, the 'GOM' – who could deliver a lengthy speech without notes at the drop of a hat – said it was impossible for him not to express his very great interest in the spectacle that had been presented to him that day. He said he believed the American Exhibition was a commercial speculation and 'hoped it would be good speculation . . . as there is nothing more desirable on this side of the Atlantic than a true and accurate representation of the American world.' On leaving, the veteran politician promised he would return to the Wild West after it had opened.

Nationwide news coverage about Gladstone's meeting with Bill and Red Shirt kept the Wild West in the headlines. Major Burke presided over daily news briefings for reporters on the Earls Court showground. He also permitted limited access to personalities connected with the show. Immediately after Gladstone's visit, he allowed a reporter from the Central News Agency, syndicating stories to different publications, to meet Red Shirt.

Referring to his meeting with the 'GOM' and speaking through his interpreter, 'Bronco Bill' Irvine, Red Shirt told the journalist:

The smallest cowboy in the company, Master Bennie Irving – son of Indian interpreter 'Bronco Bill' Irving – contemplates a full size lariat and saddle in Elliott & Fry's London photographic studio in Baker Street after appearing before Queen Victoria. (Denver Public Library)

When I saw the Great White Chief, I thought he was a great man. When I heard him speak, then I felt sure he was a great man. But the White Chief is not as the big men of our tribes. He wore no plumes and no decorations. He had none of his young men (warriors) around him, and only that I heard him talk he would have been to me as other white men. But my brother (Mr Gladstone) came to see me in my wigwam as a friend, and I was glad to see the Great White Chief, for though my tongue was tied in his presence, my heart was full of friendship. After he went away, they told me that half of this great nation of white men has adopted him as their chief. Thus I am right, for if he were not both good and wise so many young men of this nation would never have taken him for their leader.

'The Great White Chief is not as the big men of our tribes. He wore no plumes and no decorations.'

Newspaper correspondents were fascinated by Red Shirt, who they discovered was no ordinary man. He was dubbed a warrior, philosopher and poet rolled into one – his comments a combination of old-world instincts, wise observations and deep impressions about England and the English.

Thanks to Red Shirt, British newspaper readers began to appreciate that at home in the United States 'the paleface' had intruded into the 'red man's' domain. One paper commented:

In a few years hence the tomahawk and the scalping knife will be part of the heroic past. But if the white man has brought civilisation, he has also brought sickness and trouble. The Indian 'who lived free as air, whose delight was in the fight' is passing away; he has to eat the white man's food, and instead of hunting the buffalo and deer, he is even compelled to dig the ground that he might live.

Red Shirt's impression of the white man's world reads like a fragment of the Odyssey. He sees 'great villages which have no end, where the pale faces swarm like insects in the summer sun' and he marks 'the white man's lodge for the Great Spirit, whose pinnacles reach the sky, which have stood for more seasons than the red man can reckon'. It is a touching picture – this contrast between the noble savage and the new world of palefaces.

Gladstone's visit turned the political spotlight on Buffalo Bill and four days after the GOM's Earls Court rendezvous, an invitation to attend both Houses of Parliament arrived at the 'Pahaska Tepee'.

The *Bristol Times and Mirror* told its readers that Buffalo Bill:

has lightened the darkness of politics tonight. Colonel Hughes Hallett took the illustrious leader of the tomahawking Red Indians in tow, and the Radicals say that an arrangement is being made to have Mr Gladstone's scalp when he pays his promised second visit to the encampment. But apart from these ill-natured jokes about the Colonel's matinée, Buffalo Bill's fine appearance, enormous diamonds and gigantic hat attracted a good deal of notice in both Houses. He listened to the debate [*about the Crimes Bill going through the House of Commons at the time*] and dined with some members who were much interested in his visit.'

In a satirical mood, *Punch*'s weekly Parliamentary sketch – 'extracted from the diary of Toby, M.P.' – stated:

B.B. turned up punctually. Striking figure. Tall; large as to the hat; moustache much larger than Grandolph's [*Punch's satirical name for Lord Randolph Churchill*] and hair hung in little greasy curls on shoulder. Strong suspicion of use of curl papers.

'Not very lively just now', I said a little nervously, not knowing how he might take it. 'Ten minutes to spare. Would you now – ahem – would you like to go and have your hair cut?'

B.B. looked at me in a way that led me to change the subject.

Got B.B. in Distinguished Strangers' Gallery. Balfour on legs, explaining Scotch law to animated audience. Instantly fixed B.B.'s attention.

'Who's that fellow with his scalp lifted, jabbering away at the table?' he asked.

'That,' I said, 'is the former Lord Advocate for Scotland. A very good fellow. Everybody likes him.'

'Then who lifted his scalp?'

'Ah, that's a mistake. It's not what you think. It's a trick people, especially Barristers, have here of losing their hair in early youth. We have no scalping here, and this is a way Nature has of redressing the balance between the Old World and the New.'

B.B. grunted but evidently not satisfied. Presently began to unwind something from his waist.

'What's that?' I asked.

'That's a lasso', he said.

'And what are you going to do?'

'Going to fetch that chap up', said B.B., steadily unwinding himself.

Good Heavens! Here was a prospect. An ex-Lord Advocate lassoed from the gallery and dragged across the floor of the House.

'You can't do it here,' I whispered, 'you'll catch the table. Come, and I'll show you a better place.'

Got B.B. out, wandered about passages till lost ourselves, and finally got out into Palace Yard. B. didn't seem to care to go back, so packed himself up again, and set out for the Wild West by Earls Court. Felt too shaken to return, and so home.

Major Burke persuaded Bill that it was now his turn to meet newspapermen. First in line was a correspondent from the *Evening News*, a daily publication which had followed every move made by the Wild West since its arrival off Gravesend. The article is worth quoting at length as it provides an insight into life behind the scenes at the Wild West camp and a close-up of some of the personalities connected with it. It begins by commenting on progress made to the Wild West site since the paper's previous visit only days before – a sign that all would be ready for 9 May:

Today it is fast approaching the appearance of a spacious western prairie, with its undulating sweeps of verdure, its masses of rock and stone heaps, its banks of trees and shrubs, and its distant mountain ranges. Nothing is wanting to make the illusion complete, and without the slightest effort of the imagination visitors to the exhibition grounds may easily fancy themselves transported to the beauties of the western prairies of America, with its wonderful inhabitants of both men and animals. As the gates leading to the Exhibition enclosures close on the visitor,

'As the gates close on the visitor, he finds himself in an entirely new world.'

71

he finds himself in an entirely new world, and after being among the peculiar attractions of the Wild West for more than a few minutes, he finds it almost impossible to believe that he can be in the heart of London and surrounded on all sides by prosaic brick and mortar. And yet so it is; and if anything is necessary to remind him of it, he has only to listen to the shriek of the railway engines that pass along on all sides, although hidden from view, or to look about him and watch the smoke ascending from thousands of unseen chimneys.

The 'tall and manly form of Mr W.F. Cody, otherwise known as Buffalo Bill', was waiting for the correspondent 'standing on a stony prominence, clad in a long grey ulster and wide-awake hat, most gracefully tilted to one side of his handsome head'. The article continues:

'I am right glad to see you,' was the friendly greeting of the Giant of the West, stretching out a massive, yet shapely hand and grasping that of our representative in so tight a grip as to make him wince. 'Come along to my tent and have a look around.'

Buffalo Bill then led the way through a maze of white tents, most picturesquely arranged, to his own 'sanctum sanctorum' which is a similar tent to those surrounding it, only larger and handsomer in its interior. The roof is lofty and lined in a cool green canvas; the floor is covered with the most costly rugs it is possible to imagine.

'Every one of these rugs you see here, says my guide, 'has a history, and they are formed of the skins of animals, all of which have fallen to my gun. See here, for instance, is one made out of beaver; there is another of otter; this is the skin of a mountain lion. The one you are standing on is a buffalo skin, and here is the entire skin of a grizzly bear, with its claws – which the Indians think very holy – attached.

The Indian Camp

Life at the Wild West camp as captured in a series of drawings by *Illustrated Sporting & Dramatic News*, 30 April 1887.

Let me show you this chair. It is made of the horns of steers, or as you call them I believe, deer. In this tent, there are skins of nearly every animal that is to be found in America.'

Buffalo Bill then led me into an inner tent, which is raised somewhat above the other, or the reception place, by a few steps which are carpeted with rich red druggets. Here my guide commenced to perform his ablutions in a kind of primitive looking washing basin.

'You see,' said he, rubbing his dark face with a rough towel until it shone resplendent like a mirror, 'we have not yet had time to get straight, but hope to do so in the course of a few days. I would like to show you my costumes but they are not ready at hand. We wear buckskin while we go through our Wild West performance, and you will presently see the cowboys and how they are dressed.'

We then, Buffalo Bill having combed out his long hair, brushed his moustache and imperial and had his boots polished, sallied forth to have a look round. The tent of a dusky warrior was first visited, and for the first time in my life, I found myself in an Indian wigwam in all its natural barbarity. To begin with, the entrance is decidedly novel and peculiar. It is necessary, in order to get inside, to stoop your back until you are almost double, and then you must be prepared to duck yourself down at once as soon as you have passed through the slit of the canvas, otherwise you will probably get choked with the smoke rising from the wood fire burning in the centre. I believe the proper way to enter into these habitations is to crawl in on your hands and knees, but having on a favourite pair of pants I did not, neither did my guide, adopt this method.

Once inside the wigwam we sat, or rather squatted down in company with three or four Indian braves of different tribes, in a circle around the blazing fire. As soon as we were squatted on our haunches, we failed to feel any disagreeable effects of the smoke, as by the peculiar formation of the tents, and the means adopted of ventilating them, all the smoke escapes and is carried off quite easily.

Buffalo Bill.

I cannot say that my dusky neighbours impressed me very favourably, they were one and all exceedingly – almost repulsively – ugly, their naturally hideous countenances being yet further brutalised by vivid streaks of paint every shade and hue. One had a bright yellow face with the eyes outlined in blue, and the nose decorated with a brilliant red streak. His long, straight black hair fell carelessly and untidily over his shoulders, while his lanky, yet sinewy, form was enveloped in loose blue trousers with silver brandings and beads, the whole of the upper portion of the body being wrapped in a bright scarlet blanket. There were others with blue, red and green faces, but the fiendish expressions remained the same on all of them.

On leaving the somewhat close atmosphere of the wigwam, Buffalo Bill was called upon to receive and chaperône other visitors, and so handing me over to the tender attentions of his major-domo – Frankey White, another handsome Hercules – Buffalo Bill bade me farewell, but this time, with vivid recollections of his tenacious grasp, I evaded his vice-like salutation. My new guide, who is a celebrated and accomplished rider of buck jumping mustangs, took possession of me as if

I were his own particular property, and I found him a most amiable and discursive custodian. His information on all subjects pertaining to the strange kind of life led by members of the Wild West is vast and complete; he knows the ages, the histories, and all particulars of every member of the company, and as this includes some two hundred and fifty persons, his knowledge must necessarily be considerable. Under Frankey's guidance, I made my way through further rows of neat tents, until we arrived at that inhabited by Miss Annie Oakley, the champion lady shot of America. This young lady is possessed of a decidedly pretty and winsome face, of sweet and gentle manners, and a soft girlish voice. Having been formally introduced, Miss Oakley proceeded to give me a few particulars of her life and adventures.

'I am about twenty years of age', said this young Amazon, 'and have been fond of shooting from the time I was a toddling mite. At the age of twelve, I was presented with a fourteen-gauge muzzle-loading shotgun. With this I practised all day long and became so good a shot that by the time I had reached the age of fourteen I had paid off a mortgage on my father's homestead with money earned from the sale of game and skins shot and trapped entirely by myself. . . .'

Miss Oakley, having kindly showed me her numerous costly medals of which she possesses quite a magnificent collection and having assured me that she does not claim any championship, but looks upon her skill merely as a matter of dollars and cents, Frankey White bore me off to other parts of the vast camp.

En route for the stables we met with numerous members of the Wild West Company, and I do not ever remember encountering a handsomer or a finer set of fellows anywhere than are to be seen here. There is positively not an ugly man amongst them, barring the Indian element, and some of the cowboys are perfect giants in stature. Buck Taylor is 6 ft 4 ins in his stockings; while Bronco Bill also is a model of symmetry and manly grace. All were dressed in their picturesque costumes, composed of short jackets, tight breeches, high boots and sombreros and all walk with a springy gait unlike anything ever seen off the boundless prairies. Needless to say, all these cowboys are perfect masters of their horses, and it is a pleasing and edifying spectacle to see them careering gaily along over the courses like Centaurs, so beautifully do they sit their steeds.

I next visited the cookhouse, where the vast quantities of meat, &tc, are continually being cooked for the Indians, passing on my way to scrutinise a curious kind of erection set up by the dusky warriors, decorated with a war-bonnet, gay coloured ribbons, and various sorts of skins, and which they call 'medicine' or a peace offering to their gods to keep off illnesses. These erections sometimes consisting merely or pieces of stick or cane, may be found in various portions of the encampment.

One morning an official messenger personally delivered a letter addressed to Bill at the 'Pahaska Tepee':

Marlborough House,
Pall Mall, S.W., 26 April, 1887

Dear Sir: I am desired by the Prince of Wales to thank you for your invitation. His Royal Highness is anxious I should see you with reference to it. Perhaps, therefore, you would kindly make it convenient to call at Marlborough House. Would it suit you to call at 11.30 or 5 o'clock, either tomorrow (Wednesday) or Thursday? I am, dear sir,

> Yours faithfully
> (Signed) Francis Knollys
> Private Secretary.

There was panic at the Wild West camp. The company was thrilled that the heir to the British throne wanted to visit 'The Yankeeries' – but why did he request a private performance before opening day? The arena racetrack had still to be completed with soft loam added to prevent it from breaking up. Heavy rain had interrupted work yet again and the ground was in poor condition. Parts of the programme also needed more rehearsal time. 'But for all this, I determined to pull through, as the Wild West always suited me the better the more raw and wild that it was,' recorded Bill.

'I do not ever remember encountering a handsomer or a finer set of fellows anywhere than are to be seen here.'

The Prince of Wales was busy helping to organise his mother's Jubilee celebrations and had limited time to step aside from official duties to watch an entertainment. However, a visit by Bill and Salsbury to Francis Knollys at Marlborough House put the partners at their ease. They were told that Prince Edward and his wife Alexandra, the Danish-born Princess of Wales, would be pleased to see anything on the Wild West programme that they cared to present – and not to go to too much trouble on their behalf. They agreed that the afternoon of Thursday 5 May would be an ideal time for everyone – four days before the official opening.

Once again Salsbury worked hard to prepare a special 'royal rehearsal version' of the Wild West, featuring the entire company and highlights from the programme to be seen in full for the first time the following Monday. He also arranged for a Royal Box to be hastily constructed at the side of the arena, covered in American and British flags and with enough comfortable seating for the large party expected at Earls Court. Rehearsals began in earnest early in the day and continued long into the night.

In addition to the Prince and Princess of Wales, the royal party coming to the Wild West included their three daughters, Princesses Victoria, Louise and Maude of Wales, Princess Louise and her husband the Marquis of Lorne, the Duke of Cambridge, the Duke of Teck and his son Prince Francis, the Comtesse de Paris, Crown Prince Frederick of Denmark plus Lords and Ladies in Waiting and members of the Prince's royal household.

The chief of the Indian band.

THE BROMPTON BEAU

The Prince and Princess of Wales – later King Edward VII and Queen Alexandra – were the first royal guests to visit the Wild West in London and returned many more times during the Jubilee season.

A delegation from the American Exhibition including John Whitley and Bill greeted the royal party at the entrance – but the exhibition grounds were by-passed and the large group led directly across the bridge connecting the Wild West to the rest of the Earls Court showground.

Frank Richmond, the Wild West's 'orator' – or Master of Ceremonies – was stationed in front of the Royal Box to introduce and explain the performance. Nate Salsbury and Major Burke were on hand to answer questions from members of the distinguished party.

At a special signal from Salsbury the entire troop of cowboys, Indians and Mexican vaqueros charged into the arena on horseback from behind a huge scenic backdrop depicting the Rocky Mountains. The Indians were decorated in full war paint, their clothes covered in beads and feathers. The *Evening News* said, 'the sensation they produced was instantaneous and electric.'

With wild yells, they swept around the vast enclosure like a whirlwind. The wide-eyed Prince remained standing for most of the hour-and-a-half long performance, leaning eagerly over the front of the Royal Box, shouting out words of encouragement and applauding everything taking place before him. Any fears the partners may have had that the show was not ready for an audience were put to rest. Bill wrote: '"Cody", I said to myself, "you have fetched 'em!" From that moment we were right – right from the word "Go" Everybody was in capital form – myself included – and the whole thing went off grandly.'

The *Evening News* reported:

The performance opened with a general review of the company, troop after troop of horsemen charging at full speed around the arena and drawing up before the stand in which the Royal party were seated. Some remarkable shooting was then exhibited by Miss Annie Oakley and Miss Lillian Smith . . . races were run by Sioux boys, cowboys and Mexicans and a Virginia Reel was danced on horseback.

The cowboys filled an exciting twenty minutes with their amusing struggles with bucking ponies and mules, and later on gave an illustration of the pastime of roping and riding wild Texan steers. Yesterday, however, the single specimen of the wild Texan steer introduced into the arena was very tame, and might have been mistaken by the casual observer for a native cow. The great features of the entertainment were, however, the attacks made upon an emigrant wagon, a stage coach and finally a settler's hut by a troop of Indians on the war path, and the gallant rescue in each case by a company of scouts under the command of Buffalo Bill.

Colonel Cody's throwing of the lasso and shooting at glass balls thrown in the air by an attendant riding by his side, both horses going at full gallop, excited great applause; Buck Taylor, King of the Cowboys, picked his handkerchief from the ground while riding at full gallop, and also in the same way picked up a rope attached to a runaway horse.

The royal party loved every moment of the Wild West and showed their delight by applauding, cheering and giving the performers a standing ovation at the finale when the entire company, with Bill at its head, pulled up before the Royal Box, removed hats, sombreros and war bonnets and bowed from their saddles.

The Prince of Wales asked Salsbury to arrange for some of the company to be brought to the Royal Box to be presented to the Princess of Wales and himself. They included Bill, Major Burke, Lillian Smith, Frank Richmond and Annie Oakley, who later recalled:

> Our orator (Frank Richmond) beckoned me to the box and I bowed to them. I was so proud of him! His presentation speech was, 'Your Royal Highness, I have the honour to present Annie Oakley'.
>
> All I had heard of women trying to flirt with the Prince while the gentle Princess held her peace, ran before me. An English-born lady would not have dared to have done as I did – they must speak to Royalty according to the station of the Royal personages.
>
> The Prince's hand came over the low front of the box as they had all arose. I quickly proffered my hand to the Princess. She did not offer the tips of her fingers, expecting me to kneel and kiss her hand, but took my hand gently in her own, saying, 'What a wonderful little girl'.
>
> Nor was his Highness displeased at my daring. He shook my hand warmly when I turned from the Princess, and after I had bowed far enough to dare turn my back, he said loud enough for me and the entire assembly to hear: 'What a pity there are not more women in the world like that little one'.

The royals then asked to be shown around the Wild West camp and visited Red Shirt's tepee. The Prince asked him how he liked the British weather, to which he replied through his interpreter, that it was not so cold as in his country where they had many feet of snow.

The future King of England and the one-time King of the Border Men sat in a pair of Bill's comfortable armchairs and smoked fine cigars.

The *Evening News* takes up the story: 'The Prince then said: "Tell him we are immensely pleased at what we have seen." Red Shirt was gratified at hearing this. The Prince then carefully examined the huge silver medal presented to the Sioux Chiefs when they visited Washington, which bears the head of the late General Grant. Asked by the Prince how long he would remain in England, Red Shirt replied: "I came with Colonel Cody and I will stay with him as long as he stays." In answer to the Princess, who expressed her pleasure at seeing him in England, he said: "Tell the great Chief's wife it makes my heart glad to hear her words of welcome."'

Edward and Alexandra also visited Annie Oakley's tent where they chatted for 20 minutes. The Princess was impressed by a framed photograph of Annie displayed inside and 'Little Sure Shot' presented it to Alexandra as a gift. Days later, a photograph of Edward and Alexandra mounted in a hand-painted frame, a gift from the Princess of Wales, was delivered to Annie's tent at the Wild West camp.

While Alexandra, her daughters and other ladies in the royal party made a fuss of John Nelson's half-breed papoose, the Prince entered the '*Pahaska Tepee*' and was shown the gold-mounted sword presented by generals of the United States army. Inside, the future King of England and the one-time King of the Border Men sat in a pair of Bill's comfortable armchairs and smoked fine cigars.

Despite the muddy state of the showground, the royal party asked to see the stables and corral where 200 animals used in the Wild West show were kept in excellent conditions. The Prince – an earnest sportsman and rider – wanted to take a close look at Bill's 21-year-old horse, Old Charley, whom he rode in the show. Edward closely examined the famous horse, wanted to know its history and heard how Old Charley had once carried Bill 100 miles in 9 hours 40 minutes when chased by hostile Indians. The Prince was impressed with the horse, patted him and told Bill that he was a 'very fine specimen'. Said Bill: 'Charley may not have felt the compliment, but I appreciated it keenly.'

'The party then passed out of the building, where the workmen and a large crowd had assembled who cheered them heartily,' wrote the *Evening News*. 'The Prince and Princess both expressed themselves highly gratified with their visit, and signified their intention to occupy the royal box as frequently as possible during the season.'

On the way back to their carriages, the royal party met Red Shirt for a second time and Edward presented the entire contents of his cigarette case to the Indian chief who later shared the tobacco with other Indians.

It was now the public's turn to experience 'The Yankeeries' and 'Buffalo Billeries'. The weather was glorious on Monday 9 May when the gates to Earls Court were officially opened and tens of thousands of people poured through. 'All the world and his wife were there,' said the *Evening News*,'. . . or perhaps it would be more correct to say all London and his Spouse', reported *Sporting Life*. The *Illustrated Sporting and Dramatic News* described the crowd as 'everybody who is anybody, and innumerable nobodies'.

The Times estimated that 28,000 people passed through the Earls Court turnstiles on the first day. Many were admitted free by special invitation. Others paid one guinea* for the privilege of being among the first to view the American Exhibition and Wild West. From the second day onwards, the public was admitted to the American Exhibition between 10.30 a.m. and 10.30 p.m. for one shilling, or two shillings and sixpence including a seat at the Wild West. Tickets for the Wild West only – playing twice-daily at 3.00 p.m. and 8.30 p.m. – began at one shilling for a standing place in the amphitheatre and two shillings for an unreserved seat in the covered grand circle. A private box for four cost twenty-five shillings and a box seating six sold for thirty-five shillings. All reserved places were bookable in advance.

'There was a crush, and fight, and struggle amongst both quadrupeds and bipeds to reach the gates of The Yankeeries for some hours,' reported the *Evening News*, adding: 'The block in the vehicular traffic actually commenced at South Kensington Railway Station and all along the Old Brompton Road was a mass of crawling carriages of every description. Indeed to use the sidewalk (to use an expression consistent with the day) was just as bad for pedestrians. How and when I got there, I should not like to have to state on oath; but once there, I felt amply repaid for all my heroic struggles.'

* £1. 1s. in old money.

'Now then boys, this is how I want it done . . .' Nate Salsbury passes instructions to Major Burke (seated centre), Jule Keen (lying left) and members of the Wild West advertising and publicity team. (Denver Public Library)

The *Daily Telegraph* reported that:

All sightseeing London was afflicted with one of its periodical frenzies of excitement. The Underground Railway was besieged and taken by force. Down the stairs rushed well-dressed ladies waving in the air huge invitation tickets surmounted by an eagle perched on a banner; after them followed their companions of the sterner sex, who are never a match for a woman in a crowd. Every platform from the Mansion House to the distant West was packed, every train was full, and every carriage exceeded its limits of accommodation by at least half a dozen persons. However, by begging, imploring and beseeching, every one – mothers, sisters, cousins, aunts – got in somehow or other, and the proverbial good humour of English people bound on the same cheerful errand prevailed.

Once inside, however, there was general disappointment among the public and press about the American Exhibition, which was nowhere near ready to admit paying customers. 'If anyone travelled to Earls Court in the delusive hope of seeing an exhibition of American arts, products and discoveries, disappointment awaited that person at the end of his journey,' stated the *Evening News*. 'The main building in which the exhibition is to be held was a mass of chaotic confusion. Stalls half erected, others built but empty, with here and there a meagre exhibit, were the order of the day.'

Fortunately, the press understood about such matters. 'This is a matter that will be remedied before the end of the week, as nearly everyone went yesterday to have a look at the Wild West Show,' added the *Evening News*.

The American Exhibition's opening ceremony was deemed: 'About as lacking in liveliness as such events invariably are. I am afraid there was precious little attention paid to the addresses, or to the consecration prayer; but Madame Lillian Nordica's singing of "The Star Spangled Banner" and "Rule Britannia" with the band of the Grenadier Guards, brought down the house.'

After a speech of welcome from Lord Ronald Gower on behalf of the executive council for the American Exhibition and a reply by Colonel Henry Russell on behalf of the Americans, John Whitley invited the crowds to 'join us in the further development of the New World.' Taking that as their cue to leave – despite the fact that Whitley had more to say – the crowd surged towards the exit doors and stampeded towards the Wild West arena to the strains of 'Dixie'. Ten minutes later, the great hall of the American Exhibition was deserted.

As members of the first British audience ever to witness a full performance of Buffalo Bill's Wild West scrambled into the amphitheatre, they saw a vast scenic canvas backdrop depicting the western prairies, complete with mountains, rocks and trees. The press was universally complimentary about the effect, which 'imparts a remarkably good idea of wildness and distance to the surroundings'. Native trees and shrubs imported from the American frontier masked entrances and openings from which the Wild West company would shortly emerge.

A high rostrum stood at one side of the arena from which the 'orator', Frank Richmond, would welcome the audience, introduce performers, comment on the proceedings and explain aspects of western life, traditions and culture like the chorus from a Greek play. A lonely log cabin stood at the opposite side.

As the audience was shown to their seats by teams of uniformed stewards, they were offered programmes (price sixpence) and something they had never seen before

The Times correspondent wrote that Buffalo Bill's Cowboy Band 'upsets all one's previous ideas about the correct costume of musicians, but they play with spirit'. (Denver Public Library)

in a British place of entertainment – a golden, soft, chewy, salty-tasting snack which the Americans called 'popcorn'. Small conical-shaped paper containers were filled with the treat, sold for one-halfpenny. Audiences were unsure about the snack to begin with but, over a century later, it is still with us. . . .

William Sweeney took the Cowboy Band through a spirited selection of popular American tunes and light classical pieces. The bandstand was located at the edge of the arena and British musical cynics more used to the black tie and tails of a symphony orchestra or bright red uniforms of the Grenadier Guards Band had a surprise when they heard – and saw – the Cowboy Band. Dressed in clothing based on apparel worn by genuine working cowboys, they appeared in bright red double-fronted shirts, black trousers under yellow chaps, slouch hats and moccasins. *The Times* correspondent wrote: 'The Cowboy band upsets all one's previous ideas about the correct costume of musicians, but they play with spirit.'

The band included musicians playing a D-flat piccolo, an E-flat clarinet, three B-flat clarinets, three B-flat cornets – one of them played by William Sweeney – two trombones, a baritone, two E-flat alto horns, one tuba, a snare drummer and a bass drummer.[*] Contrary to some of Major Burke's publicity stories, however, most of the band were not working cowboys from the frontier, but hired from New York theatres and concert halls before the *State of Nebraska* sailed.

In the audience, 'Society in every grade was certainly represented,' noticed *The Daily Telegraph*, adding: 'Fashion, art, literature, the stage, the services, and the bar all had their representatives on the semi-circular benches or in the small private boxes on the lowest tier.'

Nate Salsbury watched this frenzied activity from a small corner inside the arena. Dressed in a light morning suit and calmly smoking a cigar, he took out his pocket watch and saw that it was 4.30 p.m. – time to begin. He signalled William Sweeney to pick up his baton and lead the Cowboy Band into the overture.

A tall man 'wearing fantastic attire and head-dress' walked out on to the rostrum. The crowd fell silent. Was this the famous Buffalo Bill? A quick glance at their souvenir programmes – nearly 70 pages in length – told them this was Mr Frank Richmond, master of ceremonies, ringmaster or, as he preferred to be called, 'orator'. Without the aid of a loud hailer and in a voice audible in all parts of the amphitheatre, he announced that Mr Levy, the cornet player, would now perform 'The Star Spangled Banner'. The crowd all stood up and American ladies in the audience waved handkerchiefs.

Frank Richmond then announced: 'Ladies and gentlemen, Buffalo Bill and Nate Salsbury proudly present America's National Entertainment, the one and only, genuine and authentic, unique and original . . . Wild West!!'

'. . . the one and only, genuine and authentic, unique and original . . . Wild West!!'

---

[*] The author is grateful to Michael L. Masterson of the Visual and Performing Arts Division at Northwest College, Powell, Wyoming, for additional information about the 1887 Cowboy Band line-up, as printed in his liner notes contribution included with the CD recording *Buffalo Bill's Cowboy Band* performed by the Americus Brass Band and available from Museum Selections at the Buffalo Bill Historical Centre, Cody, Wyoming 82414.

The audience collectively held its breath as the Cowboy Band struck up again and the full mounted company burst into view, racing around the arena at break-neck speed, yelling, whooping and shouting war cries. The programme described this as a 'Grand Processional Review and Introduction of Groups and Individual characters'. It provided British audiences with their first opportunity to see Indians tattooed and painted in every imaginable colour, wearing impressive war bonnets; Mexicans dressed in silk and velvet, sheltering under large sombreros; laughing cowgirls in brightly coloured jackets and hats and cowboys with coloured sashes, Stetsons, double-fronted shirts in all colours and leather chaps.

The *Daily Telegraph* reported: 'Next to the preliminary procession before a Spanish Bull Fight, nothing more striking has been seen than the entry of the full force of the Wild West . . . Last to enter was the Hon. W.F. Cody or "Buffalo Bill" mounted on a beautiful white horse, and looking a veritable "king of men" as fine a figure as he is an admirable and elegant horseman.' The audience needed no reminder from Frank Richmond that this was the man they had battled through London's bustling streets and in crowded railway carriages to see in person.

The audience needed no reminder that this was the man they had battled through London's bustling streets and in crowded railway carriages to see in person.

Riding Old Charley, Bill cantered across the stadium to join the rest of the company. Then together and in mid-arena they turned to face the audience and raced towards the crowds at full gallop. Could they stop in time? Of course they could. It was as if someone had applied a brake and when they came to a sudden halt, they lifted their hats, sombreros and war bonnets and waved them to the audience. The audience went wild with delight.

Frank Richmond produced a red flag and held it high in the air. This was the signal for more mounted Indians to appear. 'Sioux and Arapahos, in all colours of the rainbow – orange and red prevailing – grinning with the whitest of teeth as these painted horsemen raced helter-skelter to the saluting point in front of the grand stand,' reported the *Daily Telegraph*:

All took up excellent position and in admirable order. There was a cheer from the crowd and a yell from the tribes as Red Shirt, well-mounted and splendidly dressed, reined in his horse in front of his men, but the loudest cheer of all awaited Buffalo Bill himself, who, tossing out his curls and waving his wide hat in the air, completed the stirring picture. The brilliant horsemen vanished as quickly as they came. A word of command, a shout, and in a second, as it seemed, Indians, cowboys, girls, beads, feathers, striped mantles, and war paint had disappeared and vanished into air. They rode as if they had been born on horseback, and as if nothing could upset them.

The first spark of excitement had been lighted and Frank Richmond now took the audience through an action-packed programme beginning with a horse race around the giant arena between a cowboy, an Indian and a Mexican. Different Wild West company members took part in the daily races, which were run for real. Each day's winner was awarded a shilling.

Richmond then introduced the first of the show's two star lady sharpshooters: 'Miss Annie Oakley, celebrated shot, who will illustrate her dexterity in the use of fire-arms'. Thanks to encounters with Sitting Bull, Gladstone and the Prince and Princess of Wales, Annie was now almost as famous in London as Bill, and the audience greeted her warmly as she 'tripped' into the arena.

As a single clay pigeon was hurled into the air by a strange looking mechanical device in the centre of the arena, Annie picked up a loaded rifle from the ground, fired and smashed the missile to pieces before it landed. A pair of clay pigeons was next to sail through the air, then three and finally four; each was shot with precision using a rifle snatched up from the arena floor. Annie's ingenious mechanical contrivance – a Ligowsky Clay Pigeon device – imitated bird flight using red clay moulded into the shape of a saucer. Each pigeon measured four inches in diameter and one inch in depth. The iron trap hurled clay pigeons in any direction for Annie to shoot into smithereens.

Frank Butler, as usual, was by Annie's side, handing her rifles, looking after her ammunition and working the traps. Frank Richmond asked the crowd to be silent while Annie and Frank went through the celebrated mirror shot routine, in which Frank held a playing card between thumb and forefinger while 'Little Sure Shot' turned her back on her husband, aimed a rifle over her shoulders in his direction using a small mirror to pin-point the target. Another shooting trick involved Annie pushing the muzzle of her rifle through a playing card, rendering the sight useless, shooting off the lighted tip of a cigar held between Frank's lips twenty yards away. For years afterwards, free Wild West admission passes with pre-punched holes were known as 'Annie Oakleys', appearing as if she had used them for target practice.

Annie later wrote: 'I had been told that my success or failure depended on one critic whose name was Pen Dragon.* They told me that he was merciless, but fair and just, too. . . . I was too engrossed in catching all the small missiles that flew through the air, one, two, three and four at a time, to even think what a critic might say.'

An accurate recreation of a Pony Express ride, featuring Marve Beardsley – like Bill, a former rider with the organisation – followed. Marve galloped into the arena, changing horses and mailbags every few hundred yards. Sometimes savage Indians pursued him, other times bandits and desperados, all of whom, the audience was told, failed to prevent the mail from getting through.

Next into the arena rode an emigrant train, made up of covered wagons pulled by oxen and mule teams. The 'prairie schooners' contained families of men, women and children slowly making their way across the plains and prairies to new lives in the west. The programme informed the audience that 'the wagons are the same as used 35 years ago' while the west was still being won from the Indians.

Suddenly and without warning, a group of hostile Indians in full war paint appeared on horseback, whooping their war cries, firing rifles into the air and brandishing tomahawks. Things looked bad for the folks on the wagon train. The savages surrounded the wagons, to the consternation of womenfolk and children on board who screamed and prayed for a saviour. But new-age western men were

Things looked bad for the folks on the wagon train. The savages surrounded the wagons, to the consternation of womenfolk and children on board who screamed and prayed for a saviour.

---

*   *Pendragon* was a pseudonym for the editor of the Sunday newspaper, *The Referee.*

Bill riding his favourite horse, Old Charley, in the Earls Court arena. The Prince of Wales told Bill that he was a 'very fine specimen'. (Photograph by Elliott & Fry courtesy of Denver Public Library)

made of sterner stuff and knew exactly what to do. Quickly they steered the mules, oxen and wagons into a tight circle and took up positions from their sheltered island behind the wagons. Alas, there were more Indians than westerners, and just when it appeared as if all was lost and scalps would be lifted, a miracle occurred before the audience's eyes. Yes, it was Buffalo Bill on Old Charley with a group of cowboy and Mexican friends behind him, come to rescue the wagon train in the nick of time. One Indian after another fell from his pony following a loud bang from Bill's Winchester rifle. The rest beat a hasty retreat and galloped away to prepare for their next scene.

The wagon train was saved, and the pioneers so grateful to Bill and his rescue party that they were all invited to stay for a spell and join in a square dance – on horseback, of course.

'Places, all,' called Frank Richmond. 'From the Heights of Mount Olympus, Terpsichore may well gaze in wide-eyed wonder at a measure wildly new to her engagement list – a lively and most picturesque dance, in which gallant cowboys, graceful western girls and smart broncos participate.' The Cowboy Band struck up a tune in double time and the prairie pioneers and the great Scout all danced a most unusual Virginia reel.

A programme note told the audience: '. . . the squares are formed and away go the riders and horses in all the rollicking and intricate figures of that popular dance, the long hair and bright curls of the riders streaming on the breeze, and the alert hoofs of the spirited broncos keeping perfect time to the popular tune.'

One of the western girls had trained her horse to jump in time to the music and make it rear on its hind legs while she sat in the saddle. This was Emma Lake Hickock, daughter of Wild Bill Hickock who had been shot at Deadwood shortly before her birth.

Lillian Smith was just 16 and known to Bill as 'Young California'. She was billed in the programme as 'the champion Californian huntress' and was the youngest featured member of the Wild West company. Lillian joined the troupe a year before the London engagement and at age 15 had secretly married Joe Kidd, a Wild West cowboy, while the show was playing at Erastina, Staten Island – much to the horror of her parents. The Wild West's London season doubled as their honeymoon. Lillian had been shooting game for her family since the age of six and was now about to shoot targets for thousands of Londoners.

'Young California' ran into the arena carrying her Winchester repeating rifle and proceeded to shoot 20 glass balls flung into the air from a roving target. She then aimed at a glass ball swinging wildly and horizontally at great speed, which she smashed into tiny pieces before turning her attention to a dozen eggs, which she promptly scrambled with her 'pea rifle', to the audience's delight.

Riding a fiery mustang, Buck burst into the arena, leaning dangerously from his saddle.

Both Lillian Smith and Annie Oakley appeared together again later, riding into the arena at high speed, snatching pistols from the ground and firing at flying targets. Both lady sharpshooters became instant stars of the London entertainment scene that afternoon.

An item billed 'Cowboy Fun – picking objects from the ground, lassoing wild horses and riding the buckers' was next on the programme. While staff ran around the arena dropping handkerchiefs, sombreros, gloves and other assorted bits and pieces on to the ground, another Wild West star in the making had already mounted his horse and was waiting behind the canvas scenery for Frank Richmond's introduction. 'And now ladies and gentlemen, please welcome the "King of the Cowboys" – Buck Taylor!'

At 6 ft 4 ins tall, Buck was one of the tallest cowboys in the company and soon to become the most popular with the public – or, as the *Era* put it 'his visiting list will soon become inconveniently full'. Riding a fiery mustang, Buck burst into the arena, leaning dangerously from his saddle, first to the left, then to the right, picking up the handkerchiefs and hats placed on the ground moments before. Buck's equine feats inspired a poetical correspondent from *Sporting Life* to pen a short ode to the King of the Cowboys:

> The Cowboy King, Buck Taylor,
> Is quite an equine Nailer;
> What man dare he will dare O,
> Picks up his wide Sombrero,
> From off the ground
> While at full bound
> His steed away does tear O!

William Levi Taylor (1857–1924) – known to one and all as 'Buck' – at 6 ft 4 inches one of the tallest members of the company and the most popular with ladies in the London audience – or, as *The Era* put it 'his visiting list will soon become inconveniently full'. Buck's very public riding accident in the Earls Court arena was page one news in national newspapers – including the *British Medical Journal*. (Denver Public Library)

Then it appeared as if all hell had been let loose into the arena. Jumping ponies – or 'outrages' as Mark Twain called them – with names such as 'Indigestion', 'Dynamite', 'Suicide', and 'Happy Jack' plus a pair of angry mules were let in, each chased by cowboys, including Buck Taylor, cowgirls and Mexican vaqueros.

Frank Richmond assured the audience that: 'No cruelty is used to make the animals buck – it is simply a way they've got.' The *Evening Standard* described the scene:

A considerable amount of amusement was caused by the unwillingness of some of the ponies – for they are little more – to be mounted. Some of them nearly lay down; others circled round to the limit of their bridle, bucking and kicking furiously. Eventually they were mounted, but before the rider was fairly settled in his saddle, his steed had his head down, and went across the spacious arena bucking in the most approved form. In bucking, it may be stated for the benefit of the uninitiated, the horse gets his head down between his knees, arches his back, and springs off the ground as high as his strength will allow. A succession of these bounds does not, however, disconcert the cowboy, who sits as steady as if his horse were only walking or trotting . . . A horse ridden by a lady also proved itself an accomplished rearer and bucker, but the rider never moved in her saddle, and gained great applause for the finished style in which she rode.

The *Daily Telegraph* found the bucking ponies 'comical' and the mules 'fiendishly obstinate', adding: 'They not only kick, buck and plunge, but they leap into the air in order to dislodge their riders. The mules rush against the woodwork of the ring to crush their antagonists; the bucking ponies, with ears back and tail tucked in, plunge and tear until at last they are mastered and ridden off in triumph.'

The *Illustrated Sporting and Dramatic News* found this section the most interesting part of the Wild West. It particularly admired the bucking horse known as 'Dynamite' which was described as: 'A fiend, born a buck-jumper and encouraged in her wickedness from a foal, she humps her back like an angry tom cat, rises from the ground with her head between her hoofs, and her legs stiff as railings, and comes down with that diabolical jerk, and at that uncomfortable angle which implies, to an ordinary good rider, not only a peremptory notice to quit, but an injunction to emigrate to the adjoining parish. Her squeal is of itself sinful; it approaches bad language as near as horse ever got.'

An angry looking Texas longhorn steer wandered into the centre of the arena, where it stopped, blinked and looked around at the crowd. It had failed to spot Buck Taylor, so the 'King of the Cowboys' made his presence known by giving out a loud whoop, which focussed the steer's attention on ways and means of escaping. The animal charged towards Buck, who deftly darted out of its way like a matador. Buck uncoiled a lasso dangling from his belt, spun it around his head and hurled it towards the steer, now manoeuvring a turn in order to charge the cowboy. As the lasso landed clear over the horns and around the steer's neck, the huge animal screeched to a halt, snorted and looked angrily at its captor.

'Watch yourself, Buck,' cautioned Frank Richmond. 'He's looking angry, and you know what he's like when he's angry. He's worse than a hornet's nest.' Buck tugged on the lasso to pull in the steer – but the steer had other ideas and backed away, pulling Buck towards him. As soon as the cowboy was within arm's length of the steer, he grabbed the animal's horns and proceeded to twist them and wrestle the beast to the ground. Once on the floor of the arena, Buck held the animal until Frank Richmond encouraged the audience to give the 'King of the Cowboys' a round of applause. Four cowboys ran into the arena to steer the angry Texan longhorn back to its corral while Buck Taylor acknowledged the audience's long appreciation of his skills.

As soon as the cowboy was within arm's length, he grabbed the animal's horns and proceeded to wrestle the beast to the ground.

As Buck left the arena, another tall cowboy strode into view. Frank Richmond informed the crowd that this was 'Mustang Jack – the Cowboy Jumper with springs on his heels, the highest jumper of them all, bar none.'

'Mustang Jack' led a pair of horses into the centre of the arena. He stroked the mane and whispered into an ear of the smaller of the two. 'The smaller horse you see before you is thirteen hands high. Mustang Jack will now attempt to jump over the horse's back by a standing leap. Are you ready Jack?' asked Frank Richmond. Jack gave a wave. 'Let's help him out, shall we?' said Frank Richmond, who led a countdown as the cowboy crouched close to the ground at the horse's side – 'three . . . two . . . one!' Mustang Jack leaped high into the air and over the horse, landing on his feet on the other side of the animal.

From out of a saddlebag, Jack produced a pair of weighted dumb-bells which he held into the air for all to see. 'Each of the dumb-bells Mustang Jack is holding weighs ten pounds – that's twenty extra pounds in all. Jack will now attempt to leap over the back of the second horse – a height of sixteen hands – carrying the extra weight,' announced Frank Richmond. The weights were first passed over to four or five members of the audience who confirmed that they were extremely heavy.

Wild West performers pose for the camera in the Earls Court arena with another star attraction – the old Deadwood stagecoach. John Nelson sits at the top with one of his half-breed children and Master Bennie Irving, and coach driver Fred Matthews is perched below. Buck Taylor leans on the front wheel. Pint-size Johnnie Baker 'The Cowboy Kid' stands next to Bill and Major John Burke is behind him. (The American Collection)

There was a second countdown as Jack crouched close to the ground clutching a dumb-bell in each hand. Again, he leapt into the air, clearing the horse's back by three or four inches and down to the ground on the other side. To the sound of applause, Jack leapt onto the back of the taller horse, and taking the reins of the second, galloped from the arena.

It was now time for the old Deadwood stagecoach to be pulled into view by six mules, driven by Fred Matthews with long-bearded John Nelson also on a top seat as its scout and guard. Frank Richmond told the audience that the coach 'occupies an historic place in American history, having been baptised in fire and blood!'

Today it contained Lord Ronald Gower and other VIPs from the American Exhibition, plus a couple of pressmen. As it bounced around the arena, Frank Richmond announced: 'This is the identical Deadwood coach, called the mail coach, which is famous on account of having carried a great number of people who lost their lives on the road between Deadwood and Cheyenne eighteen years ago.' John Nelson was identified as 'the husband of a Red Indian princess and the proud progenitor of a numerous semi-royal family. John Nelson also guided Brigham Young on his first trip to Salt Lake City.'

As if to warn the VIPs, Richmond then announced that the Deadwood stagecoach would 'be attacked by a band of fierce and warlike Indians'. Yes, the Indians were back – this time determined to capture the old stagecoach, kill its drivers, scalp its passengers, steal their luggage and make off with anything else of value they could find. With the ribbons of the coach in one hand and a rifle in the other, Fred Matthews tried to deter the Indians from riding too close. But one rode up from behind, jumped from his pony on to a backboard and climbed on to the roof where he fought hand-to-hand with John Nelson while the stagecoach bounced around the arena on its ancient springs. Other Indians rode alongside, terrorising the passengers while attempting to poke rifles through the windows.

It took less than four minutes to transform the Earls Court arena into an Indian village.

Fortunately, the gunfire was heard by a group of nearby cowboys – and who should be at their head? Once again, Buffalo Bill rode in to the rescue. The cowboys chased the old stagecoach, aimed rifles in the direction of the Indians and showed them what true frontiersmen were made of. 'After a few minutes' furious fighting the Indians retired unhurt but beaten from this very vivid incident,' wrote the *Sporting Life*. All of this was played out to the sound of the Cowboy Band playing 'Garryowen', Custer's regimental marching tune.

Two other pieces involving Indians followed. The first featured a race by young braves riding bareback ponies. Frank Richmond encouraged the audience to select an Indian and cheer him on to victory. This was followed by 'Life Customs of the Indians', in which the Wild West's entire Indian company entered on horseback, transporting everything needed to establish an overnight camp on the prairie. The audiences watched squaws erect long poles and cover them with canvas and skins, while the men looked on under Red Shirt's watchful eye. It took less than four minutes to transform the Earls Court arena into an Indian village and once camp was established, the men demonstrated the art of the war dance to the beat of a tom-tom. There was also a demonstration of how to take a scalp. The *Sporting Life* correspondent found the latter item 'grotesque, not to say revolting'.

The *Evening News* noted that in skirmishes between the 'noble red man and their palefaced enemies . . . the poor Indian gets the worst of the scrimmage, which, by the way, is a healthy and pleasant change (for the white man) from what generally used to happen in real life. . . . I must confess that I should not care to be pounced upon by the redskin in his native wilds. He looks very picturesque at Earls Court and is most affable in his wigwam. I hope, if Providence should ever ordain that I meet him "nearer home", he will retain those amiable qualities. But if he is on the warpath, I solemnly promise not to intrude, knowingly, upon the sanctity of his martial enthusiasm.'

It was now time for Bill to ride into the arena for his solo spot and demonstrate 'unique feats in sharpshooting'.

Frank Richmond told the audience that Buffalo Bill: 'Will shoot objects thrown into the air while galloping at full speed on the back of Old Charley, executing difficulties which would receive commendation if accomplished on foot, and which can only be fully appreciated by those who have attempted the feat while experiencing a rapid pace when occupying a seat in the saddle.'

A mounted Indian with a basket full of glass balls attached to his saddle acted as an assistant. The balls were flung into the air for Bill to aim at and shatter, using his .44 calibre Winchester containing specially made 'shotted shells'. This unique custom-made ammunition measured just over one inch and was filled with grains of black gunpowder and a small amount of chilled shot. When fired, the shot fanned out, giving Bill a better chance of hitting up to 50 glass balls flying through the air in rapid succession at each performance.

Chief Red Shirt (centre) and some of his Indian braves pose for the plate-glass bellows camera of Messrs Elliott & Fry in London. (Denver Public Library)

Before the sound of gunfire had time to drift away, another sound could be heard approaching the arena – running hoofs heading in the direction of Bill and his Indian assistant. Into the arena ran 18 buffalo, which herded together and charged around close to each other, followed by Bill and other Indians who joined the hunting party. Frank Richmond reminded the audience that the buffalo: 'Is the true bison of the ancients. It is distinguished by an elevated stature, measuring six to seven feet at the shoulders, and ten to twelve feet from nose to tail. . . . Primitive man in America found this animal his principal means of substance, while to pioneers, hunters, emigrants, settlers and railroad builders, this fast disappearing monarch of the plains was invaluable.'

Using blank cartridges, Bill and the Indians chased the buffalo, closing in on a particular animal and steering it away from the rest of the herd. The audience was told that this would normally be the point at which the animal would be shot dead but were reminded that the great herds had now almost disappeared and only a handful remained. The animals would, therefore, live to see another buffalo hunt and were herded out of the arena and back to their corrals.

On witnessing Bill's shooting skills, *Sporting Life*'s poet in the grandstand quickly penned the following ode for the next day's edition:

'Oh give me a home where the buffalo roam'. . . Home for these buffalo is a special corral at the edge of Earls Court in 1887. Homes in the background, overlooking the Wild West showground, still stand in Warwick Road today. (Earls Court/Olympia Archives)

THE HON. W.F. CODY
(*With our Rhymist's Compliments*)

A wonderful man is Buffalo Bill,
He rides like Bil-
Ly, with great agil-
Ity, yet still
He has never a spill.
As a shootist, Bill
Has wonderful skill.
Each shot is a kill.
With marked viril-
Ity and will,
A wonderful man is Buffalo Bill.

The opening performance of the Wild West was drawing to a close, but there was one more thrilling adventure still to be seen, described in the programme as an 'attack on a settler's cabin, capture by the Indians and rescue by Buffalo Bill and the Cowboys'.

The action moved to the small log cabin positioned at the side of the arena and mounted on a base with small wheels. The entire cabin was pushed into the centre of the arena. A woman appeared at the doorway – 'Ma' Whittaker, who also doubled as head of the Wild West's costume department – to meet her husband (played by old John Nelson), riding home after a day's hunting. He ties his horse

'Squaw man' John Nelson returns to his remote log cabin with tonight's supper and is greeted at the door by 'Ma' Whittaker. Moments later the cabin will be attacked by savage Indians and the settlers rescued by Buffalo Bill. (Denver Public Library)

to a rail outside of the cabin as another family member (Ma's husband, Frank Whittaker), wanders into the arena with a recently hunted deer over his shoulders. Venison for supper tonight! However, those hostile Indians – the same savages who had tried to capture the emigrant wagon train and the Deadwood stagecoach – have followed Frank home. Now they have returned to attack a peace-loving prairie family who have set up home in Indian territory.

On seeing the Indians, the little woman screams, Frank drops the deer and they run inside the cabin and slam the door. The Indians steal 'Pa's' horse as one of them attempts to enter the dwelling from the roof. He begins to climb into the chimneystack while the rest surround the cabin, firing flaming arrows at the door and making warlike cries to terrify the folks inside.

A tomahawk-brandishing savage strides towards the door, ready to hack it down – when a loud shot rings out. Bounding in to the rescue rides Buffalo Bill and the cowboys, shooting Indians from their horses and from the rooftop of the cabin. After a great deal of powder has been fired, the Indians lie dead in the arena. The little wife opens the door and runs towards Buffalo Bill, throwing her arms around his neck. Her husband strides over to shake hands with the man who led the rescue mission. Bill modestly gestures that it was all in a day's work and he was happy to lend a hand.

After the cheers, the Cowboy Band plays the British National Anthem.

The Cowboy Band strikes up again and the 'dead' Indians scramble to their feet and run out of the scene ready for the grand finale – a salute in which all members of the company and their horses parade around the arena to thunderous applause from the public. After the cheers, the Cowboy Band plays the British National Anthem. The audience rises to its feet, the cowboys, Indians and Mexicans pull their horses to a halt, remove hats, sombreros and war bonnets and place their hands on their hearts.

After the final notes have sounded, the company bows low from their saddles and leaves the arena, the spectacular completed.

 Most of the audience headed out in the direction of the Wild West camp to take a closer inspection at everyday life in the canvas settlement. Members of the press were invited to Annie Oakley's large, flower-decorated tent, where she served a choice of American fruit juices to her guests. The *Evening News* reported: 'This champion shot is as amiable as she is clever, and I don't think I can pay her a higher compliment than that. Her shooting record is quite phenomenal, and her countrymen are justly proud of her; but all their petting and enthusiasm have failed to spoil her. She is as popular with the other members of the company, of all colours, as her performance(s) have made her with the general public.'

The same correspondent also visited Red Shirt's tepee, where: 'This grand specimen of an Indian chief was good enough to assure me through his interpreter that whenever I chose to visit the village, I was to consider his wigwam my home.'

The gentleman from *The Times* and the fellow from the *Evening Standard* were privileged to be invited to 'the tent sacred to Buffalo Bill himself . . . a wonderful combination of practical utility and luxury; the chairs and other furniture being constructed of buffalo horns and other trophies and valuable skins taking the place of carpets.'

Inside they were shown Yellow Hand's scalp, the hunting knife used to remove it and the slain Chief's war bonnet, all mounted on a special stand and positioned in a corner.

The *Daily Telegraph* reported that: 'A visit to the camp, its tents, its discipline, and its orderly arrangement, is the last privilege awarded to the visitors before they stream out and mix with the cabs and crowds of busy London again.'

Commenting on the horse-drawn traffic jams outside Earls Court, the *Sporting Life* observed: 'Such a vast concourse of the cream – or it may be as well to say the crème de la crème – of society is seldom seen at any function. The number of chariots waiting at the gates outnumbered those of Pharaoh, and the phalanx of footmen constituted quite a small army.'

Newspapers were full of 'The Yankeeries' the following morning, although Buffalo Bill's Wild West side-show generated twice as many column inches as the American Exhibition, which was supposed to be the main attraction. *The Times* said it represented: '. . . after an effectively realistic fashion, one very prominent phase of existing American life, some of it, indeed, rapidly passing away. As a mere show the display of cowboys, scouts, Indians and horses is exciting and attractive; but it is something more. These men and women are not merely trained circus people; they represent nobody but themselves and their own life in the Wild West.'

In a main leader column, *The Era* admitted that: 'The hearts of the people had flown forward to the Wild West, and were beating for Buffalo Bill.' It added that many might admit to visiting Earls Court to observe items on display at the American Exhibition, 'but nobody will believe them. They will go to see Buffalo Bill; and the vast majority will say so.'

The *Sporting Life* said the Wild West was: 'One of the most signal successes of recent years . . . there is much in the Wild West to please. There is novelty of incident, wonderful tone, colour, dextrous horsemanship, and a breezy independence of manner.'

The *Daily Telegraph* claimed: 'No sightseer has ever beheld before a picture so varied and brilliant as the processional review of the painted tribes, or those dramatic scenes of adventure which bring home to every mind the hardships and trials and innumerable dangers in the Wild West. Buffalo Bill will soon be a hero amongst the populace, and will be admired by innumerable audiences in the future for his grace, his daring, and his enterprise.'

With its tongue firmly in its cheek, *The Referee*'s gossip columnist, 'Dagonet', offered a prize of a portrait of Queen Victoria to any British newspaper published over the next few days which did not mention the words 'Jubilee' or 'Buffalo Bill'. It appears that 'Dagonet' received no entries at all.

Bill, Salsbury, Major Burke, Annie Oakley, Buck Taylor and the entire Wild West company now waited anxiously to see if the people of London agreed with the press and would turn out in force to experience 'The Yankeeries' and 'Buffalo Billeries' twice-daily for the next 23 weeks.

'Buffalo Bill will soon be a hero amongst the populace, and will be admired by innumerable audiences in the future for his grace, his daring, and his enterprise.'

'BY ROYAL COMMAND'

They say he's a darling, a hero,
A truly magnificent man,
With hair that falls over his shoulders,
And a face that's a picture to scan;
And then he's so strong and so daring,
Yet gentle and nice with it still –
Only fancy if all the young ladies
Go mashed upon Buffalo Bill!

The Referee, 1887

A ROYAL COMMAND PERFORMANCE – AN AUDIENCE WITH QUEEN VICTORIA
– HER MAJESTY IS CRITICISED – A FASHIONABLE LONDON ADDRESS – A HECTIC
SOCIAL LIFE – ANNIE OAKLEY AND THE GRAND DUKE MIKHAIL – A ROYAL
FLUSH – THE JUBILEE PARADE – A VIP RIB ROAST – SCRAPS FROM THE PRESS
– A PAIR OF NASTY ACCIDENTS – ARREST OF 'THE GIANT COWBOY' – BUFFALO
BILL IN CHANCERY – THE END OF THE LONDON SEASON

The public gave its approval to 'The Yankeeries', flocking to Earls Court by the thousand each day – but it was the 'Buffalo Billeries' they went to see. They also stayed for the American Exhibition, especially its outdoor attractions including a switchback railway – a forerunner of the roller coaster – consisting of a series of steep gradients at different angles reaching up to a height of 20 ft 9 ins, along which a car holding up to 12 screaming passengers travelled on tracks.

Another crowd-pleaser was the 'tobogganing slide', described by the *Evening News* as: 'An inclined plane of wood which is reached by a number of steps and a platform down which the cars slide. The cars – or to use the technical term, "toboggans" – seat three persons and are a modification of the ordinary sledge, having a number of rollers or wheels, working on spindles or shafts, fixed in the under frame, and a guiding or steering wheel fixed in a special manner so as to allow the car to be moved either way, that is to say to the right or the left. Once the cars are started they run by force of gravity, and as they come to the end of the plane, their velocity is so great that they are carried up the opposite incline where they are stopped by attendants.' The paper said it was 'as much like flying as human beings are ever likely to experience.' It was claimed that some toboggans could travel at up to 93 mph and they held fascination for everyone from the

Prince and Princess of Wales down to the man on the Clapham omnibus. Nothing quite like it had ever been seen in London before.

Two days after the official opening of 'The Yankeeries', an official document was delivered to Earls Court stating that Her Majesty Queen Victoria requested a private performance of the Wild West 'by royal command' on the afternoon of Wednesday 11 May 1887 at 5 p.m. Bill and Salsbury could hardly believe their luck – Buffalo Bill's Wild West 'by appointment to Her Majesty The Queen.' The performance would be the first attended by the Queen in a public venue and outside of a royal residence since Prince Albert's death twenty-six years before. The Prince of Wales had obviously given his mother a glowing report of what he had himself witnessed days before.

On the eve of her Jubilee, Queen Victoria could have ordered a royal command performance of any play, opera, ballet, concert or flea circus that took her fancy. In London that summer she could have 'commanded' Henry Irving and Ellen Terry to perform *The Bells* or *Faust* at the Lyceum; asked Richard D'Oyly Carte for a special performance of his premiere production of Gilbert & Sullivan's *Ruddigore* at the Savoy; sat in a private box at the Comedy Theatre and thrilled to Herbert Beerbohm-Tree's company in the 'romantic drama of real life' *The Red Lamp*; laughed at Marie Tempest in the hit comedy *Dorothy* at the Prince of Wales Theatre – or even gone to the Music Hall to see Herr Winkelmeier ('the tallest man in the world') and Monsieur Clive with his performing dogs at the London Pavilion. Alternatively, she could have commanded an entire company of players to perform for her at Windsor Castle. But the Queen wanted none of that entertainment – she wanted to see Buffalo Bill's Wild West at a private performance lasting not more than one hour, to be attended by herself and a few other members of her family and royal household at Earls Court.

Bill and Salsbury could hardly believe their luck – Buffalo Bill's Wild West 'by appointment to Her Majesty The Queen!'

While Bill and Salsbury were flattered by the royal command, they knew that the special performance would also create problems. A 'private' performance meant that only royal guests would be admitted – and nobody else. Only a handful of people would be seated in an auditorium designed to accommodate 40,000 people. It meant that the 3 p.m. performance on 11 May would have to be cancelled, resulting in loss of ticket sales worth thousands of pounds. Refunds could be given to those with advance tickets – mostly boxes or prime positions around the arena – or replacement tickets offered for later dates. The 8.30 p.m. performance could proceed unaltered. But there was no time to give the rest of the public advance warning that the afternoon show would be cancelled.

The partners knew that thousands of disappointed patrons would turn up at the gates of Earls Court that Wednesday afternoon and be refused admission. Still, they pondered; the British public might at least get a chance to see their Queen, a lady who had been out of public view since the death of Prince Albert. Bill later wrote:

> The Queen has cherished an invincible objection to appearing before great assemblages of her subjects. She visits her Parliament seldom; the theatres never. . . . But as with Mahomet and the mountain, the Wild West was altogether too colossal to take to Windsor, and so the Queen came to the Wild West – an honour of which

I was the more deeply sensible on account of its unique and unexampled character. I am bound to say that the whole troupe, myself included, felt highly complemented; the public would hardly believe it, and if bets had been made at the clubs, the odds on a rank outsider in the Derby would have been nothing to the amount that would have been bet that it was a Yankee hoax.

Cutting the Wild West programme down to one hour was difficult, but not impossible. With judicious pruning, pacing and combining, Salsbury managed to produce a show lasting fifty minutes, retaining the main highlights but eliminating set pieces taking time to get in and out of the arena. Out went the attack on the emigrant train. Items from 'Cowboy Fun' had to be cut – including Mustang Jack's famous leap over his horses – and the entire episode in which Indians build a village on the prairie and demonstrate scalping, although the war dance remained.

The Royal Box built for the Prince and Princess of Wales and their party a few days before was quickly reassembled, with a dais in the centre on which a special 'throne' for the Queen was positioned. Bill described the royal enclosure as an area 'draped with crimson velvet and decorated with orchids, leaving plenty of accommodation for the attendant notables. All was made as bright and cheerful as possible, and these preparations completed we waited, very much in a frame of mind like a lot of school boys attending an examination.'

Queen Victoria – 'Grandmother England' as the Indians called her – planned to arrive at Earls Court after visiting Westminster Abbey, where she was to inspect preparations made for her Jubilee Thanksgiving ceremony on 21 June. The Queen noted in her journal that the Abbey on that day was 'one mass of boarding and lumber – it looks dreadful'.

After taking a cup of tea with the Dean and Lord Chamberlain, Queen Victoria travelled 'to Earls Court, where we saw an extraordinary & interesting sight . . .'

After taking a cup of tea with the Dean and Lord Chamberlain, Queen Victoria, with Princess Beatrice, Prince Henry of Battenburg, the Dowager Duchess of Atholl, the Hon. Ethel Cadogan, Sir Henry and Lady Ponsonby, General Lynedoch Gardiner and Sir Henry Ewart, travelled 'to Earls Court, where we saw an extraordinary & interesting sight, a performance of Buffalo Bill's Wild West'.

The Queen's carriage arrived at the Earls Court Road entrance on the dot of 5 p.m. with a travelling escort from the 2nd Life Guards. One of the Indians, Black Elk, recorded that she arrived 'in a big shining wagon, with soldiers on both sides'. The royal party drove through the Wild West stables and directly into the arena, which it circled before stopping at the Royal Box. The Cowboy Band was on hand to play in the VIPs with music in waltz time. Once the party was seated, the Marquis of Lorne, husband of Princess Louise, presented Colonel Russell and John Whitley from the American Exhibition. Fourteen other British and American officials from the organisation's executive council were invited to remain and watch the performance. An audience of 26 now awaited the start of the Wild West.

Queen Victoria recorded that her party 'sat in a box in a large semi-circle. It is an amphitheatre with a large open space, all the seats being under cover.'

When asked by newsmen to describe the royal scene before the start of the performance, Major Burke stated later that besides Her Majesty and Royal

The Queen's visit to the Wild West Show at West Brompton, as realised by an artist from the *Graphic* in May 1887. Top: 'Buffalo Bill before the Queen. Horse and Rider make Obeisance.' 'The American flag: carried by Sergeant Bates.' Bottom left: 'The smallest cowboy (Master Bennie Irving, age 5 years old) kisses his Hand to the Queen.' Bottom centre: 'The Queen and the little Indian Baby Girl.' Bottom right: 'The Queen and Red Shirt.'

Highnesses, 'the august company included a collection of uniformed celebrities and brilliantly attired fair ladies who formed a veritable parterre of living flowers around the temporary throne'.

Everyone was nervous as Salsbury gave the signal for Frank Richmond to introduce 'America's national entertainment' to its smallest, but perhaps most distinguished, audience to date. Bill takes up the story:

During our introduction a very notable incident occurred, sufficient to send the blood surging through every American's veins at Niagara speed. As usual in our entertainment, the American flag, carried by a graceful, well-mounted horseman, was introduced, with the statement that it was an emblem of peace and friendship to all the world. As the standard bearer waved the proud emblem above his head, Her Majesty rose from her seat and bowed deeply and impressively towards the banner. The whole court party rose, the ladies bowed, the generals present saluted, and the English noblemen took off their hats. Then – we couldn't help it – there arose such a genuine heart stirring American yell from our company as seemed to shake the sky. It was a great event. For the first time in history, since the Declaration of Independence,

a sovereign of Great Britain has saluted a star spangled banner, and that banner was carried by a member of Buffalo Bill's Wild West!

All present were constrained to feel that here was an outward and visible sign of the extinction of that mutual prejudice, sometimes almost mounting to race hatred, that has served the two nations from the times of Washington and George III to the present day. We felt the hatchet was buried at last and the Wild West had been at the funeral.

Queen Victoria and her party then sat back to watch the full introductory parade by cowboys, western girls, Indians and Mexicans. Master Bennie Irving, five-year-old son of interpreter 'Bronco Bill' Irving, was allowed to ride with the grown-up cowboys that afternoon. The smallest cowboy in the company gallantly rode to the front of the Royal Box, kissed his hands and blew his kisses to Queen Victoria. This was Bill's cue to ride forward on the back of Old Charley. He bowed low to the Queen from his horse and said: 'Welcome, your Majesty, to the Wild West of America.'

The race between cowboys, Indians and a Mexican followed and then Marve Beardsley recreated the Pony Express ride. The two lady sharpshooters were next

Top left: 'The scene in the arena' as realised by an artist from *Illustrated London News*. Top right: 'Miss (Lillian) Smith presented to the Queen.' Bottom left: 'Red Shirt bows to the Great White Mother.' Bottom right: 'The Queen and the Indian squaws.' (Earls Court/Olympia Archives)

on the bill, Lillian Smith first shooting up glass balls and breaking eggs, followed by Annie Oakley shooting cards and cigars from Frank's fingers and lips and clay pigeons from the hurling device.

Then it was time for some cowboy fun, featuring Buck Taylor and a dozen others in and out of the saddle, roping horses and steers and attempting to tame and ride bucking ponies.

Knowing that Queen Victoria was a regular horsewoman, Salsbury scheduled two ladies from the company – Georgie Duffy and Della Ferrell – to race around the arena on ponies. Afterwards Emma Hickock, who performed fancy riding stunts on horseback and some fine dressage to music from the Cowboy Band, joined them.

Queen Victoria was having a grand time and sent word back to Salsbury that items cut from the original programme should now be restored for her entertainment – and if the performance over-ran the requested one hour, so be it.

While the Deadwood stagecoach was under attack by Indians in the arena, Salsbury and Johnnie Baker dashed about backstage, re-shaping the programme and sending word out to Frank Richmond about what to expect next.

The race between Indian boys followed and then the full war dance using all 85 Indians, who really kicked up the dust for the Queen's benefit that afternoon. Bill picked off 50 glass balls from the back of Old Charley before demonstrating how he used to round up buffalo on the plains and prairies. It was then time for the Indians to attack the settler's cabin and be shot from their horses by Bill's rescue party.

Her Majesty told Bill that she was entirely satisfied with what she had seen that afternoon.

At this point Salsbury attempted to restore sections of the show cut to fit the Queen's original request. While the company danced the Virginia reel on horseback, Salsbury began to marshal the covered wagons together for the attack on the emigrant train, at the same time scribbling a note to Frank Richmond about the revised programme order. This included 'Mustang Jack' leaping over his horses with and without dumb-bells, Buck Taylor demonstrating how to wrestle a Texan steer to the ground and a final salute featuring the entire company. Scalping, however, remained off the programme.

According to Bill: 'Under the stimulus of the Queen's presence, the performance was admirably given. The whole company seemed infected with a determination to excel themselves. Personally I missed not a single shot; the young ladies excelled themselves in the same line; the charges on the Indians were delivered with a terrific vim; and the very bucking horses seemed to buck like steam-engines under the influence of that half-minute of excitement. But perhaps this last might have been fancy.'

After the performance, the Queen issued a second 'command' that selected members of the company be presented to her, starting with the Hon. W.F. Cody. Her Majesty told Bill that she was entirely satisfied with what she had seen that afternoon. She also said other things, but 'modesty forbids me to repeat them', Bill wrote later.

The star of the show then went on to present Annie Oakley to the Queen. Annie remembers: 'I stepped near and she asked me when I was born, at what age I took up shooting and several other questions and finished by saying "You are a very, very clever little girl". To be called clever by Queen Victoria meant the highest complement, and with a "I thank you, your Majesty", I bowed myself out.'

Lillian Smith, age 16 and just married, was next to meet the Queen of England. She was still carrying her Winchester rifle when the Queen asked her to explain the weapon's mechanism. Wrote Bill: 'Her Majesty takes a remarkable interest in firearms. Young California spoke up gracefully and like a little woman.'

Nate Salsbury was then 'commanded to the presence and introduced, and took his blushing honours with all the grace of the polished American gentleman he is.'

Next came Red Shirt, 'gorgeous in his war-paint and most splendiferous feather trappings, his proud bearing seemed to fetch the royal party immensely, and when he quietly declared that "he had come a long way to see her Majesty, and felt glad," and strolled abruptly away with dignity spread all over him three inches thick, the Queen smiled appreciatively, as if to say, "I know a real Duke when I see him."'

What Red Shirt had, in fact, said to Queen Victoria was: 'I have come a long way, and am glad to look upon the Great White Mother, who has greater power than any brave in the world.'

Finally, two squaws were summoned and came racing across the arena, their tiny papooses slung behind them. The babies were shown around the royal party and Queen Victoria patted them on their heads.

And so Queen Victoria's visit to Buffalo Bill's Wild West came to an end, with a final command, expressed through Sir Henry Ponsonby, that a record of all she had seen should be sent to Windsor.

'The Wild West has basked in the smile of royalty, and the great metropolis has rushed to the show with the eagerness of children going to their first fair,' wrote *The Referee*.

What did Queen Victoria make of all this? Back at Windsor Castle that evening she confided to her journal (the spelling and grammar are all Hers):

> All the different people, wild, painted Red Indians from America, on their wild bare backed horses, of different tribes, – cow boys, Mexicans, &c., all came tearing round at full speed, shrieking and screaming, which had the weirdest effect. An attack on a coach & on a ranch, with an immense deal of firing, was most exciting, so was the buffalo hunt, & the bucking ponies, that were almost impossible to sit. The cow boys, are fine looking people, but the painted Indians, with their feathers, & wild dress (very little of it) were rather alarming looking, & they have cruel faces. A young girl, who went through the 'haute ecole', certainly sat the most marvellous plunges beautifully, sitting quite erect, & being master of her horse. There were 2 other girls, who shot with unvarying aim at glass balls. Col: Cody 'Buffalo Bill,' as he is called, from having killed 3000 buffaloes, with his own hand, is a splendid man, handsome, & gentlemanlike in manner. He has had many encounters & hand to hand fights with the Red Indians. Their War Dances, to a wild drum and pipe, was quite fearful, with all their contorsions [*sic*] & shrieks, & they come so close.

What did the Indians make of Queen Victoria? According to Black Elk: 'We stood right in front of Grandmother England. She was little but fat and we liked

'I am glad to look upon the Great White Mother, who has greater power than any brave in the world.'

her, because she was good to us. After we danced, she spoke to us. She said, "I am sixty-seven years old and I have seen all kinds of people, but today I have seen the best-looking people I know." She shook hands with all of us. Her hand was very little and soft. We gave a big cheer for her, and then the shining wagons came in and she got into one of them, and they all went away.'

As far as Bill was concerned, the afternoon had been 'a great occasion, of which the mental photograph will remain long with me'. For Red Shirt, speaking to the *Evening News* later, it had been an occasion which had resulted in all his braves sitting up through the night talking about the 'Great White Mother'. He said: 'Men who had come from my nation to the London reservation had told me of the power of this Queen, and now we have seen her. All my men know that she is a wise woman. When we return home, all the Indians will come to us to hear us tell how we saw this great woman. It pleases our hearts that she came here like a mother and not with all her warriors around her. Her face was kind and pleased us. All of my men have resolved that she is our Great White Mother.'

'We stood right in front of Grandmother England. She was little but fat and we liked her, because she was good to us.'

The article then ended on a slightly critical note: 'Let us hope our gracious Sovereign will deeply appreciate the dignity thus conferred upon her and feel a corresponding pride in these dusky additions to her already numerous family.'

Other newspapers were more openly critical of the Queen's request for a private performance, excluding thousands of her subjects also expecting to see the show that afternoon. 'The Queen's visit will no doubt give the Wild West a capital send off, but why her Majesty should have desired to escape observation on Wednesday afternoon passes my comprehension,' stated *The Globe*. 'If she wasn't ashamed to be seen by Buffalo Bill and Co., why should she have shut out the thousands of her loyal subjects, who would have been only too glad to see her? Perhaps when Victoria R. and I. has done with all the circus shows she will oblige by giving the theatres a turn.'

The Referee commented: 'The Queen, with true imperial instinct, insisted on having the Wild West all to herself, undisturbed by the gaze of the common herd; so the thousands who came to the American Exhibition to pay their money and see the show were told to go away and come again another day.'

The newspaper continued:

There is nothing to be said against the sudden closing of an exhibition for a whole day to oblige a lady; but it is rather a curious thing for an American exhibition to do. America is a Great Republic, and in Great Republics, all men are supposed to be equal. It is a droll idea for the managers of the Great Republican enterprise to say to the public, 'You can't come in. We've got Royalty inside, and we can't have ordinary ladies and gentlemen in the building at the same time.' Of course, the Queen desired this strict privacy, and the Yankees are not to be blamed for consulting the royal lady's wishes. But, seeing that it is Jubilee Year, it would not have done any harm had her Majesty, just for once, tolerated the presence of her subjects in the same public building as herself.

Punch enquired: 'Why did the Queen go for a private view to B.B.'s in Wild West Kensington, when Her Majesty could have commanded the buck jumping riders to have given their show at Buckingham Palace? Then the Queen, in bestowing largesse on the tame Wild Indians and Cowboys, could *Shakespearingly* have said: "So much for buck jumping 'em."'

British Music Hall superstar, Vesta Tilley, famous for her male impersonations dressed as a 'toff' in top hat and tails, introduced a new song into her act that summer. Called 'May Queen Victoria Reign', it contained a number of flattering verses, followed by:

> She's seen the Yankee buffaloes,
> The Circus, too, from France,
> And may she reign until she gives
> The English show a chance.
> May Queen Victoria reign,
> May she with us long remain,
> 'Til Irving takes rank
> With a war-painted Yank,
> May good Queen Victoria reign.

In a whimsical mood, *Punch* penned a poem in honour of the royal command performance, mimicking Longfellow's poem 'Hiawatha' in style and rhythm, re-naming it 'The Song of Punchiwatha':

> Would you hear how Colonel Cody
> Gave his wondrous exhibition
> Of his Indians on the war-path,
> In the sight of Queen Victoria:
> Listen to this simple story
> From the mouth of Punchiwatha.
>
> When she reached the Exhibition
> Lo! A box near the arena
> Was prepared for her reception:
> Whitley too and Colonel Russell
> And the wily Townsend-Percy
> As an escort to the lady,
> To the Empress of the North Land.
>
> Then the Indians and the Cowboys,
> And the wonderful Vaqueros,
> Raced and charged and whirled before her,
> Stopped the coach, and wheeled and circled,
> Like some birds of brilliant plumage
> Round a carcass on the mountains.
> Balls of glass were thrown and shattered
> By the Clever Colonel Cody,

Like Wabe-no the magician;
Ladies, too, there wielded rifles
Even as the strong man Kwa-sind.

To the Queen came Ogila-Sa,
Sioux Chief, and bowed before her;
He across the Big-Sea-Water
Came to see the Queen and Empress,
And will tell the wondrous story
Oft times in Wild West wigwams,
In the days of the Hereafter.

To the Queen too, the papooses,
Dusky little Indian babies,
Were presented, and she touched them
Gently with a royal finger
That the squaws, the happy mothers,
Might go back upon Kee-way-din,
On the Home wind o'er the water,
To the land of the Ojibways,
To the land of the Dacotahs,
To the Mountains of the Prairie,
Singing gaily all the praises
Of the Gentile Queen and Empress,
And the wonders of the North land.

A few days after the performance for Queen Victoria, the postman delivered a large and extremely heavy parcel to the Wild West camp addressed to Frank Richmond. Attached to the parcel was a letter containing the royal crest. He opened it and read:

The Dower Marchioness of Ely has been instructed by Her Majesty The Queen to forward to Mr Frank Richmond, Esq., a token of Her Majesty's appreciation of his very pleasant description of the Wild West. The Dower Marchioness of Ely has selected the accompanying bust of Her Majesty as a most appropriate remembrance of this occasion.

The large bust, made from Parian marble and mounted on a solid plinth, took pride of place inside Frank's tent at Earls Court for the remainder of the London season. It was admired by all – especially the Indians, who frequently congregated around the marble torso to look and to touch the bust of 'Grandmother England'.

Bill had by now been joined in London by his 21-year-old daughter, Arta, who arrived on the *Arizona* in early June. The Hotel Metropole proved to be a fine address for both of them, as Arta filled her days

Arta Cody, Buffalo Bill's
21-year-old daughter, who
travelled to London to be with
her father for the Jubilee season.
(Denver Public Library)

shopping at fashionable London emporia and taking in the city's sights, often in
the company of her cousin, Ed Goodman. Much to Bill's delight, she was also
presented at Court. But the smart hotel was unsuitable for private entertaining
and Bill began looking around for a suite of private rooms for Arta and himself to
reside in for the remainder of their visit.

The perfect address was found by Ralph D. Blumenfeld, London correspondent
of the *New York Herald*, owned by one of Bill's influential 'toff' friends, James

Gordon Bennett, the newspaper's publisher. During an interview with the American journalist, Bill casually mentioned he was seeking 'a more homely address' with easy access to Earls Court and the pleasures of the city. Blumenfeld suggested 86, Regent Street, an elegant five storey building designed by John Nash, offering a suite of rooms on two floors above Hope's, a 'gentlemen's outfitters'. The building was close to Piccadilly and London's clubland, near shops, theatres and entertainment.

Bill inspected the property with Blumenfeld and signed a short-term lease on the spot. He and Arta moved from the Hotel Metropole into 86, Regent Street later the same day and in next to no time Bill was 'embarrassed by an overwhelming mass of flowers which came hourly from hosts of female admirers'.

A valet-secretary called Jim was hired to help Bill organise his social calendar, draw up an appointment schedule, answer letters and generally run around London on behalf of his American boss. Jim must have had a wide brief. 'The boss' rarely rose from his bed before lunchtime, left for Earls Court early in the afternoon to appear in two shows, spending the rest of the day (and night) at social gatherings, including dinners, visits to clubs and 'card parties' at which large sums were lost and won playing poker. Edward, Prince of Wales, was a regular card-playing partner, and Bill is understood to have passed on tips on how to improve his game at late night suppers at 86 Regent Street.

Thanks to Major Burke's daily desire to feed reporters with good copy, gossip about Bill's hectic London social life was shared with millions of newspaper readers. *The Times* commented that: 'Buffalo Bill has found himself the hero of the London season. Notwithstanding his daily engagements and his punctual fulfilment of them, he finds time to go everywhere, to see everything and be seen by the whole world.'

A valet-secretary called Jim was hired to help Bill organise his social calendar. He is pictured wearing a fashionable Derby hat, leaning on a tent pole outside the 'Pahaska Tepee' at Earls Court. (Denver Public Library)

Sometimes there were too many engagements to fulfil. A cartoon in the *Illustrated, Sporting and Dramatic News* (see p. 65) showed the great showman, exhausted and tucked up in bed, a cigar still between his lips, his long hair flowing across the pillow with scores of invitation cards and letters spread over the quilt. A speech bubble says, 'O bother! Say I'm out!' and the caption next to the cartoon called the piece 'Done to Death'.

Bill was not the only member of the company keeping busy in between shows at Earls Court. Salsbury opened negotiations to extend the Wild West's British stay by taking it to other parts of the country for seasons stretching into the following year. Members of the company wishing to return home after the London season would be given the fare home to America – but in the glorious summer of 1887, there were few takers. Salsbury and Major Burke boarded a train and visited Birmingham and Manchester scouting for suitable locations.

At the same time, Salsbury continued to devise ways and means of improving the show. Some newspapers commented that while the Wild West played well in daylight, poor lighting spoilt the evening performances. He ordered

Relaxing outside the 'Pahaska Tepee' at Earls Court – front row (left to right): Buffalo Bill, Lew Parker (Stage Manager), Nate Salsbury with Mrs Rachel Salsbury. Back row: Carter Couturier (Advertising Agent), Major John Burke and Chief Red Shirt. (The American Collection)

Annie Oakley in front of the settler's log cabin in the Earls Court arena. Bill and Annie fell out with each other at the close of the London season and she quit the Wild West to perform in Berlin before Prince Wilhelm of Germany. She returned to England for the 1892–3 season. (Denver Public Library)

extra lighting to be installed to floodlight the arena at night, making the action visible from all parts of the amphitheatre.

Major Burke opened a permanent press box and admitted London newspaper correspondents free of charge to any performance they cared to attend. At one early performance during the London season, a columnist with *The Referee* was told by Major Burke that there had been teething troubles during the first week, which had since been rectified. The newspaper later reported that 'every performance has made things smoother and now the programme is gone through without a hitch.'

Annie Oakley was also in demand, giving regular tea parties in her tent at the Wild West camp for the children of people who had invited her and Frank into their homes. A catering company was engaged to provide refreshments and 'daintily befrilled maids' engaged to help serve teas to the children and their governesses on a small lawn laid down in front of Annie's tent. 'Two London "Bobbies" stood on each side of the tent to keep people moving', Annie recalled.

The city's gun clubs called on Annie to show off her skills and on 11 June she gave a private display to members of the Notting Hill Club 'and a select circle of their friends'. The *Evening News* reported that Annie gave a programme 'including several marvellous feats with the rifle and shot-gun . . . presented in fine style, which gave the greatest satisfaction to the many excellent shots who had assembled to witness it.'

The demonstration included breaking six balls thrown into the air in four seconds and three balls flying through the air and shot to pieces with a repeating gun. 'At the end of the programme, Captain Leighton threw a shilling in the air, which Miss Oakley hit with a bullet,' said the newspaper.

Following the display, Annie was presented with a gold medal – 'larger than a five shilling piece' – engraved with a view of the gun club's headquarters on one side and Annie's name and the date on the other.

In addition to working for Buffalo Bill's Wild West, Annie and Frank also agreed to give other private shooting displays, provided they could be completed before daily performances at Earls Court began and 'no entrance fee was charged, nor any public announcement made'. Compensation was never mentioned, but 'the following day, my husband and manager, Mr Butler, always received a cheque for £50, $250. In one week I made £750 extra,' Annie recalled.

A London gun maker offered Annie use of the grounds around his home to give private shooting lessons. 'It began when a class of five ladies asked for lessons, saying they would pay any price asked. I charged $5 per pupil,' wrote Annie.

Members of the Wild West company were invited to the prestigious London Gun Club in Wimbledon, home of the National Rifle Association, holding its annual championships at the site. 'Young California', Lillian Smith was handed a rifle and asked to pick off a few targets. The *Evening News* wrote: 'The lady seemed to find the rifle too heavy for her, and its recoil greater than she had been used to, and had to retire to a certain extent discomforted, though announcing her intention of coming again with a weapon from her own country.'

Annie Oakley arrived the following day – with one of her own Stevens rifles – having accepted an invitation to shoot live targets, including running deer and game birds in the presence of Edward, Prince of Wales. Again, the *Evening News* was on hand to tell its readers what happened: 'Miss Annie Oakley appears to have been more successful than her "comrade in arms" was yesterday,' said the paper. Nevertheless, Annie was not happy with her performance. 'The gun was about three inches drop, not bad for a target gun, but for those little blue streaks of birds that made for the high stone wall like greased lightning – never. After I shot at a string of 24, I could have been led home easily by a lingerie ribbon.'

An elderly newspaper editor watching in the audience told Annie: 'I expected to find a better shot but not so much of a lady.'

The Prince of Wales shook hands warmly with Annie and complimented her on her skills, said the *Evening News*. 'His Royal Highness is, apparently, much interested in the success of the Wild West Show as the most patriotic Western man could be. But then the Prince is very keen on good sport of all kinds,' commented the paper.

Good sport was very much on Prince Edward's mind later that afternoon when he left the Wimbledon Gun Club. He had devised a plan and for it to succeed he required Bill's approval, Annie's co-operation and the loan of the Earls Court arena for a couple of hours one morning. The Prince, by now Bill's firm friend, sent his American poker partner and drinking friend an informal note from Marlborough House. It read:

To Col. William F. Cody.

Dear Sir: Will the little girl, Annie Oakley, who shoots so cleverly in your show, object to shooting a friendly match with the Grand Duke Mikhail of Russia? We will arrive at Earls Court at 10:30 this morning. Edward.

It is not recorded if Bill, Salsbury or Major Burke told Annie in advance about the challenge, but she was given no opportunity to refuse it. She wrote: 'On the minute, four carriages drove in through the gate. There were 16 of the Royal family in the party: Edward, Alexandra, Princess of Wales; the Duke of Clarence; Prince George of Wales (later King George V); the Princess Victoria; Princesses Louise and Maude and the Grand Duke Mikhail of Russia and his suite.'

London gossips said that Grand Duke Mikhail Mikhailowicz of Russia, a 26-year-old cousin of Tsar Alexander II, wanted more from his London visit than to simply honour his distant relative, Queen Victoria. Grand Duke Mikhail, a flamboyant young man who thought he could handle a gun as well as any cowboy, was also attempting to woo 19-year-old Princess Victoria, the Queen's oldest

109

grand-daughter. Mikhail was hoping an engagement would be announced during the Jubilee celebrations, followed by a wedding shortly afterwards uniting the royal houses of Windsor and Romanov.

The Prince of Wales had other ideas and felt his daughter could do better than marry into the troubled Russian monarchy. He made it plain to anyone who would listen that he did not care much for Mikhail and did not want a Russian to place a ring on the finger of a major British royal. Mikhail's amorous overtures towards his daughter needed to be stopped, and a public humiliation would be just the thing to send him packing home to St Petersburg.

The Prince and Princess of Wales and their guests were led to the Royal Box by Bill and Salsbury while Annie escorted Grand Duke Mikhail into the centre of the arena where they briefly spoke about guns and shooting. The Prince of Wales gave the signal to begin. Annie Oakley takes up the story:

> We shot at 50 targets (clay pigeons). The score was 36–47 in my favour. Rumour had it that the loss of that match was the real cause of the Grand Duke's proffered engagement ring to Victoria being a misfit.
>
> The papers that were against the courting expedition were pink with sarcastic comments of this dashing cavalier who was outdone at his own game by a little girl from America, of this Lochinvar who was no match for short dresses and whose warlike career faded before the onset of the American kindergarten. Whether all this had anything to do with what followed, I of course, can only guess. But about that time the engagement was broken off and the opposition papers announced that 'Annie Oakley of the magic gun' had won two matches at once from the Grand Duke – the shooting trophy and the hand of the Princess.

The Prince of Wales felt his daughter could do better than marry into the troubled Russian monarchy.

The story of Annie's shoot-out with Grand Duke Mikhail has entered legend and is re-told in scores of books about 'Little Sure Shot' and Buffalo Bill Cody, including this one. The truth, however, is rather different. Despite numerous claims by other authors – and Annie Oakley herself – that the press was full of the story next day, only one British newspaper – Bill's old friends at the *Evening News* – mentions the shooting match in a small paragraph tucked away inside the 17 June 1887 issue. Annie Oakley's own account of her life with the Wild West in London clearly recounts the famous story, although no mention of it appears in anything written by Bill – or his ghost writers – in later editions of his autobiography. Annie Oakley's name is never once mentioned in volumes attributed to Bill's pen. It is true that the two American personalities fell out with each other towards the end of the 1887 London season, as will be seen later in this story. Nevertheless, they were later re-united and Annie and Frank became loyal friends with Bill for the rest of the great showman's life. Yet, despite numerous revisions and re-prints of his autobiography, references to Annie Oakley were never included or restored – and no mention made of a shooting contest between the little girl from Darke County, Ohio, and the dashing Grand Duke from the Imperial Russian Court.

The 'shoot-out' was by no means the end of royal patronage for Buffalo Bill's Wild West. A few days before Jubilee Day – 21 June

1887 – another royal equerry arrived outside the 'Pahaska Tepee' at Earls Court with a request for a third 'command performance' – this time for 'the royal pleasure' of half the crowned heads of Europe paying homage to Queen Victoria in London that week.

The message asked if 'a private exhibition' could be given on the morning of Monday 20 June; and, after reading a list of who would be in the audience, Bill and Salsbury agreed that 'surely, never before since the world commenced has such a gathering honoured a public entertainment'.

Queen Victoria felt that her guests needed some light, amusing and diverting entertainment before the following day's climax to her Jubilee celebrations, a long, solemn service at Westminster Abbey and parade through London's streets.

'I was getting fairly hardened to royalty by this time,' said Bill. 'I had exhibited before it; I had met it at private parties and at club houses . . . but this was to be a knock-down in the royalty line – a regular wholesale consignment – a pack of cards, all pictures and waited on by the brightest, best and bravest and most beautiful that all Europe could produce.'

The Queen herself would not be in attendance on this occasion, but Edward and Alexandra, the Prince and Princess of Wales, would lead the royal party, with Prince Albert Victor, the Duke of Edinburgh, and Prince George. Their guests would include the Kings of Denmark, Saxony, Greece and Belgium, plus the Queen of Belgium, Crown Prince Rudolph of Austria, the Prince and Princess of Saxe-Meiningen, the Crown Prince Wilhelm of Germany (later the Kaiser Wilhelm) with his Crown Princess, Crown Princes of Norway and Sweden, Princesses Victoria, Margaret and Sophie of Prussia, the Duke of Sparta, Prince George of Greece, Prince Louis of Baden and Princesses Victoria and Maude of Wales, Marie Victoria and Alexandria of Edinburgh and – no stranger to Earls Court – Grand Duke Mikhail Mikhailowicz of Russia. Countless other lords and ladies in waiting would also attend with a strong military escort.

Said Bill: 'I've held four kings, but four kings and the Prince of Wales makes a royal flush.'

On this occasion the old Deadwood stagecoach, 'baptised in fire and blood' on the plains, carried four passenger-Kings inside plus the Prince of Wales sharing the ribbons on top with Bill during the Indian attack. Bill instructed the Indians to make the adventure as real as possible for the royal passengers. They were to create as much din as they wanted, poke rifles through the windows and fire all their blank cartridges, paint gruesome face patterns with war paint and really 'shake 'em up' inside the old coach as he 'cut 'er loose' around the Earls Court arena.

After being rescued by cowboys and recovering his breath, the Prince of Wales – who had just been taught by Bill how to play draw poker – told his friend: 'Colonel, you never held four kings like these before.'

Said Bill: 'I've held four kings, but four kings and the Prince of Wales makes a royal flush, such as no man never held before!' The man later to become King Edward VII roared with laughter, and then attempted to translate the story into different languages for the benefit of the foreign royal passengers, now climbing out of the Deadwood stagecoach, their legs turned to (royal?) jelly! No doubt, the exchange suffered somewhat in translation.

In a rare letter home to Lulu, Bill later told his wife:

What do you think, Mamma? I've just held four kings! And I was the joker! It wasn't a card game, either. You remember the old stagecoach? Well, I got a request from the Prince of Wales to let him ride on the seat next to me, while inside would be the kings of Denmark, Saxony, Greece and Austria. Well, I didn't know just what to say for a moment. I was a little worried and yet could I tell the Prince of Wales that I was afraid to haul around four kings, with Indians shooting blanks around? So I just said I was honoured. . . .

And, Mamma . . . we sure did rock around that arena, with the Indians yelling and shooting behind us, fit to kill. And Mamma – I wouldn't want to say it out loud – but I'm pretty sure that before the ride was over, most of those kings were under the seat. It sure was fun.

On 22 June 1887 Bill received the following letter from Marlborough House:

Dear Sir: – Lieut. General Sir Dighton Probyn, Comptroller and Treasurer of the Prince of Wales' household, presents his compliments to Colonel Cody and is directed by his Royal Highness to forward him the accompanying pin as a souvenir of the performance of the Wild West, which Colonel Cody gave before the Prince and Princess of Wales, the Kings of Denmark, Belgium, Greece and Saxony and other royal guests on Monday last, to all of whom, the Prince desires Sir Dighton Probyn to say, the entertainment gave great satisfaction.

As a gesture of thanks the Prince of Wales made sure that everyone had ringside seats for his mother's own Jubilee spectacle on 21 June.

The pin referred to in the letter took the shape of the Prince of Wales' three feathers worked in diamonds, with the motto '*Ich dien*' ('I serve') beneath.

As a gesture of thanks to the entire Wild West company, the Prince of Wales made sure that everyone in the troupe had ringside seats for his mother's own Jubilee spectacle on 21 June, when a huge cavalcade of carriages carrying royalty and heads of state from around the world would parade through London's streets on their way to and from Westminster Abbey. Jubilee day was declared a national holiday and thousands of people from around Britain travelled to the capital on special trains to get their first public glimpse of their sovereign for over 30 years.

Passes were provided allowing company members to watch the parade from VIP grandstand enclosures lining the route of the procession. Carriages were hired to take the Wild West stars to their places. Years later Black Elk recalled: 'They put us in some of those shiny wagons and took us to . . . a very big house with sharp, pointed towers on it. There were many seats built high in a circle, and these were just full of Wasichus (*white people*) who were all pounding their heels and yelling "Jubilee! Jubilee! Jubilee!" I never heard what this meant.'

After being seated, a beautiful black carriage pulled by black horses appeared and drove around. 'I heard . . . the Grandmother's grandson, a little boy, was in that wagon. . . . Next came eight buckskin horses, two by two, pulling a shining black wagon. . . . There were soldiers with bayonets, facing outward all around this wagon. Now all the people in the seats were roaring and yelling "Jubilee!" and "Victoria!" Then we saw Grandmother England again. She was sitting in the back of the wagon . . . her dress was all shining and so were the horses. She looked like a fire coming. . . . We sent up a great cry and our women made the tremolo.'

It was Bill and Salsbury's turn to show their appreciation to scores of people who had made the Wild West the London entertainment success story of 1887. In typical Cody–Salsbury fashion, it would take the form of a grand-scale Fourth of July Independence Day feast, involving every company member acting as hosts, waiters or cooks. Guests would include London-based Americans who had provided assistance or used their influence to bring the enterprise to England, plus members of London society who had entertained Bill.

The partners planned a large-scale rib-roast breakfast at the Wild West camp. Guests were told that food would be prepared by Indians 'after the manner of their cooking when in their native habitat', and the event would be 'a novel entertainment that would serve the double purpose of regaling appetites while affording an illustration of the wild habits of many Indian tribes.' Invitations were much sought after.

Promptly at 9 a.m. guests arrived and were shown to the massive dining tent, which had been festooned and decorated for the occasion with flowers and flags. A large fire had been lit in front of the tent. A hole had been dug and a bed of coals laid, over which a tripod was positioned from which ribs of beef had been suspended.

Long trestle tables and benches were arranged and while the Cowboy Band played in the background, the cream of London society sat down to eat a 'typical breakfast' of ribs of beef cooked Indian-style, grubsteaks, salmon, roast beef, roast mutton, ham, tongue, stewed chicken, lobster salad, American hominy, sweet-corn, potatoes, coconut pie, 'Wild West' apple pie, popcorn and peanuts.

Members of the Wild West management team relax in the shade of Jule Keen's tented office at Earls Court – complete with money safe and portrait of Annie Oakley – after counting cash takings in between daily performances. Pictured (left to right): Albert Sheible (Business Representative), Nate Salsbury, Jule Keen and Major John M. Burke. (Denver Public Library)

'The whole of the Indian tribes in camp breakfasted with the visitors, squatting on straw at the end of the long dining tent,' wrote Bill. 'Each brave had a sharp white stake in front of him, on which he impaled his portion of rib when not gnawing it from his fingers. Some dozen ribs were cooked and eaten in this primitive fashion, civilised and savage methods of eating confronting each other.'

One account of the breakfast claims that Bill insisted that cutlery be kept hidden until the last minute to create an impression that guests would have to eat using the same sharp white stakes as the Indians. He was heard to say aloud to anyone listening: 'All the world knows that fingers were made before forks.' It was only when Salsbury sensed some unease and social distress among the smartly dressed guests that knives, forks and spoons were hastily produced and rushed on to the table, to everyone's relief.

Speeches were made by Bill, Salsbury and Red Shirt and an Indian dance performed. Guests were then invited to remain at Earls Court for the afternoon performance of the Wild West.

London 'Bobbies' and Police Inspectors were assigned to the Wild West at Earls Court for the duration of the Jubilee season. Front row: (left to right) Nate Salsbury, Superintendent Fisher, Jule Keen, Buffalo Bill, Superintendent Foinett, Major John M. Burke, Chief Red Shirt, Inspector Cronin. Back row: G. Duck, E.M. Stuart, Albert E. Sheible (Wild West Business Representative), W.E. Wood, D.A. Jones, L.H. Skinner, Carter Couturier, Lew Parker, Harry Lee, W.C. Hayler, W.D. Snyder, Unidentified. (Earls Court/Olympia Archives)

Business continued to boom at the 'Buffalo Billeries' and hardly a day seemed to pass without an incident of one kind or another providing reporters in the press box with good copy for their columns. Here are some typical tales, some kind and others not so generous, published by various journals from the time:

14 May: The Indians feed on the same things as the rest of the camp, as a rule. But, when they can get the chance, they open out the customary commissariat

in the direction of roast dog. They have, by some means, made a capture of a white dog, and concealed him somewhere on the premises. They were fattening him up when I last heard of him, and I expect by this time he has gone the way of all flesh. The word, therefore, to the wise of Kensington – look after your dogs! — *The Dramatic Review.*

14 May (again): No alcohol in any shape is allowed within the camp. An Indian with a skinfull of English/Scotch whisky will probably upset the underground railway. And no Indian is allowed outside of the camp without a white man as his companion. (*This was later relaxed – Author.*) — *The Dramatic Review.*

5 June: The joke in America just now is that the London Post Office has had to be enlarged to meet the demand made upon its space by the Buffalo Billy-doux addressed to the cowboys and vaqueros of the Wild West by the fair maids of the metropolis. — *The Referee.*

9 June: Red Shirt has a very poor opinion of Parliament. Blanket, feathers, moccasins and paint, he accompanied his interpreter under the escort of Mr Justin H. Cathy to the House of Commons one night this week. The famous Sioux was introduced to the Baron Henry D'Worms, who doubtless by the way of being polite, asked him what he thought of the British Parliament. Red Shirt mused in philosophic quiet for a few moments and then he said he did not think it a very magnificent institution. 'Laws could be made much more quickly in my country than in England', he said. Our opinion agrees with Red Shirt's. If the business of this journal were managed in the dilatory fashion of the House of Commons, our Ascot race specials would appear on or about Christmas day! — *The Sportsman.*

11 June: It is satisfying to know that Buffalo Bill is having a good time. He has communicated his views to a friendly journal in America and expresses himself as delighted. Buffalo Bill says he likes England and has been splendidly treated, not only as a showman, but also as a soldier and a gentleman. He thinks the House of Commons very like the House of Representatives, and the London theatres far ahead of those in America, especially the details of stage management. English audiences applaud the same parts of his show as the Americans; but are more fond of the shooting and the horse racing, upon which they make heavy bets. The Queen is lovely – just like a good-natured mother, eagerly questioning him about frontier life and promising him another visit to the camp. 'No man', he enthusiastically asserts, 'not even a brother, could have done more for a stranger and his business than that greatest of great actors, Henry Irving has done for me.' He laughs at the statements of some English papers that his bucking horses are trained, and invites anybody to try to ride them. A party of hunting men accepted the invitation recently and were promptly unhorsed. — *Illustrated Sporting & Dramatic News.*

12 June: Buffalo Bill has taken in hand that dangerous weapon, the pen, and has been treating his admirers to some Wild West Reminiscences. In his last essay he tells how he slew Yellow Hand, the most terrible of the Cheyenne race, and a man who had scalped more white men than any member of his tribe. Yellow Hand, it seems, challenged B.B. to single combat, and Bill took him at his

'It is satisfying to know that Buffalo Bill is having a good time. He has communicated his views and expresses himself as delighted.'

word, went out and fought him and left him lifeless on the sward. Very good, so far; but look at this, ye duchesses and dames of high degree, who are lavishing caresses on the boss of the *Wild West Show*. Look at it, and then perhaps you will think twice before you put your dainty and delicate hands into that big fist that is stained with blood spilt in barbarous – perhaps I may say in this instance barber-ous – fashion. 'His bullets missed me; mine hit him and he reeled and fell, dying; but before his end had come, I ran up to him and, with ready knife, scientifically scalped him in something like five seconds!!!' — *The Referee*.

18 June: (referring to the fact that Indians in the Wild West company were banned from drinking alcohol inside and outside of the camp):

AT THE SCALPERIES

A whopping big Indian, last week at the 'Show,'
Was treated to plain 'Irish neat,'
The camp was soon painted a deep crimson glow,
And peace it was on the retreat.
John M. Burke got angry – belligerent, too,
And ready for all sorts of strife:
He picked up a club, just as mad people do,
That 'Injun' is so better for life.

— *Topical Times*

'The flames were applauded by the audience, some of whom looked upon them as a portion of the programme.'

25 June: Rumours have been freely circulated that smallpox, scarlet fever and other infectious diseases are prevalent at the Wild West Camp. I took the opportunity of having a chat upon the subject with the medical officers attached to the exhibition . . . 'I have had a letter from The Lancet on the subject, and here in my pocket I have numerous others asking the same question', said Dr. Maitland Coffin, medical officer to the Wild West. 'There is not the slightest truth in the report,' he added, 'I consider sanitary conditions at the camp to be most admirable in every respect. Drainage could not be better. In the camp all tents are pitched upon elevations. People who know about these matters – military men and others – are well aware of the fact that living under canvas is the most healthy mode of existence for any class of men, no matter whom. I have not had a case of illness since the camp was pitched. I do not think you could find anywhere, in the same number of people living any life, a more healthy condition than those in this camp.' — *Topical Times*.

30 June: The 'fat-boiling cowboys' made a blaze on Thursday evening at the Wild West camp which might have been attended by more serious results than those which fortunately transpired. Somebody was boiling a cowboy – or was it a cow? – and having got rid of the lean, nothing remained but the fatty substance which is generally combustible under certain conditions. The conditions, it seems, were sufficiently favourable for the fat to ignite and a high old fire ensued for some time. The flames were applauded by the audience, some of whom looked upon them as a portion of the programme, while others thought them a glimpse of Red Shirt. But the sight of the firemen, drilled under the special eye of Buffalo William – Col. The Hon. W.F. Cody as he has been christened in England – led the people to think that there is more reality than is usually exhibited at the Wild West Show. There have been many rumours afloat regarding the presence of some fell disease or other among the dusky warriors of the West, but this actual burning will go far to contradict a growing belief that these rumours were a portion of a plan of advertising devised by the bland and childlike American. — *The Sportsman*.

9 July: (following a legal action served on the Wild West by Mr Garland, who lived near the Earls Court site, requesting all rifle shooting to be 'restrained'): Mr Justice Chitty has postponed until next Friday the hearing of an application to restrain an alleged nuisance caused by rifle shooting at Buffalo Bill's Wild West Show. — *Evening News*.

13 July: (following a visit to the home of Oscar Wilde, who was said to be envious of the attention Bill received from other guests): An infamous libel has been circulated with regard to Buffalo Bill. It stated that he eats peas with his knife. An indignation meeting of peeresses has been held, and a fund raised to be spent on tracing the libel to its source. English society, in the person of its leading lion, is outraged by the statement. — *The Referee*.

16 July: (Mr Garland's action comes to court): Buffalo Bill probably imagined before coming to this country that he knew what a 'tight place' was; but he was mistaken. He knows now, or will soon know, for he has got into Chancery – not metaphysically, but literally. Alas poor William! You had better have faced a herd of mad bison or a tribe of Red Indians on the warpath, than have suffered yourself to be driven within these gloomy portals above which Dante's famous line concerning the abandonment of all hope, might fittingly be inscribed. — *Evening News*.

17 July: I have asked several of my American friends what has astonished them most in this country, and they nearly all answer, 'the fuss that is being made in Society with Buffalo Bill.' As a matter of fact the accounts which have been cabled to the States of Mr Cody's dinners with duchesses, evenings with earls, picnics with princes, frolickings with fashion, and rollickings with royalty, have been looked upon as the work of an advertising agent with a strong imagination. But the Americans who come over here find that the cables 'are all true' and that the ex-scout and present circus proprietor is really an honoured and fêted guest in the houses of the great. — *The Referee*.

26 July: Visitors to the Wild West were somewhat astonished yesterday at the prowess of an Englishman, who requested to be allowed to mount one of the buck-jumping horses. The cowboys and vaqueros were only too delighted to have a little sport with the stranger, whose performance they calculated would last about two seconds. But the rough and homely-looking young Britisher 'sold' them; for he not only succeeded in mounting the horse that used to give Antonio Esquivel so much trouble, but when once there he 'stuck on' and rode his wild steed twice around the arena and himself into the hearts of the cowboys. John Bull scored one! — *Evening News*.

2 August: Buffalo Bill's Indians are getting on, and learning how to adapt themselves to the circumstances of civilisation with a vengeance. Not only eyes,

'An infamous libel has been circulated with regard to Buffalo Bill. It stated that he eats peas with his knife.'

but opera glasses were levelled from tents at the visitors yesterday. The spectacle of a painted brave stretched flat on his stomach, and whilst fancying himself un-observed, sweeping the throng with the binoculars, was one that would have startled Fennimore-Cooper. — *Evening News*.

12 August: At 10:45 a.m. yesterday morning, Mr D.G. Mills was travelling on the District Railway between West Kensington and Earls Court Station, exactly opposite the 'Rocky Mountains of the Wild West'. 'I was considerably startled by a loud report, accompanied by the smashing of glass and felt a stinging sensation in my left cheek, from which blood was spouting profusely over my clothes. On arrival at Earls Court, I gave information of the occurrence to the inspector who at once accompanied me to the Wild West Show. We had an interview with Colonel Cody who denied the possibility of the missile having been fired from his establishment, and kindly supplied me with a collar, my own being covered in blood. As a matter of fact there can be no doubt that a bullet had passed through the compartment in which I was and I felt I had been struck with a splinter of broken glass; and though the hole was very small, both myself and the gentleman sitting opposite were covered with pulverised glass.' — *Evening News*.

14 August: Colonel W.F. Cody will do the public a service if he will get an injunction to restrain boys from playing the new game of 'Buffalo Bill'. In this, the boy who is the buffalo has to allow the other boys to butt him in the stomach. A boy named Grant played 'Buffalo Bill' and was the buffalo. At the Inquest the jury returned the verdict of 'accidental death'. — *The Referee*.

" Our Turn Next."

'Only one word in the Hon. Cody's ear – I should let the Indians win now and then, just for a treat', commented *Punch* in its 4 June 1887 edition.

In the rough and tumble world of Buffalo Bill's Wild West, it is remarkable that more people did not experience serious injury or death performing daring deeds on horseback in the giant arena. Nevertheless, two of the company's principal performers suffered serious accidents in London, both of them in front of capacity crowds.

The first blow fell when Buck Taylor, 'King of the Cowboys' and a leading heartthrob among lady admirers of the Wild West, was injured in a riding accident. The incident took him away from the show for many months and nearly ended his career in the saddle. It was not Buck's famous daredevil feat in which he leaned from the saddle to snatch hats, gloves and handkerchiefs from the ground, which caused the injuries.

The accident happened during a relatively passive section of the show when Bill, Buck, two other cowboys, and four western girls danced a complicated 'Virginia reel' on horseback. While manoeuvring his horse through a particularly tricky turn in which the riding performers hold hands as in a square dance, Buck's horse swerved, bringing his knee into contact with the saddle of another horse ridden by Della Farrell. When the cowboy urged his horse to move forward, his right leg was thrown up and twisted across his horse's back. Buck yelled with pain and heard his bone snap as Della's horse reared on to its back legs, out of control. Buck's horse charged across the arena with the 'Cowboy King' slumped forward in the saddle, his arms around the animal's neck. As the crowd fell silent and the Cowboy Band stopped playing, Buck sat up, tipped backwards in the saddle and fell unconscious to the ground.

Bill immediately galloped across on Old Charley and jumped down next to where Buck was laying face-upwards in the dust. Word quickly spread through the audience that the 'King of the Cowboys' was dead.

The Wild West's own resident medical officer, Dr Maitland Coffin, rushed forward and improvised a splint for Buck's injured thigh. Major Burke urged Frank Richmond to tell the audience that Buck was alive and his injuries were 'not as bad as they may have appeared'. A collective sigh of relief passed through the crowd, followed by applause and the show continued while the injured cowboy was loaded on to a horse-drawn ambulance and taken to nearby West London Hospital, Hammersmith, where he was admitted to Mr Keetley's accident ward. There it was discovered that Buck had fractured bones in his thigh, just beneath the hip and also sprained some neck muscles. Early announcements stated that Buck would be in hospital – and out of the show – for at least six weeks.

Buck Taylor's accident became headline news and Major Burke ensured that daily bulletins about his condition were made available to newspapers. Even the *British Medical Journal* felt compelled to provide its readers with a 'surgical synopsis' of Buck's injuries: 'A simple and perfectly transverse fracture of the right thigh-bone was discovered at the junction of the upper with the middle third of the shaft. The shortening hardly amounted to half an inch, owing probably to the direct violence which had broken the bone, without the aid of muscular action, and also to the transverse character of the fracture. The chief point of interest,

Word quickly spread that the 'King of the Cowboys' was dead.

however, in this case, is the production of the fracture by direct force applied to the outer aspect of the thigh . . .' And so on.

The medical bulletin, however, ends on a happy note: 'Buck Taylor is quite the hero of the hour, and receives daily large numbers of visitors including many persons of high social position and culture, who take an interest in an unsophisticated child of nature.'

Buck remained in a private hospital ward for two months, sleeping in a specially extended bed large enough to accommodate his 6 ft 4 in frame. His food was prepared by Wild West catering staff and brought to him freshly cooked three times daily. Eventually he was discharged and allowed to return to the Wild West camp, where the company and a gathering of press people awaited him. The *Evening News* observed: 'He was met on arrival by Buffalo Bill, who gave a most hearty greeting to his old chum, and expressed himself pleased to see him once more in their midst. This welcome was general all round, and during the handshaking which went on, the Cowboy Band played a pleasant and cheering serenade in honour of the return of their chief. Buck is now thoroughly convalescent, looks extremely well, and is quite cheery. He cannot, of course, as yet, expect to resume his old place amongst the Wild West performers, but there is every hope that ere long he will be sufficiently recovered to get about with ease and freedom.'

Five weeks later, the 'King of the Cowboys' was still hobbling around on crutches. The *Evening News* paid him an unexpected visit late one evening and found him sitting in the doorway of his 'uncommonly comfortable' tent, the injured leg slung over a chair. 'Two lengthy, brass-mounted crutches stood against a neighbouring table, telling their own sad tale,' noted the reporter.

In a front page story published on 22 August, the paper reported:

The interesting invalid looked handsomer than ever, and his temporary removal from the scene of the camp does not appear to have wrought any havoc in his bodily strength or activity of mind. Mr Taylor was dressed in a crimson silk jacket, beautifully embroidered in flowers of different hues, his legs being encased in a pair of dark coloured trousers, and his feet in Morocco slippers. His mass of brown hair was combed back from his open forehead and fell in graceful locks on his shoulders. No wonder as he sat there, sadly contemplating the moon and listening wistfully to the distant sounds of revelry from the neighbouring tents, he attracted the attention of all passers by.

The reporter was invited inside and was surprised to find 'every possible adjunct in the shape of furniture, and fixtures known to modern civilisation. A spacious bed stood in one corner, a large chest of drawers and a table covered with books and pictures, photos and coloured prints, stood in another, while several chairs and couches filled up the vacant space, and the flooring and deal boards was covered with a fine thick carpet.'

Buck was asked if he was glad to be out of hospital. 'Well, not for some reasons, but I can tell you I was magnificently treated while I was there,' he told the paper. 'The best of everything to be got, I had, and the committee even broke through their rule, and gave me a private room a week after I was brought there.

Buck Taylor never did recover sufficiently to ride with the Wild West again in London.

I can't very well tell how grateful I feel for all their kindness and attention, and I am not likely ever to forget it. Of course, I was there quite a while, but I was so comfortable, the time seemed to slip by wonderfully quick. It will be very nearly three months since I met with this accident; that's long enough, anyhow.'

Buck Taylor never did recover sufficiently to ride with the Wild West again in London. He remained confined to his tent until he was fit enough to appear in Manchester several months later.

The dashing Mexican vaquero, rough rider and trick roper, Antonio Esquivel, was involved in two separate accidents in the Earls Court arena. On 10 July, *The Sportsman* reported:

'Happy Jack' came very near to killing a man on Wednesday night at West Kensington. 'Happy Jack' is one of the mustangs belonging to the Wild West Show and he gained his sobriquet by the 'playful' manner in which he endeavours to dispose of his riders and the pleasure the feat seems to give him. Others of these brutes seem to get angry when the sanctity of their backs is invaded by the longhaired cowboy or wild settler on the last western prairies. On Wednesday the Mexican rider, Antonio Esquivel endeavoured for some time to bestride this festive buckjumper. Having at length accomplished his purpose, he rode triumphantly around the enclosure and finally attempted to dismount. His right foot caught in the stirrup and 'Happy Jack' playfully started off at full speed kicking all the time at the unfortunate Mexican. As soon as possible 'Happy Jack' was lassoed and Esquivel released from his uncomfortable position. He was borne out of the grounds and examined by a couple of doctors who found, to their astonishment, that the man has received no more injury than a thorough shaking up. He pluckily returned to the arena, upon being assured that he was not hurt and mounting another mustang rode off amid the cheers of the crowd.

Esquivel was not so lucky one month later. The show was almost over and the troupe riding out of the arena whooping it up, as usual, after the finale and shooting blanks into the night sky. Cowboy Jim Kidd, husband of 'Young California', Lillian Smith, accidentally fired his revolver full into Esquivel's face. The shot was so close to Esquivel that the wadding of the blank charge severely wounded the side of the Mexican's forehead, blinding him in his right eye and damaging his left.

Esquivel was rushed to his tent and Dr Coffin summoned. He was taken to St Thomas's Hospital, where his wounds were found to be more serious than originally thought. An emergency operation took place to save the sight of his left eye.

Tony Esquivel, champion vaquero and Wild West cowboy star, was injured in a shooting accident during the London season. Despite serious injuries to one eye, Esquivel was back in the saddle again the following day. (Denver Public Library)

As usual, the *Evening News* told Londoners the full story. 'The medical report states that the celebrated rider will lose the sight of his right eye entirely, and great care and skill will be required to save the other. The affair was purely accidental, and the unintentional perpetrator of it is completely down with regret for the painful calamity he has brought upon his friend.'

The paper added: 'Esquivel is one of the most popular men in the camp, among both white men and Indians, so that the sad event has cast an unusual gloom over the little community. His splendid feats of horsemanship and his indomitable courage under the most trying circumstances had made him an immense favourite with the audiences at the Wild West, and his loss to the show will be a very serious one indeed.'

Less than a week later, Antonio Esquivel was back in the saddle, bandages covering his blinded right eye and wounded forehead, but the sight saved in his left eye. He would ride with Buffalo Bill's Wild West for many more years.

Meanwhile another cowboy was hitting the headlines – by getting into trouble with the law. Dick Johnson was something of a loner and known to all as 'the giant cowboy' because of his tall, thickset appearance. He decided to go for a drink alone at the Lillie Arms pub in nearby Fulham Road on the evening of 21 July following the show.

Shortly after midnight, Johnson was approached by William Payne, an inventor from Islington, who claimed he invited the cowboy to drink with him. While Payne was taking money from his wallet to pay for the drinks, Johnson is said to have 'called him by an offensive name', struck him and knocked out a false tooth. The Lillie Arms then turned into something resembling a scene from one of Ned Buntline's western stories, with Payne staggering backwards, crashing into tables, chairs and tipping over drinks.

Payne picked himself up, fled from the pub, and quickly found Police Constable Alfred Botley walking his beat. Seeing blood flowing from Payne's mouth, he went to the Lillie Arms with the injured drinker to confront the cowboy. Inside, other drinkers stood clear of Johnson and the pub fell silent when PC Botley and Payne walked in.

The policeman asked Johnson to accompany him to the station, where he would be charged with assaulting Payne. Johnson refused to move, punched the constable in the face with his fist and strode out of the pub. PC Botley followed, along with half of the drinkers, and caught hold of Johnson who punched him again. A second policeman – PC Owen Davis – arrived on the scene, only to be kicked in the stomach by the cowboy, who then took off down the road pursued by an angry crowd. When Johnson was caught, he lashed out violently 'and it was only by the use of their truncheons that the prisoner was got to the station house', the court later heard.

Johnson spent the rest of the night locked in a police cell. At daybreak, word was sent to the Wild West camp that one of their cowboys was under lock and key and would later appear in court.

The Wild West's resident sheriff Con Groner went to the police station where he found Johnson protesting his innocence. The 'Giant Cowboy' told the frontier

The Lillie Arms then turned into something resembling a scene from one of Ned Buntline's western stories. . . .

sheriff that before turning in for bed he had gone out for a quick drink and in the pub invited Payne to join him. Johnson said that Payne refused the drink, saying that he would buy his own 'and anyway, I don't drink with no cowboys.'

Johnson was remanded on bail and allowed to return to the Wild West camp providing he did not leave the showground. On 19 August he appeared at Middlesex Sessions charged with assaulting PC Davis 'and inflicting upon him grievous bodily harm and assaulting him while in the execution of his duty' and also with assaulting Payne. He pleaded not guilty to both charges and was represented in court by a solicitor called Geoghegan, who put up a vigorous defence for the cowboy.

The *Evening News* reported that the court was 'unusually crowded during the hearing, and several members of the Wild West company attended, including Buck Taylor, who came into court on crutches following his recent accident.' Several company members were called to provide character witnesses, and each spoke highly of Dick Johnson. The jury, however, thought otherwise and delivered a guilty verdict. The cowboy was sentenced to six months' hard labour in London's notorious Pentonville Prison.

The Wild West company was outraged at the severity of the sentence and organised a petition asking for the judgement to be turned into a fine. They protested about police conduct and how truncheons had been used to 'calm the cowboy down'. The judge was unmoved: Dick Johnson remained in prison, was discharged early the following year and quietly re-joined the Wild West after it had moved north to Manchester.

The cavalry scout meets the Household Cavalry in the *Illustrated London News*.

Meanwhile, Buffalo Bill and Nate Salsbury were preparing for a court appearance of their own. In the wake of the Wild West's London success, a small-time British touring circus owner called George Sanger had put together an entertainment called *Scenes From Buffalo Bill's Wild West* using one or two real buffalo, two or three unreal Indians, some mules and a rickety stagecoach. While imitation might be a form of flattery, the partners were worried that Sanger's uses of the phrase 'Buffalo Bill's Wild West' in publicity material made his show appear suspiciously like their own. They were concerned that an inferior entertainment was being passed off 'in such a manner as to induce public belief that the representation was that of the plaintiff'. Legal advice was sought and the partners were forced to take out an injunction to stop Sanger using the phrase. He agreed – then continued using the phrase hoping that no one outside of London would notice. But they did.

The case of 'Buffalo Bill's Wild West Company v. Sanger' came before Mr Justice Kekewich on 30 August 1887, when the circus owner told the court he had pasted notices over his posters stating that his Wild West show had no connection with the London version. He claimed that he did not intend to mislead the public.

The Judge ruled that while Bill and Salsbury were entitled to exclusive use of the words 'Buffalo Bill', they had no claim over the words 'Wild West'. Sanger was permitted to continue using the phrase, provided he continued pasting notices over his posters denying connection with the 'real' Wild West show. Sanger was given a week to alter his advance publicity material. If he failed to make the alterations, he would be held in contempt and brought back to court.

In August Major Burke told British and American reporters that Bill and Salsbury would take the show to Paris for six months.

Bill and Salsbury picked up the court costs, but kept close watch on Sanger's publicity campaign. A week later, the unscrupulous circus owner was still trying to pass his show off as the genuine article and was hauled back before the court and fined £100. This time Sanger paid the court costs. The case brought him a certain notoriety which he later capitalised on, changing his name to Lord George Sanger and creating a large circus empire which toured successfully for many years.

The partners' main concern was that arrangements had been finalised to take the Wild West to Birmingham and Manchester following the close of the London season in October. They were worried that Sanger, and other Wild West imitators, would get there first, attempt to pass off their small-scale efforts as the real thing and dilute the Cody-Salsbury profits.

In August Major Burke told British and American reporters at the Wild West camp that, following the London season's close, Bill and Salsbury would take the show to Paris for six months, followed by Vienna, Rome, Constantinople, Jerusalem, China and Australia. In reality, the plan was not so ambitious, although the Wild West would, eventually, cover 63,000 miles travelling around Britain and Europe from the United States between the years 1887 and 1904. Next on the touring plan would be a special season at Aston Lower Grounds in Birmingham, followed by a Christmas and New Year season at Salford Racetrack in Manchester. A final show would be given in Hull before the company sailed home to New York in May 1888, fourteen months after arriving on the *State of Nebraska*.

 There would be one more London court appearance for the Wild West. Towards the close of the Earls Court season, Barnet Police Court heard that Henry Broad, age 13 and described as 'an errand boy', was found in possession of a silver six-shooter owned by Buffalo Bill. The boy was charged with stealing the revolver from the Wild West camp and publicly boasting about how it came into his possession. The police were alerted and the boy arrested. On examination, police found that the revolver was inscribed 'Colt's Frontier six-shooter – property of Buffalo Bill'.

The *Evening News* reported: 'Henry Broad was charged with unlawful possession of the weapon, and then stated he went to the Wild West on the 3rd inst., having in his possession a fan made of peacock's feathers. The Indian chiefs "Blue Horse"

and "Flies Above", he said, admired this fan, and intimated by signs a wish to possess it, offering the revolver in exchange. The bargain was struck, and he returned to Barnet with the pistol.'

Police went to the Wild West camp to conduct their own inquiries and found that Flies Above had returned to the United States three weeks before; while Blue Horse, through his interpreter, denied all knowledge of the transaction.

The revolver was shown to Bill, who immediately identified it as his own missing six-shooter. Further inquiries revealed that Henry Broad's mother worked as a waitress at a Wild West refreshment stall and the lad was a frequent visitor. One of the cowboys, Jim Mitchell, was sworn and identified the weapon as one used by him in the show. He had accidentally left it on some rocks in front of the scenic backdrop and when he returned, discovered it had gone missing.

The bench remanded the young thief for a week before giving him a good telling off and fining him £4. His mother was later reported to have 'taken him home and given him a good fourpenny one across the ears.'

As the London season drew to a close, royalty continued its fascination with the Wild West. The Prince and Princess of Wales and their sons and daughters returned to the Earls Court arena several more times.

On one occasion, Princess Alexandra sent Bill advance notice that she would like to ride in the Deadwood stagecoach and word was sent back that she would be a welcome VIP passenger that evening. When the old stage stopped in front of the Royal Box, the Prince objected to his wife climbing inside.

Bill later recorded: 'When a lady will, she will and there's an end on't, as the old proverb says, and so the gentle Alexandra was booked for inside passage, and took it smilingly. Her spouse seemed much relieved when we delivered her up safe and sound after her exciting expedition; for herself she seemed highly delighted, and thanked me effusively for the novel pleasure she had experienced.'

On another occasion, the Princess turned up unannounced at the 'Buffalo Billeries' with a party of friends and persuaded Bill to let some of the gentlemen in her party ride the mustangs and hunt buffalo. A reporter from *The Referee* got to hear about it – thanks to Major Burke – and also discovered that guests were afterwards treated to long drinks at the American bar. Her generosity won the approval of the paper. 'The royal relations who came over with dire and fearful visions of taking out their Jubilee in Westminster Abbey must have been agreeably surprised when they found themselves, thanks to the forethought of their charming hostess, enjoying all the fun of the fair, and winding up with pineapple punches, brandy swizzles, champagne cobblers, flashes of lightning, old chum revivers and claret sangrias, bosom caresses and Jubilee cocktails.'

Princess Alexandra also penned a note to Bill stating that she wished to visit the show alone and *incognito* and would prefer as few people as possible to know. 'For a royal lady whose face is as well known in London as that of Big Ben at Westminster, this seemed considerably cool,' recalled Bill.

For once Major Burke was lost for words, apart from stammering that the visit was 'a middling tight fix'. When the Princess arrived with a gentleman aide in

The Princess persuaded Bill to let some of the gentlemen ride the mustangs and hunt buffalo.

an ordinary carriage, Burke asked if they would not prefer to sit in the Royal Box. 'No, sir', replied the Princess. 'Your band will play the national anthem, and then I am in plain view, you see, discovered.'

Burke asked if the Princess had any particular part of the amphitheatre in mind from which to watch the show. 'Certainly, yes,' she replied. 'Put me amongst the people. I like the people.'

Burke seated the Princess in the press box, which that evening was free of newspapermen. Minutes after the performance begun, however, three reporters arrived with a lady guest. Burke admitted that by now he was 'dancing on thorns' and certain that word about the royal visit would find its way into the press – perhaps back to the ears of the Prince of Wales.

During a break in the performance, one of the newspapermen asked Major Burke who the other guests were. 'I never saw such a likeness in my life to. . .'.

'I know what you're going to say,' said Burke, 'the resemblance really is rather striking. But come along, I'll introduce you.'

The Princess and her aide were introduced as 'Colonel and Mrs Jones, friends of mine from Texas.'

Bill recalled: 'The Princess took the joke with becoming gravity, although her companion seemed horribly disturbed. She confessed afterwards that it was one of the pleasantest and funniest evenings she had ever spent in her life. As to Major Burke, he was in a cold perspiration until he had steered his onerous charge through the departing crowd of sightseers and seen her comfortably seated in her carriage. His attempt at a murmured apology was cut short by a silvery laugh, as the Princess remarked the "evening has been most enjoyable and the adventure one grand success", and so, as the Frenchmen say, "the incident closed itself".'

 Despite his hectic social and professional life, Bill stayed in constant contact with his family by letter. He may have been the lion of London society, but his letters demonstrate that his thoughts were increasingly on his home, Scout's Rest Ranch: his horses and cattle, raising the new barn, recruiting help for brother-in-law, Al Goodman, to gather in the hay. Lulu, as usual, was proving difficult.

'Sometime I will bring you all over to this lovely orderly law-abiding country on a visit,' he told Al in a letter from London in July 1887. 'If you see a good place where I can invest some money, I can send it for we have a few scads now – and am liable to have more . . . there is lots of money to be had in this country for 3 per cent – and if you hear of a big syndicate that has got a good honest thing that requires lots of money, I believe I could float it over here. I am running with such men as the Rothchilds now. I have been offered a million dollars for the Wild West providing I stay with it three years.'

In August Bill packed his daughter Arta and nephew Ed Goodman off on a six-week European tour. While they were away Bill was invited to a late evening entertainment at which a number of theatrical people were present, including a young and unknown American actress called Viola Katherine Clemmons. Bill later told friends that she was 'the finest looking woman in the world'.

Viola Katherine Clemmons,
who, Bill told his friends, was
'the finest looking woman
in the world'. (Buffalo Bill
Historical Centre)

Viola had made her stage debut at San Francisco's Grand Opera House just the year before in a stage adaptation of Dumas's *Gabrielle de Belle Isle*. Her wealthy parents decided that she had talent and sent her off to London to learn more about acting from some of Britain's top drama teachers, including Emile Banker, Walter Lacy and Herman Vision.

Bill and Viola began seeing a great deal of each other. He introduced her to everyone as his niece. They met for late-night suppers and occasional morning outings. She came to Earls Court to see him shoot glass balls, save the emigrant wagon train and ride to the rescue of the pioneer family in the log cabin. He escorted her around the Wild West camp and entertained her in the 'Pahaska Tepee'. With Arta and Ed still away in Europe, Viola became a regular visitor to 86 Regent Street. Everyone connected with the Wild West from Nate Salsbury and Major Burke down to programme sellers and popcorn vendors noticed that Bill and Viola had eyes only for each other.

By the time Buffalo Bill's Wild West prepared to close the Jubilee season in London, its organisers and many of its star performers had become household names with the British public. References to Cody, Salsbury, Major Burke, Annie Oakley, Lillian Smith, John Nelson, Frank Richmond and Jule Keen were cleverly woven into a poem about their London visit in the newspaper, *Topical Times*:

Bill and Viola began seeing a great deal of each other.

THE WILD WEST ALPHABET

A is America, with stripes and with star,
B are the buffaloes, brought from afar.
C stands for Cody, the 'great all-round man,'
D are the deeds, so well known to his clan.
E is for Esquivel, vaqueros with pluck,
F is their firmness while taming a 'buck.'
G are the girls, to perfection they ride,
H are the horses, when galloping stride.
I are the Indians, with whoop and warpaint,
J are their jokelets, less polished than quaint.
K is Jule Keen, at finance quite the boss,
L stands for Lillian, a match for our 'Ross.'
M are the mustangs, which show 'cowboy's fun.'
N is John Nelson, the veteran gun.
O stands for Oakley, who bangs 'all creation.'
P is her pluck, she's the pride of her nation.
Q is her quickness, which makes her rejoice,
R stands for Richmond, with stentor-like voice.
S is Nate Salsbury, who all do esteem,
T is Buck Taylor, now back on the scene.
U is the union, displayed by them all,
V is their valour, not heeding the falls.

W is the welcome we give to the 'Show,'
X is its 'excellence' which we all know.
Y is our yearning to see it again
Z is their zeal – and long may it remain.

The Wild West played the last of its 300 performances of the Jubilee season at Earls Court on 31 October 1887. Two and a half million people paid to see the show in London and Bill had not missed a single performance, although there must have been times when self-inflicted exhaustion or an evil hangover made him long for a day off. Luck had been on his side from the start. Britain's summer weather had been the best for 30 years, its people in a holiday mood and the show given the royal stamp of approval many times over. Thousands more British people would now turn out to see Bill's cowboys, Indians, vaqueros and western girls in the provinces.

On the day after the final London performance, *The Times* wrote:

The American Exhibition, which has attracted all the town to West Brompton for the last few months, was brought yesterday to an appropriate and dignified close. A meeting of representative Englishmen and Americans was held, under the presidency of Lord Lorne, in support of the movement for establishing a Court of Arbitration for the settlement of disputes between this country and the United States. At first, it might seem a far cry from the Wild West to an International Court. Yet, the connection is not really very remote. Exhibitions of American products and a few scenes from the wilder phases of American life certainly tend in some degree at least to bring America nearer to England. . . . The two things, the Exhibition and the Wild West Show, have supplemented each other. Those who went to be amused often stayed to be instructed. It must be acknowledged that the show was the attraction, which made the fortune of the Exhibition. Without Colonel Cody, his cowboys and his Indians, and without the collateral fascination of the Switchback railway and the Toboggan slide, it is conceivable that the Exhibition might have reproduced the Wild West in one feature at any rate – namely, its solitude – with rare fidelity. But the Wild West was irresistible. Colonel Cody, to the amusement of some of his more superfine compatriots, suddenly found himself the hero of the London season. Notwithstanding his daily engagements and his punctual fulfilment of them, he found time to go everywhere, to see everything and be seen by all the world. All London contributed to his triumph, and now the close of his Show is selected as the occasion for promoting a great international movement. . . . Civilisation itself consents to march onwards in the train of Buffalo Bill. Colonel Cody can achieve no greater triumph than this, even if he some day realises the design attributed to him of running the Wild West Show within the classic precincts of the Coliseum in Rome. . . . It is no paradox to say that Colonel Cody has done his part in bringing America and England nearer together. The nearer they are brought together, the less likely they are to quarrel.

'It is no paradox to say that Colonel Cody has done his part in bringing America and England nearer together.'

HEADING NORTH

Who from the west to east have come
To show us what the Yanks call 'some,'
And make us say we think they're rum?
Why, Buffalo Bill's Crowd.
Who'll, breaking all our salient laws,
On wives and daughters lay their claws,
And turn them into Indian squaws?
Why, Buffalo Bill's crowd.
Who'll draw a million souls to see
The strange things from Amerikie,
And only charge a modest fee?
Why, Buffalo Bill's crowd.

Topical Times, 1887

ANNIE OAKLEY QUITS – HORSEMEN VERSUS WHEELMEN – A LUKEWARM WELCOME IN BIRMINGHAM – THE WORLD'S LARGEST THEATRE IN MANCHESTER – 'FRIENDS OF TEMPERANCE' TRY TO BAN BUFFALO BILL – OPENING POSTPONED – A NORTHERN SENSATION – AN INDIAN TRAGEDY – AUDIENCES GET SMALLER – AN INDIAN CHRISTENING – AN OUTDOOR 'FAREWELL' – A HIGH TIME IN HULL – HOMEWARD BOUND – FAREWELL TO OLD CHARLEY

While Salsbury supervised dismantling the Wild West in London and transferring it 110 miles north to Birmingham, Bill took time off to visit Italy with Arta. He would probably have preferred to travel in the agreeable company of Viola Clemmons, but felt a fatherly duty to give his attractive teenage daughter some of his time before embarking on the next stage of his public and private British conquests.

The Times's comment about staging the show in Rome's Coliseum intrigued Bill and he planned to visit the old Roman ruin to see if it were possible. But in Rome Bill found what millions had already discovered – the Coliseum's floor had been plundered and collapsed generations before, leaving underground passageways and tunnels exposed to the skies above.

The continental holiday gave Bill time to rest and reflect. The business of being Buffalo Bill Cody in London during the Jubilee season had been hard work and he needed to distance himself from both the enterprise – and Viola – for a while.

In a letter home to Julia, Bill had complained about the British climate 'which I don't believe agrees with me at all and if I don't get my health back soon I will be tempted to leave it and come back to my own good country. I could do a great business if I could get back to open in New York next May. I believe it would pay better than to stay over here. Oh, how I would love to spend a month with you at the ranch.' The climate disagreeing with Bill was caused by London's sulphurous smog, which hung in a pall over the city thanks to coal-burning fires roaring up three million domestic and industrial chimneys across the capital.

The London season had made both Bill and Salsbury rich men, but the partners had doubts about how profitable their forthcoming open-air winter visit to Birmingham might be due to a lack of similar facilities for their big show. The Birmingham engagement was designed as a short fill-in before moving further north to Manchester, where the Wild West would play inside a new, purpose-built, steam-heated stadium for five months.

Back in England, Bill discovered that Annie Oakley and Frank Butler had quit the Wild West. Following the London season, Annie and her husband accepted an invitation to stay at the country home of British gunmaker R. Edward Clark and his wife in Shrewsbury. They spent 12 days roaming over Clark's 5,000 acres, shooting partridge, pheasant and other wild birds in hills and valleys surrounding the estate.

Before leaving for Shrewsbury, Annie and Frank agreed to visit Berlin to give an exhibition shooting match for Crown Prince Wilhelm. Annie had discussed the engagement with 'Fritz' while he was in London for the Jubilee and told him she would be delighted to visit when the season closed. She also accepted a five-week booking in Paris and, while relaxing in one of one of Mr Clarke's comfy armchairs, the Butlers decided not to return to the Wild West and travel directly to Berlin instead.

Back in England, Bill discovered that Annie Oakley and Frank Butler had quit the Wild West.

Their reasons for quitting the show are unclear. Annie wrote: 'I severed my connections with the Wild West at the close of the London season, the reasons for so doing take too long to tell.' She may have left for monetary reasons. Annie could earn as much from giving demonstrations and private shooting lessons as she could in the public arena. It is possible that she left the show in a state of high dudgeon after Bill and Salsbury objected to her taking leave to appear elsewhere and missing the start of the Birmingham season.

Perhaps Annie Oakley was homesick for America, where she was equally as famous as she had become in England? Or was Bill jealous of her success with royalty, the public and the press? There are reports of Bill flying into rages and storming off to sulk in the 'Pahaska Tepee' whenever Annie received more public acclaim than he did – but it is unlikely. In London in 1887 nobody received more acclaim than Buffalo Bill, who was too busy having a grand time in London with Viola Clemmons and his new club friends to worry about who was getting more column inches than he. Although Annie received her fair share of good notices and recognition for her remarkable shooting skills, she remained in Bill's shadow – and always appeared happy to be so.

While Bill was returning from his holiday for the start of the Birmingham engagement, Annie wrote that she and Frank were shooting for the cream of

German royalty in Berlin, including 'princes, princesses, dukes, duchesses, Bismarck and other potentates'. On the journey from Germany to Paris Annie became unwell. A doctor told her she was exhausted and needed complete rest. The Parisian booking was cancelled and the Butlers sailed home to America.

 Two cowboys also remained in London to accept an unusual challenge – a 48-hour endurance race between American horses and modern-day bicycles, held over six days for a prize purse of £300. Salsbury encouraged former Pony Express rider Marve Beardsley and cowboy 'Bronco Charley' Miller to accept the challenge. It was a nice way of generating Wild West publicity between the close of the London season and the start of northern engagements.

The race was held on an indoor track laid down inside Islington's Agricultural Hall.* The cyclists, riding the latest 'penny-farthing' models with a large front wheel and a smaller one at the rear, were World Champion cyclist, Richard Howell of Leicester, and W.M. Woodside of Philadelphia, America's cycling champion.

A large audience turned out to see the unusual spectacle of cowboys on horseback racing against cyclists sitting on very different saddles.

A large audience turned out to see the unusual spectacle of cowboys on horseback racing against cyclists sitting on very different saddles. Only one horse and one cycle were permitted to race at a time, but riders could change over whenever they wished, usually every hour. The bicycle track on the outside edge and made from timber measured eight laps to the mile; while the wide horse track, made from soft tan, was one-seventh of a mile in circumference. Salsbury loaned Marve and 'Bronco Charley' 30 of the Wild West's best horses for the marathon.

On the first day 'Bronco Charley' wore a jockey jacket and red and gold cap, while Howell 'wore ordinary cycling dress'. But when it was Marve's turn to jump into the saddle, he was thrown from his horse, injuring his ankle. Less than one hour later he was back, only to be thrown for a second time that day. After the first eight hours, 'the wheelmen' had covered 138 miles and the horsemen 137 miles.

By the end of the second day, cowboys were leading by 220 yards and the spectators were favouring Buffalo Bill's boys over the cyclists. Day three ended with cowboys taking a slight lead of 406 miles to cyclists' 405 miles and by day four little had changed – cyclists 536 miles and cowboys 535 miles. On the fifth day the cowboys took the lead again – 655 miles to cyclists, 636 miles.

The hall was packed to the rafters for the final day and the *Evening News* noted 'the sport was of an interesting and exciting character, and the men in better condition than is usually the case at such a late stage of a contest of this description.' The race ended with the horsemen completing a marathon 674 miles and cyclists 673 miles and 1,320 yards.

Although the cowboys won the prize, the horse and cycle race proved little apart from the fact that a man-made machine could just about keep up with a

---

* Now, the Business Design Centre.

horse. The cowboys would probably have argued that it was impossible to ride a bicycle up mountain trails, cross a prairie or a shallow river – but the cyclists might equally have replied that a bicycle needed no feed or water. . . .

The Wild West arrived in the industrial heartland of Birmingham, Britain's second city, on 4 November 1887 to a very different reception. They were to give their first performance to a West Midlands audience on the meadow at Aston Lower Grounds two days later. The arena was the same size as Earls Court, but the 'grandstand' – as football-mad 'Brummies' preferred to call it – was much smaller because the season was to last only three weeks. It could accommodate around 4,000 spectators, each paying one shilling admission.

The weather had turned cold and instead of bivouacking on open land next to the arena, the company's tepees and tents were pitched inside the Great Hall and galleries running the full length of Aston Hall, a striking architectural brick mansion built between 1618 and 1635 in the centre of the park. The City of Birmingham owned the property, which today includes the home of Aston Villa Football Club.

Fires were banned inside the Jacobean surroundings of Aston Hall.

The Indian tepees were pitched in the centre of the floor, having first been scrubbed down to remove months of soot accumulated from open fires burning inside throughout the London summer. Fires were banned inside the Jacobean surroundings of Aston Hall. Cowboy tents surrounded the wigwams on the hall floor and upper galleries, while Bill's 'Pahaska Tepee' was erected on a stage overlooking the rest of the company, like a headmaster surveying his students.

Horses and mules were housed in a large roller skating rink, converted into temporary stables. The remaining animals lived in specially created corrals close to a large mess tent erected opposite the mansion's kitchen, which Wild West caterers commandeered for the duration of their stay. As in London, the public would be allowed to walk around the outdoor site to view the animals, and peer through Aston Hall's open doors at the tented village inside.

The Birmingham show was identical to that seen in London, the exception being pint-sized Johnnie Baker – 'The Cowboy Kid' – now replacing Annie Oakley as a featured sharpshooter. Bill had taught Johnnie how to shoot and Annie and Frank had turned him into an exhibition marksman. His 'party piece' was to lie on his back, arching his body off the ground supported by his head and his feet, and fire his rifle from the upside-down position. He rarely missed his target.

The *Birmingham Daily Gazette* was at Aston Lower Grounds to watch the Wild West company settle in. 'A visit last night to the Aston hunting grounds was fruitful of a series of odd sights and unusual sounds,' reported the paper. 'In the hurry and bustle of preparation one saw the show behind the scenes, the cowboys as common mortals, and the chiefs without their paint. They looked a curious and heterogeneous congregation.'

On the evening before the first performance, Bill and Salsbury treated the entire company to an evening out at Birmingham's Grand Theatre, where they saw a performance of the musical comedy *Human Nature*. The cowboys were also invited

Johnny Baker

Champion Shot

Johnnie Baker seen here performing one of his famous routines, leaning over backwards to fire at a target from the upside-down position. He rarely missed his mark. (Buffalo Bill Museum and Grave, Lookout Mountain, Golden, Colorado)

to watch a football match played by one of Birmingham's home teams, but they declined. They had work to do.

A visit to a football game might have better prepared the company for Birmingham audiences. In the large sprawling city, known as 'the workshop of the world' and producing everything from pen nibs to steam engines, 80 per cent of the population worked in factories. Part of the region had long been known as the 'Black Country' thanks to the grime and soot polluting the air from factory furnaces and mines. For factory workers, football was the stuff of life. The 'Brummagems' as Bill called them, lived, ate, slept, watched and played football – and nothing would keep them from seeing their favourite teams play. Not even Buffalo Bill's Wild West.

The first performance took place at 3.00 p.m. on the afternoon of Saturday 6 November. It was a misty day and rain drizzled down on to Aston Lower

134

Grounds. The 'grandstand' was hardly full, thanks to competition from two cup-ties played simultaneously in the city at Small Heath and Cape Hill. The football matches attracted 13,000 spectators. The Wild West attracted less than 5,000.

The show's orator, Frank Richmond, was ill-prepared for a British regional audience. London spectators had been enthusiastic and appreciative, while the Birmingham audience brought a football match mentality with them that afternoon, keeping up an active banter with the master of ceremonies throughout the proceedings.

'Is them Indians genuine?' and 'Buffaloes ain't up to much,' were two of the loud and public comments overheard by the *Birmingham Daily Gazette* in the audience. The paper added: 'In spite of London's lavish praise, they insisted on their right to criticise. They were not at all sure that the Wild West should not be described as a mixture of circus, menagerie, and melodrama. Even the Orator didn't impress them overmuch; and this was surprising, for very few entrepreneurs in this country find room in their travelling companies for an Orator. Mr Frank Richmond, the Cicero of the Ring, did his best to prove that the "Wild West" is beyond comparison – that it is to be considered not a vulgar exhibition for money, but an important object lesson, a glorified drama. The genius of the place was against him, and the thousands smiled at his sentiments, cried "Off-side!" when the Indians and cowboys forgot in fighting the rules that generally govern combats at Aston, and cheered with plebeian gusto the dusky kings who deigned to gallop by for their entertainment.'

The paper was also critical of the horse race between a cowboy, Indian and Mexican: 'Nobody could swear which won. Probably when the show gets to Manchester, where a book is made on every event from a cat race to a fly hunt, cards giving particulars of age and weight and so on will be issued. A race is nothing unless you know which you want to win.'

Despite the reviewer's observations, the people of Birmingham generally liked the Wild West. 'Fortunately the show is so good that it can stand all the banter applied to the Orator, and all the mirth provoked by the splendid superlatives on the programme', the same writer stated, adding, 'the "Wild West" may be written down as a good deal less dangerous than a well fought match at football.'

The short season was not the success Bill and Salsbury had hoped for and the grandstand was full for just a few performances. Business was particularly dismal on Saturday afternoons at the height of the football season, although Sunday afternoon and early evening concerts given by William Sweeney and The Cowboy Band attracted good audiences.

There were fewer social engagements in Birmingham for Bill to attend – which probably pleased him – and the company spent most of their daytime hours rehearsing new pieces to be added to the show in Manchester. Off-duty hours were spent playing cards in Aston Hall's rarefied surroundings. By now the Indians had become skilled at both dominoes and cards and gambled large sums of money on poker games which went on for hours, especially when Red Shirt was away from camp attending one of the civic functions he was invited to in Birmingham with his interpreter.

The football matches attracted 13,000 spectators. The Wild West attracted less than 5,000.

The *Birmingham Daily Gazette* noted: 'It is satisfactory to know that they (the Indians) are fairly paid and have their wants supplied in a way that will leave a pleasant "pile" of dollars for them to return home with.'

Eighty miles away from Birmingham behind the main grandstand at Manchester Racecourse, workmen were putting the finishing touches to 'the world's largest theatre' – a gigantic brick and timber auditorium, designed to seat up to 8,000 spectators with standing room for a further 3,000 in three galleries. Several private boxes were also included. The striking new building measured 600 ft long, 200 ft wide and 80 ft from floor to ceiling and cost £15,000 to build.

The interior resembled Earls Court, with an indoor arena in the centre facing spectators sitting in a large semicircular amphitheatre. Unlike Earls Court, there was also a 140 ft long stage, backed by a semicircular frame through which scenery could be changed.

A pen and ink sketch from a Manchester magazine called *The Parrot* of what was claimed to be 'the world's largest theatre' at Manchester Racecourse, Salford – a purpose-built, centrally heated indoor venue for the Wild West's spectacular 1887–8 winter and spring season. After the show returned to America, the building was demolished. (Manchester Department of Libraries and Theatres, Local Studies Unit)

The building in Manchester's Salford district, would be Buffalo Bill's happy hunting ground for the next five months. As it turned out, the Wild West was the only major event ever presented there. After a failed attempt to use it for indoor racing, the huge theatre was demolished when the company returned to the United States the following spring.

Over 1,000 ft of piping was installed to heat the building by steam throughout Manchester's bitterly cold winter, controlled by a 30 horsepower boiler. Lighting was powered by electricity, which had never been used on such a large scale in Manchester before. Fireproof paint was used on walls both inside and out and it

THE WILD WEST SHOW.

was claimed that in an emergency, a capacity crowd could be evacuated from the auditorium in less than three minutes through 12 emergency exits.

The Wild West's Manchester engagement was designed to attract people from across the north of England. Like Birmingham, Manchester was a working class region at the centre of northern England's textile industry. Manchester Racecourse was easy to reach thanks to a network of railways linking the city to other parts of the region and Bill and Salsbury expected capacity crowds on excursion trains travelling in from Liverpool, Lancashire and Yorkshire.

However, not everyone was in favour of having the Wild West in Manchester. Attempts were made by a Salford 'Friends of Temperance' group to ban the show, on the grounds that alcohol would be sold and performances given on Sundays, putting a double-dose of temptation in the way of the city's chapel- and churchgoers.

At Henry Irving's suggestion, Richard Mansell, manager of Manchester's popular Queen's Theatre, and his business partner, William Calder, were retained by Bill and Salsbury to anticipate problems which might have arisen during construction of the giant building. They were also to steer the project through to the awarding of a theatrical licence required for indoor entertainment and only granted once the building was at a sufficiently advanced stage of completion. Mansell and Calder became partners in the Manchester engagement. When the licence hearing came before the court at Salford Town Hall, the anti-alcohol and pro-chapel lobby was out in force, led by the Revd James Clarke, Chairman of the Salford Board of Guardians.

Thanks to Mansell and Calder, Aldermen and councillors sitting on the bench that day had already inspected the giant building at Manchester Racecourse during a site visit. There they met Salsbury and Major Burke, who suggested they all retire for lunch at a nearby hotel to discuss the matter. Over roast beef and copious amounts of beer, Salsbury and Burke enthused about the Wild West's educational qualities, its family values and how it provided people with a rare opportunity to see native Indians and wild animals at close quarters. They were reminded that the show had enjoyed royal patronage – surely a seal of approval if one was needed.

Major Burke emphasised that the Wild West was not a play with dialogue or a circus with clowns, but: 'consists of dramatic episodes, illustrating the progress of civilisation in America'. The civic dignitaries were won over and promised to give the enterprise their approval, but there would be some restrictions in order to placate the show's opponents.

The licence was granted, but alcohol banned from the Wild West site. Sunday performances were also prohibited, along

Punch, 4 June 1887.

Manchester was covered with brightly coloured posters announcing that the Wild West was coming to town, carefully avoiding stating exactly when.

with shows on Christmas Day, Ash Wednesday, Good Friday 'and days appointed for public fast and thanksgiving'. The site had to be cleared by 11.00 p.m. every evening and 'police constables when dressed in uniform and other constables when not so dressed if known as such to the manager or his servants, shall be permitted to have free ingress to the theatre at all times.'

The Wild West rode into Manchester by train early in December and set up camp inside a 200 ft long by 80 ft wide purpose-built structure next door to the massive theatre – tepees down the centre aisle, cowboys' tents at either side, and the 'Pahaska Tepee' at the top end providing Bill with a good view of the entire layout (when not staying overnight at a private house he rented for Arta and himself in Howard Street, Salford). Hot water pipes allowed tents and tepees to be heated to a cosy 68 degrees. Gas jets were fitted for lighting. As in London, the public would be allowed to wander around the camp before the start of the twice-daily show.

Horses were stabled in buildings attached to the Racecourse, and corrals created at the rear of the theatre for remaining livestock.

Performances were scheduled to commence in early December, but the opening was postponed after Salsbury insisted on making extra rehearsal time available for elaborate new portions of the show. Many sections had to be radically altered for the Manchester arena and new equipment – including a giant wind machine – perfected, while the huge electric lighting rig purchased directly from the American Exhibition in London was installed and made to work properly. Uncertainty persisted over the precise opening date.

Bill, Salsbury and Major Burke turned Mansell and Calder's offices at the Queen's Theatre into their own headquarters, from where they issued final instructions to architects, Messrs Magnall and Littlewood, on last minute changes needed for the opening performance – whenever that might be.

Punch, 4 June 1887.

Manchester was covered with brightly coloured posters announcing that the Wild West was coming to town, carefully avoiding stating exactly when. The posters depicted thrilling scenes from Bill's life hunting buffalo, fighting Indians, leading wagon trains and working as an army scout – a life one million miles removed from those lived by ordinary folk in working class Manchester.

The *Salford Chronicle* paid the Wild West camp a visit on 9 December and described the scene in an article the following day:

The Indians and company which Buffalo Bill has gathered round him have taken kindly to their new quarters on our Racecourse. . . . The Indians have now settled down in their encampment, in which they are provided with comfortable quarters, being situated near the

See-you Chief combing his Wig-wam.

principal part of the building. Everything has been done to promote the comfort and convenience of the Indians, the camp being heated by hot water pipes. Each tent contains accommodation for 15 persons, and the height measures 12 ft. When necessary huge fires are provided for the tents, the contented occupants gathering round in their own peculiar manner. . . . The cowboys have taken up their residences in marquees. The equestrian proportion of the establishment is of gigantic dimensions, there being about 230 horses, including some Broncos and mustangs, the latter being of a wild nature.

The *Manchester City News* was fascinated by off-duty Indians relaxing in front of their wigwams. 'Most of the day they spend lolling on mattresses, or playing cards and smoking in front of their tents. . . . The passion for gambling and smoking cigarettes almost amounts to a mania, and has evidently been acquired by contact with civilisation. Even the young children possess it, and smoke with all the gravity, if not with the avidity of their elders. . . . But rigorous precautions are taken to guard the Indians from intoxicating liquors, and the closest watch kept to prevent them getting any fire water.'

By the time the train pulled into Liverpool's Lime Street station, a crowd of 30,000 awaited them.

On 8 December the Mayor of Salford, Alderman Alfred Dickens plus local magistrates and the Chief Constable, visited the Wild West theatre and 'expressed themselves thoroughly satisfied with the building and general arrangements'. In the arena they were introduced to Bill, admired his hunting trophies, Indian weapons, curiosities and colourful flags and banners used to decorate the interior. Bill, Salsbury and Mansell were invited to call on the Mayor for tea at his parlour at Salford Town Hall the next day.

As a reward for their hard work licking the new show into shape, Bill and Salsbury took the company on a railway day excursion to Liverpool. They rode from the racecourse to the Exchange station in a fleet of omnibuses hired from the Manchester Carriage Company, and were watched by thousands of people as they passed along Chapel Street.

Fast as an arrow, word raced along the Manchester–Liverpool train route that Buffalo Bill and his Wild West would be passing through their towns. Crowds began to gather on railway platforms at Wigan and St Helen's stations. By the time the train pulled into Liverpool's Lime Street station, a crowd of 30,000 awaited them. A great roar went up from the massive welcoming party as the company climbed down from carriages on to the platform.

Over 100 policemen were drafted into Queen's Square to keep crowds back as members of the Wild West filed into the Court Theatre to see a matinée performance of William Calder's drama, *Shadows of a Great City*.

By the end of the performance, Queen's Square was a mass of human faces, all wanting to see Buffalo Bill, Red Shirt, Buck Taylor (still limping, but no crutches in sight), cowboys, Indians and Mexicans. A police escort was provided to take them back to Lime Street station and crowds on railway platforms turned out again to watch the Wild West steam past on their return to Manchester. If Bill and Salsbury had any doubts about the warmth and enthusiasm of northern audiences, they were dispelled for the time being.

THE POSITIVE INAUGURAL DATE

December 17th

To the Public of Manchester and Salford, all Lancashire and Yorkshire

Messers. Calder & Mansell are pleased to announce positively

The definitive Completion of the

GIGANTIC PREPARATIONS OF MONTHS

For the Advent of

THE WORLD FAMOUS

B U F F A L O B I L L ' S

(Colonel Wm. F. Cody)

W I L D W E S T,

And are thus enabled to name

Positively the Opening

on

Saturday Evening, December 17,

of the

COLOSSAL BUILDING

(heated by Steam and Lighted by Electricity)

at

MANCHESTER RACECOURSE

Presenting the entire great aggregation of

Genuine Historical American Characters

including

Colonel W. F. Cody (Buffalo Bill)

Indian Scouts, Cowboys, Hunters,

Frontier Girls, Marksmen, Mexicans,

Herds of Indian Ponies, Wild Buffalo,

Texan Cattle, Elk, Deer, Bear, &tc.,

that were the

LONDON JUBILEE SEASON'S SENSATION.

All the Features of that

Remarkable Engagement

And in addition

THE LARGEST SCENERY

EVER PAINTED

depicting in

Seven Animated Tableaux

Scenes, Incidents and Episodes

in the

STORY OF THE SETTLEMENT OF AMERICA

forming the

Grandest Combination of Art and Nature Known in the World's

History

For further particulars see Future Announcements

Nate Salsbury, Director

John M. Burke, Gen. Manager

On 14 December the first advertisement announcing the opening performance of the new Wild West exhibition appeared on the front page of the *Manchester Evening News*.

At around the same time as the advertisements appeared, tragedy stuck the Wild West Camp. A 22-year-old Sioux Indian known as 'Surrounded' developed an inflammation in his lungs. He was visited by the camp's own Medicine Man and the squaw elected 'mother of the camp'. When the red man's medicine failed to work, a white man's doctor was summoned who insisted on transferring the young Indian to a nearby infirmary.

A second Indian and 'Bronco Bill' Irving travelled to the hospital with Surrounded, where he later died. A dark shadow fell over the encampment, especially among Sioux members of the company.

'Bronco Bill' told the *Manchester Evening News* that Surrounded – described as 'a fine fellow, being 6 ft 7 ins in height' – received his unusual name when, as an infant, his parents' settlement was attacked and he was carried by his father through fire and smoke while 'surrounded' by enemy warriors.

The paper stated that: '"Surrounded"'s remains will be interred in the Salford Borough Cemetery and an imposing funeral ceremony will be witnessed.' The *Salford Chronicle* claimed that the body would be conveyed to London at Buffalo Bill's expense for burial in Brompton Cemetery, near Earls Court.

No record now exists as to what finally happened to Surrounded's last remains. It is likely that he was brought back from the Infirmary to the Wild West camp, where a period of mourning followed by a Native American ceremonial service took place out of public gaze. He was not buried in Salford's own cemetery, any others in the immediate neighbourhood or anywhere else in the city of Manchester. Although other Indians were to be buried at Brompton cemetery, as will be seen later in this story, Surrounded did not find his final resting-place in London, either.

Poor Surrounded was probably interred somewhere in a common grave – one without marker or headstone – now lost in the mists of time. It is even possible that, over 120 years after Buffalo Bill and company sailed home to America, young Surrounded is still beneath the ground at the site which once housed Manchester's Racecourse. . . .

No record now exists as to what finally happened to Surrounded's last remains.

Meanwhile, Wild West imitators could still be found hanging on to the fringes of Buffalo Bill's buckskins. A few days before the Manchester opening, the *Salford Weekly News* ran a story with the headline: 'Attempted Murder at the Wild West Show'. It told the story of a third-rate outfit called 'Mexican Joe's Wild West Show' which was appearing in Sheffield. 'At a performance on Monday, an Indian named Running Wolf, said to be the most savage of the troupe, shot at Colonel Shelly while he was impersonating "the death of the lone scout". Instead of using cartridges, the Indian had used a hard substance which had struck Col. Shelly under the left eye and inflicted a slight wound, from which blood flowed rather freely. Col. Shelly was able to appear again later and was loudly cheered. This is said to be the fourth attempt by Running Wolf to shoot his employer.'

Salsbury ignored the story. Advance bookings for the Wild West in Manchester were healthy and the number of special excursion trains booked to travel in from

Sheffield proved that 'Mexican Joe's' pathetic attempt to copy the genuine article was hardly worth bothering with.

What was new about Buffalo Bill's show in Manchester? It was certainly more spectacular than any other version of the Wild West presented before or after, including seasons at Madison Square Garden and Staten Island. The indoor presentation gave Salsbury an opportunity to create an epic entertainment with stunning scenery and effects that could not be ruined by England's unpredictable weather. Electric lighting allowed stage managers to quickly change from one scene to another and introduce startling new effects, including a realistic prairie fire, a 'real' tornado, and more wild animals, including bears.

The arena was dominated by a vast canvas – one of several used at each performance – created at a cost of over $40,000 by British artist Matt Morgan who had sailed to America to seek fame and fortune. Now his work was being appreciated for the first time in his native England – seven giant canvas panoramas, each over 200 ft long, hoisted into position by a network of pulleys, drums and rollers concealed in the flies above the large stage. When it was time to change the panorama, a canvas silently floated up into the roof to be replaced by another quickly slipping into position. The *Manchester Examiner and Times* told readers that the 'colossal stage has given scope to the scenic artist to produce effects of perspective and other illusions which even the stage pictures in a Christmas pantomime or a modern melodrama could never eclipse.'

The scenic panoramas rose and fell behind a foreground of Rocky Mountains, complete with fully grown trees and plants. Rocky pedestals jutted out from either side of the panorama; each supporting some expertly stuffed buffalo, which looked down on the audience.

There would be other modifications to the show, including seven different tableaux representing 'pages of passing history'. High spots from the Earls Court version remained, but were radically developed, adapted or opened out to suit the wide-open spaces of the indoor arena.

The first Manchester performance was a private matinée at 2.30 p.m. The audience was made up of specially invited influential guests, including Members of Parliament, mayors, magistrates, aldermen, councillors, vice-consuls, professional gentlemen, merchants, tradesmen and the press – plus their families – from across Manchester and other northern towns. Many more guests than were originally expected turned out that afternoon to welcome Buffalo Bill and the auditorium was inconveniently packed to the rafters. Nevertheless, the *Manchester Evening News* rated the enterprise 'the most novel and realistic performance ever given in the North of England'. The *Manchester City News* said: 'Manchester never before beheld such a remarkable scene.'

It was like opening day in London had been all over again, and Salford's streets were choked with horse-drawn tramcars, buses, cabs and private carriages hours before the performance began.

'Manchester never before beheld such a remarkable scene.'

Following the usual stirring opening by the Cowboy Band, Frank Richmond was again first to be seen by the public. In Manchester he addressed the audience from his own rocky ledge 30 ft above ground – and this time there were no football hooligans in the audience to ruin his impeccable delivery. Richmond was commended for his powerful voice, 'which can be heard with ease all over the building', providing humorous and clever descriptions about what was going to happen next. He told the audience: 'Ladies and gentlemen, for the first time in England, the Wild West presents the unique and unparalleled spectacle of western life and history – the drama of civilisation!'

The lights were lowered, the giant curtains parted and the Grand Processional Review involving the entire company on horseback began. It was similar to that which had impressed London audiences several months before, but now refined to provide a more effective build-up for the entrance by the show's three stars – Red Shirt, Buck Taylor and Buffalo Bill.

Red Shirt, fully adorned in war-paint, was 'conspicuous by the luxuriance of his feathery adornments and leading his gorgeous warriors through many evolutions, and they all whooped and galloped and intertwined till the air was again filled with thunders of applause.'

Buck Taylor galloped into the arena, waving his hat, blowing kisses to female members of the audience and spinning a lasso furiously in the air.

Frank Richmond then announced: 'Ladies and gentlemen, the Wild West presents the great plainsman, the great hunter, the great Indian fighter, the greatest scout of the old west – Colonel William F. Cody . . . Buffalo Bill!'

Orator Frank Richmond addresses the audience from his own rocky ledge.

The *Manchester Examiner and News* described Bill's arrival in the arena on the back of Old Charley: 'He burst bravely into sight mounted on a long-tailed horse, galloped forward into the arena with many heroic gestures, halted suddenly in front of private boxes, from one of which he received a splendid bouquet, and then made a most impressive exit by forcing his horse backwards with surprising rapidity. Buffalo Bill looks as great a hero in his person as he looks in his pictures. For months to come he will remain the hero and the idol of all right-minded boys.'

The company then intermingled and galloped around the arena, whooping, shouting, giving out war cries at the top of their lungs and displaying their equestrian skills until the curtain closed again and they quickly disappeared from view. After the applause had died down, the audience fell silent.

According to the *Manchester Examiner and News*, what followed next 'was altogether wonderful – the curtain slowly rose on a scene of great beauty. This was the primeval forest at midnight before the arrival of the white man, a scene which was not only a splendid example of the powers of the scenic artist, but a stage picture very skilfully managed. . . . A brown bear is seen prowling across the path, and disappears as the day begins to break. While the gradual dawn is flushing through the foliage, the figures of deer and elk steal in and a stampede of buffaloes is attempted. . . . Presently a noise of whoops and strange shouts is heard and Red Shirt and his savages charge into the arena.'

At this point the section known as 'Life Customs of the Indians' on the original programme takes place, featuring dances in celebration of the rain, antelope and grasslands. There is also a battle between rival tribes, ending with dead Indians littering the ground. The stage falls into darkness.

It is time for two tableaux – the first showing the Pilgrim Fathers stepping from the *Mayflower* on to Plymouth Rock witnessed by large groups of Indians at either side of the stage. The Indian princess Pocahontas is then seen saving the life of Captain John Smith.

Now the Indians are back, leading two ox-drawn carts laden with skins and long poles. They unload the cargo and the squaws begin to construct tepees while the braves watch, perform more dances to the sound of tom-toms and run races up and down the arena.

'The next must be regarded as the finest episode of them all', wrote the *Manchester Examiner and Gazette*. 'It is a sunlit prairie stretching far back to an illimitable distance, where the mountains seem but faint shadows. Buffalo run in followed by Buffalo Bill. The animals scamper all over the arena covered by a blazing fire of rifle shots.'

The emigrant trail slowly makes its way across the arena, pulled by mules and bullocks led by old John Nelson. The wagons halt by a pool, campfires are started and a meal is prepared. Before the pioneers bed down for the night, there is a little entertainment. Emma Hickock – 'America's Queen of the side-saddle' – displays her talents on her dancing horse. The cowboys and western girls join forces and dance the Virginia reel on horseback to the accompaniment of their accordions and banjos, plus the ever-present Cowboy Band.

As darkness falls over the prairie and the pioneers climb into their bedrolls, a slight red flicker on the horizon lights up distant hills. Then a blaze springs up, roaring across the prairie, burning nearer and nearer to the sleeping wagon train. It appears as if the whole landscape is a mass of fire. Frightened buffalo, bear, deer and elk stampede across the arena and out again until the pioneers control the fire using blankets, rugs and coats. The emigrants prepare for a hasty departure and a general stampede of men, women, children and cattle follows. 'It is', said the *Manchester City News*, 'a veritable triumph of stage management and scenic display'. The applause is loud and prolonged.

This remarkable effect was achieved by simple illusion. Different layers depicting grass were set out in tiers, 3 ft high in the front to 26 ft at the rear, giving an appearance of immense distance. The fire, controlled by gas jets, began at the back and gradually moved forward. Steam was pumped under pressure into pipes running under the full length of the stage, and out through hundreds of holes drilled through the top. Rising steam provided a safe and realistic smoke effect. The frightened beasts were driven from the wings in front of the steam pipe, giving the appearance of animals running for their lives through smoke and fire.

There is now an interlude, provided by Master Johnnie Baker 'The Cowboy Kid and celebrated American marksman' and Miss Lillian Smith going through her paces, shooting balls flying through the air while swinging wildly on the end of a rope.

A sunlit prairie stretching far back to an illimitable distance, where the mountains seem but faint shadows.

Now it is time for some 'Cowboy Fun', and although Buck Taylor's London injuries prevent him from leaning dangerously from the saddle to snatch items from the arena floor, he is still able to lasso Texas steers and wrestle them to the ground. It is left to other members of the company to copy original stunts perfected by the 'King of the Cowboys' while Buck watches from the sidelines. The bucking horses are as popular in Manchester as in London and Frank Richmond says that if anyone cared to bring 'a refractory horse' over to Salford the cowboys would have pleasure in riding it.

We are back at the settler's lone log cabin on the prairie. A group of farmers are chopping wood and womenfolk draw water from a well. In the background, farm hands are hard at work ploughing fields. The Indians attack, but are overpowered by a rescue party led by Buffalo Bill.

Another item new to England follows – announced by Frank Richmond as 'General Custer's Last Fight at the Battle of Little Big Horn, in which the brave General and his command are slain, not one living to tell the tale – the reddest page of savage history was written at this time.'

The scene opens with a scout arriving in front of General Custer's fort. He brings news to the longhaired General – played by Buck Taylor – that a camp of hostile Indians has been discovered. The scene moves to Chief Sitting Bull's camp, where the Sioux leader – played by Red Shirt – is surrounded by his warriors. Troopers enter to the sound of the Cowboy Band playing 'Garryowen', the 7th Cavalry's own marching song. The scenic panorama shows the rolling grasslands of the Little Big Horn. Enter the Indians, who ride rings around the troopers, killing them to a man. Firing from behind his dead horse, Custer is the last to die in a hail of bullets and arrows. Night falls and the battlefield is seen at twilight, dead 7th Cavalry soldiers lying motionless in the moonlight. The episode closes with other troopers, led by Buffalo Bill, riding into the arena, finding they have been unable to prevent the massacre. On the panorama above, the words 'Too late! Too late!!' are projected as a light slowly fades on Bill, his head bowed, hat in hand and standing motionless over the body of his dead friend.

This episode later appeared so real to 400 boys from St Joseph's Industrial School that they believed the palefaces had been slaughtered by Indians in the arena before their eyes. The *Salford Weekly News* said: 'Many manifested signs of deep sympathy and anxiety to take part in the action.'

BUFFALO BILL'S WILD WEST·

CONGRESS, ROUGH RIDERS OF THE WORLD.

JOHNNIE BAKER,
THE MARVELOUS MARKSMAN.

Johnnie Baker (1869–1931) 'the marvellous marksman' who met Buffalo Bill as a small boy and remained with 'The Colonel' for the rest of his life. (Denver Public Library)

It was then Bill's turn to shoot up a storm with his rifle, smashing glass balls both on foot and from horseback, and lassoing the neck of an Indian 'brave' enough to try and kidnap a young trapper's daughter.

The final episode moves to the wooden miners' camp of Deadwood City, placed in front of a scenic panorama of pine trees and snow-topped mountains. The miners have a day off and hold a shooting match, have a gunfight, capture a horse thief and welcome the arrival of Marve Beardsley and the Pony Express.

'Buffalo Bill has come, we have seen, and he has conquered.'

On comes the old Deadwood stagecoach, which disgorges its passengers, receives new ones and departs. Indians attempt to hijack the coach as it approaches a canyon and they seem to be winning the day when Buffalo Bill and the cavalry appear in the nick of time and rescue the old boneshaker. The Indians know when they are beaten and flee in terror.

The stagecoach returns to Deadwood City as the daylight starts to fade. A wind begins to blow, leaves, tumbleweed and sagebrush blow across the stage. The wind intensifies, turning into a destructive cyclone, destroying the log cabins and uprooting tents from their guy ropes, blowing the Deadwood stagecoach sideways out of the arena, strewing the stage with wreckage. This last effect was created using three powerful 6 ft-high Blackman air propellers standing in the wings, creating a 50 mph wind.

There is a blackout, and when the lights come back on, the entire company is on horseback in the centre of the giant arena surrounding Bill, as the applause shakes the very rafters of the gigantic theatre.

The *Salford Reporter* told its readers: 'Buffalo Bill has come, we have seen, and he has conquered. The great Jubilee Exhibition has been succeeded by the great Jubilee Show. . . . Nothing more vividly illustrative of a phase of human life from which civilised Europe is removed by a thousand intervening years was ever presented to the British public before the advent of Colonel Cody and his little army of cowboys and Indians.'

On Christmas Eve the paper urged any readers who had not already seen the show to go along over the holidays. 'Already thousands upon thousands of people of every class and all ages have seen what is the foregoing we have attempted briefly to depict, and we may be certain their first visit will not be their last. We do not entertain the least doubt as to the complete success of the venture; we believe it is assured because it is so well deserved.'

 The Wild West enjoyed bumper business in Manchester over the Christmas and New Year holidays, stealing business from seasonal pantomimes, traditional choral and brass band concerts. In January, Salsbury sailed from Liverpool to New York to begin preparations for the company's next American summer season. Shortly after his departure, the British weather turned bitterly cold and Manchester audiences began to get smaller. Bill developed bronchitis, but refused to miss any performances. Letters home from nephew Ed Goodman claimed that Bill was homesick, yearning for North Platte's wide-open spaces.

There was talk of closing the show early and taking it back to London for a short season before cutting their losses and sailing home. But in a letter to his parents in March, Ed Goodman said the idea had been abandoned. 'You see they have captured London once and should they go back and not capture it again it go hard with them. So they are not going to go, but stay here and stand it out. Everyone seems to think we will do better business when we have better weather. We have been having some terrible weather here for a long time. I hope we will for I hate to see them lose money,' wrote Ed.

Ed also reported that Bill had gained 18 lb since coming to Manchester and now weighed 218 lb. 'I believe it is only home sickness that is the matter with him,' suggested Ed.

The weather warmed up in March and audiences returned to Salford. Ed told his parents that: 'we may come out of the hole here alright yet and not lose any money but I doubt it.'

 Manchester Evening News, 9 February 1888: 'Yesterday at the Indian camp at the Wild West Show, the squaw of Little Chief (who ranks next to Red Shirt) gave birth in the morning to a female child. This is the first birth which has taken place during the sojourn of the Indians in this country. A Council was held in camp during the day, and a name quickly decided upon – Frances Victoria Alexandra – in honour of Mrs Cleveland (wife of US President Cleveland), Queen Victoria and the Princess of Wales. The Indians celebrated the event with the rejoicing usual on such an occasion. Major Burke telegraphed the news to Red Cloud, the great chief of the Sioux Indians, at Pine Ridge Agency.'

From the *Salford Weekly News*, 18 February 1887:

A 'papoose' or Indian infant was baptised on Wednesday at St Clements Church, Salford. This was a remarkable occurrence in many respects. It was one of the curious spectacles which the presence of Buffalo Bill's Wild West at Manchester Racecourse has been responsible for. The ceremony was not unusual in form, but altogether quite novel in its attendant circumstances.

The infant was baptised according to the rites of the Church of England, the first of its race so privileged with such a good start in civilization, because it was the first of its race ever born in the British Isles. The mother, Goodrobe, presented this addition to the population on the Wild West Camp on 8th February. Goodrobe is the wife of Little Chief, who is next in command to the great Red Shirt, the Chief of the Sioux nation. Both father and mother belong to the Oglala tribe. Children of that tribe and all other of the Indian race have hitherto received their names amid rejoicings distinguished by the luxury of a roast dog banquet and other native festivities; but the little papoose of which so much was made on Wednesday, began life on a higher scale. The affair had got wind in the district around the Wild West camp, and there was quite a large congregation assembled in St Clement's Church.

A certain theatrical element was present in the whole proceedings; but it could not be otherwise when there were so many strange figures

Punch, 4 June 1887.

Squaws and Squawls.

among the congregation. A group of squaws first made their appearance, among them was Goodrobe and her child. The infant was not, like others, tied on the back of its mother, but carefully carried in her arms, encased in something that looked something like a very large slipper, beaded and embroidered all over the surface. Red Shirt, in full-feathered war paint, next arrived accompanied by about fifty more Indians, including Little Chief, the father of the child, distinguished also by a splendid display of plumage. They all wore their blankets and the choicest adornments in the wardrobe of the camp. A great deal of time had evidently been spent on their toilet, much more time than usual, for Wednesday being Ash Wednesday and a holiday in the Wild West. Their complexions were brightened up with nice fresh paint, and they all looked as if they appreciated the importance of the occasion.

'Little Chief had assumed an ash white complexion for the occasion. . . .'

Buffalo Bill was there himself, too, and Major Burke, Buck Taylor, Bronco Bill and others. The child was christened Frances Victoria Alexandra after Mrs Cleveland, wife of the President of the United States, The Queen and the Princess of Wales. But she will be known among her race as 'Over The Sea'. By some such suggestive or poetical sobriquet are all good Indians known such as Red Shirt, Eagle Heart, Little Bull, Blue Horse and other inhabitants of the camp. Those individuals mentioned have each promised a present of a pony to the child, in accordance with the Indian custom – a custom which has some connection with the wonderful horsemanship of these natives.

Little Chief had assumed an ash white complexion for the occasion and he looked very grave during the ceremony. He and his wife, Goodrobe, stood at the baptismal font beside the clergyman, the Revd J.J. Scott; the godfather, Mr A.M.H. Gardiner of Salford, and the godmothers, Mrs Whittaker and Mrs Gardiner. Bronco Bill interpreted. There was much lively curiosity exhibited by the congregation, but none by the Indians. The effects either of well-drilled order or of stoical temperament were visible in their demeanour, while the rest of the congregation were standing on the seats and straining their glances to the ceremony at the front near the door, the Indians sat cowering under their blankets, their faces to the altar, without once turning around to catch a glimpse of what, to them, must have been a strange ceremony. Most of them toyed with the prayer books, or puzzled themselves over the pages. They were called to action soon: when the hymn 'Nearer my God to Thee' was announced. A Sioux translation had been carefully rehearsed and led by Bronco Bill, and they sang it in unison in a deep bass tone. A short sermon was preached on the text 'Our Father'.

Then came the offertory to which the Indians liberally contributed. The benediction was pronounced but the audience did not seem inclined to depart, as they wanted to see the baby. This desire became evident to the Revd Mr Scott and he announced that 'if they would keep their seats the baby would be shown around'. There was great satisfaction at this intimation and a loud hum of expectancy filled the church. Mrs Whittaker carried it around in its big bead-embroidered case and the female portion of the congregation were merry and delighted. Many of them wanted to kiss the child, and in trying to do so they seriously disturbed its repose. Finally, Major Burke, standing in the chancel, held it aloft to the view of the congregation, which then filed out of the church well satisfied. Among the presents the child has received is a handsome necklace made of coins of the realm, gilt and enamel, presented by Mr Gardiner.

Bill had been elected into the Grand Order of Freemasons in Nebraska in 1870 and attended Masonic meetings in Manchester. The Prince of Wales was Grand Master of the Freemasons in England and loved all the ceremony and ritual that went with it – especially when he was permitted to bestow honours on friends. During an official visit to Manchester, the Prince honoured Royal Arch-Mason and Most Excellent Master William Frederick Cody at a special ceremony in the city and presented his American friend with a gold watch.

There was another American-style rib roast for VIP guests at the racecourse and Bill was presented with a rifle by local dignitaries in appreciation of business brought to Salford in the wake of the Wild West. Boston pork and beans, Maryland fried chicken, hominy and popcorn were served. This time, Bill really did insist that guests ate in true Indian fashion using two sticks – one sharpened and acting as a fork and the other flat and used to scoop up food.

Shortly after the rib roast, Salford Town Council proposed naming three small streets near Manchester Racecourse in honour of Buffalo Bill – Cody Court, Buffalo Court and Bill Street. Some councillors were opposed to the idea and thought the names 'grotesque'. They were outvoted and the streets were duly re-christened in honour of the man who brought cowboys and Indians from America to industrial Salford. Cody Court and Buffalo Court still exist today.

The final performance in the giant theatre was given on 30 April to a packed house which Bill remembered as: 'One of the most enthusiastic audiences I ever appeared before; bouquets were presented to various members of the company and when I appeared I met with one of the warmest receptions of my life: bouquets were thrown, handed and carried into the arena to me while the vast audience cheered, waved hats, umbrellas and handkerchiefs, jumped upon their feet, and in fact the scene was very suggestive of pandemonium. It was fully five minutes before the noise subsided sufficiently to enable us to proceed with the performance.'

Next day Bill took the Wild West outdoors on to the racecourse for a special 'farewell' edition of the show. Afterwards everything would be packed away ready to be taken by train to Hull, from where one last open-air performance would be given at a local football ground. Then everything would be loaded on board the steamship *Persian Monarch* departing for New York with the company and animals on the early morning tide of 6 May.

Over 20,000 Mancunians turned out to see races between cowboys, Indians and Mexicans, but the high spot of the afternoon was a race over ten miles between American broncos and British thoroughbreds. There would be one rider for each set of ten horses, each rider changing his mount every half-mile. The winner would receive £400.

Mexican vaquero, Antonio Esquivel, rode Bill's horses. Thoroughbreds, owned by Mr B. Goodall, a horse breeder from Altrincham, were ridden by Mr J. Latham. Betting was heavy and Manchester's bookmakers had a field day. The *Manchester Evening News* reported: 'The English horses ran much better than the broncos, but

'I met with one of the warmest receptions of my life: the scene was very suggestive of pandemonium.'

149

the Mexican was much smarter than his opponent in getting on and off. At the half distance, the Mexican was a little in advance. A slight accident lost him his lead, and later on he fell and the Englishman finished the race alone.'

Bill was furious and demanded the race be run again the next day – with the prize purse increased to £500. The bookmakers were out in force again at the racecourse – and this time Esquivel won the day, romping past the winning post 300 yards ahead of the Englishman. The rest of the company must have been glad; the chances were high that Bill would have delayed the sailing still further until the Mexican had eventually ridden to victory.

The high spot of the afternoon was a race over ten miles between American broncos and British thoroughbreds. The winner would receive £400.

Northern England's top newspaper editors broke a life-long rule when they invited two non-pressmen to be their guests of honour at a special supper held at the Manchester Press Club a few days before the close of the season. The guests were Buffalo Bill and Major Burke, both of whom had provided the newspapers with an abundance of good copy for the last five months – and the editors wanted to show their thanks in grand style. For once Major Burke was permitted to step into the limelight because, in the words of the *Salford Weekly News*, 'he has come much more into contact with the pressmen of the city than the Colonel has done.'

In appreciation of his work, the pressmen presented Major Burke 'with a token of esteem in the shape of an exceedingly pretty gold locket bearing an appropriate inscription'. Following a toast, Major Burke was called upon to reply – and for once the great publicist was at a total loss for words and 'became fairly overcome by his feelings'.

The next morning Major Burke left Britain by the Holyhead mail steamer on his way to New York, via Dublin and Queenstown, to prepare for the Wild West's grand opening in New York. His work had been successful, recognised and celebrated by newspapers across the United Kingdom and he sailed home to America a happy man.

Before the Wild West left Manchester, some props and animals no longer required or considered unsuitable for the long sea journey to America were auctioned. A pair of bay carriage horses was purchased by Mr Goodall for £80 and various circus owners and proprietors engaged in spirited bidding for a single buffalo, sold to Mr Cross of Liverpool, who also purchased four elk for prices ranging from £20 to £25 and a bear at £20. Circus owner George Sanger, still trying to pass off his version of the Wild West as 'the real thing', bought two reindeer, two mules and two American deer for £71. He is reported to have stayed well out of Buffalo Bill's way at the auction.

People in the East Riding seaport town of Hull would witness a single performance of the Wild West at 3 p.m. on Saturday 5 May at the Holderness Road football ground. To guarantee a seat, thousands began arriving for the 'final performance in England' at 9 o'clock in the morning.

The company steamed into the town's Alexandra Dock railway station 48 hours before the opening, cheered by crowds all along the route between Manchester and Hull. The following afternoon Bill was spotted with Buck Taylor, 'Bronco Bill' Irving and Frank Richmond 'riding and pedestrianising' in the port.

Hull's Station Hotel became the show's headquarters for the short engagement. Members of the company lodged at the Queen's and Manchester Hotels, while the Indians bedded down in the emigrant shed on the Alexandra Docks quayside.

As was now usual, large crowds turned out to witness the Wild West's arrival at their local railway station and the public was promised a grand procession through Hull's streets from the quayside to the football ground the next day.

Local men interested in working as temporary roustabouts before, during and after the performance were offered a fee of 3s 6d each – a small fortune for a single afternoon's work. A small advertisement in the *Eastern Morning News and Hull Advertiser* called for fifty strong men to turn up at the football ground at 1 p.m. By 10 a.m. over 500 were queuing to offer their services.

Local men interested in working as temporary roustabouts were offered a fee of 3s 6d each – a small fortune for a single afternoon's work. By 10 a.m. over 500 were queuing to offer their services.

Another advertisement for fifty lads to sell programmes for a fee of two shillings also appeared and nearly one thousand boys scrambled over each other for a chance to work for Buffalo Bill that afternoon.

The grandstand was full hours before the show began. The *Eastern Morning News* noted that there was: 'A fashionable assembly on the grandstand, many of Hull's best known citizens being noticeable. A very large concourse of the fair sex were also to be counted amongst the onlookers. The vast audience was largely composed of visitors from the country, who had been brought in by special trains by the various local railway companies.'

A long line of tramcars, waggonettes and cabs blocked roads leading to the football ground. Visitors arriving on foot reached the ticket office first.

The Hull show closely resembled that presented at Earls Court for the first time over a year before and many acts not seen since the Birmingham engagement were revived for the afternoon. The Wild West still worked its magic on the crowd, who cheered the cowboys, booed the Indians, blew wolf-whistles at the western girls, yelled their approval when Bill, Johnnie Baker and Lillian Smith hit their targets and wildly applauded when broncos attempted to dismount their riders. It was the perfect way to close the British season.

After the show, performers rode back through Hull's streets to the Alexandra Dock, pursued by crowds who could not get enough of Buffalo Bill's Wild West.

Animals, props, costumes, saddles, guns, tents, wagons and the old Deadwood stagecoach were immediately loaded on board the *Persian Monarch*, now moored to the quayside. After Wild West passengers had found their cabins, they appeared on deck to wave goodbye to the crowds.

At midnight the quayside was still crowded with people determined to stay until the ship slipped its moorings and sailed on the 3 a.m. tide for New York. They called long and loud for Bill to make a final personal appearance on deck – but the Wild West hero remained in his saloon until the *Persian Monarch* quietly pulled out of Hull and into the North Sea under the cover of night. It would journey south into the English Channel and then out into the North Atlantic's rough breakers and onwards in a westerly direction to New York.

There was to be a personal tragedy for Bill a week into the homeward voyage. On the morning of 14 May, Bill went below decks to inspect the animals and see how they were faring on the journey. Old Charley, the horse that had become almost as famous as Bill himself, had developed a chill. A groom was ordered to stay with the horse, but Old Charley's condition worsened and he died during the early hours of 17 May. His death cast an air of sadness over the whole ship.

Old Charley was twenty years old and had been bought for Bill as a five-year-old in Nebraska. From that time onwards he had become Bill's best four-legged friend. For a wager of $500, he once carried Bill one hundred miles over the prairie in nine hours and forty-five minutes. The bet stated that the journey could not be covered in less than ten hours. He had been with Bill at the start of the Wild West and was the undoubted 'star' horse of the company, admired by royalty, presidents, politicians and plain ordinary folk on both sides of the Atlantic. Now he was gone.

In an article in the *American Agriculturist*, Bill later recalled this sad event in his life:

'Men tell me you have no soul; but if there is a heaven, and scouts can enter there, I'll wait at the gate for you old friend.'

A human being could not have had more sincere mourners than the faithful and sagacious old horse. He was brought on deck, wrapped in canvas and covered with the American flag. When the hour for the ocean burial arrived, the members of my company and others assembled on deck. Standing alone with uncovered head beside the dead was the one whose life the noble animal had shared so long. At length with choking utterance he spoke, and Charley for the first time failed to hear the familiar voice he had always been so prompt to obey.

In a moving on-deck funeral oration to his dead horse, Bill eulogised:

Old fellow, your journeys are over. Here beneath the ocean billows you must rest. Would that I could take you back and lay you down beneath the verdant billows of that prairie you and I have loved so well and roamed so freely; but it cannot be. . . . How oft at break of day, when the glorious sun rising on the horizon has found us far from human habitation, have you reminded me of your need and mine, and with your beautiful ears bent forward and your gentle neigh given voice as plainly as human tongue to urge me to prepare our morning meal! And then, obedient to my call, gladly you bore your burden on, little knowing, little reckoning what the day may bring, so that you and I but shared its sorrows and pleasures alike. Nay, but for your willing speed and tireless courage I would many years ago have lain as low as you are now, and my Indian foe have claimed you as his slave. Yet you have never failed me. Ah, Charley, old fellow, I have had many friends, but few of whom I could say that. Rest, entombed in the deep bosom of the ocean! May your rest never more be disturbed. I'll never forget you. I loved you as you loved me, dear old Charley. Men tell me you have no soul; but if there is a heaven, and scouts can enter there, I'll wait at the gate for you old friend.

Old Charley was then allowed to slide gently down a pair of skids into the Atlantic surf, and Bill spent most of the remaining days of the *Persian Monarch's* long voyage home alone in his saloon.

 The Wild West returned to New York in triumph and immediately set up shop on Staten Island for another summer season. Thanks to Major Burke, American newspaper readers had been kept informed about Bill's British success. They took the ferry across to the island in their tens of thousands to welcome him home, eager to see the same entertainment witnessed by Queen Victoria, the Prince and Princess of Wales, crowned heads of Europe and pillars of Victorian British society. In New York, Bill took a suite at the Waldorf Astoria, where he held court each night after the performance, hosting lavish dinner parties and long poker sessions.

Following the New York season, Salsbury arranged engagements in Philadelphia, Washington, Baltimore and at the Richmond Exposition on the James River in Virginia. At the close of the season, the Indians returned to the foothills of Dakota to tell their tribes stories about the things they had seen and the people they had encountered in the white man's world. The cowboys journeyed home to Texas, Wyoming, Nebraska and Montana while the Mexicans headed towards the southern valley of the Rio Grande. Bill came home to his ranch at North Platte for his first break in over two years. Stock now grazing on his pasture and living in his new barn included prize cattle from England and Scotland, bought from the profits of the London season. It was time for a long rest.

DOING EUROPE

It was a pleasant day
As near the first of May
As days come in pleasant April weather,
That Miss Annie Oakley shot
Her hundred pigeon pot
When the record and the clays broke together.
And may all the days she knows
As through the world she goes
Be as lucky for her all time through,
As that pleasant day in spring
When she showed us she could wing
One hundred birds in minutes six and seconds thirty-two!

By H.C. Bunner and dedicated to Annie Oakley

ANNIE RE-JOINS THE SHOW – PARIS BOUND – PRISONERS OF THE
BARCELONA EPIDEMIC – DEATH OF FRANK RICHMOND – ESCAPE TO ITALY
AND 'GERMANLAND' – THE 'GHOST DANCE' – AN INDIAN CLAIMS POOR
TREATMENT – FAREWELL TO BUCK TAYLOR – HOME TO HELP SITTING BULL
– MASSACRE AT WOUNDED KNEE

Bill and Salsbury wanted Annie Oakley back in the show for its 1890–2
European tour. Since parting company with the Wild West at the close of
the 1887 London season, Annie had continued to earn good money from
appearing at shooting matches and joining Pawnee Bill's Frontier Exhibition, a
show closely resembling the Cody–Salsbury version.

Annie also agreed to take a leading part for five weeks in a western drama called
Deadwood Dick, or the Sunbeam of the Sierras, described as 'the greatest and most
thrilling border drama ever produced, featuring Bold Border Boys, Bad Bucking
Broncos, and Masterless Mexican Mustangs.'

She recalled: 'The backer said he would guarantee the play would be first class.
The money offered was good. I learned after that he was simply gambling on
my reputation to clean up a few thousand. I never understood just why the press
abstained from vegetable throwing but they threw not one carrot. One of them
wrote: "Through all the strife, the beautiful character of Sunbeam, taken by Annie
Oakley, was a poem hewn in rocks".'

Annie was relieved to receive a letter from Salsbury, asking if rumours about her joining another Wild West Show were true. 'He said he would fight any company I joined,' wrote Annie. 'My husband's reply was, "You cannot afford to fight my wife. I might tell the reasons for cancelling her contract with your company." Then Mr Salsbury said, "No, I will not fight her in any way," and we parted friends. In a short time he opened negotiations and a different contract was signed.'

Annie and Frank re-joined the company for the European tour, to include a seven-month season in Paris followed by engagements in Spain, Italy, Austria and Germany. The Butlers would stay with the Wild West for the next ten years, appearing throughout the United States and Europe, thrilling everyone from Kings and Queens to ordinary people with their shooting skills. Annie remained a star of the company and helped the Wild West attract huge audiences on both sides of the Atlantic.

The opening of the Eiffel Tower was the other great attraction in Paris that year.

Johnnie Baker now stood in for Lillian Smith as the second star rifle artist to be featured in a solo spot on the programme. Red Shirt, a household name in England during the 1887/88 visit, stayed at home with his people at Pine Ridge, South Dakota, and sent in his place Long Wolf, a Sioux Chief said to have taken part in the Battle of Little Big Horn.

The company, along with their horses, cattle and wagons, sailed from New York to Le Havre on the *Persian Monarch*. On arrival, a chartered train transported them to Paris to appear at the Great Universal Exhibition for seven months as part of the city's anniversary celebrating one hundred years since the French revolution. The opening of the Eiffel Tower was the other great attraction in Paris that year.

The company rented a large open space owned by 32 different tenants between Courcelles and Port Maillot in the city's Neuilly district near the Bois de Boulogne. Local residents, worried about horse-drawn traffic congestion coming their way, raised objections – but a generous 40,000 francs donation to the local poor of the parish soon changed their minds.

The French edition of the Wild West wielded the same magic on Parisians as the British version had on Londoners four years before. President Carnot and his wife, plus his entire cabinet and their families, attended the opening performances.

While in Paris, Bill was re-united with Black Elk, who with five other Indians had somehow managed to miss the boat home when it sailed from Hull to New York in May 1888. After discovering the ship had departed, Black Elk made his way to London where he found a job with Mexican Joe's Wild West, another Buffalo Bill imitator touring the suburbs with an inferior show. When it was announced that the genuine Wild West would be playing in Paris, Mexican Joe decided that he, too, would cross the Channel with his cowboys and Indians and cash in on the western craze before Bill's version arrived.

While in the French capital, Black Elk fell ill and Mexican Joe's show moved on without him, leaving him stranded far from home for a second time. The Indian was cared for by a French family who nursed him back to health, and then took him to meet his old boss between performances in Neuilly. Black Elk later said:

Bill and Salsbury wanted Annie Oakley back in the show for its 1890–2 European tour. Annie remained a star of the company for the next ten years and helped the Wild West attract huge audiences on both sides of the Atlantic. (The American Collection)

'He was glad to see me. He had all his people give me three cheers. Then he asked me if I wanted to be in the show or if I wanted to go home. I told him I was sick to go home. So he said he would fix that. He gave me a ticket and $90. Then he gave me a big dinner. Pahaska has a very strong heart.'

With their Parisian success still ringing in their ears, Bill and Salsbury took the company on the road for a successful tour of southern French cities before crossing the border into Spain. A Christmas–New Year season was planned in Barcelona, the city to which Christopher Columbus had returned after his great 'discovery' of the Americas 398 years before.

Columbus had arrived in Barcelona in triumph. It was a different story for Buffalo Bill's Wild West, which arrived on a chartered ship from Marseilles to discover Barcelona in the grip of a smallpox and influenza epidemic. Disease was claiming scores of lives in Barcelona daily and the last thing anyone wanted was to expose themselves to large crowds, which threatened to spread the disease.

The show opened to small audiences. Spanish nobility who had promised to attend the first performance and occupy the best seats in the stadium stayed away. After several days and in desperation, Salsbury slashed admission prices by half in order to attract a half-decent audience. The city's beggars descended on the Wild West camp pleading for food outside the company's mess tents. They even raided its dustbins in the hope of finding something to fill their empty bellies. Barcelona's filthy streets and poverty-stricken people horrified Indians in the company. They knew what it was like to be poor, but they had never before seen anything so appalling and on such a scale.

Plans were made to close the season early and flee from Barcelona as fast as they could – but before leaving, half the company complained of feeling ill. Many had developed a fever and were ordered to remain in their bedrolls. An American doctor in the city was called and spent days going between tents and tepees in high winter gales doing whatever he could for the sick wild westerners.

Salsbury was told that the company would be placed in quarantine and prevented from leaving Spain until public health officers were satisfied that the cowboys and Indians could no longer spread the diseases they had contracted.

Over Christmas ten Indians and three cowboys died of influenza or smallpox. Frank Richmond, the Wild West's popular orator and ringmaster, also contracted influenza and spent several days with a burning fever before dying. All were buried in a lonely Barcelona cemetery thousands of miles away from the plains and prairies of home.

The company stayed in quarantine for a month before Salsbury was allowed out to search for a vessel prepared to take his company, animals and equipment out of Spain. Few ships had been permitted to enter Barcelona's port during the epidemic, so only a few vessels were available to take the company to their next engagement in Naples, most of them unsuitable for the needs of the Wild West.

An ageing steamer, half the ideal size required, was found and Salsbury negotiated a week-long charter with the Captain. Back at the Wild West camp he warned the company that while the next few days would be uncomfortable, they would at last get out of Barcelona. After animals, equipment and passengers were loaded on board, it was obvious to the Spanish Captain that the ship would be overloaded and in danger of capsizing before it left the harbour. The Captain changed his mind when Salsbury threw more money on the table and headed his listing steamer out into the wintry Mediterranean for the crossing to Corsica, Sardinia and onwards to Naples.

In Italy an enterprising confidence trickster had printed thousands of Wild West tickets and sold them at discounted prices, causing confusion when the turnstiles opened for the company's first performances on Italian soil. Fortunately the Italians liked what they saw and the Wild West began to regain some of the vigour and energy it had lost during its unfortunate Barcelona engagement.

In Rome the company had an audience with Pope Leo XIII at the Vatican, who blessed the cowboys, Indians and Mexicans. They were photographed taking a gondola ride in Venice, and played to large and appreciative crowds in Bologna, Milan, Florence and Turin. In Verona, the city's own 45,000-seat Coliseum provided a natural open-air amphitheatre for the Wild West.

The company then crossed the Alps to play in what Major Burke called 'Germanland', including Innsbruck, Munich, Vienna, Berlin, Dresden, Leipzig, Magdeburg, Hannover, Brunswick, Hamburg, Bremen, Dusseldorf, Cologne, Koblenz, Frankfurt and Stuttgart.

In October 1890 the Wild West moved into winter quarters in an old castle in Banfelt, near Strasbourg, where they planned to remain until spring when the European tour would continue. The Indians prepared to camp outdoors in tepees erected in the castle's orangerie, while the rest of the company spent the winter indoors, with their horses and cattle safely tucked up in well-equipped stables and barns.

Indians not classed as troublesome 'prisoners of war' could leave the Wild West whenever they wished, given money and a ticket home to America. The majority stayed with the show. Never before had they been better fed. They did not have to hunt for food or even prepare it. A chance to tour with the Wild West gave them an opportunity to earn money for their families and experience people and places denied to most Americans.

But news reached the winter quarters that a 'Messiah' craze was sweeping across the western prairies. They heard that a new religious cult started by an Indian prophet called Wovoka promised that dead Indians would rise, the buffalo would return to the plains, the white man would leave them in peace allowing them to return to their old ways. Wovoka said that his messages had been passed on from

The Captain changed his mind when Salsbury threw more money on the table. . . .

'your fathers the ghosts, that they are marching to join you, led by the Messiah who came once to live on earth with the white men but was killed by them.'

Followers of the mystical religion grew. Converts were told to abstain from alcohol, renounce violence and wear shirts covered with painted mystical symbols said to repel the white man's bullets. The Indians were encouraged to perform a 'ghost dance' in large circles for several days at a time, chanting and appealing to the spirits of their ancestors.

Indians were dancing everywhere and when Sitting Bull was told his people must also join the 'ghost dance' he became concerned that soldiers would return to restore order. But his people joined the dance and government-appointed Indian agents started sending urgent telegrams back east telling the Bureau of Indian Affairs that the tribes were preparing for war.

The Indians in Buffalo Bill's Wild West wanted to go home and become part of the 'ghost dance' movement. An Indian called White Horse resigned from the company and returned to the United States, where he told the *New York Herald* that Buffalo Bill's Indians in Europe were being starved, treated cruelly and crammed into steerage cabins while the rest of the company lived in luxury saloons. The story found its way back to European newspapers, which launched their own investigations.

Major Burke immediately fired off an angry letter of denial to the *New York Herald*'s Paris Bureau:

The Indians wanted to go home and become part of the 'ghost dance' movement.

The statements and general inference about starvation and cruelty in the Wild West camp are ridiculously untruthful, and unjust to Cody and Salsbury. I appeal to your sense of justice to fully deny the same. The Wild West is under the public eyes daily, and in all the countries and cities visited, under rigid police and health inspection. Our cuisine is the same as in New York, Paris and London, and has challenged the admiration and astonishment of the citizens of every place visited for its quality and quantity. Our contracts and beef bills will bear witness as well as the United States consuls and local officials, and thousands of others who have daily visited our camp. Our pride as well as our interest lies in the good food and good health of our people. As regards the steerage passage, the steamships don't want to give cabin passages to Indians. Many a good white man has gone across the ocean in the steerage. Would that every white man in the world was as well fed, clothed and looked after as our red tourists on Buffalo Bill's Wild West.

At Major Burke's invitation, a delegation of three European-based American diplomats was dispatched to the camp on their own fact-finding mission. After questioning Indians closely about food, living conditions, health, wages and overall status within the Wild West company, the following statement was issued:

We take great pleasure in stating that we visited Buffalo Bill's Wild West Show and have seen the Indians both in their tents and during the performance. They are certainly the best looking and apparently the best fed Indians we have ever seen.
(Signed) W.H. Edwards, Consul General
(Signed) Chas H. Johnson, US Consul at Hamburg
(Signed) C. Coleman, Secretary of Legation, Berlin.

The *New York Herald* was quick to print a denial of the story with a dispatch from its European Bureau: 'The friends of Buffalo Bill are delighted with the authoritative denial of the charge of cruelty to his Indians, cabled to the Herald this morning. It shows the value of an international paper that stories wilder than the Wild West itself can be so promptly sat upon and refuted. His accusers have not yet produced that statement bearing out his charges, and it looks now as if their good nature and charity has been buncoed by the wily White Horse.'

Although a retraction had been published, the earlier negative newspaper story had damaged the Wild West's reputation in America and Bill decided to sail home with Major Burke during the winter break to repair cracks caused by the allegations with the Commissioner of Indian Affairs. He took all 100 Indians in the company back with him, inviting anyone who wanted to question them about their treatment in Europe to ask anything they wished. Those wishing to return to Europe could join him again in the spring for the voyage back.

Buck Taylor also decided to quit the show at this time and return to America to run his own Wild West outfit. He would soon discover that it was one thing to be a star member of a company and have everything done for him, but something different running the entire operation. Buck's attempt to mount a Wild West rival was an expensive failure. He spent the rest of his life working with horses on various ranches, never again achieving the same level of fame, fortune and adulation bestowed on him as the 'King of the Cowboys' with Buffalo Bill's Wild West. He died in 1924.

Bill returned to North Platte for a short holiday, while Major Burke travelled to Pine Ridge with the Indians to recruit new braves for the remainder of the European tour. Meanwhile, back in Strasbourg, Salsbury was masterminding the Wild West's next chapter, including a return to England beginning in the provinces and ending in what was planned as a triumphant return to London.

The US Army, however, had other plans for Bill.

The US Army, however, had other plans for Bill. There were signs that thanks to the 'ghost dancers' the Sioux were again on the warpath. Ever since the Battle of Little Big Horn, the Indians had been confined to reservations, prisoners on land which had been theirs for centuries. No Indian living in the west could now claim freedom on land they had signed away for a promise that they would be looked after, provided with rations and their treaties honoured. Sitting Bull warned his people that the promises were false ones and the white man would try to take every bit of land for himself. He told his people to stand together 'as one family as we did before the white people led us astray'.

The Sioux were starving. Their rations had been reduced and their crops failed during a long, dry summer. Measles, influenza and whooping cough killed hundreds of children in an epidemic and Indians everywhere were 'ghost dancing', asking spirits to drive the white man away.

The US government lived in fear of an Indian uprising and dispatched 5,000 troops to territory near Standing Rock to secure peace. Troops included Custer's old command, the 7th Cavalry under the command of Bill's friend, General Nelson Miles.

When word of the army's arrival reached Sitting Bull, the chief urged his people to dance like they had never danced before. The army immediately accused Sitting Bull of inciting his people to act in a rebellious fashion.

Bill was back in New York planning the Wild West's next overseas tour when he received a telegram from General Miles asking him to come to Chicago as soon as possible for an urgent meeting.

A day and a half later, Bill met with General Miles who told him that a major Indian war was just around the corner. He badly needed information about Indian territory known as the Badlands, and the mood of its people. Miles knew that Bill was highly regarded by Indians, especially Sitting Bull, and asked the former Chief Scout to travel to the region, find Sitting Bull, talk him out of waging a war and get him to sit around the table with General Miles.

Bill was delighted to think that the army's top brass still rated him as a man able to stop an Indian war single-handed and that his show business years had done nothing to diminish his authority on the frontier. It was like something out of a Buffalo Bill dime novel, and the great showman would, no doubt, capitalise on this upcoming adventure at a later date. But as Bill took a train east to Standing Rock with written orders from General Miles in his pocket, it had not occurred to him that he was being asked to arrest Sitting Bull in the middle of Indian territory and bring him to the nearest army fort.

Bill was delighted to think that the army's top brass still rated him as a man able to stop an Indian war single-handed.

The Indian agent at Standing Rock, James McLaughlin, was aghast when Bill arrived with orders to be given every assistance to bring Sitting Bull in. McLaughlin felt his own authority was under threat and he sent a telegram to Washington demanding they withdraw Bill's orders, leaving him to find Sitting Bull by his own devices.

McLaughlin needed to delay Bill until he had received a reply and promptly instructed army officers to 'entertain' Colonel Cody at their club and fill him with so much drink he would be unable to set off as planned the following morning. Bill, always happy to 'share a glass of cheer' with the army, gratefully accepted their invitation and drank the officers under the table. By the time they awoke next day with evil headaches, Bill was on his way, his saddlebag full of the candy Sitting Bull had acquired a taste for while appearing with the Wild West.

McLaughlin's reply from Washington arrived hours after Bill had departed, stating that Colonel Cody should be recalled before he reached Sitting Bull's camp. He was located on the road, told about the change in orders and returned to the fort. Meanwhile 43 members of the Indian Police, made up of Sioux tribesmen, were dispatched to persuade Sitting Bull to come peacefully into the fort. A detachment of soldiers, plus a Hotchkiss gun, would be positioned 18 miles away and 'the prisoner' handed over to them and escorted to Standing Rock.

Indian police arrived at Sitting Bull's camp during the early hours and found their way to the Chief's wooden cabin. They knocked on the door, waking Sitting Bull and telling him he was under arrest. He agreed to go with them and they urged him to get dressed and prepare his horse before the alarm was sounded. But the sound of barking dogs and the cries of one of Sitting Bull's two wives, woke others in the camp who rushed to his aid. Shots were fired and Sitting Bull fell to the ground. A bloody fight between the Indian Police and other Indians from the tribe broke out.

In the noise and confusion which followed, something bizarre happened. Sitting Bull's horse, a gift from Bill during the Chief's Wild West days, thought it was back in the arena. On hearing the sound of shooting it recognised its old cue, and all alone without a rider, the horse sat down in the middle of the carnage going on all around, and began performing tricks before its master, now lying dead on the ground. The Indian police are reported to have been terrified, thinking that Sitting Bull's spirit had passed into the horse.

The horse was unhurt and ridden back to the fort. Bill later re-introduced it to the Wild West. The story was not so happy for the Sioux. The following month on 29 December 1890 – during the Moon of Popping Trees – soldiers at nearby Wounded Knee Creek gunned down 300 Indian men, women and children of the 'ghost dance' movement. As they fled, many with small children in their arms, bullets ripped through the special dance shirts, which, they were told, would protect them from the white man's weapons of death.

All alone without a rider, the horse sat down in the middle of the carnage and began performing tricks before its master, now lying dead on the ground.

THE BUFFALO BILL EXPRESS

Hail! Hero, hunter of the West,
To bonnie Scotland's strand;
Well hast thou stood the fiery test
In thy wild western land.
Hail to the land where storm clouds dwell
Around the mountain crest;
The land where heroes fought and fell –
Hail! Hunter of the West.

A poem for Buffalo Bill, by E. Hartley –
Glasgow, December 1891

PRISONERS OF WAR IN ENGLAND – GEORGE C. CRAGER 'IN CHARGE OF INDIANS' – ANOTHER BRITISH INVASION – THE BUFFALO BILL EXPRESS – SCALPING, TWICE-DAILY – MANCHESTER BENEFIT FOR BALACLAVA VETERANS – THE TOUR TAKES ITS TOLL – PAUL EAGLE STAR – WILD WEST IN WALES – STORMS IN BRIGHTON – VIOLA CLEMMONS AND 'WHITE LILY' – TO SCOTLAND – AFRICAN NATIVES JOIN THE SHOW – CRAGER SELLS ARTEFACTS TO GLASGOW MUSEUM – ENTRY OF THE COSSACKS – WILD WEST AT WINDSOR – DEATH OF CHIEF LONG WOLF – ANNIE'S LETTERS OF PROPOSAL – THE BUFFALO BILL LINE

While Bill received no fee for his aborted Sitting Bull mission, expenses amounting to $500 were repaid and he made his way back to North Platte to prepare for the rest of the European tour.

Travelling back to Europe with the Wild West would be 23 prisoners of war from 'ghost dance' disturbances, assigned to Bill as part of an 86-strong Indian group released to appear with the show. The US War Department placed the Indians into Bill's care with a special letter signed by Acting Secretary for War, L.A. Grant. The Indians were turned over to Major Burke and told 'that in accordance with the recommendation of the Major General Commanding the army, I beg to advise you that when these prisoners are relieved from your services, they will not be permitted to return to their reservations without authority from the War Department.'

Prisoners on the payroll included Short Bull and his brother-in-law Kicking Bear, Lone Bull, Mash the Kettle, Scatter, Revenge, Paul Eagle Star and his cousin, Bull Stands Behind. Others included Plenty Wolves (also known as Yankton Charlie) and Black Heart. They were all described in the show's publicity material as 'warriors of the greatest celebrity and all participants two months ago of the last page in the blood-stained history of the white and Indian races in America.'

Head Chief of Buffalo Bill's Wild West in 1891 was Long Wolf, the Oglala Lakota Sioux warrior who had joined the show with his squaw, Wants, and daughter Lizzie Long Wolf in 1886, and had never left.

A group of nine 'Indian policemen' headed by No Neck were recruited to keep a close eye on the prisoners and deal out their own brand of punishment when required. They appeared the same as the other Indians, but wore white star badges and a ribbon to mark them out from the rest of the group.

A small Indian boy 'of seven summers' called Johnny Burke No Neck also travelled with the company. Wild West publicity material claimed that the child was one of two young survivors of the Wounded Knee massacre, found as papooses in the arms of their mothers lying dead on the frozen ground. Major Burke and No Neck, the Indian police chief, had jointly adopted him. The small boy would play an active part in the show that year and his cheerful manner and winning smile make him a firm favourite with audiences all over England.

Long Wolf with his squaw, Wants (right holding baby) and daughter Lizzie Long Wolf (left) in 1886. Long Wolf later died in London and was buried in Brompton cemetery. (Denver Public Library)

Breaking with tradition, Bill and Salsbury recruited a British orator to guide the public through the Wild West show, explain who was who and the significance of what was going on in the arena. Henry Marsh Clifford, replacing the much-missed Frank Richmond, was a Shakespearean actor and singer with a strong and commanding voice guaranteed to be heard loud and clear across Wild West arenas in England, Wales and Scotland over the next two years.

Joining Annie Oakley and Johnnie Baker was a third marksman, Claude L. Daly, a 25 year-old champion crack-shot from Pennsylvania – '5 ft 10 ins tall with the biceps of a gladiator', read his publicity material – who would demonstrate pistol and revolver shooting skills. It was also claimed that Daly had not taken part in any shooting matches in recent years 'for the good and sufficient reason that he cannot find an opponent'.

Hammitt would take on the fancy riding and roping tricks which had earned Buck Taylor wide acclaim back in 1887. And, like Buck, Hammitt would also be a hit with ladies in the audience. . . .

Replacing Buck Taylor as chief of the cowboys was Frank Hammitt: '23 years of age, stands 6 ft 1 in. in his stockings and weighs over 200 lbs. He speaks English, French and Spanish, is a native of Colorado, and before joining the show was a Bronco buster, or wild horse breaker.' Hammitt would take on the fancy riding and roping tricks which had earned Buck Taylor wide acclaim back in 1887. And, like Buck, Hammitt would also be a hit with ladies in the audience. . . .

Each company member was required to sign an agreement stating that in return for regular employment over an agreed period of time, they would be paid regular wages, given transport, food and lodging, provided they accepted the rules and regulations of Buffalo Bill's Wild West Company. It was clearly stated that good behaviour was expected at all times. Fines of between $1 and $5 would be taken from the pay packets of anyone heard 'swearing or using boisterous language about the establishment, in cars, hotels or other places'. There were also fines for spitting, fighting, 'or any other behaviour deemed unsuitable by the management'.

A new Indian interpreter, George C. Crager, age 35, travelled with the company in 1891. A former journalist with the *New York World*, Crager accepted the job because he wanted to visit Europe and write about his travels. He claimed to speak thirteen different Indian dialects, had run away from home as a child and been accepted into a Sioux tribe by a Chief called Two Strokes. He drifted from one tribe to another, learning different languages and customs, how to hunt, ride and fend for himself in hostile territory. Later he joined the army as a courier, clerk, guide and interpreter before a newspaper accepted some articles and he became a frontier correspondent, the first reporter to enter Wounded Knee after the previous year's massacre.

When not acting as interpreter between scores of Indians in his care and their paleface bosses, Crager could always be found in his tent writing about his life with Native Americans and travels with the Wild West. Thanks to Crager, we have some insight into how Indians appearing with Buffalo Bill in 1891–2 were regarded and treated. In an interview with a British newspaper, the interpreter admitted that he had 'not yet recovered from the surprise at seeing them treated with such unexampled consideration'. Some of Crager's comments are politically incorrect by today's standards, but in 1891 the interpreter had no idea that his

Prisoners of war from 'ghost dance' disturbances were assigned to Bill as part of an eighty-six-strong Indian group released to appear with the show. Bill (centre) and Major Burke (seated right) are pictured with some of them at the Pine Ridge reservation, with new Indian interpreter, George C. Crager (front row – third left) who was later responsible for selling valuable Indian artefacts to a Glasgow museum. (Denver Public Library)

comments would appear in print once again over a century later when attitudes and values would be somewhat different. . . .

> The Indians on their reservation are treated like dogs by the United States government. Were the Indians to receive one half of the rations and goods allotted them it would be all right. But there is too much red tape to allow them doing so. When they join this company, however, the treatment becomes too good. They are petted and courted and fed too well, and the trouble we have to contend with is in consequence of their too good treatment and overfeeding. There is no work for the men to do except in the arena during the performance. Even their tepees are put up by the women. There is no place of interest in any town we visit that they are not taken to see, and neither pains nor expense spared in this matter. Colonel Cody's motive for doing this arises from the belief that travel is always the best educator of mankind. He wants to make them appreciate the fact that they are but a small body incapable of successfully opposing a civilised nation, and so he takes them everywhere in order to demonstrate the greatness of the white man.

Crager admitted that Indians who had been most aggressive during recent conflicts with the army and white settlers were the most docile while in Bill's employment and keen to learn 'the arts and industries of civilisation'. Said Crager:

> The Colonel hopes these means will wean them from their former hostile ways. Over 800 Indians have been connected with the Wild West during the last five years, and on their return to reservations it has always been found that they have become pioneers of civilisation among their own people. Take the Pine Ridge Agency for

instance. See the Indians who have been most successful in agriculture there. See who it is follows the plough. It is the Indians who have been with Buffalo Bill's Wild West. See who are most advanced in education; whose children are sent to school. It is the Indians from the Wild West show.

Indians on the tour, said Crager, 'were paid $3.50 to $10 per month, besides which everything is found for them, even portable bathing vans, so they need not put their hands in their pockets for a penny. When the white man wanted a bath, however, he had to go into the town and pay for it.'

Crager also told newsmen that transport was always provided whenever an Indian wanted to visit a nearby town, 'whereas other members of the company, from Colonel Cody and Mr Nate Salsbury downwards, were content to ride on a tramcar. If an Indian has a headache or a toothache, medical attendants are provided and he is excused from performing. When an Indian terminates his contract with the Wild West he is given a civilised outfit sufficient to last for two years, and is sent back to his own land.

But Crager was later to be seen as not quite so supportive of the Indian cause when it came to the disposal of native artefacts.

 The European tour resumed in April 1891, starting with an engagement in Stuttgart, before playing towns in the Rhineland region, then crossing the border into Holland and Belgium in late spring.

By late June, a steamship carrying the Wild West had docked at Grimsby ready for a second British 'invasion' and a long tour of its populous industrial cities, giving two performances daily, 'rain or shine'. The tour began in the north of England, moving down to the Midlands and across to Wales and onwards to the south coast before travelling north again for a New Year season in Scotland.

For many cowboys and Mexican vaqueros in the Buffalo Bill company, this would be a third winter away from home.

For many cowboys and Mexican vaqueros in the Buffalo Bill company, this would be a third winter away from home. After Scotland, Bill and Salsbury planned a return to the scene of their previous London triumph at Earls Court – and, hopefully, the same warm reception – before returning to the United States in the autumn. Advertisements told the public that this was: 'Positively the last time this aggregation of Western American Characters will appear in Europe, being a Positive Farewell presentation of this interesting page of passing history'.

Three special 'Buffalo Bill Express' trains pulling a total of 72 passenger and freight carriages were chartered to transport the Wild West between locations. Two trains carried 100 tons of scenery, properties and the four-legged stars of the show while the third transported two-legged members of the company in comfort. When trains pulled into a station during the early morning hours, an artillery of horse-drawn carts and wagons would be waiting to move performers, animals, scenery, properties, accommodation tents and tepees, food and a portable grandstand – tiered, covered and large enough to seat 15,000 people – to the showground. Twelve hours later, the Wild West would be fully rigged up and ready to admit the public through its turnstiles.

At the end of an engagement, roustabouts would dismantle the grandstand and pack everything back on to carts and wagons for the journey back to the station where trains would be waiting to travel on to the next booking. The first train usually departed around midnight – less than three hours after the public had left the showground. Setting up and breaking down the Wild West in England in the late 1880s was a triumph of project management and logistics, involving skilful planning, speed, efficiency and an energy which modern-day, open-air touring shows would find difficult to match.

The first British engagement of the new season took place at Cardigan Fields, Leeds; a city surrounded by woollen mills in the heart of England's clothing manufacturing industry and close to the South Riding coalmines. Special excursion trains would bring the public in from surrounding areas of Yorkshire and Lancashire for the next two weeks.

Setting up and breaking down the Wild West in England in the late 1880s was a triumph of project management.

On 19 June Major Burke showed the city's press around the Wild West camp in Leeds. Nate Salsbury greeted them at the entrance and when asked why he had started a Wild West show with Buffalo Bill replied: 'The first object we had in view was to make money; the second was to demonstrate to you across the ocean the great change brought by civilising influences among the North American Indian tribes.'

The *Leeds Daily News* was quick to point out that the Indians in Buffalo Bill's show were far from savage or without intellect:

The fact is quite the contrary. A short conversation, through an interpreter, with one of Buffalo Bill's braves soon convinces one that in many cases, he is gifted with a thoughtful mind and an observant eye. Yesterday, Short Bull, leader of the ghost dancers and high priest of the 'Messiah Craze' made a speech through the medium of an interpreter, which clearly showed that civilisation had made him a philosopher. At one time he was a fanatic of the most dangerous type. It was curious to see him and his fellow braves bedecked in their gaudy garments of variegated colours and their faces besmirched with paints of every hue, listening with half closed eyes to all that was said. Not a word could they understand, but their wonderful power of interpreting a gesture or a facial movement, no doubt, gave them a clue to the conversation. With all their war paint they are very simple folk and their conversation consisted mostly of reminiscences of home, and simple but evidently heartfelt gratitude to Colonel Cody and his colleagues who had, as they naively put it, been so kind as to take them to different countries to see rare and wonderful sights.

The Leeds reporter was also amused to catch sight of an Indian brave 'making himself agreeable to two pretty Yorkshire lasses. He was most courtly in his demeanour. Conversation was impossible, but the graceful fold of his blanket and the expressive look on his well-ochred countenance were more eloquent than all the English or Ogalala (*sic*) that was uttered ever since the world began. The lasses seemed to regard the novelty with a fair degree of pleasure and complacency.'

BUFFALO BILL'S
WILD WEST
AMERICA'S NATIONAL ENTERTAINMENT.
AN ILLUSTRATED TREATISE OF HISTORICAL FACTS & SKETCHES.
PUBLISHED BY
BUFFALO BILL'S WILD WEST COMPANY.

COL. W. F. CODY (BUFFALO BILL), PRESIDENT.   NATE SALSBURY, VICE-PRESIDENT & DIRECTOR.

JOHN M. BURKE ... . General Manager	JULE KEEN ... ... Treasurer
ALBERT E. SHEIBLE ... ... Business Representative	LEW PARKER ... ...Contracting Agent
CARTER COUTURIER ... ... Advertising Agent	WILLIAM LANGAN ... ... Supply Agent

PROGRAMME.

OVERTURE - "Star Spangled Banner" - COWBOY BAND, WM. SWEENY, Leader

1.—**GRAND PROCESSIONAL REVIEW** and introduction of Groups and Individual Characters.

2.—**HORSE RACE** between a Cowboy, a Mexican and an Indian, on Spanish-Mexican Horses.

3.—**MISS ANNIE OAKLEY,** Celebrated Shot, who will illustrate her dexterity in the use of Fire-arms.

4.—**HISTORICAL ADVENTURE IN THE LIFE OF "BUFFALO BILL."** The famous Single Combat with "YELLOW HAND," Chief of the Sioux, at War Bonnet Creek, Dakota, and the downfall and death of the same on July 17th, 1875, in presence of the Indian and American Troops.

5.—**PONY EXPRESS.** The Former Pony Post Rider will show how the Letters and Telegrams of the Republic were distributed across the immense Continent previous to the Railways and the Telegraph.

6.—**ATTACK ON AN EMIGRANT TRAIN BY INDIANS, AND REPULSE BY THE COWBOYS.** At the conclusion of this Scene the "Virginia Reel" will be danced by Cowboys and the Prairie Girls on Horseback.
N.B.—The Waggons are the same as used 35 years ago.

7.—**JOHNNY BAKER,** Celebrated Young American Marksman.

8.—**COWBOY FUN.** Picking Objects from the Ground. Lassoing Wild Horses. Riding the Buckers.

9.—**PISTOL & REVOLVER SHOOTING.** Introduced by Mr. CLAUDE L. DALY.

10.—**RACING BETWEEN AMERICAN BACKWOODS WOMEN.**

11.—**CAPTURE OF THE DEADWOOD MAIL COACH BY THE INDIANS,** which will be rescued by "BUFFALO BILL" and his Attendant Cowboys.
N.B.—This is the identical old DEADWOOD COACH, called the Mail Coach, which is famous on account of having carried the great number of people who lost their lives on the road between DEADWOOD and Cheyenne 18 years ago. Now the most Famed Vehicle extant.

12.—**RACING BETWEEN INDIAN BOYS ON BAREBACK HORSES.**

13.—**LIFE CUSTOMS OF THE INDIANS.** Indian Settlement on the Field and "Path."

14.—**Col. W. F. CODY ("Buffalo Bill"),** in his Unique Feats in Sharpshooting.

15.—**BUFFALO HUNT,** as it is in the Far West of North America—"BUFFALO BILL" and Indians. The last of the only known Native Herd.

16.—**ATTACK ON A SETTLER'S CABIN**—Capture by the Indians—Rescue by "BUFFALO BILL" and the Cowboys

17.—**SALUTE.**

NATIONAL ANTHEM.—CONCLUSION.

An action-packed programme – the Wild West running order from the 1891–2 British season programme. (Earls Court/ Olympia Archives)

At 3 p.m. the next day the Cowboy Band opened the show 'with a large infusion of that restless energy which usually characterises their countrymen, and they get a lot of hard work into the overture and other compositions which they perform.'

A gentleman 'with a white sombrero and a voice like a foghorn' then mounted a platform and announced that the show would now begin. Henry Marsh Clifford, the new British 'orator', had just made his first appearance with the Wild West.

Clifford was well-known as an actor on northern stages and immediately found favour with the reporter from the *Leeds Daily News*, who wrote: 'I was very much interested in this gentleman, not only on account of the information which he imparted from time to time, but because he could make more noise than any other man I ever encountered. He certainly needs all the lung power he possesses and he is the most conscientious shouter that ever "did the gag" for a show.'

The show closely followed the well-tried and tested formula which had been so successful in England and Europe, with one or two new features included. A re-staging of the famous hand-to-hand duel between Bill and Yellow Hand at War Bonnet Creek in July 1875 was new to British audiences.

It began with American troopers riding into the arena, with their scout, Buffalo Bill, at the head. When they reach the far end, there is a discussion and two soldiers are sent back in the same direction. Enter a band of mounted Indians, loudly yelping and waving spears, rifles and tomahawks in the general direction of the two approaching soldiers. A rifle is fired into the air and the two soldiers bring their horses to a halt and see the savage Indians lying in wait for them.

One of the Indians, handsomely dressed as a war Chief, separates himself from the rest of the group and begins riding up and down in front of the others, yelling at the soldiers in general – and Buffalo Bill in particular.

Clifford tells the audience: 'This Indian is called Yellow Hand, and he is calling to Colonel Cody. He is challenging him to fight. He is saying, "I know you Pahaska; if you want to fight, come ahead and fight me."'

Audiences up and down the land loved this gruesome episode in the show.

Bill accepts the challenge and gallops towards the centre of the arena. Yellow Hand also advances and the scout and the Indian Chief eyeball each other from the back of their horses. They raise their rifles and shoot. Yellow Hand's horse falls to the ground and Bill's own steed does a passable imitation of stepping into a rabbit hole, allowing Bill to roll over, quickly get on to his feet and raise his rifle at the Indian who is reaching for his own weapon. Bill shoots. There is a scream from the crowd. The Indian cries out, staggers, falls to his knees and drops dead on the ground.

Bill races towards the Indian and produces a giant hunting knife from his belt. He holds it high into the air for everyone to see. Clifford tells the audience: 'Buffalo Bill drives the keen-edged weapon up to its hilt into the Indian's heart. Jerking his war bonnet off, the great Scout scientifically scalps the Indian in about five seconds.'

The crowd cheers. Bill swings the Indian's topknot and war bonnet into the air and shouts: 'The first scalp for Custer!'

Audiences up and down the land loved this gruesome episode in the show. It helped sell thousands of copies of Bill's first autobiography, *The Life of Buffalo Bill*, which included a detailed re-telling of the story along with his history right up to the time he became an actor. Copies were on sale, price one shilling.

'Buffalo Bill Express' trains next took the company to Liverpool, Britain's most prosperous seaport, where the Wild West set up camp on 6 July in Newsham Park next to Balmoral Road in the city's Fairfield area for another two-week engagement. The *Liverpool Mercury* visited the showgrounds as the last of the artillery of horse-drawn carts and wagons arrived from the station. The reporter noted that the 'enterprise is one of magnitude' and marvelled at the speed adopted by the construction crews, likening it to a military campaign.

Like everyone else in England, the paper was also fascinated by the Indians, 'who immediately on their arrival wrapped themselves up in their cloaks and distributed themselves all over the grounds, some seeking greater comfort in the heaps of straw laying about for the accommodation of the cattle. It is a remarkable instance of the way these men can hide themselves with nothing as it were. When it is pointed out that they are hardly noticeable when they are on the ground or when approached closely, they have the appearance of "old clo".'

It was not unusual for Bill and Salsbury to offer benefit performances for worthy local causes, or admit large groups of poor and needy people into the show for free. In Liverpool, 350 boys and girls from the city's Bluecoat Hospital School, a charitable foundation, were invited to a performance on 15 July. The children marched in to the sound of the school band, and after being seated were treated to 'liberal amounts of lemonade and ginger beer, given to them by Mr Charles J. Jones, President of the Bluecoat Brotherly Society'.

The youngsters obviously enjoyed the show, along with inmates from the Liverpool Home for Aged Mariners who were also there at Bill's invitation. The *Liverpool Mercury* joined them in the audience and reported: 'The continued cheering of the children throughout the performance and at its close demonstrated the pleasure they received and their gratitude to Colonel Cody for the rare treat he had given them.'

A star attraction in Liverpool was a new wild horse from South America called 'Untamed' which was said to have killed four men and could find no horseman

Another equine 'star' of the show, 'Untamed' was said to have killed four men. (Photograph by A.R. Dresser reproduced courtesy of Denver Public Library)

brave enough to control it. Cowboy Chief Frank Hammitt gave it a try that afternoon and 'amid great excitement, mounted the animal and after a wild career across the vast field, resumed complete control'.

Another benefit performance was given when the 'Buffalo Bill Express' transported the Wild West back to Manchester in late July for a three-week long engagement – the first British city to welcome the show for a second visit. Benefiting from ticket sales at a performance held on 31 July at Brook's Bar, Whalley Ridge, would be 19 ageing veterans from the Charge of the Light Brigade, the bungled battle at Balaclava fought 46 years previously, when over 600 of Lord Cardigan's cavalrymen charged Russian artillery, and 257 were killed or wounded and 500 horses were lost.

An advertisement in the *Manchester Evening News* announced the event:

'INTO THE VALLEY OF DEATH RODE THE 600'

Extraordinary Combined Attraction for the Balaclava Veterans' Benefit
This Friday evening, July 31st at 8.00 p.m.
By kind permission of Col. N. Wardrop of H.M. 12th Lancers
A detachment will give a mounted lance drill and sword exercise
Band of the 12th Lancers in Concert
By kind permission of Col. Thompson
The 'miniature volunteers' aged from 6–10 years in an exhibition drill with
miniature brass band
This feature opens the performance sharp at 7.45 p.m.
Unique Military Spectacle – Historic Heroes of the Past – England's Defenders of
the Present – Soldier Lads of the Future
Plus experienced Red and White Warriors of the West under Col. W.F. Cody
Three bands – 12th Lancers, the miniatures and the Cowboys
The unique event of a lifetime
Help the cause! Come – attend!!

A capacity crowd turned out for the occasion and hundreds of pounds was raised for the local Balaclava Fund, which needed the cash to support local veterans. The old soldiers, wearing their original uniforms, sat in VIP boxes and later shared a 'glass of cheer' with Bill in the 'Pahaska Tepee'.

The 'Buffalo Bill Express' continued south and in mid-August pulled into Sheffield, a city of smoke and fire, where men had been employed producing steel for two centuries and manufacturing plate cutlery in more recent years. Those not employed near burning steel furnaces worked underground in mines. The Wild West was scheduled to perform for one week in a park in Penistone Road, next door to a local tram terminus.

The strain of giving two daily performances, travelling from one city to another and supervising such a massive operation, began to take its toll on Bill. In a letter home to his sister written in Sheffield on 14 August, Bill told Julia: 'I have been

The old soldiers, wearing their original uniforms, sat in VIP boxes and later shared a 'glass of cheer' with Bill in the 'Pahaska Tepee'.

171

In July 1891 the Wild West gave a Manchester benefit performance for nineteen survivors of the Charge of the Light Brigade. Bill (centre), with Major Burke and Indians from the show are pictured with some of the veterans plus members of HM 12th Lancers who gave a mounted drill and sword display in the arena. (Denver Public Library)

feeling poorly again.' Two weeks later he wrote to brother-in-law, Al Goodman, that, 'from the time I enter my grounds in the morning until I leave after the night show it's a continual strain and I am becoming very nervous, although strange to say I am shooting better than I ever did in my life.'

Once again, Bill was homesick for his North Platte ranch. In a letter to Julia he begged her to 'sit right down & write me a long letter, all about the haying, new barn, land, stock and everything.' He admitted that his 'health is not good, I worry a great deal.'

Anyone passing the Sheffield showgrounds on the morning of 14 August would have witnessed a rare sight – something never seen before or since in England's fourth largest city. The date coincided with the middle of the eighth moon, the season when the buffalo casts its hair and all hunting stops while Indians celebrate Buffalo Dance Day.

A reporter from the *Sheffield Evening Telegraph and Star*, more used to covering industrial stories, local murders, court cases and council meetings, was permitted to witness the festivities, standing discreetly at the back of one of the larger wigwams in the company of interpreter George Crager who explained the proceedings:

Half a dozen Chiefs and braves were tum-tum-tumming on their drums, and now and then trying the voice in accompaniment in accordance with the practise of more civilised orchestras. There was a stirring among the tents, a coming and going which denoted that something unusual was in progress. . . . Every visitor who entered the wigwam would recline and listen to the strains of the orchestra, apparently in a serious meditative mood. . . . The orchestra, a curious group, some sitting cross-legged, tailor fashion, some with their legs stuck out in front of them, kept up a ceaseless monotonous low beating on their drums, a species of tambourine made large without the jangling appendages.

Anyone concerned that another 'ghost dance' craze was in the making in Sheffield need not have worried. By lunchtime the Buffalo Dance was over and the Indians were back in the ring for the matinée.

Disaster struck that afternoon. As the Indians galloped into the arena to attack the Deadwood stagecoach, the horse carrying Paul Eagle Star, a 25-year-old Sioux brave and one of the prisoners of war, stumbled on to its fore-feet and collided with the wooden fence surrounding the arena. The horse's belly scraped along the ground with the Indian's right ankle caught between the horse and the floor of the arena. Paul's foot was almost wrenched from the rest of his body.

Paul Eagle Star was immediately rushed to Sheffield Infirmary where surgeons fought to save his foot and lower leg. Bill, Salsbury, Indians and cowboys turned up at the infirmary to see him, but the young brave was too ill to receive visitors. The *Evening Telegraph and Star* reported: 'He is a docile patient, bearing the most agonising pain with customary Indian fortitude.'

It was time for Wild West trains to leave Sheffield and roll onwards to Nottingham, but the Indians were reluctant to leave Paul alone in the infirmary. Bill instructed George Crager to stay with the injured brave and rejoin the show later.

Crager sat with Paul around the clock. In waking moments, Paul told the interpreter that he knew he was going to die and wanted his wife, back at the Rosebud Indian agency in South Dakota, to be informed. He asked for her to be told that he had received the greatest kindness from surgeons and nurses at the white man's hospital. Paul instructed Crager to thank 'Pahaska' and 'Little Big Man' Salsbury for taking him with them across the great waters to see more of the white man's world. The interpreter replied that in a few days he would be able to thank them himself, as he was certain to recover thanks to paleface medicine.

Tetanus set in the following day and doctors were forced to amputate Paul's lower leg in an attempt to save his life. Paul begged Crager to stay with him in the operating room, and not leave him alone. The interpreter held the Indian's hand throughout, telling him to be brave, assuring him that everything would be fine. Paul Eagle Star died shortly after the operation, murmuring the words, 'Jesus, Jesus' softly to the man still holding his hand. His body was unable to sustain the shock of amputation and its after-effects.

Crager sent a telegram to Bill and Salsbury in Nottingham breaking the news, which the *Evening Telegraph and Star* reported 'caused much consternation at the Wild West camp . . . news of his untimely death has cast a deep gloom over the encampment.'

Paul Eagle Star died shortly after the operation, murmuring the words, 'Jesus, Jesus' softly to the man still holding his hand.

Bill and Salsbury instructed Crager to remain in Sheffield to represent the Wild West management at an inquest, held at the infirmary on 24 August. He was joined by Major Burke who travelled to Sheffield with Kicking Bear, Black Heart, Lone Bull and Paul's cousin, Bull Stands Behind. 'The Indians, particularly Bull Stands Behind, displayed much emotion on seeing the dead body of their comrade,' reported the paper.

Major Burke told the inquest that: 'Colonel Cody was considerably upset on receiving news of the Indian's death and has since been quite prostrated and unable to come over to Sheffield to make the necessary arrangements in person.' Bill sent his personal thanks to the infirmary's medical staff for the care and attention given to the Indian in their charge 'and intends to send a marble bust of himself to the infirmary as a token of his indebtedness to them.'

Verdict of the inquest: 'accidental death'.

Paul's body was later placed in 'a stout coffin' and taken by horse-drawn hearse to the Midland Station where it was loaded on to a train bound for Nottingham, where Buffalo Bill and company waited on the platform for its arrival.

At Nottingham station the coffin was removed from the train and carried to a private waiting room where the rest of the company paid their last respects to Paul Eagle Star. At 11.35 a.m. the coffin was placed in a private carriage and with George Crager, Major Burke, No Neck, Kicking Bear, Black Heart, Bear Growls and Bull Stands Behind as escorts, travelled south to London's St Pancras station. There, an open hearse pulled by black stallions was waiting to carry the young Indian's remains through London's busy streets to Brompton cemetery, next door to Earls Court.

Paul Eagle Star was buried in a common grave, without a headstone or marker in an area which was becoming the British cemetery's equivalent of 'Boot Hill'. He remained there for the next 108 years.

 The show was so successful at Nottingham's Trent Bridge Close that the *Nottingham Evening News* predicted: 'In twenty years time, men with grey hair will remember the drama of Buffalo Bill's Wild West with the romantic interest with which we now regard the cross-bow and broad-sword battles of our forefathers. The children who watched with excitement, not untinged with alarm, will have for their manhood a memory of wild phases of western life in a time that is fast fading away.'

The reaction was the same when the Wild West returned to Birmingham's Aston Lower Grounds for a second visit. *The meadow where the company had performed four years previously had now been converted into a housing estate,* but the local council drained a lake large enough to create a second meadow and the show played where fish had previously swum and ducks paddled.

Instead of pitching tents and wigwams in the Great Hall, the company created an open-air camp, the Indians erecting eight large tepees in a clump of trees near the Great Hall and the cowboys in an area next to an ornamental garden at the other side of the building.

Over 10,000 people bought tickets for the opening performance and about the same number gathered on rising ground surrounding Aston attempting to see the show for free. The 12-day Birmingham season was more successful than the previous visit – even on Saturday afternoons at the start of the football season.

Leicester's Belgrave Road Grounds became home to the Wild West the following week before trains steamed into Wales for six days of shows at the Marquis of Bute's estate at Sophia Gardens Park, Cardiff, beginning on 21 September. Although suffering from a heavy cold, Bill led the company on a parade through Cardiff's streets. The city was brought to a standstill by the Indians, Mexicans, cowboys and western girls, plus the Deadwood stagecoach pulled through the city by a mule team. The *Evening Express* said it was 'the most interesting and realistic sight ever seen in the streets of Cardiff.'

After the parade, Salsbury travelled north to Glasgow to open discussions with the local council about staging an expanded version of the Wild West in a massive

Derby-hatted visitors to the Wild West on the Marquis of Bute's Estate in Cardiff prepare to take a spin around the arena in the Deadwood stagecoach, driven by John Nelson (on the top driver's seat) and defended by Buffalo Bill. (The American Collection)

indoor arena in a production set to rival the 1887–8 Manchester engagement. At the same time Major Burke travelled to Bristol to generate pre-show publicity in the city where the show would play the following week.

Later that day, Bill agreed to be interviewed by a reporter from the *Evening Express* who found him coughing and sneezing inside the 'Pahaska Tepee'. 'I found him a soft-voiced gentleman, with the bearing of the cavalier he looks, with his long grey locks and sweeping beard.'

Bill told the reporter that he had brought the show to Cardiff at the suggestion of the Spanish–Italian coloratura singer, Madame Adeline Patti, whom he had met in New Orleans, where she told him about her home in Wales. 'I mentioned that I proposed making a trip to England and she advised me, if I did, to be sure to come to Cardiff, which was the outlet of a very wealthy country. I said we would come, and here we are . . . and very good business we have done here, too,' said Bill. Madame Patti, who was also appearing in Cardiff, was expected to visit the Wild West before the end of its Welsh engagement.

'The people of Cardiff appear to be very intelligent – much more so than the people in the north of England.'

The same reporter also interviewed Annie Oakley, who told him that in her opinion no other country produced gun barrels as good as those made in England. She also reflected on the cities she had visited on tour with the Wild West and openly expressed her likes and dislikes of Europe and Europeans.

Annie told the reporter that she had liked Paris very much:

> . . . especially the better class Parisians, but the lower class I don't like at all; they all seem so rude and forward. Austria I liked, but Germany and Berlin only indifferently. I cannot say why because we were treated kindly, but there it is all the same. Italy was agreeable, and Milan and Florence, but Rome – oh, the people were like heathens there. . . . There is no place like England. It was as if we have come home. There is not much difference between the English and the Americans in matters of dress and manner, but, of course, the language as spoken differs considerably. As for Cardiff, we are all delighted with it. The people appear to be very intelligent – much more so than the people in the north of England – and their behaviour is wonderfully good. Another good reason for liking Cardiff is the business done – the best of all the towns.

The Cardiff engagement, in fact, netted Bill and Salsbury £10,000 in ticket sales, amounting to something like ten times that amount in modern day box office income. The portable stadium was not large enough to seat all those who wanted to come, so six large wagons full of extra chairs had to be hired for later performances. Still more people came, and there was standing room only, with hundreds turned away disappointed.

Cardiff proved to be the most successful engagement of the tour so far. Over 200,000 people saw the Wild West in Wales – 160,000 coming in from outside of the city, making a tidy profit for railways, hotels and shops benefiting from the extra trade brought into the neighbourhood by Buffalo Bill. One restaurant claimed to have served 15,000 extra dinners to Welsh families travelling to Cardiff to experience the Wild West.

Someone else expecting to make money from the Wild West in Wales was Henry Ellis, described by the local newspaper as:

. . . a respectably dressed man, age 38, charged with frequenting the entrance of the Wild West show on September 22nd with intent to commit a felony and assaulting Detective Constable Roddy. He was seen loitering near the entrance to Sophia Gardens Park and his conduct was such that a constable handed him over to Detective Constable Roddy. He was taken to the Police Station and when in Westgate Street, he tripped Roddy, who did not allow him to get away. . . . It was found that he had a criminal record and the professional pick-pocket was given three months hard labour for the first offence and one month for the assault.

The Wild West might have remained in Cardiff playing to packed houses for another week, but Bristol beckoned and the 'Buffalo Bill Express' pulled into Temple Meads station during the early hours of 27 September. As usual, a welcome party of ordinary people was waiting on the platform to greet the company and lead them to the Gloucester Road showground at Horfield. The *Western Daily Press* claimed that the line of carriages and wagons – each pulled by eight to ten horses – taking the company, its goods, chattels, and cattle from station to showground, stretched for one mile.

The old friends smoked a cigar together in a railway station waiting room while the Indians performed a dance.

In Bristol, Bill was reunited with his old friend, actor-manager Henry Irving who had been appearing in the same city with Ellen Terry and the Lyceum Company in the dramatic double bill of *Nance Oldfield* and *The Lyons Mail*. Accompanied by No Neck, his stepson, Johnny 'No Neck' Burke, Short Bull and Lone Bull, the old friends smoked a cigar together in a railway station waiting room while the Indians performed a dance designed to protect Irving and Miss Terry on their journey home to London.

On the way back to Gloucester Road, the carriage carrying Bill and the Indians ran into heavy horse-drawn traffic a mile away from the Wild West camp. When their driver asked another about the cause of the delay, he was told it was due to thousands of Sunday drivers and sightseers turning out to catch a glimpse of Buffalo Bill. In order to prevent further horse-drawn traffic congestion, Bill ordered the carriage blinds to be drawn so they would not be seen. Young Johnny 'No Neck' Burke soon became bored with sitting in a darkened carriage and kept lifting the blinds to wave to the crowds. It took over two hours to travel the final mile to the showground gates – and by that time Buffalo Bill and his passengers were all fast asleep.

A street parade was planned for the following day, and people began to take time off from work to line pavements hours before the 3 p.m. commencement. Healthy advance bookings at the box office proved that the Wild West's Bristol engagement would be another success.

Heavy rain fell over Bristol that night and throughout the following day. The arena was saturated, but this did not stop over 100,000 people from travelling into the city to see Buffalo Bill during the week of 28 September. Special excursion trains brought passengers to the city from all parts of the west and southwest of England, and Bill promised performances 'rain or shine'. In Bristol it was mostly in the rain – and the public still couldn't get enough of his cowboys and Indians.

The weather remained wet and windy as the 'Buffalo Bill Express' convoy moved south to the naval dockyard city of Portsmouth, to set up camp on 4 October for one week at the North End Showgrounds. The *Hampshire Telegraph* reported that the visit was 'a somewhat unfortunate one, not from any lack of attractiveness on the part of the show itself or from a lack of desire to witness it on the part of the inhabitants of Portsmouth and the neighbouring district, but simply on account of the singularly untoward state of the elements.'

Onwards to Brighton, where Wild West roustabouts battled against driving rain and bitingly cold winds to create a camp and performing area at Hove Street Meadow in Church Street on 12 October. The *Argus* newspaper paid no attention to the weather and said that the visit was 'on the lips of everyone for weeks past; boys and young people generally have been waiting the advent with feverish impatience, while their elders have been almost as eager to see in reality what they have read so much about. Neither will be disappointed.'

Severe gales, however, stopped the show in Brighton for two days – the first performances lost through bad weather since the Wild West arrived in England. The wind was blowing so furiously that Bill decided against putting the canvas roof across the top of the portable grandstand, fearing it would blow away or become damaged. Elsewhere in Brighton, chimney stacks were blown down, tiles were ripped from roof tops, trees were blown down and small craft lifted clean out of the sea and dropped unceremoniously on the beach.

Bill was heard to comment that while he was happy to perform 'rain or shine', he drew the line at typhoons!

On the night of 13–14 October, Brighton experienced gales, thunder, lightning, hail, and unusually large flakes of snow followed by rain. Throughout the following day there were fitful gleams of sunshine and more wind and rain – all of it bad for open-air show business. Bill was heard to comment that while he was happy to perform 'rain or shine', he drew the line at typhoons!

The Indians became so afraid at the ferocity of the gales that throughout the night they were heard singing prayers of deliverance to the Great Spirit. On 15 October their prayers were finally answered, the rain stopped, the sun grudgingly appeared and the crowds at last trooped to see a dampened Wild West on a waterlogged Hove Street Meadow.

The sun shone a little brighter when the 'Buffalo Bill Express' steamed into East Croydon railway station on 19 October to play for a week on a 15-acre public recreation ground in Waddon Marsh Lane – and if any local people needed reminding where this was located, advertisements reminded them that it was 'next to the gas works'.

Hundreds of children from local parish schools were invited to see the show for free, sitting in the one-shilling seats under cover from rain, which threatened to spoil the outing. Croydon's Mayor, Councillor Fred Edridge, led the children into the showground and a fife and drum band followed him. But the evening performance had to be cancelled and most of the company spent the evening watching someone else working for a change from the stalls of the Theatre Royal, at a performance of the play *Sweet Innisfail* by Walter Reynolds.

Advertisement in *The Stage* – October 22 1891:

Buffalo Bill and Viola Clemmons had remained in touch by letter. At home in America and while on tour in Britain, Bill was always anxious for news of Viola's activities from London friends keeping an eye on her public and private affairs. He was not always pleased by what he heard from his correspondents. The actress had other 'gentleman friends and admirers' and was fond of boasting aloud how she had conquered the famous Buffalo Bill.

Bill was always anxious for news of Viola's activities. He was not always pleased by what he heard from his correspondents.

But in 1891 Viola had her heart set on theatrical stardom, and Bill would be her route to fame and fortune. Dissatisfied with playing small roles in minor London productions and second-rate provincial tours, Viola planned to use her considerable charms to persuade Bill to finance her entry into theatrical management, staging productions starring herself in meaty leading roles designed to show off her acting talents.

Bill found it hard to say no to anyone, especially the glamorous young actress who assured him that pumping money into an American melodrama about a girl abducted by Red Indians, rescued by cowboys and starring herself in the title role of *Onita, The White Lily* would be profitable for all concerned. Viola argued that the play was similar in style to those Bill had successfully performed during his Buffalo Bill Combination days before the Wild West – and if they had been popular in the United States, consider how they would be received by English audiences who could not get enough of genuine cowboys and Indians.

Viola said that the play, new to British audiences, would provide her with an opportunity not only to show off her acting talents, but also give her a chance to sing, take part in a war dance, perform tricks on a horse, shoot a rifle and wear a variety of dazzling costumes before the public.

But Viola wanted more than just money to mount an epic production of *White Lily*. She also wanted to borrow a dozen Indians from the Wild West to give the cast authenticity and publicity value. Her sights were also set on the loan of some of the show's trained horses for various equestrian scenes. Members of the Wild West's stage management team were wanted to organise and promote the production, which would first tour the provinces before coming into London, where stardom surely awaited Viola's arrival.

M ISS CLEMMONS'S,
"WHITE LILY" CO.

Grand Success.

GENUINE PRAIRIE HORSES.

Only full-blooded Sioux Indians in this country excepting
those held by Col. W. F. Cody (" Buffalo Bill ") as Prisoners
of War.

Now Booking for 1892.
A few Spring Dates vacant.
November 2nd vacant.

PRINCE OF WALES THEATRE, GREENWICH,
Week of October 26th.

Miss Clemmons's permanent address,
Law's Exchange, Charing Cross, London.

TO CIRCUS PROPRIETORS AND SHOWMEN.
The Summer Season of

BUFFALO BILL'S WILD WEST
will close on Saturday, October 24th, 1891.
MESSRS. LYON and CO. have been instructed TO SELL
BY AUCTION the whole of the travelling Plant and
Material of this world-renowned combination. The Pro-
prietors call the attention of Showmen generally to the
great value of this Plant, which includes a splendid
PORTABLE GRAND STAND,
in perfect condition and the most practical construction of
the kind in Europe.
Catalogues of all the material can be obtained from
Lyon and Co., 315, Fulham-road, S.W.,
on Monday, October 26th.
THE SALE
will take place on the Wild West Grounds, at Croydon,
at 1 p.m. sharp on Wednesday, October 28th, 1891.
BUFFALO BILL'S
WILD WEST WINTER SPECTACLE
will open in
GLASGOW, November 9th, 1891.

Side-by-side – classified: 'Miss Clemmons's White Lily Co.' announces availability for 1892 bookings in a small classified ad in the theatrical newspaper *The Stage*, on 22 October 1891. Below is an advertisement for a sale by auction at Croydon of plant, materials and the grandstand used by Buffalo Bill's Wild West.

Salsbury, a seasoned actor and theatrical impresario, wanted nothing to do with the venture. He refused to put any of his own money into *White Lily*, but agreed to loan out one of his stage managers, Sherman Canfield, to act as company manager for Viola's theatrical venture. He also reluctantly agreed to hire out some of the company's performing horses and release twelve Indians on the strict understanding that they would be fed, looked after, and kept away from alcohol. Both Canfield and the Indians, under the supervision of a minor

A signed lithograph produced early in 1904 for Buffalo Bill's final farewell tour of Britain which ended at the Agricultural Show Fields, Birches Green, Hanley, near Stoke-on-Trent on Friday 21 October 1904 – *'Positively the last two performances of Buffalo Bill's Wild West in England – EVER!!'* said the *Staffordshire Sentinel*.

A cardboard souvenir game featuring Buffalo Bill, cowboys, Indians and the Deadwood Stagecoach, could be purchased in London and provincial showgrounds during the 1902/04 seasons. Each figure came with its own miniature stand, allowing Edwardian children to have hours of fun recreating the Wild West in their own playrooms. The Indian pictured here defending his territory is the only survivor from a complete set given to an English landowner by Buffalo Bill and passed down to his own son and later grandson. (Michael Bailey Collection)

Portrait picture of Buffalo Bill on a souvenir postcard produced around 1892. (Denver Public Library)

Front cover of a map showing the touring route taken by Buffalo Bill's Wild West throughout the United Kingdom between 1902 and 1904. Drawing by Adrian Jones. (Jim Carey Collection)

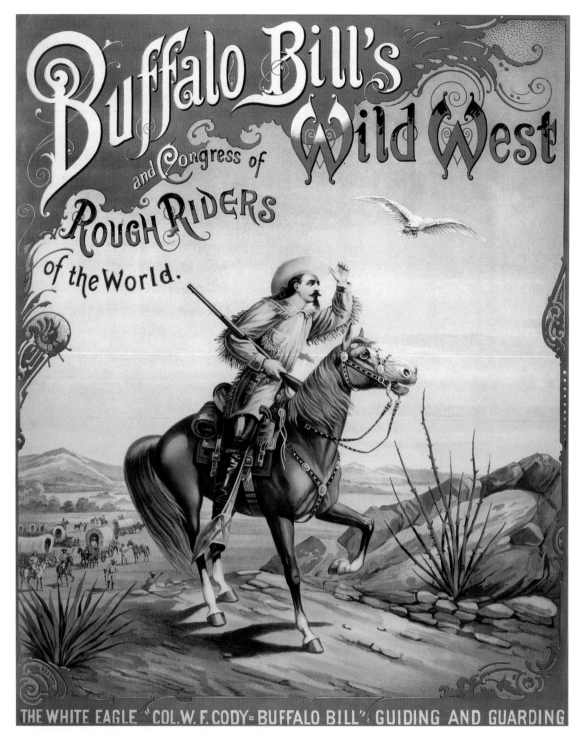

'The White Eagle' – alias Buffalo Bill – was one of a pair of lithographs showing Bill 'guiding and guarding' a wagon train of pioneering settlers to new lives in the west. A second lithograph showed an Indian called Red Cloud, described as 'The Red Fox – waiting and watching'. The lithographs were produced in 1893 for the Chicago World's Fair.

A typical cover drawing by Robert Prowse from the 1949 edition of *More Adventures with Buffalo Bill*, edited by Wingrove Willson (alias G. Clabon Glover, Nat Knowlden and Buck Ingham) published in London by Aldine of Chancery Lane. (Author's Collection)

Opposite and this page: Started by Ned Buntline, Prentiss Ingraham and many other imitators, the fad for Western novel adventures grew worldwide, helping to perpetuate the legend of Buffalo Bill. (Author's Collection)

THE WHITE CITY.

BUFFALO BILL

AND CONGRE

WORLD'S
WONDROUS
VOYAGES

FROM PRAIRIE TO PALACE
CAMPING ON TWO CONTINENTS

DISTANCE TRAVELLED, 63,000 MILES

OR NEARLY THREE TIMES ROUND THE GLOBE

BUFFALO BILL AND THE FIRST AMERICAN
INDIANS THAT HAVE VISITED THE ADRIATIC

EARL'S COURT LONDON   JUBILEE 1887 FAREWELL 1892

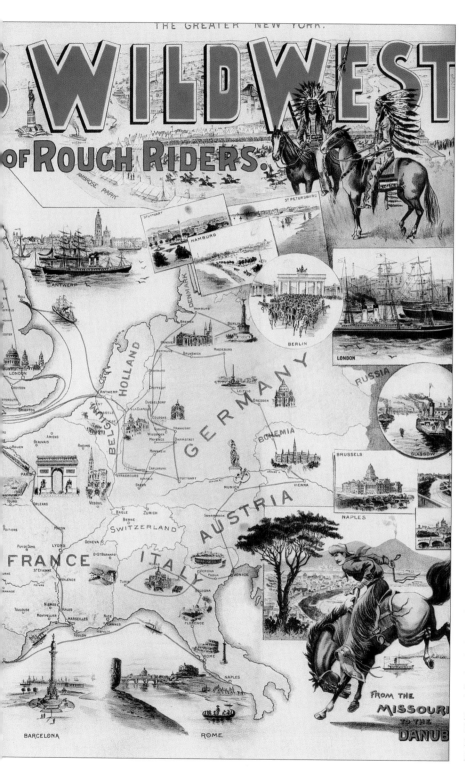

'The world's wondrous voyages – from prairie to palace, camping on two continents, distance travelled, 163,000 miles' – the outside back cover of a programme used in the Wild West's 1895 American programme and produced by A. Hoen and Company of Baltimore. The image was later turned into a poster.

An English guardsman with a Union Jack and an American cavalry officer with the Stars & Stripes flank Buffalo Bill on a poster for the 1903–4 'final farewell tour' of the United Kingdom by Buffalo Bill's Wild West and Congress of Rough Riders of the World. (Denver Public Library)

The Wild West BUFFALO BILL ANNUAL

Colour plate by Denis McLaughlin from the 1951 edition of the *Buffalo Bill Wild West Annual*, written by Arthur Groom and published by The Popular Press of Cockspur Street, London. (Author's collection)

Number 86, Regent Street (beneath the Union Jack), an elegant five storey building designed by John Nash, offered Buffalo Bill and his daughter, Arta, a suite of smart rooms on two floors above Hope's, a 'gentlemen's outfitters'. The building was close to Piccadilly and London's clubland, near shops, theatres and entertainment. Shortly after moving in Bill reported that he was 'embarrassed by an overwhelming mass of flowers which came hourly from hosts of female admirers.' (Alan Gallop)

Irving Berlin's stage musical, *Annie Get Your Gun*, probably did more to introduce Annie Oakley to new audiences than any other medium since her years with Buffalo Bill. The show, originally produced in 1946 with Ethel Merman as Annie, ran for three years on Broadway and has since been produced all over the world, including a Tony award-winning revival in New York in 1999. The show was filmed starring Betty Hutton in 1950. (Irving Berlin Music Company)

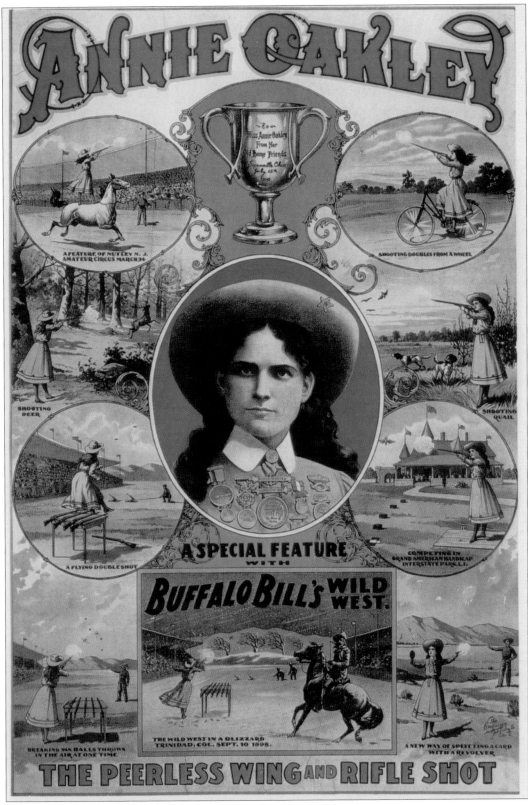

Annie Oakley – The Peerless Wing and Rifle Shot – demonstrates her many shooting skills on a colourful poster produced by Nate Salsbury to promote his star female attraction. (The American Collection)

A musical divertissement in honour of Buffalo Bill: 'The Buffalo Bill Polka – composed for and dedicated to the Hon. W. F. Cody by special permission – by May Ostlere – Metzler & Co, 42 Great Marlborough Street, London, Price 4/-'. Other versions were available in 1887 for a full orchestra, brass band and military band. (Earls Court/Olympia Archives)

'Le Legende de Buffalo Bill' lives on twice daily at Marne-la-Vallée on the eastern outskirts of the French capital – better known as Disneyland Resort Paris. (Jenna Louise Gallop)

'Historical Sketches and Programme' cover for the 1892–3 British season. (Earls Court/Olympia Archives)

Chief Long Wolf, who died in London in 1892, was buried in Brompton cemetery – the city's most fashionable and crowded cemetery. His resting-place reflected his status and was marked with a tall stone cross containing the inscription: 'Chief Long Wolf, North American Indian with Buffalo Bill's Wild West Co. Died June 11th 1892, aged 59 years. Also Star, who died August 12th, 1892, aged 20 months.' Carved onto the stonework was the figure of a wolf, included as one of the old Chief's two last wishes. It would be a further 105 years before his second wish, to return home to be buried among his people, was granted. (Alan Gallop)

chief called Black Heart (who would play the role of an evil Indian named after Bill's old foe, Yellow Hand, in the drama), were told they could return to the Wild West company and their old jobs at the end of Viola's theatrical season, which Salsbury suspected would be a short one.

An advertisement in *The Era* announced that a new theatrical company had been formed. It stated:

Miss Viola Clemmons's
White Lily Company
will present
The Wild West on Stage
in
The First and Only Appearance of
Miss Viola Clemmons
and her Anglo-American Combination
In the high-class 4-Act Indian Border drama entitled
'WHITE LILY'.
An artistic and financial success.
For this elaborate production
Miss Clemmons has secured
A PARTY OF RED INDIANS,
which are the only genuine Indians ever brought to this country,
except those now held by
COL. W.F. CODY (Buffalo Bill)
As Prisoners of War.
The band consists of member of the Ogalla and Bruh[*] Sioux Tribes,
and were all participants in the late Messiah Craze and at
The Battles of Pine Ridge and Wounded Knee.
SPECIAL AUTHENTIC SCENERY,
TRAINED PRAIRIE HORSES,
and all the supernumeraries travel with the Company.
EXHIBITION OF TROPHIES
taken from the Battle Fields of Wounded Knee and Pine Ridge will be on view.

The advertisement listed venues and dates where the production was scheduled to appear on its first tour. They included engagements at theatres in many regions where the Wild West had already appeared to great acclaim, including: Derby, Oldham, Preston, Leicester, Greenwich, Bromley, Bath, Plymouth, Swansea, Manchester, Ashton-under-Lyme, Burnley, Hanley, Accrington and Northampton between 24 September and 31 December 1891. Readers were told that Miss

---

* Brulle.

Clemmons 'is now taking bookings for 1892. A few Spring dates vacant. Nov. 2nd vacant by misunderstanding.'

Theatres interested in booking *White Lily* were told to write to Miss Clemmons 'at her permanent London address at Low's Exchange, Charing Cross, London'.

Prior to arriving in Preston, Sherman Canfield sent a telegram to the manager of the Theatre Royal, Preston, asking him to 'kindly notify hotel proprietors that we earnestly request them not to supply our Indians with intoxicating drinks during our stay in Preston.'

Not having the publicity skills of a Major Burke on hand, Canfield took out a small advertisement on the front page of the *Preston Chronicle* on 10 October 1891 stating that Miss Clemmons and her company of Indians would be arriving at Central station 'by special train about 4.15 p.m. Sunday'. Viola, no doubt, was expecting the same kind of enthusiastic turnout on the Preston station platform that Bill and the Wild West always enjoyed whenever they steamed into town. It is not recorded how many Preston citizens turned out on that chilly October Sunday afternoon to greet their arrival from London.

The *Preston Chronicle*'s drama critic, however, was in *White Lily*'s first night audience at the Theatre Royal and liked what he saw. He reported that the Indians 'are a really grand body of men, possessed of a certain innate gracefulness, in the staining of their bodies, in the way of arranging their striking and picturesque dress. To see them on stage in their full war paint, among their wigwams, to go through their peculiar, essentially barbaric dance, to engage in mimic combat, is indeed a scene indescribable in its attractiveness.'

He added: '*White Lily* is a melodrama possessing intricate merits. Perhaps not the least of these is the fact that there is not too much claptrap, and in Miss Clemmons, too, who plays the part of Onita, we have a heroine who doesn't play in that trammelled stilted sort of way in which the heroines of this style of play are supposed to. Indeed, her unaffected, charmingly natural, unconventional manner is distinctly pleasing, and imbues her part with a special attractiveness. Certainly it is a unique performance and doubtless will be played to full houses.'

Later that month, *White Lily* opened at Horton's Theatre, Greenwich, on London's outskirts and Bill arrived at the opening night with a party of friends. *The Stage* newspaper was also in the audience to write about the occasion:

> This week we have another change from comic opera to American drama in the shape of *The White Lily*, produced by Miss Viola Clemmons' company. This piece is on much the same lines both as regards plot and situations as *On The Frontier*, which was here a few weeks back. Miss Clemmons herself plays Onita, The White Lily in a natural girlish manner quite in keeping with the character. . . . One of the principal attractions put forward in connection with this company is the engagement of a band of Sioux Indians who form an important feature in the entertainment. Their native dances to the accompaniment of the 'tom-tom' are very interesting and will, no doubt, prove a draw in the provinces. The company carries some highly effective sets with them, particularly that of The Ranch in Act II. On Monday Col. W.F. Cody – 'Buffalo Bill' – was present. He, with a party of friends, occupied two private boxes. During the evening, the lessee, Mr W. Horton, appeared before the curtain and made

Viola was expecting the same kind of enthusiastic turnout that Bill and the Wild West always enjoyed whenever they steamed into town.

a little speech relative to the visit of so well known a man as Buffalo Bill. He concluded by asking Col. Cody to step forward to the front of the box, upon doing which BB was received with much applause.

Other reviews throughout the tour were mixed. Critics in Manchester managed to write about the play without mentioning its leading lady at all. It also cast doubts on *White Lily*'s literary worthiness. The *Manchester Evening News* did point out, however, that the play seemed to be 'a crowd pleaser', especially for people in the gallery who loved the gunfire and predicted that the show would enjoy good business.

When the show played in Hanley, Viola was thrown from her horse in a daring scene performed on a narrow platform 20 ft above the stage and hidden behind scenery depicting rocks running along the edge of a canyon. The regular horse used in this scene had become lame earlier in the day and another animal, unused to performing on narrow wooden ledges and under the glare of harsh lighting, shied and tossed Viola from its back 20 ft down to the stage below. But the audience thought it was all part of the plot and loved every moment of it. Fortunately when members of the company rushed to her aid and found her shaken but uninjured, there was some rapid 'mugging' by other actors and the show went on. Viola limped through the rest of the performance.

White Lily closed at Northampton's Opera House on New Year's Eve 1891 following a short post-Christmas season, and failed to re-open. There were no New Year engagements and Viola and *White Lily* never found their way to London and stage stardom. Instead, the production sank with all hands on the road before it had a chance to recoup its enormous touring costs.

While Viola spent the autumn and winter touring in provincial theatres, Bill was preparing to take the Wild West north to Scotland. Viola returned to London and prepared to spend the new year holidays alone. But she vowed to follow Bill across the Atlantic when he returned home after the close of the Glasgow season. As a Christmas gift, she sent him the copy of a script she favoured called *A Lady of Venice*, a blank-verse drama 'about love and intrigue in Medieval Italy' by Richard Zouch Troughton. Viola told Bill that if London's playgoers did not appreciate her talents, she would try her luck in America with the play – and be close to the Wild West wherever it happened to be appearing.

Second Seats (Reserved), 2s; Admission, One Shilling

THEATRE ROYAL, PRESTON.

"WHITE LILY."
"WHITE LILY." MONDAY, Oct. 12.—SIX NIGHTS
"WHITE LILY." ONLY.
"WHITE LILY." THE WILD WEST ON THE
"WHITE LILY." STAGE.
"WHITE LILY." FIRST and ONLY APPEAR-
"WHITE LILY." ANCE of
"WHITE LILY." MISS VIOLA CLEMMONS
"WHITE LILY." And her ANGLO-AMERICAN
"WHITE LILY." COMBINATION, in the HIGH-
"WHITE LILY." CLASS INDIAN BORDER
"WHITE LILY." DRAMA entitled,
"WHITE LILY." "WHITE LILY."
"WHITE LILY." For this Elaborate Production
"WHITE LILY." Miss CLEMMONS has secured
"WHITE LILY." A PARTY OF RED INDIANS,
"WHITE LILY." Which are the only genuine
"WHITE LILY." Indians ever brought into this
"WHITE LILY." country, except those now held by
"WHITE LILY." COL. W. F. CODY (BUFFALO
"WHITE LILY." BILL)
"WHITE LILY." As Prisoners of War.
"WHITE LILY." The Band consists of Members
"WHITE LILY." of the lOgalla and Bruh lSioux
"WHITE LILY." Tribes, and were all participants
"WHITE LILY." in the late Messiah Craze and at
"WHITE LILY." the Battles of Pine Ridge and
"WHITE LILY." Wounded Knee.
"WHITE LILY." SPECIAL AUTHENTIC
"WHITE LILY." SCENERY,
"WHITE LILY." TRAINED PRAIRIE HORSES,
"WHITE LILY." And all Supernumeries, travel
"WHITE LILY." with the Company.
"WHITE LILY." EXHIBITION OF TROPHIES
"WHITE LILY." taken from the Battle Fields of
"WHITE LILY." Wounded Knee and Pine Ridge
"WHITE LILY." now on View at the
"WHITE LILY." GRAND CLOTHING HALL,
"WHITE LILY." FISHERGATE.
"WHITE LILY." POPULAR PRICES.

SPECIAL NOTICE.

COPY OF TELEGRAM.
Handed in at the Oldham Post Office at 8 35 p.m.
Received here at 8 55. 7.10.91.
To Trevalion, Theatre Royal, Preston.
Kindly notify Hotel Proprietors that we earnestly request them not to supply our Indians with Intoxicating Drinks during our stay in Preston.
Will arrive Central (L. and Y.) Station, by Special Train, about 4 15 p.m. Sunday.
SHERMAN CANFIELD,
Manager White Lily Co.

The *Preston Chronicle*'s critic liked what he saw. . . . Audiences were persuaded to attend with classified advertising and reassured that the Indians would be sober. (Author)

Around midnight on 24 October, the Wild West company climbed back into their railway carriages to travel through the night and most of the next day from Croydon to Glasgow. In Scotland they would appear for an extended Christmas and New Year season opening on 9 November. The company was given time off from performing to explore their new surroundings, while Bill, Salsbury and Major Burke worked around the clock adapting the show to its new surroundings at the East End Exhibition Building in Duke Street, Dennistoun.

The 270 ft long by 225 ft wide building, constructed to house exhibitions demonstrating Glasgow's industrial achievements, had stood empty for some time, too large to attract touring circus or music hall shows. With major modifications, it would make an ideal base for the Wild West, and Salsbury entered an agreement with the local council to share the cost of converting the building into 'the grandest amphitheatre in Europe, seating 7,000'. To do this they employed hundreds of local tradesmen to raise the roof a further 21 ft over its previous height using steel lattice girders to support it. The building also had to be extended on one side, central heating and tiered seating installed – an expensive undertaking which had to be funded and completed before the company could move in to rehearse.

Sergeant George Partridge (left inside boxing arena) of the 5th Royal Irish Lancers and doubling as a rider in the Wild West, takes part in a friendly off-duty sparring match, watched by a mixed audience of cowboys, Indians and fellow soldiers. (Roger Partridge Collection)

Work converting the building to the Wild West's requirements commenced six weeks before the advertised opening night. Advertisements in Scottish newspapers told the public that: 'This is the Final, positively the Last, Absolute Farewell exhibition of this organisation in Europe previous to departure for America – NEVER TO RETURN, ergo Scotland's last chance.'

But it was clear that the building would not be ready for 9 November – so the first night was pushed back a further four days 'to ensure perfection in this stupendous production.' Builders, carpenters, bricklayers, plasterers, painters and men from a dozen other trades worked into the night converting the building from an exhibition hall into a comfortable, centrally heated theatre suitable to stage the largest show on earth. The arena stage would measure 150 ft wide, 210 ft deep with a proscenium 70 ft wide and 32 ft high.

While Bill and Salsbury battled with builders in Duke Street, the cowboys, Indians, Mexicans and western girls settled into their new indoor quarters in a former reformatory opposite the auditorium. Stables and corrals were constructed for the animals between the two buildings.

On 12 November an advertisement in the *Glasgow Herald* told the public that:

The delayed opening did nothing to harm advance ticket sales in Glasgow, helping instead to fuel 'Wild West fever' which spread across the city.

The management of *Buffalo Bill's Wild West* sincerely regret to announce another postponement. Having been under great expense for the last two weeks ready to fulfil to the letter their public promise, circumstances beyond their control (relative to the building which should have been handed over to them on 2nd November), there has been another delay and the management therefore, throw themselves on the indulgence of the Scottish public, with the assurance that it is in the interests of their future patrons' comfort and that Monday 16 will positively be the inaugural exhibition. Those who have already purchased tickets can have them transferred to Monday or any another evening or have money refunded on application to Messrs Patterson & Son, 152 Buchanan Street, Glasgow. Trusting that any inconvenience unnecessarily created will be excused owing to the magnitude of the enterprise. Remaining yours respectfully, Cody and Salsbury.

The delayed opening did nothing to harm advance ticket sales in Glasgow, helping instead to fuel 'Wild West fever' which spread across the city. On opening night, all 7,000 seats were filled with wildly excited Scots, including the Lord Provost John Muir and leading city magistrates, who occupied VIP boxes to enjoy what the latest advertisements described as 'the Acme of Instructive Amusement'.

Ticket prices ranged from twenty-five shillings for a box seating six people, five shillings for a single box seat and between one and four shillings for a grandstand seat. Special 'Wild West' horse-drawn tram services operated from all parts of the city to the auditorium's front door – the last trams timed to depart at 10.18 p.m. giving the audience time to leave their seats and get home at a reasonable hour.

Bill and Salsbury again opened their doors to worthy causes and gave a benefit performance to 6,000 local orphans, who stood in their seats and sang 'Yankee Doodle' to the Wild West company at the close of the show in appreciation of their afternoon treat.

The show played to 'house full' notices over Glasgow's Christmas and New Year holidays and to avoid losing audiences during January and February as had happened in Manchester three years before, new attractions were added to stimulate repeat business and encourage new audiences. The new acts were also designed to keep the public happy while the star attraction left the Wild West for a short visit home, returning in time for the London opening in May.

Bill wrote to sister Julia from Glasgow: 'Am sorry to say I am off again. I have got the Hay fever or Grippe or something, & being so worn out and so much to do & to think of its hard. I am now trying for new attractions to put in this place to fill my vacancy when I have to leave here for my trip home. I want to leave my company playing here while I am gone. . . . I am so anxious to get in a country where I can feel & see the Sun again . . . I expect to spend most of my time at the Ranch when I come.'

Ten weeks into the Scottish season, the *Glasgow Herald* carried an advertisement telling readers 'extraordinary additional attractions will be appended to the grand natural exhibition of *Buffalo Bill's Wild West* from Monday 18th January.'

It continued:

> First appearance in Scotland, Direct from the Continent
> And for the first time in the world's history in conjunction with
> the American Indian
> 30 Shulis Warriors and Amazons
> from the Interior of Darkest Africa
> And Lockhart's Six Burmese Elephants –
> The most perfectly trained animals of their kind.

'The Red men sent out Chief No Neck, Short Bull and Kicking Bear who met with three of the black chiefs and soon the two tribes were upon the most friendly terms.'

Anglo-American journalist and explorer, Henry Morton Stanley, had brought the dancing Shulis to Europe from Nzenza, an area north of Lake Victoria (now part of Uganda) and was anxious to find a performing venue for the troupe before shipping them home again. The *Glasgow Evening News* takes up the story in an article published on 16 January:

While preserving in its entirety the unique exhibition of Wild West scenes and doings, Buffalo Bill has decided on a novel additional attraction which will, if possible, make the show at Dennistoun, more acceptable to the public than ever and yesterday an impressive reception was given at the building by Colonel Cody to a large number of invited guests including many of the leading clergy, professions and others in the city. In addition to the large party of Indians who have been included in the camp, 30 Shulis warriors and amazons from darkest Africa have been added to the show and the most interesting part of the gathering yesterday was the witnessing of the meeting between the two races, the one from the extreme east and the other from the extreme west, a meeting which has, perhaps, never had parallel. The Red men sent out Chief No Neck, Short Bull and Kicking Bear who met with three of the black chiefs and soon the two tribes were upon the most friendly terms being

able to converse, after a fashion, with each other. The savages went through their various songs and dances before each other and friendliness reigned for the black men applauded the red men and vice-versa. The new departure in entertainment takes place on Monday and also includes Lockhart's six Burmese elephants who give an extraordinary performance, the huge animals acting like trained dogs or cats, exhibiting an intelligence which even in these days can only be classed as marvellous. The cowboys, too, will vary the entertainment by riding Texan steers and sabre exercises will be gone through by a detachment of English Lancers.

Annie Oakley in action wearing rehearsal clothes, observed admiringly by one of her many Indian friends, during a pre-show run-through in the Earls Court arena in 1892. (Denver Public Library)

The new attractions worked their magic on Scottish audiences and ensured that the Wild West played to good houses until the season closed at the end of February. Once again, the *Glasgow Herald* was there to witness the African tribe make their debut: 'These dark skinned eastern savages present a strange contrast to the haughty and noble looking Red Indian from the west, and they gave an exhibition of their native dances and songs. These were most acceptably and warmly received by the large audience. The grotesque looking dresses with beads, shields and spears gave a vividly realistic and true effect. All together the Wild West has been most popularly improved by these fresh performances.'

On 17 December, Indian interpreter George Crager borrowed a sheet of official Wild West stationery with Buffalo Bill's picture at the top and wrote a letter to 'Mr Paton, Curator' of Glasgow's 'Calvin Grove (*sic*) Museum'. Describing himself as 'in charge of Indians', Crager stated: 'Hearing that you are empowered to purchase relics for your museum, I would respectfully inform you that I have a collection of Indian relics (North American) which I will dispose of before we sail for America. Should you wish any of them after inspection I would be pleased to have you call at my Room at the East End Exhibition Building – Please answer when you can come.'

In December 1891, Indian interpreter George Crager wrote to 'Mr Paton, Curator' of Glasgow's 'Calvin Grove (sic) Museum', offering to sell Indian relics before sailing home to America. (Reproduced courtesy of Glasgow Museums: Art Gallery & Museum, Kelvingrove)

The curator of the Kelvingrove Museum arranged to meet Crager the following month. At the meeting Crager produced a box containing 28 different Native American artefacts, including a bloodstained, beige coloured cotton cloth shirt with a fringe decoration around the neck, cuffs and seams. A group of feathers was attached to the inside seam at each elbow and there were more feathers and some fur around the throat. Crager claimed the shirt had been 'blessed by Short Bull, the High Priest of the Messiah' and that it had been ripped from the back of a fallen warrior after the massacre at Wounded Knee Creek. The 'ghost shirt' was said to have shielded whoever wore it from bullets, but gave no protection when the 7th Cavalry opened fire slaughtering hundreds of Sioux, including the shirt's original owner.

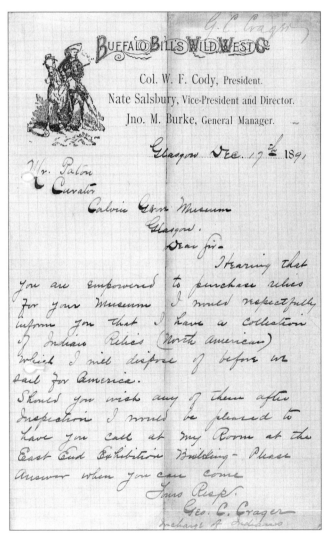

He also produced a head-dress made from feathers and horsehair, purses made from buckskin and decorated with beads, some arrows, a decorative canvas shield claimed to have once been owned by Chief Lone Bull, a pair of ornamented buckskin leggings, beaded moccasins and a woven baby's cradle.

When asked to whom the artefacts belonged, Crager stated they were from his own collection and he could do with them as he wished. He accepted £40 from Mr Paton for fourteen artefacts. The museum's own archives record that Crager 'donated' a further fourteen items.

Indians in the company would have been alarmed if they had ever learned that their interpreter had sold native artefacts without consulting them, particularly the 'ghost dance' shirt, which, they claimed, acted as a spiritual link with its original owner.

It was never clear who the rightful owners of the property might have been. Were they Crager's own property or did he steal the shirt as a souvenir from an Indian lying slain on Wounded Knee's snow-covered ground while visiting the site as a frontier reporter? Had some of the artefacts once been the property of Paul Eagle Star, who had died in Sheffield Infirmary while holding on to Crager's hand?

Shortly afterwards, various members of the company returned to the United States. George Crager never again worked for Buffalo Bill's Wild West.

While the animals were put into winter quarters and some members of the Wild West appeared in British variety theatres during March and April 1892, Bill returned home to try and make sense of what was happening at Scout's Rest Ranch in North Platte.

Arta, who had travelled to England with Bill on his first visit, was now married. Lulu encouraged the newlyweds to take over the running of the ranch, even though Arta's husband, Horton Boal, had little experience of working on such a large property. Bill was worried that a change of management would put his sister Julia and her husband Al Goodman on to the street after successfully running the spread for six years. The Goodmans eventually moved back to their Kansas ranch, but a bad winter ruined their crops and they were forced to move in with their son Ed – one of Bill's original programme sellers in England – in Denver.

Family arguments made Bill glad to be on the high seas heading for England once again.

Family arguments probably made Bill glad to be on the high seas heading for England once again, and in mid-April 1892, he was back at Earls Court with Nate Salsbury, re-creating the scene of their earlier Jubilee triumph.

In London, Shulis warriors from Africa were replaced by Cossack horsemen from the Russian Caucasus and a team of Gauchos from the Pampas grasslands of Argentina.

The Cossacks, under the leadership of Prince Ivan Rostomov Macheradse, were hired on the recommendation of entertainment agent, C.M. Ercole, who negotiated with the Russian government to bring them to England. In the show they would present a 12-minute act in which they performed breathtaking acrobatic feats on lithe steppes horses – a programme to rival Bill's own company of skilled western roughriders.

The Gauchos, wearing Spanish-style costumes including tremendous cotton pantaloons and colt-skin boots, performed a comedy-style act riding wild bucking horses which they would deliberately fall from and then chase their steeds around the giant arena, jumping back into their saddles while the horses charged at full gallop. It was funny to watch, but required expert horsemen to accomplish.

In place of an American Exhibition as a next-door supporting attraction, the Wild West was to appear alongside the International Horticultural Exhibition – 'an exhibition devoted mainly to the illustration of the various phases of the horticultural arts, and to bring together in one grand display not only the representative styles of different countries as they exist today, but reproductions of English and foreign gardens of former periods', stated publicity material. 'The Yankeeries' had given way to 'The Floweries'.

London was again covered with posters featuring images of Bill's face and scenes from his adventures. Major Burke went to work on his old London newspaper contacts to ensure that the 1892 event received almost as much build-up as that generated in 1887.

The Wild West's 'positive farewell after a triumphant five years' campaign on two continents' opened as 'the Mecca of the Citizens of the Metropolis for the summer of '92' on Saturday 7 May 1892.

The royal box at Earls Court was re-built and put in regular use throughout the six-month long London season. The Prince and Princess of Wales, their children and visiting dignitaries were again regular visitors.

There was little sign that the public had become tired of cowboys and Indians, apart from a *Punch* cartoon (below) showing an exhausted looking buffalo and a bronco horse standing in front of tents at the Wild West camp. The caption reads:

The Wild West's 'positive farewell' tour opened on 7 May 1892. *Punch* greeted it with a certain weary cynicism, but the public seemed happy.

Old Buffer: 'Ugh! I'm tired to death of being hunted. Blessed if I'll run away from those blank cartridges again!'
Bronco: 'Yes, you bet! And I've made up my mind to quit bucking. Its perfectly sickening having to do it from year's end to year's end!'

To promote their second London season in May 1892, Bill and Salsbury printed 100,000 copies of the *Wild West Courier*. The four-page broadsheet include excerpts from glowing press reviews from 'The Buffalo Billeries' first UK tour. (Alan Gallop)

Bill also printed 100,000 copies of his own newspaper, the *Wild West Courier*, written by Major Burke and handed out free to passers-by buying evening newspapers on London's busy streets. The four-page broadsheet 'advertorial' featured a busy masthead depicting episodes in the life of Buffalo Bill. The contents included excerpts from glowing press reviews written when the company was last in London. The International Horticultural Exhibition also received mention in a half page article, written in glowing prose which could only have been composed by Major Burke. The article, waxing lyrical about the peace and tranquillity which can only be experienced in a garden, appeared next to a gory drawing of Bill scalping Yellow Hand, blood pouring from the Indian's head and lifted scalp – the perfect signal to draw the crowds to Earls Court for a second dose of 'The Buffalo Billeries'.

In June 1892 a message was delivered to the 'Pahaska Tepee' at Earls Court from Queen Victoria's Equerry, General Sir Henry Ponsonby, stating that 'Her Majesty will be highly honoured if the Wild West Managers could make it convenient to let their Cossack riders come to Windsor and show their wonderful proficiency on horseback to Her Majesty, members of her family and the Royal Household.'

Nate Salsbury later recalled: 'This polite request was constructed, as it always is in England, to be a mild sort of command. . . . As the Cossacks only consumed about twelve minutes in their performance, I concluded that, no matter how startling it would be, it would hardly compensate for all the trouble of getting them down to Windsor, so I determined to take the whole outfit, and do something worthy of the occasion.'

Salsbury immediately swung into action and on Saturday 25 June chartered a special train plus a dozen passenger and freight carriages – paid for by Queen Victoria – 'and loaded enough of our outfit to give a representative performance, leaving enough members of the company in London to satisfy the public, which was easily done, when it was explained to the afternoon audience that Colonel Cody had gone to Windsor by Royal Command.'

Salsbury arrived in Windsor ahead of the company and reported to Colonel McNeill, the Queen's duty equerry, who showed the American producer around the castle grounds allowing him to pick any large open space he wished for the royal show. Salsbury selected a spot opposite the east terrace on a place formerly known as the Prince's Recreation Ground where Prince Albert had once played cricket with his children. It was now used for occasional garden parties.

Staff from the royal household began to improvise a large oval-shaped arena for the Wild West on the lawn, using small moveable rail fences borrowed from one of

Prince Ivan with his Ukrainian Cossacks who performed alongside cowboys and Indians during the 1892 British season. (Denver Public Library)

Queen Victoria's nearby farms. While this took place, a large marquee was being erected at the other end of the lawn in which a lavish buffet would be served to the company.

A canvas pavilion for Queen Victoria and her guests overlooking the arena was created on a promenade along the castle's battlements. A carpet was spread over the stone paving and a number of comfortable chairs brought out. A stone stairway led down to the area soon to represent the American frontier, now transferred to the grounds of the Queen of England's castle in the heart of Berkshire.

News that Buffalo Bill, his Wild West company, horses and buffalo would be arriving in Windsor was not made public, but word spread through the town that something special was planned up at the castle that afternoon – and whatever 'it' was, 'it' would be arriving at Riverside station by train at lunchtime. Either a gossipy 'insider' from the royal household or a railway official sending word down the South Western Railway track from London finally gave the game away. Official confirmation that Buffalo Bill was on his way to Windsor arrived when a detachment of mounted guardsmen and other foot soldiers marched down the hill to the station. A mass of men, women and children followed them. By the time the 'Buffalo Bill Special' pulled in, both the platform and street winding up to the castle was thronged with excited people.

A Russian Cossack stands in the dirt road at the Wild West Camp. Cowboys used the rectangular tents on the right while larger tepees on the left housed over 80 Indians travelling with the company that season. The tent on the far right is the entrance to Buffalo Bill's 'Pahaska Tepee'. The large building with a roof behind is the rear outside wall of the spectators' arena. (Denver Public Library)

Hundreds cheered as Bill, riding his white horse 'Billy', led the company up the hill and through the castle gates. Word was sent that the Wild West 'awaited Her Majesty's pleasure' and shortly afterwards Queen Victoria arrived in her pony carriage and took her seat on the promenade along with Prince and Princess Christian, Prince Henry and Princess Beatrice of Battenburg and their children Princess Victoria of Schleswig-Holstein and the Prince of Leiningen. Also present were assorted Generals, Major Generals, Majors, Colonels, Admirals, Countesses, Right Honourable Gentlemen and Ladies, plus the Dean of Windsor and over 20 other members of Victoria's Court at Windsor. The *Windsor & Eton Express* reported that: 'The Queen had also very kindly allowed the Castle and park servants and their families to see the performance.'

Salsbury prepared to give the signal to began and later reported that at this point Major Burke 'let his hair down, and we knew the afternoon was bound to be a success, for whenever the Major let his hair down the world stood in awe.'

Queen Victoria requested that someone connected with the show should join the royal party on the battlements to explain anything she might not understand. Salsbury volunteered and was escorted 'with much ceremony' to the royal presence. He later wrote:

A mounted British Lancer carries a Union Jack around the arena, followed by Indians in a section of the show celebrating horsemanship from around the world. (Denver Public Library)

Don't suppose for an instant that I look back on that experience with any but feelings of respect and admiration, for the methodical conduct of the whole affair. While there was much ceremony, there was also much courtesy shown to us. As I entered the pavilion, I removed my hat, as any gentleman would do in the presence of ladies in an enclosed place. After I was introduced to the Queen, I gave the signal to begin, and took my place beside the Queen's place as Scout, Guide and Interpreter for the occasion. Noticing that I was standing, and uncovered, Her Majesty said, 'Mr Salsbury, please put on your hat, as I feel a strong draught here, and please take a chair.'

'Your Majesty', said I, 'I am very comfortable.'

'But I would be more comfortable if you would take a chair.'

The Queen appeared interested in everything she saw and plied Salsbury with one question after another about what was taking place on her lawn. When Bill took centre stage to shoot glass balls thrown into the air by an Indian, she asked Salsbury about the 'arm' he was using. 'He is using a Winchester rifle, Madam,' said Salsbury, 'an American firearm.'

'Ah, a very effective weapon, and in very effective hands,' replied the Queen.

At the point in the performance where Cossacks were performing tricks on horseback Prince Henry of Battenburg said to the Queen in German: 'Mamma, do

Rising above a giant painted panorama of hills and mountains are the chimneys of houses bordering the Wild West arena at Earls Court. In the foreground, Bill and his horse 'Billy' pose for Mr Dresser's camera with other members of the company. The same houses still stand in Eardley Crescent today. (Denver Public Library)

you think they are really Cossack?' Before the Queen had time to reply, Salsbury – a fluent speaker of German, French and Spanish – replied: 'I beg to assure you, sir, that everything and everybody you see in the entertainment are exactly what we represent it or them to be.'

The Queen turned to the Prince and said: 'I think we had better speak English for the rest of the afternoon.' Salsbury takes up the story: 'Princess Beatrice, who was sitting besides the Queen, was much amused at her husband's discomfiture, and smilingly said to him, "Mon Cherie, vous avez reçu' votre premiere leçon americaine." I immediately replied, "Oh Madame, j'espère non." At this there was a general laugh, which I wish Burke could have heard, for he could have used the incident in his own way in his description of the affair.'

When the show was over, the Queen called for Bill and Major Burke to be presented to her, and after thanking Salsbury for helping her enjoy the Wild West once again, she rose to greet the star of the show as he climbed the stone stairs, still wearing buckskins and spurs. She complimented him highly for his work that afternoon and told her she had enjoyed every moment.

As was always her custom, Queen Victoria retired to write up her journal. That evening she recorded:

Bill (centre), the Cossacks (left) and Indians (right) at Windsor Castle to entertain the Queen for the afternoon, June 1892. (Denver Public Library)

We went on to the East Terrace, & watched from a tent, open in front, a sort of 'Buffalo Bill' performance, on the lawn below. It was extremely well arranged, & an excellent representation of what we had also seen 5 years ago at Earls Court. There were Cow Boys, Red Indians, Mexicans, Argentinos taking part, & then a wonderful riding display by Cossacks, accompanied by curious singing, & a war dance by the Indians. There were extraordinary buck jumping horses, shooting at glass balls by Col: Cody (Buffalo Bill), & display of cracking huge whips. The whole was a very pretty wild sight, which lasted an hour. At the conclusion of the performance, all advanced in line at a gallop & stopped suddenly. Col: Cody was brought up for me to speak to him. He is still a very handsome man, but has now got a grey beard.

While the Wild West company tucked into a feast fit for a King (or a Queen) prepared by the royal kitchens, Bill and Salsbury were invited to the Equerry's private apartment for lunch. Bill had taken the pledge (again) that summer, and politely refused a glass of wine. Salsbury, a life-long teetotaller, recorded: 'We compromised by another act of self-sacrifice on my part . . . I did duty for both of us in a glass of wine. The whole thing was delightfully informal, and wound up by our each being presented with a memento of the occasion in the Queen's name. Cody received a beautiful watch charm, and I was complimented with a scarf pin, set in diamonds, and bearing the Royal monogram.'

On the railway journey back to London in time for the evening performance at Earls Court, Salsbury reflected that: 'The higher you ascend the social scale in England, the more delightful do you find the surroundings. . . . Of course there was ceremony, but it was the purely perfunctory kind that goes with all court proceedings in Europe, or for that matter in all monarchies.'

Newspapers reported that London was suffering from 'a plague' of scarlet fever. . . .

Tragedy struck the Indians at Buffalo Bill's London Wild West Camp twice more in the summer of 1892.

Newspapers at the time reported that London was suffering from what the *Evening News* described as 'a plague' of scarlet fever and pneumonia, which daily claimed the lives of both young and old in the city. One of the oldest Indian members of the Wild West company was Schongamaoneta Haska, also known as Long Wolf, who was 59 years old when he contracted the disease.

Long Wolf had grown up at Wounded Knee in the shadow of Dakota's Black Hills, an area conceded to the Indians by a land and peace treaty signed in 1868. The old Indian had been a signatory of the treaty, although his name was wrongly translated as High Wolf. The US government, the railway companies, the army and eastern settlers all ignored the treaty, leading to decades of warrior campaigns – known as the Indian wars – and eventually the white man smashed the Sioux nation into defeat.

It is believed that Long Wolf was a sub-Chief to either Chief Crazy Horse or the fearsome warrior known as Man-Afraid-Of-His-Horse, and was a Scout prepared to fight at the battlefront – which is probably how he received his name. He is known to have taken part in the Battle of Little Big Horn and the defeat of Custer and the 7th Cavalry in 1876.

Schongamaoneta Haska – also known as Long Wolf – who was aged 59 when he died of the scarlet fever and pneumonia which was daily claiming the lives of London's young and old in 1892. (Denver Public Library)

He joined Buffalo Bill's Wild West in 1886 with his wife, Wants, and daughter Lizzie Long Wolf. It was a means of escaping confinement, poverty and near-starvation on their reservation. His first season for Bill was at Staten Island and they were part of the company chosen to visit England in 1887/8. By 1892, Long Wolf and his family were Wild West veterans, having performed all over the US East Coast, across Europe and twice in England.

Bill liked Long Wolf and the old Indian felt the same about the man he called 'Pahaska,' even though he had to participate in re-enactments of scenes he had actually once been part of, including twice-daily recreations of the Battle of Little Big Horn.

When Long Wolf and another Indian became ill at the Wild West camp, the resident Medicine Man was called, but could do nothing for them. Scarlet fever was beyond the Medicine Man's magic, and camp medical officer, Dr Maitland Coffin – whose services had been retained for a second time – was charged with carefully checking the health of every single company member throughout the epidemic. The last thing the Wild West managers wanted was more deaths on the Barcelona scale and medical attention was on hand at Earls Court day and night. A canvas medical centre containing beds and a fully equipped surgery for Dr Coffin was established, and the doctor made daily rounds of all tents and tepees checking the health of everyone involved in the show.

Doctor Coffin arranged for the two sick Indians to be transferred to the West London Hospital, Hammersmith, on 5 June 1892, where the fever could be contained and there would be no danger of passing the illness to others in the company.

The second Indian responded to treatment, but Long Wolf's health deteriorated after he developed pneumonia. He told his wife and daughter that he wanted to return home to die among his people in his ancestral lands, but he was too ill to be moved. The old Indian knew he was going to end his life in a strange land. He asked for a pencil and paper and drew a picture of a wolf, with instructions that the picture should be reproduced on his headstone marking his 'temporary' resting place. As he slipped into unconsciousness, he whispered that he hoped his remains might be returned to his native land one day.

Long Wolf died on 11 June – the same day as the second Indian was discharged, fully recovered – and preparations were made to transfer his body back to the Wild West Camp for ritual ceremonies before burial. While examining Long Wolf's body, Dr Coffin noted that he was covered in sabre cuts and gunshot wounds – permanent reminders of the Indian's encounters with white men while defending the land his people had inhabited for centuries.

Arrangements were made to bury Long Wolf in Earls Court's local graveyard at Brompton cemetery, London's most fashionable and crowded burial place. His resting place would reflect his status as a Chief and eventually be marked with a tall stone cross – unlike the 'common grave' without any marker in which Paul Eagle Star lay buried two hundred yards away. He would also share the earth in his resting-place with tens of thousands of palefaces, including scores of eminent Victorians, many laid to rest in large Gothic mausoleums, others in the shadow of Greco-Roman columns.

Bill paid £23 for the plot, a large sum in Victorian times when an average worker earned just £1 per week. A 13 ft deep grave was prepared and his funeral took place at 10.30 a.m. on the morning of 13 June when Bill walked through the gates of the cemetery across the road from the Wild West showground at the head of a large and solemn procession. Six handpicked Indians, wearing full ceremonial face paint and eagle feathered bonnets, carried Long Wolf's coffin behind him. They entered the cemetery gates slowly in time to the single beat of a deerskin drum.

Bill liked Long Wolf and the old Indian felt the same about the man he called 'Pahaska'.

A pen and ink sketch from an unknown London newspaper of Long Wolf's burial at Brompton cemetery, near Earls Court, 13 June 1892. An Anglican clergyman reads the burial service over the coffin, watched by Bill and his Indians.

Walking behind the coffin were the rest of the company, headed by 'Little Big Man' Nate Salsbury with Long Wolf's widow and daughter, the rest of the Indians, cowboys, Mexicans, Cossacks, roustabouts and a large slice of London society now associating itself with Buffalo Bill's Wild West.

A clergyman read prayers over the coffin while a shaman or medicine man prayed in the Sioux language. The Cowboy Band played hymns and then Long Wolf was lowered into the ground and the deep hole filled with London clay.

Two months later the grave was re-opened to admit a second Indian lying in a small coffin which was placed on top of Long Wolf's. This contained a 20-month-old Indian girl called White Star Ghost Dog, whose parents were also part of the Wild West company. In the section of the show known as 'Life Customs of the Indians', depicting Indian life on the plains, White Star was placed in a saddlebag slung across the back of a horse and paraded around the arena with other small children from the camp. On 12 August, White Star fell from the saddlebag and landed on her head. Both Dr Coffin and the Medicine Man were called – but neither could do anything to save the life of the tiny child. Later that evening the child died in a tepee at the Wild West camp, amid much wailing from the Indians.

White Star's father, Ghost Dog, pleaded with Bill not to allow his infant daughter to be left to wander alone with strange spirits beneath the earth of a foreign land. Bill and Salsbury obtained permission from the authorities to open

White Star's father pleaded with Bill not to allow his daughter to wander alone with strange spirits beneath the earth of a foreign land.

Long Wolf's grave to admit a second coffin lowered on top of the Chief's. The spirits of the old man and the infant could then keep each other company until the time came for them to be brought home to their native soil and their spirits set free.

The authorities agreed and on 19 August the small coffin containing White Star was lowered into the deep hole and rested on top of that containing Long Wolf. After it was filled, a tall stone cross was erected. On it was inscribed:

'Chief Long Wolf, North American Indian with Buffalo Bill's Wild West Co. Died June 11th 1892, aged 59 years. Also Star, who died August 12th, 1892, aged 20 months.'

Carved on the stonework was the figure of a wolf, included as one of the old Chief's two last wishes. It would be a further 105 years before his second wish, to return home to be buried among his people, would be granted.

Annie Oakley continued attracting audiences to Earls Court in her own right – especially gentlemen admirers, unaware that 'Little Sure Shot' was really Mrs Annie Butler. Letters of proposal from fans wanting to meet and marry Annie arrived at her tent at the Wild West camp each week. One was from a young man claiming that he had not missed one of Annie's twice-daily performances since the company had returned to London. She later recalled that he had written to tell her 'that I was the one little girl he could ever love and that he had never dreamed until that day that there was another in my life. He said he was leaving for South Africa as he could not keep away from the show if he remained in London.'

The distinguished American artist, Frederic Remington, visited the Wild West in London in 1892 to produce sketches and write accompanying text for *Harper's Weekly*. He is pictured here (centre) strolling with Nate Salisbury (left) and Major Burke (right). (Earls Court/Olympia Archive)

A month later 'a woman of breeding came to call. She was the mother of this boy. She looked at me, kissed me, and said, "I knew that my boy would never love any girl who was not of the highest type."'

Another letter arrived from a Welshman, containing his photograph. 'He had seen me shoot. Would I marry him? He had a little money and guessed that I had saved up some. "Yours until death us do part, your Darling Ducky." If I had been a spinster of 80, toothless and had long since lost my last chance of connubial felicity, I could not have said "yes" after one look at that printed chin.

'I asked my husband to come to the arena with his rifle and hold the photograph for me. He held it by one corner while I sent a .22 bullet through the place where brains should have been. I then wrote across the narrow chest of the rest of the picture, "Respectfully Declined" and off it went.'

The distinguished American artist, Frederic Remington, visited the Wild West in London to produce sketches of Earls Court activity and write an accompanying story for *Harper's Weekly*. His first impression of London life was that before visiting the Tower of London, Houses of Parliament and Westminster Abbey, everyone wanted to visit the Wild West.

At present everyone knows where it is, from the gentleman in Piccadilly to the dirtiest coster in the remotest slum of Whitechapel. The cabman may have to scratch his head to recall places where the traveller desires to go, but when the Wild West is asked for, he gathers his reins and uncoils his whip without ceremony. One should no longer ride the deserts of Texas or the rugged uplands of Wyoming to see the Indians and pioneers, but should go to London.

Remington also told his American readers that the Wild West:

. . . was the evolution of a great idea. It is a great educator, and with its aggregate of wonders from out of the way places, it will represent a poetical and harmless protest against the Derby hat and starched linen – those horrible badges of the slavery of our modern social system, when men are physical lay figures, and mental and moral cog-wheels and wastes of uniformity – where the great crime is to be individual and the unpardonable sin is to be out of fashion.

Salsbury invested some of his Wild West profits into other large-scale theatrical ventures, which proved less than successful in America. The remainder of his fortune went into creating a fine home for his family near the beach in New Jersey, while Bill sank huge sums into any venture which seemed like a good idea at the time.

By 1892, Bill's North Platte ranch had become one of the most successful in Nebraska; and while in England that year, he began to consider other investment opportunities. Perhaps it was the high cost of chartering railway locomotives and scores of carriages to move the Wild West from place to place, or recognition of a real investment opportunity, which prompted both Bill and Salsbury to consider building their own British railway network in the summer of 1892.

Annie Oakley was always
careful with her money, but
enjoyed buying fashionable
clothing from London's top
dressmakers and milliners.
She is pictured here in London
wearing one of her smart
new outfits and her prized
gold medal around the collar,
awarded on 11 June 1887 by
members of the Notting Hill
Gun Club. The medal – 'larger
than a five shilling piece' – was
engraved with a view of the
club's headquarters on one side
and Annie's name and the date
on the reverse. (The American
Collection)

Using fast-moving trains to travel between engagements was nothing new to the
Wild West. Salsbury had been using America's rapidly growing railway network to
transport the enterprise from one state to another for several years. In 1890, Max
Eberhard Schmidt, a Chicago businessman in need of funds to create new railway
links between eastern American cities and new communities springing up in the
west, approached Bill and Salsbury. Schmidt's company, the Multiple Speed and
Traction Company, needed an inexhaustible supply of investors to keep their ideas
afloat – and large railway users seemed like favourable investors.

Bill and Salsbury were too busy touring their show to pay attention to Schmidt's ideas. But the cost of transporting the Wild West around Britain in 1891–2 on 'Buffalo Bill Express' trains made the partners realise how much money could be generated by enterprising private railway companies, still in their infancy and funded by rich entrepreneurs. They realised that public demand for rail travel was growing and new routes were needed.

Schmidt was in England in 1892 taking a closer look at privately owned railway systems, attempting to raise capital to develop new branch lines outside of London. He was so confident of success that he took out a patent – number 18,622 – to develop single track lines between main line railway networks and towns not yet connected by railway services.

A contract signed in London on 8 July 1892 between 'The Multiple Speed and Traction Company and Col. W.F. Cody and others' to construct 'Buffalo Bill' railway lines linked to main line British railway tracks. The project failed to progress any further than the initial contract signing. (Bryan Mickleburgh Collection)

Schmidt visited the 'Pahaska Tepee' at Earls Court to pitch his idea of a 'Buffalo Bill Line' to the Wild West bosses. He explained that new branch lines in England would be more viable than in the United States because shorter cross-country routes would produce a faster return on investment than lengthy routes crossing America's mountains, plains and deserts.

Schmidt introduced Bill and Salsbury to Henry Dodson, a City of London financier, who had already successfully invested in railway projects. Dodson was anxious to join other investors in financing new networks and was delighted to enter into partnership with the famous Buffalo Bill.

A syndicate to build a 'Buffalo Bill Line' linked to main line track owned by a private railway company was created between the Multiple Speed and Traction Company and 'Col. William F. Cody and others' (Salsbury and Dodson), using Schmidt's railway patent licence. It was stated that an estimated sum of £12,000 was required to lay track on a route determined by Multiple Speed. The eight-page document (see page 204), containing twelve separate clauses, was signed by Bill, Salsbury, Dodson and Schmidt and their legal witnesses on 8 July 1892 at the offices of Messrs Foss & Ledsam, at 3, Abchurch Lane, London EC.

The agreement stated that Schmidt would be paid £500 immediately upon signing and once an operational line was completed and revenue matching the £12,000 development costs generated from trains using the track, he would be paid 10 per cent of future profits. The document insisted that accounts be carefully recorded and made freely available for Schmidt's inspection at 'any reasonable time during business hours by the representatives of the company appointed for this purpose'.

The legal document stated that Multiple Speed would send its chief engineer from Chicago 'to superintend construction and installation of the said railroad and plant', and paid a monthly salary of £75, plus all travelling and living expenses by the Cody–Salsbury–Dodson syndicate.

It was agreed that once the Buffalo Bill Line was completed, the syndicate could purchase the property outright for the sum of £100,000 – half to be paid into Multiple Speed's Chicago bank account and the balance in either negotiable bills of exchange or promissory notes made out to Schmidt.

The contract permitted further Buffalo Bill Lines to be constructed in England, provided the first track was installed to Multiple Speed's satisfaction and additional royalties paid to Schmidt at the rate of £500 per mile 'or fraction of a mile on which a car is run on single track'.

It is not known what became of the Buffalo Bill Line, the Multiple Speed and Traction Company, Schmidt or Dodson. The line was never built, and the Wild West ended up paying privately-owned British railway companies thousands of pounds in rental fees for trains, carriages and the privilege of running them on someone else's tracks.

The Wild West ended up paying British railway companies thousands of pounds for trains, carriages and the privilege of running them on someone else's tracks.

The railway exercise was a waste of Bill's time and money – and the beginning of a series of financial disasters and business failures that would hang over the head of Buffalo Bill Cody for the rest of his life.

The Wild West sailed from London's Tilbury Docks on the American steamship *Mohawk*, leaving their popular British orator, Henry Marsh Clifford, behind. The actor was offered the chance to sail with the rest of the company and continue acting as master of ceremonies with the Wild West in the United States. But Clifford pined for the legitimate theatre once again and had accepted a leading part in a play at London's Drury Lane with the Augustus Harris Company. Clifford spent the rest of his life appearing in Shakespeare, comedies, tragedies and pantomimes in London and regional theatres and was fondly known to theatrical friends for the rest of his life as 'The Foghorn' and 'Buffalo Bill's Man'.

The *Mohawk* landed at Jersey City to the usual tumultuous welcome. The cowboys led their horses down the gangplank, Bill holding the reins of Billy, the horse he had appeared with before tens of thousands of people across continental Europe and Great Britain. Billy also appeared with Bill on Wild West show posters plastered across a thousand walls from Munich to Manchester.

As Bill stepped on to the quayside, Billy fell to the ground and was pronounced dead, Buffalo Bill's second horse to die after a long sea voyage from England. Major Burke later wrote: 'However small it may seem, this pathetic incident will always be remembered by the returning voyagers, as Billy and Charley were favourite members of the "Old Guard".'

Act Four Scene One

POSITIVELY, DEFINITELY AND PERHAPS THE FINAL FAREWELL

You bet I know him, pardner, he ain't no circus fraud.
He's Western born and Western bred, if he has been late abroad;
I knew him in the days way back, beyond Missouri's flow,
When the country round was nothing but a huge Wild Western Show.
When the Injuns were as thick as fleas, and the man who ventured through
The sand hills of Nebraska had to fight the hostile Sioux;
Those were hot times, I tell you; and we all remember still,
The days when Cody was a scout, and all the men knew Bill.

William E. Annin – February 1891

A BROADWAY FLOP – VIOLA CLEMMONS MARRIES A PLAYBOY – A TOWN
CALLED CODY – THE CAMPO BONITO GOLD MINE – A CONGRESS OF ROUGH
RIDERS OF THE WORLD – SALSBURY BOWS OUT – ENTER JAMES M. BAILEY –
ANNIE OAKLEY INJURED IN TRAIN CRASH – LONDON AND OLYMPIA – DEATH
OF NATE SALSBURY – A LONDON CHILD RECALLS THE WILD WEST – INJURED
ON TOUR – THE WETTEST WEATHER FOR A CENTURY – 'MOVING PICTURES'

Chicago's Columbian Exposition – a six-months-long, open-air world's fair – notched up another success for Buffalo Bill. Viola Clemmons' American stage debut in *A Lady of Venice* was another failure.

For months New York's theatregoers had been promised an opportunity to see Viola Clemmons in person in a suitable vehicle which would show off the acting talents she had mastered in England. Whether or not New York playgoers actually wanted to see Viola is debatable, but popular newspapers, including the *New York Times*, led their readers to believe that her metropolitan debut would be sensational and similar to that made by Henry Irving and Ellen Terry years before.

Using Bill's money, A *Lady of Venice* was booked to open at the Fifth Avenue theatre on 12 February 1894. On the run-up to opening night, Viola was photographed modelling some of the expensive gowns she would wear in the production. The pictures appeared in most of the New York popular dailies. Stories appeared about duels that had been fought for Viola's hand by various suitors and how she had been thrown by the horse while appearing in England, but carried on performing like a trouper.

It had also not gone unnoticed 'that Miss Clemmons owes her fame and position on the stage to the faith and money of Mr Buffalo Bill who is her backer. Doubtless he thinks she has genius and he has done all can for her'. On the eve of her opening night the *New York Times* proclaimed: 'Her beauty has been so loudly and persistently proclaimed that well-seasoned playgoers tremble at the mention of her name.'

An advertisement in the same newspaper promised that *A Lady of Venice* would be 'the greatest production ever put on the stage'. Audiences were promised 'grand Venetian scenery, handsome costumes and working gondolas on the Grand Canal'.

The opening night of *A Lady of Venice* coincided with a blizzard raging over New York. The Fifth Avenue theatre, however, was packed to the rafters with expectant playgoers. The following day's *New York Times* review sounded the death-knell for the play:

'She has an interesting face, a large quantity of pale hair, a large mouth which is generally wide open and a full set of very handsome teeth.'

The threat of the first appearance of Miss Clemmons as a star actress has been hanging over New York for nearly a year. In that period, the amiable portion of the press has been worked industriously on her behalf. . . . Those persons who braved the terrors of a blizzard to go to the Fifth Avenue theatre found that she is not so hard to bear after all. To be sure, Miss Clemmons is scarcely an actress in respect to art. That she is an actress in respect to trade is undeniable for she has learned to speak the words of a part on the public stage with some appropriate gestures and poses. She is self-possessed and graceful in a heavy sort of way. Her beauty has been over advertised in advance. Sanguine folks found that the advance plans and specifications of Miss Clemmons were misleading. Yet the croakers were actually agreeably disappointed for she is, to quote Joe Gargery, 'a fine figure of a woman.' She has an interesting face, a large quantity of pale hair, a large mouth which is generally wide open and a full set of very handsome teeth. Although she has no large share of dramatic aptitude and has probably little stage experience, her actions are not restricted and positively awkward.

The paper said the play had been written 'in antique, bombastic black verse and this is spoken very badly by Miss Clemmons and most of her associates'. Theatre lovers were warned that printed copies of the play 'can be bought for the reasonable sum of 15 cents. That is probably what Mr Buffalo Bill paid for the play – unless he was badly fooled.'

On the morning after the opening night Viola sent a telegraph to Bill in Chicago: 'Play roasted. Company roasted. I more than roasted.' Viola's starring vehicles on both sides of the Atlantic were said to have cost Bill $50,000, but had turned her into 'a name' and other parts in other productions followed. All of them were critical and box office failures. Later Bill was heard to comment: 'I would rather manage a million Indians than one soubrette.'

A Lady of Venice closed at the end of the following week and was replaced by Viola Clemmons in another starring vehicle, *Mrs Dascot* – 'a 4-act society drama' by General Lloyd S. Bryce and Stanislaus Strange. Fortunately Bill had no part in financing this 'comedy drama of the present day, with a young wife, an old husband and a young and fascinating lover.' It was just as well. The New

York critics universally panned the piece, about which the New York Times complained: 'A worse piece has rarely beed inflicted on first nighters. Not only was its subject hideous but the treatment was clumsy, unimaginable and inexpert beyond reason.

Mrs Dascot closed four nights later and effectively ended Viola Clemmons' theatrical career, its only claim to fame now being that it helped to launch the career of Maurice Barrymore — father of John, Lionel and Ethel, later known as Broadway's 'first family of the theatre'.

Viola stayed on in America, later marrying a rich young Wall Street playboy called Howard Gould, whom she had first met when the Wild West was appearing on Staten Island. Gould, president of nine railway companies and a director of the Western Union Company, was a friend of Bill's. An expert horseman, he liked to visit the Wild West camp to ride Bill's famous horse, Isham and spend time with the cowboys. One day while Gould was trotting Isham around the arena, Viola arrived on the scene and enquired who the handsome young rider might be. When told that his name was Howard Gould, she asked if he was related to the late Jay Gould, head of one of America's richest families. When she discovered that he was, indeed, of the same family, the object of her affections suddenly shifted from the ageing showman to the young playboy.

Gould was flattered by her attentions and, when he crossed the Atlantic with a group of friends for a grand tour of Europe, Viola followed him. Racy and sensational stories about their time together in Europe started appearing in popular newspapers, much to Bill's embarrassment. He was aware that Mrs Cody also read the newspapers and that a great deal of harm was being done to the name and reputation of Buffalo Bill.

Shortly after their return, and much against the Gould family's wishes, Howard and Viola were married in a private service at New York's fashionable Holland House hotel. No members of the bridegroom's wealthy family were present, although Viola's mother, Mrs J.W. Dayan (she had re-married after her first husband died) attended the ceremony and told the *New York Times* that her daughter would now give up the stage 'in deference to Mr Gould's wishes — not because he has any objections to the theatrical profession, but simply because it is unnecessary for my daughter to continue working'. The newlyweds left for honeymoon on Gould's private racing yacht, *Niagara*.

 Despite losing a small fortune in the theatrical disasters, Bill continued investing in projects he believed in, especially those on the Great Plains where he felt he could earn a second fortune while making the region prosperous at the same time. In the 1890s when he was said to be worth $3 million, Bill backed his judgement by buying up a large parcel of empty green and fertile land in the Big Horn basin of northwest Wyoming and for a second time attempted to build a town. Other investors agreed to construct saloons, homes, trading posts and dig irrigation ditches. The spot, on a bend in the Shoshone River and near the gateway to Yellowstone National Park, was named Cody after its famous founder.

In the 1890s when he was said to be worth $3 million, Bill for a second time attempted to build a town.

The Burlington Railroad Company was persuaded to construct a railway line to Cody and the government built a main road linking the town to Yellowstone. Brochures were printed promoting Cody as a 'Colossal Pleasure Garden of Entrancing Scenic Revelations'. People bought land and built homes. Bill built a two-storey hotel out of sandstone and named it 'The Irma', after his youngest daughter, installing a huge mirror from France to decorate its 36 ft long cherrywood lounge bar. Cody, Wyoming, became a boom town, with schools, churches and its own weekly newspaper. Nephew Ed Goodman became the new town's first postmaster.

For his own corner of peace and quiet, Bill purchased more land further along the Shoshone and built a ranch, called the TE, named after the cattle brand carried by his herd brought into Wyoming from South Dakota. A whitewashed lodge building was constructed to house his friends – cowboys, Indians, politicians, celebrities, writers and artists.

Later he would also pay for a large, two-storey lodge to be built from hewn logs, called the 'Pahaska Tepee' – or 'Long Hair's Lodge'. Bill believed that Yellowstone Park and the spectacular Wapiti Valley nearby would become a tourist attraction and visitors would want to stay in quality accommodation offering traditional western hospitality.

Using his share of the profits from the Wild West, Bill invested in a coffee factory in La Crosse, Wisconsin, and opened a second hotel and livery stables in Sheridan. He built a new house next to Scout's Rest Ranch – called the Welcome Wigwam – after the first one burnt down. And he poured money into a gold and tungsten mine called Campo Bonito near Oracle, Arizona, which very nearly bankrupted him.

By 1893, Bill and Salsbury had extended the name of their enterprise to 'Buffalo Bill's Wild West and Congress of Rough Riders of the World' in recognition of the international performers now featured in the company – Cossacks, Arabians, Mexicans, South Americans, soldiers on leave from the 7th United States Cavalry, veteran French Chasseurs, British and German Lancers – plus 130 cowboys, cowgirls, Indians and 20 members of the Cowboy Band. From time to time expert riders from Puerto Rico, the Philippines, Japan, Cuba, Hawaii and Hungary would further reinforce the cast.

The high cost of running such a massive operation began to squeeze Bill's cash reserves.

The Wild West now counted '640 eating members' on its payroll. The name 'rough riders' was borrowed from President Theodore Roosevelt who, as a Lieutenant Colonel in the 1st US Volunteer Cavalry, adopted the name after the famous battle at San Juan Hill in Cuba, an incident which was later incorporated into the show.

The high cost of running such a massive operation, combined with other investments, began to squeeze Bill's cash reserves and the Wild West started losing money. The show now cost $4,000 a day to operate and in July 1894, while appearing at Ambrose Park, South Brooklyn, Bill admitted in a letter to his sister that: 'This is the tightest squeeze of my life. Don't mention it to anyone, but it's close papers this time. But I hope to struggle out of it some way. But I tell you I am not sleeping well now – do nothing but think and try to plan some way out of it, and you can imagine my state of mind.'

There had been a crop failure at one of Bill's ranches, an irrigation ditch had flooded and the promised group bookings at his hotel in Sheridan failed to materialise. The coffee factory had to be closed and the premises put on the market. There were no takers.

By the end of the 1894 season Salsbury had been taken ill with a serious stomach ailment and was never again able to take an active part in the daily management of the Wild West. Occasionally he sat on the sidelines, assisted by Johnnie Baker, directing new additions to the programme and providing advice when required, but the day-by-day running of the organisation now fell entirely on Bill's broad shoulders. Bill wanted to quit, but a pressing need to keep other business interests afloat prevented him from leaving. Like it or not, he was now permanently lassoed to the Wild West.

The ailing Salsbury urgently needed to find a suitable new partner to take on his business responsibilities and in 1895 struck a deal with James M. Bailey – the second name in the famous Barnum & Bailey circus empire – who agreed to provide transportation and local expenses for a speculative share of the profits.

Bailey – known as 'the little Napoleon of show business' – was a circus man through and through. He admitted to anyone prepared to listen that he cared for nothing but success from his chosen business. As a boy he had run away to join a travelling circus and later

Nate Salsbury – a studio photograph taken shortly before his death in 1902. (Denver Public Library)

started his own sawdust ring empire, which became a serious rival to the 'Greatest Show on Earth' operated by P.T. Barnum. The two circus organisations merged in 1881, Bailey's managerial astuteness complementing Barnum's promotional abilities. Together they made their circus the most successful enterprise of its kind in the United States.

Long seasons in one place were not Bailey's style of business. In order to guarantee full circus tents, his shows played one-day engagements before packing up and moving on somewhere else the next day. It is said that the first thing Bailey did when he picked up his morning newspaper was turn to reports about the prices of wheat, butter, eggs, potatoes, and other farm produce, because that was his barometer of conditions along his circus routes. If prices were good, his circus tents would be full of happy customers. If prices were low, box office takings would reflect the depression.

To pull the Wild West out of debt, Bailey used his circus railway cars to move 'America's National Entertainment' to 131 cities in 190 days covering a 9,000-mile route. While the Barnum & Bailey Circus was away on a triumphant European tour, 42 railway cars owned by the company – plus a further ten – would be used on the Wild West's American tour.

Buffalo Bill would rather have been at home at Scout's Rest Ranch than on a train rolling towards another town along the tracks.

The one-day tours were a brilliant success, but Bill hated the constant travelling, which exhausted him. He was now in his early 50s, his hair thinning and beard turning white. Buffalo Bill would much rather have been at home at Scout's Rest Ranch or at the old TE than on a train rolling towards another town along the tracks – it mattered little to him what it was called, they all merged into one and the same nameless showground.

On the night of 28 October 1901, following a performance before 12,000 people in Charlotte, North Carolina, members of the Wild West company boarded the three show trains for the night ride to Danville, Virginia – the last engagement of the year. They were looking forward to a winter rest.

The locomotives and carriages pulled out of Charlotte in three separate sections. The first transported the animals and departed at midnight. The second, carrying Bill and the rest of the company in sleeping cars, departed two and a half hours after the first train. A third section, pulling freight cars full of scenery and seating, would follow later. Somewhere along the route the second train pulling the sleeping cars missed a telegraphic order instructing the driver to divert into a siding. On the outskirts of Lexington at 3.30 a.m. the second locomotive collided with the rear end of carriages pulled by the first.

The impact smashed the wooden Pullman cars into splinters. A railway worker said it looked as if one train had tried to devour the other. Wreckage was strewn along the track for over half a mile and the remains of railway cars lay smashed in a ditch.

There were no fatalities among Buffalo Bill's company, but over 100 horses perished or had to be shot, including Bill's own mounts Old Pap and Old Eagle. Only two horses survived the disaster. Four trainmen were injured and Annie Oakley, asleep in her private compartment with Frank, was thrown from her bed into the side of a trunk containing her guns and costumes.

The third train pulled into a siding and was used as a temporary hospital carriage until help arrived. Frank carried Annie along the line, and on the way she complained that she could not feel any movement on her left side.

Annie was rushed to St Michael's Hospital in Newark, New Jersey and underwent urgent surgery. She remained hospitalised for several months and endured numerous operations. There were fears that she might never perform in public again. Little did she know, but 'Little Sure Shot' had fired her last gun for Buffalo Bill's Wild West.

In 1902, Bailey sent the Wild West across the Atlantic to England once again. Between December 1902 and October 1903 the show would travel nearly 3000 miles to nearly 100 different locations, starting with a long season at London's Olympia, then shorter stays in Manchester and Liverpool before a series of one- and two-day engagements in England and Wales.

At the same time as Barnum & Bailey's Circus was returning to the United States from England, Buffalo Bill's Wild West was crossing the ocean ready to undertake its own tour travelling in the same Pullman cars used by the folks from the sawdust ring. Bill would have preferred to remain in America, but Buffalo Bill's Wild West without Buffalo Bill himself was unthinkable. Besides, too many people depended on 'the boss' for their livelihood and he would not desert them. And Bill's other business interests needed a constant source of income to keep them afloat. So the Wild West remained on tour, sapping Bill's vitality, which was often missing when he was away from the arena, but always returned when he rode out into the spotlight.

Bill would have preferred to remain in America, but Buffalo Bill's Wild West without Buffalo Bill himself was unthinkable.

Before leaving the United States, Nate Salsbury was re-united with the company for one last time to revive items on the programme new to British audiences – 'The Battle of San Juan Hill', using some of the men who had actually taken part in the Spanish-American war under the command of Teddy Roosevelt; and 'The Guardians of Neptune's Stormy Coast', featuring US Life Savers.

Salsbury's 'stomach trouble' (it is not known if it was ulcers or cancer) had become worse, and doctors ordered him to take things easy. But he missed the Wild West, its daily dramas, triumphs and tribulations. On paper, Salsbury was still the organisation's Vice President and a major shareholder in the enterprise. Although his name remained on posters and programmes, he had reluctantly entered semi-retirement two years previously. In order to give himself something to do, Salsbury began to draft his memoirs with a view to publishing them at a later time. He also invested $200,000 of his savings in building a group of smart seaside cottages for successful theatrical people – known as the 'Reservation' – near his home in Long Branch, New Jersey, and accepted the unpaid job of President of the local property owners' association.

Salsbury was glad to be involved with the Wild West again. He travelled into New York from Long Branch to rehearse the performers. It was clear to everyone that the pale looking man, who once had had more energy than six cowboys, was now frail. He directed action scenes from a chair and when too weak to shout instructions, received help from Johnnie Baker, who had become adept at reproducing Salsbury's original directions.

In West London the Wild West moved into a massive indoor grand hall covering four acres, Olympia. The centrally heated

Illustrated London News artist, Ralph Cleaver, was invited in to sketch the Wild West in rehearsal at the London Olympia before it opened on 26 December 1902. Top panel: Buffalo Bill, Mexican Vaqueros and Russian Cossacks. Centre panel: Sioux braves racing around the arena. Bottom panel: A cowgirl, cowboys saddling and riding buckjumpers, and Sioux Indians Sandrock and Red Star.

venue was perfect for shows during winter months, taking place beneath a giant iron and glass roof measuring 450 ft long by 250 ft wide.

By the time the Americans arrived, Queen Victoria had been dead for over a year, succeeded by her son and Bill's old friend, Edward, Prince of Wales. The age of Queen Victoria had made way for the short-lived Edwardian era, which had not begun well. Britain was in the grip of the Boer War, a conflict in which half a million British men were sent to South Africa to fight 88,000 rebels in the independent Dutch republics of the Transvaal and Orange Free State. There were heavy casualties on both sides so, by December 1902, Londoners needed cheering up – and Buffalo Bill was just the man to do it.

The Wild West now projected the personalities of Buffalo Bill, with its usual mix of cowboys, Indians and the 'Congress of Rough Riders of the World', and James Bailey's circus performers, including a team of 'freaks' – Nouma Hawa 'the World's Smallest Midget, along with the Egyptian Giant and other famous Curiosities in the Side Shows'. Later in the season they would be joined by a 'bearded Venus and human Ostrich man with a Giraffe neck'. Such side-shows could have injured the integrity of the Wild West. Fortunately, they did not seem to.

Londoners needed cheering up – and Buffalo Bill was just the man to do it.

The first performance was scheduled for 26 December 1902 playing through until 4 April 1903 before touring. Johnnie Baker, who had taken over Salsbury's duties, was now responsible for making sure the show was ready to open. In addition to his job as 'Arenic Director', Johnny also dropped his name of 'The Cowboy Kid' to become 'the celebrated young American marksman' when he appeared with his rifle in the arena.

Heading the 100-strong Indian delegation, including 75 Sioux from four separate tribes, were Red Star, Sandrock, High Bear and Walks Under Ground. Their interpreter was also an Indian, Luther Standing Bear.

The official London programme, a sixpenny guide to the life and frontier adventures of Buffalo Bill, his performers and western life, running to 60 pages, also carried advertisements for the first time (not many of the claims would be permissible today!):

The Hand that Rocks the Cradle buys the Soap. Let it be Wright's Coal Tar Soap. It protects from Infectious Diseases – smallpox, measles, etc.

Dunn's Famous 3s 9d Hats – we save our customers at least 30 per cent on every purchase.

Tomce – the one minute cure for toothache, the only real cure. Wm. Harris who suffered for three months writes – 'Tomce cured me in a few seconds. That is now five months ago and my tooth has not ached since'. Send 1s 4d to the Quick Cure Company.

There were also advertisements for *The Last of the Great Scouts* – 'contains the most Thrilling Incidents in the Career of Col. William F. Cody as told by his sister, Helen Cody Wetmore, replete with anecdotes of Heroism and Adventure with illustrations by Frederic Remington, price 2s 6d from attendants at each performance'. Bill claimed that this was, by far, the most truthful book about him ever written. 'The rest is fiction', he told a reporter, presumably referring to dime novels about his adventures and not his own autobiographical works.

Audiences could also buy a flat cardboard box containing one-dimensional coloured cardboard figures of Buffalo Bill, the Deadwood stagecoach, cowboys and Indians, complete with a small round metal stand to keep them standing upright.

The pieces allowed children to re-create the Wild West all over again when they returned home. Costing 1s 6d per box, they were quickly snapped up by more affluent parents taking their children on an outing.

As the company gathered backstage at Olympia on 26 December ready for the first 2.00 p.m. performance of the 14-week season, a telegram was delivered addressed to Bill. The contents shook the showman from the top of his sombrero to the toes of his fine leather boots. Nate Salsbury was dead.

The stomach illness which had plagued Bill's business partner for the last fourteen years of his life, had finally killed him. He had died with his wife and four young children at his bedside at Long Branch on Christmas Eve, age 56, and was buried at New York's Woodlawn Cemetery – just as the Wild West was preparing to open in London. Like Bill, Salsbury had also been a freemason and entitled to a private Masonic funeral. Leading show business figures attended and over 100 wreaths surrounded his coffin, including an enormous broken column made from flowers, sent from London by Bill.

As the company gathered backstage a telegram was delivered addressed to Bill.

Bill wanted to cancel that day's performances, but Johnnie Baker persuaded his boss to carry on, claiming that Salsbury would have been horrified by the suggestion if he had been in London with them. With a heavy heart, Bill agreed to continue and called together company members who had known Salsbury and gently broke the news to them. They agreed to lower scores of flags fluttering around Olympia to half-mast and drape the Stars and Stripes, carried around the arena at the start of the show, with a streamer of black crêpe.

A British programme advertisement for *The Last of the Great Scouts* (Earls Court/ Olympia Archives)

The company then prepared to mount their horses, smile for the public and ride into Olympia's spotlight for the spectacular Grand Processional Review. It was hard work – but thousands of excited Londoners taking their children on a post-Christmas treat to see the great Buffalo Bill awaited them and their cheers and applause got them through the day.

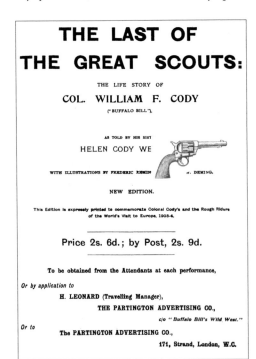

THE LAST OF
THE GREAT SCOUTS:

THE LIFE STORY OF

COL. WILLIAM F. CODY

("BUFFALO BILL"),

AS TOLD BY HIS SIST

HELEN CODY WE

WITH ILLUSTRATIONS BY FREDERIC REMIN   ... DEMING.

NEW EDITION.

This Edition is expressly printed to commemorate Colonel Cody's and the Rough Riders of the World's Visit to Europe, 1903-4.

Price 2s. 6d.; by Post, 2s. 9d.

To be obtained from the Attendants at each performance,

Or by application to

H. LEONARD (Travelling Manager),

THE PARTINGTON ADVERTISING CO.,

c/o " Buffalo Bill's Wild West."

Or to

The PARTINGTON ADVERTISING CO.,

171, Strand, London, W.C.

London newspapers noted that although it had been ten years since his last London appearance, Bill could still attract the crowds. *The Times* wrote on 26 December 1902: 'All roads seemed to lead to Olympia, the great building, so long wrapped in silence and desolation, was filled to capacity and the vast space under the ample glass roof rang with the shouts of 14,000 people.'

Youngsters who had marvelled at the Wild West in 1887 and 1892 were now grown-up and brought their own children to Olympia to see the same show they fondly remembered from their youth.

Bill's old friends at the *Evening News* commented that the Wild West was 'no longer a revelation to London' but

BUFFALO BILL'S WILD WEST

10th EDITION

. . . AND . . .

CONGRESS OF ROUGH RIDERS OF THE WORLD.

COL. W. F. CODY
"BUFFALO BILL"

STAFF OF "BUFFALO BILL'S" WILD WEST COMPANY

COL. W. F. CODY ("Buffalo Bill") PRESIDENT and DIRECTOR-GENERAL.

JOHN M. BURKE . GENERAL MANAGER. JULE KEEN, Business Manager and Treasurer.
JOHNNIE BAKER . . Arenic Director. WM. McCUNE . . Officer of the Day.
JOE ESQUIVELL . . Chief of Cowboys. WM. SWEENEY . Leader of Cowboy Band.
F. DANGERFIELD . . Scenic Artist. M. B. BAILEY . . Chief Electrician.
L. E. DECKER - - - - - Representing Col. W. F. Cody.

PRESS BUREAU.

MAJOR JOHN M. BURKE, HARVEY L. WATKINS, CHARLES S. WELLS, DEXTER W. FELLOWS.

STAFF OF BARNUM & BAILEY, LIMITED.

GEORGE O. STARR, *Director.*

FREDERICK B. HUTCHINSON, *Manager.* CLARENCE L. DEAN, *General Agent.*
ALFRED D. STARR, *Treasurer.* HARVEY L. WATKINS, *General Press Agent.*

PARTINGTON ADVERTISING CO., Publishers of Official Programme and Book of Historical Sketches.

A page from 'Buffalo Bill's Wild West and Congress of Rough Riders of the World' 1902–3 British programme. (Earls Court/ Olympia Archives)

welcomed the fact that 'a new generation has arisen since the celebrated Colonel Cody made his first bow to a London multitude fifteen years ago and there must be many thousands of metropolitan residents who did not visit the Wild West when it was here in its second visit in 1892–3. For these, the remarkable exhibition has all the attraction of complete novelty.'

The paper was quick to point out that the show 'has undergone the power of Time in these ten years. There have been many changes of personnel, the march of events putting a more modern aspect on the programme and furnishing new entertainment for all.'

The press was in full agreement that: 'in one thing, the Wild West changeth not. Colonel Cody . . . still sits in his saddle with the manly dignity of a vigorous soldier, and gives proof that he remains as clear-sighted and true a marksman from horseback as ever.'

The Times was as impressed with Bill in 1902 as it had been a decade and a half earlier. 'After all the performers have taken up their allotted places in the ring, Buffalo Bill rides forward amid shouts and applause and advances to the Royal Box, occupied by the Duke and Duchess of Argyll and the children of Princess Henry of Battenburg and announces: "Ladies and gentlemen, permit me to introduce you to a congress of rough riders of the world."'

A new Deadwood stagecoach now rattled around Olympia's arena. The previous model had become worn out and was given by Bill to Washington's Smithsonian Institution for permanent exhibition. The new version was similar in appearance and Wild West fans were none the wiser.

The public had plenty to entertain them during the 1902 Christmas holiday season. London's music halls were at their peak during the early years of the twentieth century, and over Christmas dropped much of their bawdiness to accommodate family audiences. Dan Leno starred in *Mother Goose* at Drury Lane, Marie Lloyd could be seen in the title role of *Aladdin* at Peckham's Crown Theatre and Harry Lauder topped the bill in *Down South* at the London Pavilion. But the Wild West had lost none of its crowd pulling power and enjoyed good business for the remainder of December and throughout January.

Writer and historian Godfrey James visited the Wild West at Olympia as a boy and nearly half a century later recalled the great impression Buffalo Bill's company made on him in *London – The Western Reaches*, published in 1950:

> My brothers and sisters and I were greatly excited when Buffalo Bill was in possession. There were two shows a day, but our funds were low, and though we should have liked, had we been able, to attend the performances daily, we had to be content with one visit.
>
> I remember a thrilling scene in which a rickety and ancient mail coach drove from one end of the arena to the other, being ambushed about half way by Red Indians. There was a great deal of noisy powder play, guns being let off in profusion not only by the attacking Red men, but also by the mail guard and his passengers in self defence. Of course, everything ended satisfactorily for the coach and its crew, and the bodies of many braves studded the centre of the ring as smoke clouds and their accompanying acrid fumes dissolved to the great glass roof above.
>
> I remember Buffalo Bill himself, in his picturesque cowboy-like outfit, a handsome and commanding figure as he shot from his horse (I believe it was a white one) with a rifle at glass balls thrown into the air as targets as he galloped across the arena. His precision was wonderful to see, and not many of his inanimate victims fell to the ground intact.

'His precision was wonderful to see, and not many of his victims fell to the ground intact.'

But although we witnessed the show once, we re-constructed our thrills at second hand. For nightly, as we lay listening intently in our beds, we could hear the sound of the shots which heralded the progress both of the attack by the Redskins and of the Colonel's own spectacular display.

We got another thrill by strolling round to the back of the building, where the stabling quarters actually adjoined the block of flats in which we lived. Doors were often left open, and we used to creep in, as unobtrusively as possible, to see the horses fed and groomed, and to hope for a glimpse – often rewarded – of the Red Indians ready in their war paint for the next performance. Whether they were real Redskins or whether they were 'palefaces' made up for the occasion, I do not remember. I know we used to like to think they were the genuine article and so, again at second-hand, achieve yet another thrill.

 On 26 February 1903, Bill celebrated his 57th birthday in London. After the matinée audience had gone home, word was sent to 'the TE Ranch, London' – the name given to Bill's private office at Olympia – asking him to return to the arena where the entire company was waiting.

The Cowboy Band launched into a spirited rendition of 'For He's a Jolly Good Fellow' as the boss walked through the doors. Major Burke stepped forward and – according to *The Sphere* – 'assured the Colonel of the high esteem in

Mexican vaqueros at London's Olympia in 1903. (Denver Public Library)

219

which he had ever been held by all of his employees. He then handed the Colonel a magnificent solid silver coffee and tea service suitably inscribed, each of the various pieces being marked with the letters 'T.E.'.

Minor royalty were regular visitors to the Wild West, but it was not until 14 March 1903 – three weeks before the Olympia season closed – that King Edward VII, who as Prince of Wales had done so much to promote the show during his mother's Jubilee year, attended with Queen Alexandra. The Dukes of Connaught, Wales and York, Princess Mary and the King's grandson (later King Edward VIII and Duke of Windsor), accompanied them.

After the show, the King and Queen came backstage for a re-union with Bill and Johnnie Baker. The youngest member of the company, eight-year-old Moses Red Star, was also presented to the royal couple. The *Illustrated London News* reported that 'Moses was rather shy when he was presented to the Queen, but he took most kindly to King Edward, gaily toying with the King's umbrella. The little boy also gave one of the clay balls which Buffalo Bill shoots at in the arena, to Prince Edward of Wales.'

The company turns out for Bill's 57th birthday presentation at Olympia, 26 February 1903. (*The Sphere*)

On leaving, the King was overheard to say that 'George and Mary simply must see this', referring to his son and daughter-in-law – later King George V and Queen Mary – not present that afternoon. And so four successive British rulers attended Buffalo Bill's Wild West in London.

In a letter to his sister on 17 March 1903, Bill told Julia that 'the King and Queen sent me a great big very valuable diamond pin, (showing) their crown and Edward VII's, studded with diamonds and rubies.'

Another letter from the 'TE Ranch, London' – says, 'We have drawn so many thousands of people here during this long stay we have about worn the Jubilee out.' Bill still craved news from home, especially about everyday things and asked Julia: 'Do you have milk from the cows at the barn, does Christy bring eggs? I like to hear of these little things.'

His mind was also on the Campo Bonito gold and tungsten mine in Arizona; and in March Bill received a cable announcing that, after months of tunnelling, his miners were expecting to strike a rich vein any day. Success was almost guaranteed. 'It seems like a great load had suddenly been taken off me – I don't believe money makes anyone happier but it's kind of a safe guard to have a little around, eh?' wrote an elated Bill to Julia. Later he asked his sister: 'Say, isn't it

Buffalo Bill in the front passenger seat of a steam-powered Gardner-Serpollet car, giving a lift to Wild West Treasurer Jule Keen (back seat – left) and Major Burke. Eustace Gray took the photograph at the London Olympia on 18 February 1903. (Motor Transport Collection)

221

glorious to think your old brother is a millionaire? Now I can do good – and make others happy . . .'

Two days later Bill was telling Julia that business at Olympia had fallen off and 'I am a little cramped for ready cash just now, but when I think of the millions I have banked in that gold mine, which I will commence to draw on in about four months time, I feel encouraged. But it will be a little hard sledding till I get on the road with the show.'

The Olympia season ended in early April 1903 with poor houses, but Bill was far from discouraged. Although business was poor he looked forward to a good summer tour and 'then quit the show business for ever. We have got a gold mine . . . and as soon as we can build a mill . . . have a steady income.'

 On 10 April, the Wild West loaded its human and animal cast, a self-contained portable arena complete with covered seating for 12,200 people, tons of scenery, properties and a special electric lighting plant, on to Bailey's three show trains pulling a total of 150 carriages north to Manchester. A three-week open-air season would take place at Brooks Bar, a stretch of open land near the centre of the city.

The Wild West played in all weather conditions – and in 1903 most of it was in the rain.

Touring with the company was a small delegation from the Barnum & Bailey organisation, including James Bailey's nephew, Fred Hutchinson, whose job was to supervise rail transportation and the rapid erecting and dismantling of the Wild West in each town.

Hutchinson had learned his skills in America working with his uncle's touring circus. While Bill and Johnnie Baker took credit for what went on before the public, Hutchinson must take credit for the incredible speed with which the Wild West went about its business on tour. Within hours of trains pulling into a town on tour, a canvas city with an international population of 800 plus scores of animals, was created. Covered seating for thousands was put in place and two daily shows presented before the canvas city was dismantled and returned to the station. The entire operation would then steam out of town onwards to the next engagement, where the process was repeated all over again. The Wild West played in all weather conditions – and in 1903 most of it was in the rain.

A description of what happened when the Wild West prepared to leave town after a performance appeared in the *Staffordshire Sentinel*, a newspaper circulating in a region in which Hutchinson chose to quarter the show's animals and a handful of staff during the winter months:

Before the last spectators had left the grounds, the area was in possession of 180 men whose sole business was to take down the show. The painted scene at the lower end of the ground disappeared as if by magic and within ten minutes the blacksmith's shop and stable behind had vanished from the face of the earth. One section of men dealt with the ropes, while another party rolled up the canvas and another took the poles in charge. Then there appeared on the field a long string of wagons and into these the ropes, canvas and poles were loaded, and one by one the vehicles set off for the station.

Turning from the stables to look at the great dressing tent where the 'actors' in the

Buffalo Bill visited the Buckingham Palace Road studios of top London society photographer Carl Vandyke in February 1903 for this full-length portrait. It was later used in several newspapers and magazines to promote the lengthy British tour about to follow. He wears embroidered buckskins, gauntlets and soft leather boots and holds his ever-familiar Winchester rifle. (Vandyke Collection)

show donned and doffed their warpaint and feathers, I was not in the least surprised to find that this, too, had been dismantled while our backs were turned and the men were already taking to pieces the seating, which ten minutes before had accommodated thousands of people. Working with a wonderful quietness and method, they furnished a typical example of the extraordinary agility and perseverance for which the Yankee is so famous.

In a quarter of an hour half the place was down and in half an hour it was almost completely razed to the earth, packed and loaded onto wagons. One of the most laborious tasks was to disinter the long tent posts – 800 in number – which were each driven four or five feet into the earth. This was accomplished by a single and dextrous process using a long lever on wheels. Attached to the working end of the lever was an iron chain, which was given one or two turns around the post to be drawn up. Then the men bore heavily on the other end of the lever and in a trice the post was uprooted. The 800 posts were up and carted in an absurdly short time, and the dismantling process grew quicker and quicker as time went on, for as soon as one part of the show had been dealt with, the men who had been engaged upon it were able to concentrate their efforts on the remaining part and assist those already there.

Where were, one asks, the Americans, Japanese, Cossacks, Bedouins, Indians, Mexicans and Gauchos? Out in the meadow near the road . . . with their horses, quietly awaiting the signal to move off. The men sat quite immovable on their backs until the word of command was received.

The word was given and the whole body of mounted men silently moved out of the ground and directed their course to the station. By the time we arrived, 400 horses had already been loaded and their riders snugly ensconced in the sleeping compartment and were already in the land of dreams. Three special trains were driven into the goods yard for the purpose of conveying the show to its next engagement, where it opens later today. The train comprises 150 trucks, including 18 sleepers, 7 for staff and 11 not quite so elaborately fitted for the less important members of the company. The loading of the rest of the show was again an object lesson in simplicity and smartness. As each wagon arrived, the draft horses were unhitched and taken back to fetch another consignment. The team of horses was then attached to the wagon left behind and drawn up the slope on to the bogie carriages which make up the greater portion of the trains and the wheels of the wagons having been fixed in steep blocks, it was then ready for the journey.

By half past twelve the first train was sent away. Half an hour later the second followed and finally after the last consignment had been loaded up at half past one-o-clock, the whole establishment, Buffalo Bill himself and all his horses and show had disappeared like a vision of the night leaving not a trace of it behind.

> 'Buffalo Bill himself and all his horses and show had disappeared like a vision in the night.'

When trains pulled into Manchester's Longsight station that afternoon, hundreds of spectators waited to welcome the company, expecting a spectacular cavalcade of cowboys and Indians to pass through to the showground two miles away in Upper Chorlton Road. But no such parade had been planned. The company arrived in Manchester early to settle into new surroundings and adapt parts of the show to the open-air arena. The last thing they expected was a welcome committee and their arrival date had been deliberately kept vague, the only public announcement being for the opening performance on 13 April – Easter Monday, and the Wild West's 21st anniversary.

The crowd patiently waited while horse-drawn wagons and carriages came and went from railway sidings transporting goods from the train to Brooks Bar. But the crowds refused to depart and Bill hastily called a meeting on board the train to discuss an action plan.

It was agreed that the company would change into costumes not already unloaded and ride their horses through the streets to the showground, waving to crowds along the route. The goodwill gesture was sure to stimulate ticket sales during a cold snap, which threatened to bring snow to the north-west that week.

The appreciative crowd, many of whom had been waiting in the cold for several hours, cheered enthusiastically as the rough-riders of the world, with Bill at their head, met the Manchester public two days ahead of schedule as darkness descended over the city. After that time, street processions were always scheduled whenever weather permitted the Wild West to stay longer than two days in a town or city.

The *Manchester Evening News* was again a keen observer of Wild West activity before the show opened. The paper's correspondent was particularly impressed with the self-contained nature of the set-up.

To pull the Wild West out of debt, James Bailey used his Barnum & Bailey circus railway cars to move 'America's National Entertainment' around America and the United Kingdom. Between December 1902 and October 1903 the show would travel nearly 3,000 miles to nearly 100 different British locations on three show trains pulling a total of 150 carriages. (Denver Public Library)

Except for food, the management are dependent on no one. If a tent was ripped in two, it could be repaired on the spot. If a wagon wheel came off, the wheelwrights would have it fixed up right away, if a pony cast a shoe or had a cough it could be doctored for either discomfort. And if all the electric light in Manchester suddenly

Indians from Buffalo Bill's
Wild West take over a
Manchester Corporation
Tram for a short excursion
during their 13 April–2 May
1903 engagement in the city.
Bill does not appear on the
photograph, having injured
his foot in a riding accident at
the start of the engagement.
(Manchester Department of
Libraries and Theatres, Local
Studies Unit)

227

failed, the Wild West would still be illuminated as Colonel Cody carries his own plant in duplicate. The organisers leave nothing to chance. If a whirlwind swept away the thousands of square feet of gleaming white canvas, which covers the brightly painted seats around the arena, a telegram to the stores would bring reserve canvas on the next train to Manchester.

On 12 April, Bill wrote to his sister from the Queen's Hotel, Manchester, stating that he was pleased to hear that she was well, and 'I wish I could say that I did. But I am going to get out of this business that is just wearing the life out of me. There is such a nervous strain continually and the thing has got onto my nerves. And this must be my last summer. Today it's snowing here and we open outdoors tomorrow.'

There was a seat price at the Wild West in Manchester and on tour to suit every pocket or class of person. Nearly 4,000 seats were on sale at one shilling each and a further 3,680 at two shillings, all unreserved. Just under 3,000 reserved seats were sold for three shillings each, 1,560 at four shillings and 324 box seats at seven shillings and sixpence per box. Seats were numbered and when all were sold, 'house full' signs were positioned outside and no further members of the public admitted.

The star of the show tried in vain to stand up, but was unable to get on to his other foot.

Special Buffalo Bill excursion trams to Brooks Bar were operated by Manchester Corporation, alongside regular service trams, horse-drawn omnibuses and hansom cabs. Every vehicle 'plus waggonettes, carriages, cabs, bikes and conveyances of every description, carried the multitude to one of the greatest shows on earth' on opening day.

The gates were scheduled to open at 1 p.m. but the public was admitted earlier to avoid crowding at the entrance. Just as the performance commenced, snow began to fall on Manchester.

Everything started well enough and the crowd went wild when Bill rode into the arena to introduce his congress of rough riders. But as he turned to ride out, his horse shied at a piece of scenery being moved, slid on the slippery grass and reared up on its hind legs unseating Bill, who slid from the animal's back. The horse slipped again and fell on to Bill's right foot, crushing his boot under its weight. The star of the show tried in vain to stand up, but was unable to get on to his other foot.

Two medical orderlies from a nearby hospital were in the audience that afternoon and rushed to assist. They lifted Bill out of the arena to a tent where they removed his boot to reveal a badly swollen foot. Within minutes his foot and toes had doubled in size and a cold compress was placed over the injury to reduce the swelling.

Bill's second appearance later that afternoon was cancelled and the painful swelling had not gone down in time for the evening performance. Never one to disappoint his public, Bill gritted his teeth and rode around the arena in an open carriage, smiling and waving to the crowd. He expected to be back in the saddle the following day, but it was a further five weeks before Bill could take an active part in the Wild West arena again.

On 4 May the Wild West arrived in Liverpool for a three-week season at the Old Exhibition Grounds on Edge Hall Lane Estate. The Bishop of Liverpool, Dr Chavasse, who had seen the Wild West in London, had written to Bill suggesting an open-air Sunday service be held at the showground. Bill agreed and on 10 May a large congregation turned up at Edge Lane in their Sunday best to sing hymns in the company of cowboys and Indians.

The *Liverpool Daily Post* was also in the congregation and next day reported:

Unfortunately the weather is no respecter of either persons or creeds and the atmospheric conditions on this occasion were neither better or worse than had prevailed for many days past, a cold and drizzling rain falling which rendered the open-air meeting of this description very uncomfortable for all concerned.

Those forming the congregation – and there was numerous attendance – were better off than the principal figure and well protected from the driving rain by the canvas cover, while the Bishop, calmly unheedful of discomfort, stood along with other clergy with him.

When the Bishop delivered his address, he approached the congregation and was practically sheltered from the rain by an umbrella held over his head by Major Burke, general manager of the show.

A large male-voice choir led the congregation in singing 'Rock of Ages', 'O God, Our Help in Ages Past', and 'Onward Christian Soldiers', and the *Liverpool Daily Post* noted that 'many of the dusky Chiefs, seated with Buffalo Bill in the front row with their squaws and children, followed the service with much interest and it was noticeable that many joined in the hymn singing.'

Bill braced himself for the next stage of the tour, a gruelling visit to nearly 90 different railway towns, starting in Warrington on 25 May and ending in Burton-on-Trent on 23 October. The show would then be put into winter quarters at Hanley, near Stoke-on-Trent, until 25 April 1904, when it would begin touring almost non-stop until the following autumn. So much for quitting 'the show business for ever'. Bailey had other ideas for Bill and the Wild West.

So much for quitting 'the show business' for ever. Bailey had other ideas for Bill and the Wild West.

For the next five months, the Wild West played to audiences of farm labourers, metal workers, cotton mill weavers, fishermen, coal miners, glass blowers, lace makers, milliners, stevedores, shipbuilders, railway navvies, brewers, shopkeepers, domestic servants and their masters and mistresses plus people engaged in a hundred other trades in Edwardian England.

Most towns on the 1903 tour were close to each other, and the railway convoy had only to travel short daily distances to reach the next stop. Showgrounds were located as close as possible to railway stations or sidings, allowing Bill's roustabouts to arrive in a new town, set up the show, dismantle and move on to the next location in the fastest possible time. Recreation grounds, parks, football fields, vacant meadows and empty spaces – all free from trees – were hired to present the show. It was a long way from the giant indoor and outdoor arenas used by Bill and Salsbury during the Wild West's hey-day – but the show still

Buffalo Bill drives a horse-drawn carriage through New Street, Birmingham, as part of a parade through the city centre in June 1903. (Birmingham Central Library, Local Studies & History Service)

produced the same excitement and production values in Barnsley, Bristol, Bangor and Berwick-on-Tweed as it had in Boston, Bremen and Brussels.

Advertising stated that the Wild West was 'now making its Absolutely Final tour of Great Britain – and will Positively Never Return! Don't Miss the Last Chance!' Announcements told local people that the show would arrive in 'Three special trains, containing 500 horses, 800 people . . . The entire Grand Programme will positively be presented undivided and uncurtailed.'

To ensure that everyone knew that Buffalo Bill's Wild's West was coming to town, Major Burke recruited an advance publicity team whose job was to visit towns ahead of the show, co-ordinate advertising in regional newspapers, liaise with bill-poster companies and deliver pre-written press stories into the hands of local newspaper editors. By the time the Wild West steamed into town, everyone would have known about the show and more expensive seats snapped up in advance from appointed agents.

Corn merchants throughout England and Wales were hired to provide forage for the animals. Farmers with room to spare in their barns and meadows were paid handsomely to shelter and feed 500 horses and dozens of cattle for an occasional night or two when the show was not travelling – often over a weekend. Some cowboys and Indians also pitched their tents and tepees in fields for a night in order to escape the confined sleeping areas in the Pullman carriages.

There was no shortage of landowners keen to do business with Buffalo Bill. He was often invited to be the house guest of farmers and fellow freemasons who were well paid for their hospitality. Many were given signed photographs of Bill as a souvenir – not a few exist today, proudly owned by the great-grandchildren of Britain's Edwardian gentry.

Suppliers of animal feed were not slow to offer their services to the Wild West, which required an ongoing daily supply of 10 tons of hay and straw, 10 quarts of oats plus other animal feed for horses and cattle.

Like an army, the Wild West travelled on its stomach and contractors were hired to supply the company with daily deliveries of 1,400 lbs of meat, 1,450 lbs of bread, 700 lbs of potatoes and 300 lbs of other assorted vegetables. Meat was delivered overnight and stored in a refrigerated compartment in one of the Pullman carriages. Huge quantities of butter, milk and eggs were purchased locally.

The company's 80-strong catering team was always first to leave the train whenever it arrived in a new town. Their 14 ft-long, four-wheeled wood- and coal-burning stove was always the first piece of equipment unloaded and dispatched to showgrounds. While roustabouts constructed the giant mess tent – seating 575 – around the mobile kitchen, caterers were busy cooking up a hearty breakfast of steaks, chops, bacon and eggs for 800 hungry wild westerners. Men installing

An army marches on its stomach. Wild West caterers cooking up stew for 800. (Denver Public Library)

Two adult Indians and two children photographed outside their tepee by Alfred Juggins at a muddy Wild West Camp at Perry Bar, Birmingham, June 1903. (Birmingham City Library)

seats, building the arena, with its canvas-covered stables and dressing rooms, were first to be fed, sitting in their own section of the dining tent. Performers ate later in their own area.

Everyone ate the same food. Dinner was served in two sittings before gates were opened admitting the public to afternoon performances. Supper was taken before the evening show. When the Wild West made its third appearance in Birmingham in 1903, the *Birmingham Daily Gazette* was invited to eat with the company and noted that everyone enjoyed a substantial meal of plain food. The reporter found little demand for cakes or pastries but reported that 'everything is done on a large scale and everything is done well'.

In July, when the Wild West arrived in Bristol, Bill was in low spirits. Physically he was one-third of the way through the tour with 60 towns still to play. Mentally he was at home on the TE Ranch. He wrote to his sister: 'I am here in my car, it's Sunday. I do not go to hotels any more for I haven't the strength to be even talked to. The only ray of pleasure I have is when I get to thinking of dear old TE and the rest I am going to get there.' The letter outlined his plans for a new kitchen, dining room and furniture for the ranch. Bill also revealed that he was seeking legal separation from Lulu, giving her 'everything at North Platte and a yearly allowance besides'. He signs off saying he is tired and 'will lie down and think of us at TE'.

The tour rattled on down the tracks and people still turned out in their thousands.

The tour rattled on down the tracks and, despite the wettest weather on record for over a century, people still turned out in their thousands to welcome Buffalo Bill to their towns. In the small Welsh town of Aberdare, the *Aberdare Leader* described the Wild West's visit as 'the social event of the year, if not the century'. Far more people than could be accommodated in the grandstand turned up from surrounding communities to spend the Fourth of July with the Wild West in Wales. Next day when the show moved 23 miles along the railway track to Cardiff for its second visit, hundreds followed in its wake.

The tour visited Devon, Dorset, Hampshire, Surrey and Kent during the rest of July and August before moving into Bedfordshire, Norfolk, Suffolk, Cambridge, Northamptonshire, Lincolnshire and Yorkshire for the autumn months.

By October, Bill was writing home from Bradford telling his sister about:

Fifty hours steady of the worst cold rain and wind storms I have ever experienced in all my life. We stood it off for 43 hours but had to give up and tonight have lost our first show of this season. We commenced pulling at 8.15. At 8.37 a house adjoining our big top [*at Leeds Road, Thornbury*] was blown down and fell on our seats. Had we had an audience in, they would have been killed so we were lucky not to attempt a show. I have been cold & wet since early Monday morning its now Tuesday eve 1045 I am in my car and the wind ain't doing a thing to it. Altogether your old brother is having a lively time . . .

In Bradford Bill spoke to the *Weekly Telegraph* about his attitude towards native Americans. He told the paper's correspondent at the Leeds Road showground:

I don't think there will be any more uprisings by the Indians. You know the brave is a peaceful man, as a rule. He loves to roam about at will and is an ardent follower of the chase. Lots of people call him savage, crafty, cruel and bloodthirsty, but I have always found him a man of great intelligence, with a good deal of dignity about him. He resents the idea of being forced to live in reservations and live by the spade and the plough instead of the lance and the bow and arrow. But he is gradually blending with other people and it is quite feasible to expect in the course of time they will be entirely similated with cosmopolitan Americans.

There may have been occasions when the Indian has massacred his opponents and made war on settlers but it is idle to accuse the Indian of being the embodiment of treachery when instances can be given of similar or worse cases from the late Boer

Red Star, a Sioux Chief with the Wild West, in the photographic studio of Alfred Juggins in Aston, Birmingham in June 1903. He is wearing full native dress, including feathered war bonnet and holds a traditional pipe. (Birmingham City Library)

War. An Indian, just like a European, if he is a skilful strategist, will take advantage of every opportunity to gain a point in his fight with the enemy, and who shall blame them? We would do it ourselves. The Medicine Man is the real cause of these uprisings. He is a political agitator, nothing more.

 As the season came to a close, arrangements were made to find accommodation to stable the horses and cattle in special winter quarters between October and April, when touring would continue. A large estate called Etruria at Hanley, near Stoke-on-Trent, Staffordshire, provided the answer. Etruria was once the village home of potters employed by Josiah Wedgwood, whose factory had been built nearby on the banks of the Caldon Canal and Trent and Mersey Canals. The purpose-built village was named after a region in northern Italy which had inspired some of Wedgwood's designs. A handful of cowboys and stable hands remained behind – on full pay – to exercise and care for the animals and carry out repairs to the show's equipment, while the rest of the company returned to America for the winter.

Etruria provided six months of shelter in barns and stables, meadows and grazing land plus comfortable living quarters for the cowboy caretakers in cottages on Wedgwood's former estate.

The 1903 season wound up with a final performance at Dallow Lock, Burton-on-Trent on 23 October. Between shows, Bill hosted a festive luncheon for the company and guests including top brass from the Barnum & Bailey organisation, the Wild West's British bankers and a reporter from the *Burton Mail*. The dining tent was covered with flags and flowers and after the meal Bill stood up and addressed his troupe:

Once more we are closing one of our many seasons and I want to compliment members of the company for their loyalty to their duty and uncomplaining work throughout these months of rain and mud. I want to say that I hope in the spring to meet many familiar faces back in the arena.

You are now about to depart to your various homes, a journey which takes you many thousands of miles apart. I am in hope that you will occasionally remember the season of 1903 in good old loyal England (*cheers from the company*) where we have been treated so kindly by everyone we have come into contact with. I have no hesitation in saying that there are no more loyal people under the sun than the English people. I know that you join me in heartfelt thanks to His Majesty the King and Her Majesty the Queen of England, both of whom came to see the performance while we were in London (*more cheers from the company*).

Although it has been a very rainy season, we have had less sickness in our company than we have had for many years, even in America. It has been very disagreeable at times – very disagreeable – and we have all longed for the sunshine that did not come very often (*laughter from the company*). I do not think that will prevent us from coming back to try again another year (*cries of 'hurrah' from the company*).

I hope you all reach your homes in health, that you will get a good rest and you will enjoy yourselves in whatever occupation you take up. You will have my kindest regards and sympathy for your welfare and your health. (*Lusty cheers, cowboy calls, war whoops and yells of appreciation in many different tongues and keys.*)

'I have no hesitation in saying that there are no more loyal people under the sun than the English people.'

The tour closed after its 333rd performance, having travelled 2,881 miles around England and Wales by rail. The company disappeared in all directions – to Germany, Argentina, Arabia, Mexico, Texas and South Dakota. Cossack and Japanese horsemen had found professional engagements in American circuses that winter and sailed with Bill, the cowboys and Indians from Liverpool to New York on the *Lucania* – another 3,025 mile voyage. On arrival, they said their farewells on the quayside and boarded trains to different destinations. Bill caught a train to

'Buffalo Bill arrived at Liverpool on Saturday night from New York on the *Lucania* with his troupe of Japanese and Cossacks (friendly for once, at least), Red Indians, cowboys, Mexican and American soldiers,' reported *The Sphere* on 23 April 1904. The drawing, by Ernest Prater, shows Major Burke welcoming the boss back to Britain on the quayside.

Wyoming and the peace and tranquility which could only be enjoyed at *'the dear old TE.'*

Bill returned to Liverpool on the *Lucania* in April 1904, refreshed and ready to resume the Wild West tour. Newspaper photography was still in its infancy at this time, but line drawings could be reproduced in larger newspapers. Ernest Prater, a well-known magazine illustrator, was commissioned by Major Burke to make sketches of 'the boss' and some performers – in full costume – arriving on the quayside. The sketches were then copied on to printer's blocks and circulated to newspapers and magazines published in towns and cities featured on the early part of the tour.

Stretching out before the company were a further 132 engagements covering 4,000 miles from Cornwall to Inverness.

Stretching out before the company were a further 132 engagements covering 4,000 miles from Cornwall to Inverness. Most tour dates would be one-day stands, with occasional two-day engagements in Cardiff and Hull and week-long bookings in Newcastle, Glasgow and Edinburgh. The season would end on 21 October as it began on 25 April – in Staffordshire.

Before opening at the Old Racecourse, Bootham Bar, Stoke-on-Trent, Bill invited the Mayor of Hanley, Councillor H.B. Shirley, to bring his entire council to watch a dress rehearsal at Etruria. It was a way of thanking them for making the cowboys who remained behind so welcome in their community. The civic dignitaries arrived in two electric tramcars chartered for the occasion.

There they witnessed cowboys putting horses through their paces in the paddock, demonstrating fancy rope tricks and bronco busting. Afterwards the Mayor expressed delight that the Wild West had chosen to spend the winter in his borough. He said that the cowboys who had remained behind had 'been of good conduct, even if one of them had been taken to the Police Station. We were not sure if he was drunk or sober, so we let him go.'

Mayor Shirley had every right to be pleased. Wintering the animals at Etruria had cost Bill and Bailey $150,000, which had gone directly into the coffers of local traders supplying hay, oats, animal feed and stabling plus food, board and lodging for cowboys looking after them.

The councillors were the first to witness a new act – Carter the Cowboy Cyclist 'in his wonderful bicycle leap through space'. Carter's party piece was to mount his cycle and take up a position at the top of a steep incline curling upwards at the far end. On reaching the end of the ramp, the bike left the curl and hurtled through the air, 15 ft off the ground, for a distance of 40 ft.

The civic leaders were also introduced to some of the Indians newly recruited into the company, including Young Sitting Bull – a son of the famous Chief – Charging Hawk, American Horse, Whirlwind Horse, Too Elk and Lone Bear, Chief of the Indian Police. The new recruits from Pine Ridge would also take part in the re-creation of the Battle of the Little Big Horn – Young Sitting Bull playing the part of his famous father and Johnnie Baker (wearing a long blond wig and built-up boots) in the role of General Custer.

Major Burke's advertisements and handbills for the 1904 tour heavily promoted this section of the show with the following understated copy:

THE BATTLE OF THE LITTLE BIG HORN
The Awful Reality of Furious Conflict and Massacre in Savage Warfare
Presented with Perfect Historical Accuracy of Detail
Introducing 800 Indian Chiefs, Braves and Warriors, Soldiers, Scouts and Horses
With every Accessory of Arms, Accoutrement and Savage Decoration,
Whose Inconceivably Overpowering Apotheosis of Mortal Combat
Is the Illustrious Tableaux of
CUSTER'S LAST STAND AND HEROIC FALL
The world will never see its like again!
Everything Presented is Realism Itself

Audiences throughout England, Scotland and Wales loved every moment of it.

The tour began in pottery-making industrial towns near Hanley before turning west into Wales where the Wild West played in Llandudno, Holyhead, Caernarfon, Portmadoc, Dolgellau and Aberystwyth before side-stepping into Chester, Wrexham and Oswestry and back into Wales to play at Builth Wells, Carmarthen, Pembroke Dock, Llanelli, Neath, Bridgend, Barry Dock and Cardiff. Gloucestershire, Devon, Cornwall, Dorset, Hampshire, Buckinghamshire, Berkshire, Sussex, Surrey and London suburbs followed.

'Carter the Cowboy Cyclist in his wonderful bicycle leap through space,' which hurled him 40ft through the air. Carter was a popular novelty attraction during the Wild West's later tours of the United Kingdom. (Buffalo Bill Museum and Grave, Lookout Mountain, Golden, Colorado)

The Wild West in Surrey – Buffalo Bill with two Indian chiefs, photographed by Thomas Dane between performances at a one-day engagement in Redhill, 17 June 1904. (The American Collection)

Throughout the tour, Bill continued writing letters to his family, friends and business associates. He still demanded news from home and encouraged everyone to correspond with him, however trivial their letters might be. The Campo Bonito gold mine in Arizona was still on his mind. Despite earlier indications that it was on the brink of turning Bill into a millionaire, it had still to yield enough ore to make a profit and he was permanently frustrated trying to keep track of his commercial interests back in America using the mail. To keep them all afloat, Bill continued touring, attempting to generate sufficient funds to keep his enterprises going and his family in the manner to which they had always been accustomed.

In June, Wild West trains steamed north again to Lancashire, Newcastle and Berwick-on-Tweed before crossing into Scotland for a two months long tour of towns and cities in the Highlands and Lowlands. The trains headed south in mid-September, travelling down England's west coast to Barrow-in-Furness, Kendal, Lancaster and Blackpool, through industrial Lancashire and Yorkshire, ending back in Hanley for a final performance at the Agricultural Show Field, Birches Head, on Friday 21 October 1904 – 'Positively the last two performances of Buffalo Bill's Wild West in England – EVER!!' said the *Staffordshire Sentinel*.

It added: 'As a mark of affection for Buffalo Bill, it has been suggested that the popular song of affectionate remembrance "Auld Lang Syne" be sung as a wind-up after the performance.' And, if anyone needed reminding, the words of Robert Burns' old Scottish lament of fondness and farewell was printed in the paper, designed to be cut out and brought along to the showground.

Audience eye-view of the 'Grand Processional Review' at the start of the Wild West viewed from the grandstand at Penzance, Cornwall in 1904. (Denver Public Library)

Following the final performance, the Wild West would be dismantled for the last time on British soil, carted off to the station where Bailey's trains would depart for Liverpool and the steam-ship *Campania* take them to New York. 'All England will join the *Sentinel* in wishing them "Bon Voyage", a long life and prosperity,' said the newspaper.

The *Staffordshire Sentinel* considered it an honour to be the last place in Britain ever to witness a performance by Buffalo Bill's company: 'After tomorrow, Colonel Cody will never again be seen in England as a public character. He expresses the hope that he may in some not far distant day, be permitted to visit the country in a private capacity and enjoy quietly the scenes, the exigencies of his business has prevented him getting the full benefit of.'

The 1904 British tour had been more successful and profitable than the previous year's experience in the wet. Attendance at each performance exceeded the local population in each town by three or four times. Crowds were drawn to shows from scores of surrounding communities and in many cases the amount of cash in circulation was far greater after the Wild West had been in town than it was before. As well as spending money at the turnstiles, cash also changed hands in restaurants, hotels and public houses, in cabs, on trains and in shops. A complaint often heard was that town traders were unable to see the Wild West because they were too busy catering to the needs of customers visiting the show. Tens of thousands of business enterprises of all sizes benefited from having the Wild West visit their hometowns in 1887–8, 1891–2 and 1902–4.

On 2–3 November 1904, the Highland Railway carried nearly 12,000 excursionists to the Wild West in Inverness – nearly 500 coming from the Orkney and Shetland Islands over 200 miles away. Huge numbers also visited from the Isle of Skye.

In his annual report, the Chairman of the Cambrian Railway in Wales stated that the last quarter's 'highly satisfactory' business was largely owed to a visit to Welsh towns by Buffalo Bill's Wild West.

Between 11 and 16 March, Newcastle's tram receipts on the line leading to the Wild West showground were £600 in excess of any other six days in the corporation's history. On 18–19 March, Sunderland's tram receipts were up by £238 ($380).

Major Burke told the *Staffordshire Sentinel*: 'Colonel Cody and the Wild West are public benefactors and bring money out of secret hiding places and put it into circulation. There is always enough money in any country, and if it is in circulation, times are good. If it is kept locked up, times will be hard. Therefore, the man or institution who keeps it in circulation is certainly a friend of the people and should be welcomed as such.'

Bill and his Indians meet a pair of young Cornish children in the Wild West showgrounds in Penzance, May 1904. (Denver Public Library)

As a permanent reminder of the Wild West, the British Bioscope Company made over 300,000 'moving pictures' showing every movement of the entire performance, from William Sweeney and the Cowboy Band playing the Star Spangled Banner and the introduction of the rough riders by Bill, to the final salute and God Save the King. The films were shown to Bill and the press in Manchester before the final performances in Hanley. Colour and sound were, of course missing, but Bill told British Bioscope managers that anyone watching the picture show could easily imagine they were actually attending a performance of the Wild West.

British Bioscope presented Bill with a 'moving picture machine' and ten reels of film containing the entire show to take home to America. The same presentation was later shown up and down Britain in theatres, public halls and other places of entertainment, which a few years later would be given a new name – *cinemas*.

From the *Staffordshire Sentinel*, Saturday 22 October 1904:

Colonel Cody as Buffalo Bill came before an English audience for the last time in Hanley on Friday evening. The audience was an immense one, but it by no means over-taxed the vast seating accommodation. Many were present because they once again wished to look on the face and figure of one of the most wonderful men of his day. Nobody's attention could stray when the Colonel was in the ring. He came on in the grand manner, which is such a remarkable feature of the show, riding like a king into the arena, while his congress of rough riders of the world were already assembled. The audience, as soon as they saw him coming on his beautiful brown charger, which he handled so splendidly, raised a large cheer enough to please the veteran no end.

He made his usual introductory speech in a fine full voice which was distinctly audible to the entire assembly, and the cavalcade got into motion and the audience saw in the searchlight a vast kaleidoscope of colour moving in intercepting circles.

Then followed the usual items, which were remarkable and sensational and after the attack on the settlers' cabin, the entire congress re-appeared, took a turn around the arena and retired, the Colonel, amid great cheers, backing his horse with profound bows until he overtook his departing Indians, and wheeling with a final wave of his hand, he was gone.

There was no final bow. Instead, Bill and his company of 800 rough riders of the world, Indians, roustabouts, blacksmiths, cooks, train drivers, programme and refreshment sellers, remained silently behind the great canvas prairie panorama and listened to 12,500 people singing to them from the arena:

> *Should Auld Acquaintance Be Forgot*
> *And Never Brought to Mind?*
> *Should Auld Acquaintance Be Forgot*
> *And Days o' Lang Syne.*
> *For Auld Lang Syne, my Dear,*
> *For Auld Lang Syne,*
> *We'll Tak' a Cup o' Kindness yet*
> *For Auld Lang Syne . . .*

Opposite: Indians next to a poster advertising the Wild West in the small Cornish town of Bodmin in 1904. Advertising stated that the Wild West was 'now making its Absolutely Final tour of Great Britain – and will Positively Never Return! Don't miss the Last Chance!' Local people were told that the show would 'arrive in three special trains, containing 500 horses, 800 people . . . the entire Grand Programme will positively be presented undivided and uncurtailed.' (Denver Public Library)

243

THE LAST ROUND-UP

I haven't seen him much of late; how does he bear his years?
They say he's making ducats now from shows and not from steers.
He used to be a judge of 'horns', when poured in a tin cup,
And left the wine to tenderfeet, and men who felt 'well up'.
Perhaps he cracks a bottle now, perhaps he's had his fill.
Who cares; Bill Cody was a scout, and all the world knows Bill.

William Annin

A PUBLIC DIVORCE – ESCAPE TO EUROPE – STUCK WITH 'THE SHOW BUSINESS' – BILL AND THE BOTTLE – THE TWO BILLS – ENTER HARRY TAMMEN – THE BAILIFF'S MEN – MOVING PICTURES – A CIRCUS ATTRACTION – DEATH OF BUFFALO BILL – A MOUNTAIN BURIAL – MAJOR BURKE DIES OF A BROKEN HEART

Bill returned to Wyoming determined to go hunting with his pals, including old army friends, some wealthy Englishmen, Major Burke and Chief Iron Tail, who would lead the Wild West's Indian troupe on later tours. He had also promised to take 12-year-old nephew, Walter Goodman, on his first hunting trip, where the boy bagged an elk. 'Uncle Bill' later had the head mounted for the boy.

Bill's daughter, Arta, who had travelled to London to be with her father on his first visit to England, died in Spokane, Washington, in January 1905. Bill used the occasion to send an olive branch to Lulu, suggesting that they bury their differences for the sake of their child and attempt a new life together. Lulu replied that Arta's death was thanks to Bill and his talk of divorce, which had broken her heart. While Bill and Lulu travelled on the same train to their daughter's funeral, Mrs Cody refused to talk to her husband or his sisters. She said she would see them all 'so low that even the dogs would refuse to bark at them', and threatened to denounce the Cody family over the grave of her daughter.

Bill was prepared to surrender any money he had left to buy his freedom and happiness, provided Lulu would quietly divorce him. But no sooner had Bill re-assigned most of his property to Mrs Cody, than the lady turned tail and refused to go along with her estranged husband's wishes.

A divorce trial was held in Cheyenne, Wyoming, in February and March 1905, where there was much talk about Bill's remarkable capacity to consume liquor, his unreasonable behaviour, and accusations of 'intimacy with other women'. Viola

Clemmons' name was mentioned. By now she had divorced her playboy husband and taken a $100,000 settlement. The court heard how Lulu had given Bill a 'love potion' called 'dragon's blood', obtained from a gypsy and poured into her husband's coffee. The potion made Bill violently ill, but Lulu told the court that she had not intended to kill her husband but make him love her more and other women less.

The court was told that Lulu 'was of a quarrelsome nature' and had also turned to the bottle, insulted Bill's guests at Scout's Rest Ranch, verbally abused her husband in front of other people and frequently used 'language so vulgar that it would not bear repeating in front of gentlemen, let alone ladies.'

The court also heard how Bill had always provided for his family. It was revealed that Bill had twice returned to various hotel rooms to find them wrecked by Mrs Cody, who expected – wrongly, as it turned out – to find other women in the room. It was even suggested that Mrs Cody was jealous of attention given to her husband by Queen Victoria, but the judge ordered all references to British royalty removed from the record.

The divorce hearing came to an inconclusive end, and the case was dismissed. Both Bill and Lulu left the court still married, having hung their dirty washing out in public for nothing.

The court heard how Lulu had given Bill a 'love potion' called 'dragon's blood', obtained from a gypsy and poured into her husband's coffee.

Bill fled to Europe with the Wild West on another 'farewell tour' visiting Paris for three months and a long tour of French provincial towns. Bill and Bailey then planned to take the show to Italy, Austria, Hungary, Bavaria, Bohemia, Prussia, Germany, Holland and Belgium. He was reluctant to visit Europe again, but James Bailey wanted the Wild West out of the way so it would not offer competition to his circus interests.

Bailey now owned 75 per cent of the entire Wild West enterprise, having acquired all of Salsbury's shares in the organisation and 'promissory notes' from Bill for large sums of money borrowed to keep his business interests afloat. He was now well and truly stuck with 'the show business' and wrote to a friend in 1906 that following the tour he would 'take everything back to America for several years touring before I retire. . . . Then I hope to live long enough to spend a few years in the land we both love – the dear old Rockies and Plains.'

An outbreak of glanders, a contagious equine disease, killed 200 of the Wild West's 300 horses when the show appeared in Marseilles. The cost of disposing of the animals in an incinerator and buying new horses plunged the show into debt.

In March 1906 while the Wild West was appearing in Rome, news came through that James Bailey had died. While Bailey's wife inherited her husband's share in the enterprise, Bill was left as sole manager and star of the entire Wild West organisation. Mrs Bailey soon made it clear that she intended to sell her share of the business, but until then, the full burden of responsibility for the enterprise rested entirely on Bill's shoulders – and could she please have the money he owed her late husband?

Bill sank into a deep depression – and reached for the bottle.

It is true that Bill Cody enjoyed a drink, but accounts of his drunkenness are probably exaggerated. Buffalo Bill was not an alcoholic. It is unlikely that he was ever drunk immediately before or during a performance, although there may have been occasions when he was 'hung over'. He was too aware of his public persona and status as a role model to young people to allow the smell or effects of liquor to stand in the way of his heroic image.

As a young man out on the plains, in wooden lean-to frontier towns and remote army forts, he enjoyed the company of whisky. He probably enjoyed the contents of a bottle as a touring actor and during his early days with the Wild West. But Nate Salsbury's sobering and sensible influence controlled his drinking, even if it failed to wean Bill completely from the bottle. Thanks to Salsbury, there were long periods when Bill went on the wagon and refused liquor for many months on end. There were other times when he fell off the wagon and sought solace from a bottle.

Stories of Pullman carriages taking Bill and the Wild West across America and Europe stacked to the roof with crates of bourbon are also unlikely. There is evidence that when VIPs were occasionally invited to Bill's private saloon in the train, someone had to be sent out to buy alcohol to offer guests. None was on board. Neither Salsbury nor James Bailey would have tolerated it.

Bill mixed with too many members of the royal family, politicians, artists, writers, actors and civic dignitaries, to have been drunk in public. He would have been shown the door and hounded out of town if he had ever appeared under the influence of drink in the company of eminent Victorians and Edwardians.

But in private and in his own private saloon car, hotel suite or in the 'Pahaska Tepee', when off-duty or a guest of others, he was entitled to relax and let his long hair down and enjoy a drink or two, or three – or more. He could certainly hold more drink than most men, but this author believes that Buffalo Bill Cody was not a drunk, even if liquor sometimes kept him company through the night on never-ending railway journeys on tour.

In later years, Bill realised that heavy drinking affected his work and he needed his wits about him. Without the wise council of either Salsbury or Bailey, Bill had to rely on his own intuition running the Wild West and numerous other business interests. He was determined to remain sober, keep a clear head and make sure others stayed away from the bottle, too. The man who had once loved to drain bottles of whisky with his cronies had little time for drunks in his later years.

By 1905, following his divorce hearing and with financial problems hanging over his head again, Bill Cody was a sober man indeed. In a letter to Julia written from France, he says that in his old age (he was by now 60) he had 'found God . . . and realise how easy it is to abandon sin and serve Him. . . . I have quit drinking entirely. And quit doing rash things simply by controlling my passion and temper when I find myself getting angry, I calm myself down first. . . . This is a pretty decent outfit, no drinking, gambling or swearing in this show. No quarrelling so there is no fighting.'

A more serene Buffalo Bill arrived home in the United States in October and straightaway went to work organising a season in

In his own private saloon car, hotel suite or in the 'Pahaska Tepee', when off-duty he was entitled to relax and let his long hair down and enjoy a drink or two, or three – or more.

Madison Square Garden, New York, followed by two years' of non-stop American touring with one- and two-day performances. By now Bill's fine head of long white hair was thinning and he was forced to wear a hair-piece in the arena to keep up the illusion of looking the same in his 60s as when he first appeared in public as a young man decades before.

Bill now owned just one-third of the Wild West, and that was heavily mortgaged to the bank. In 1906, Bailey's estate began selling off parts of its entertainment empire. Ringling Brothers bought its circus interests while soundings went out to anyone seeking to buy or merge with the Wild West and reduce its huge overheads.

Bill now owned just one-third of the Wild West, and that was heavily mortgaged to the bank.

Gordon W. Lillie – known as 'Pawnee Bill' – ran a Wild West Show, which competed with Bill's version. In 1888 Lillie had worked as an Indian interpreter with Bill's show and left to form his own company. It quickly ran into trouble and folded. In 1890 he tried again and this time made a success of the enterprise, closely copying Bill's formula of combining scenes from western life with horsemanship, fancy rope tricks and slices of Indian culture.

Lillie suggested a Wild West merger, but Bill refused when his rival insisted on changing the show's name to include 'Pawnee Bill's' in the title. Meanwhile, the Baileys started to make life even more difficult for Bill and threatened to close the show. In order to prevent years of hard work disappearing like smoke signals into the sky, he agreed to merge his interests with Lillie's. In 1908, 'Buffalo Bill's Wild West company with Pawnee Bill's Great Far East' – generally known as 'the Two Bills' show' – made its debut. The Bailey estate still retained financial control.

The Two Bills first appeared at New York's Madison Square Garden, where Lillie commissioned thousands of dollars worth of scenery and stage effects, leaving no room for wagons or stagecoaches to enter the arena. Johnnie Baker, in his role as arena director, was furious with Lillie. Bill was reported to be close to tears as opening night approached.

Fortunately the staging problems were resolved and the show played to good houses, before the Baileys appeared on the scene again, insisting that Johnnie Baker and Major Burke be fired. Lillie was offered a chance to buy the entire outfit for $666,666 and become sole owner and Buffalo Bill a mere employee of the show carrying his name. Lillie, however, was a reasonable man and offered Bill half his shares, to be paid from his partner's earnings. Together, the Two Bills dispensed with Bailey's circus and freak show components. The enterprise became a Wild West entertainment once again, with some of Lillie's own acts, 'inspired by scenes from the Orient', thrown in. It was a good compromise. The one time 'Cowboy Kid' and American entertainment's most original publicity man also stayed with the enterprise.

The 1910 season was promoted as Bill's farewell tour – 'positively my last appearance in person in the towns and cities of the present tour. . . . On the honour of Buffalo Bill, my present visit will positively be my last "Hail and farewell" in the saddle to you all,' stated publicity material. He meant it, too, and even made a moving farewell speech from the arena in Madison Square Gardens, telling the public that he was going home for a well-earned rest, to be with his horses, cattle, Indian friends and green fields. 'To my little friends in the gallery and the grown-ups who used to sit there, I thank you once again. God bless you all. Good bye.' Two years later, Bill was still saying goodbye. . . .

The Two Bills made money from their show. Like Salsbury, Lillie invested his profits in property while Bill used his to prop up the ailing Campo Bonito mine in Arizona, ever hopeful that one day it would strike Eldorado. Despite earning good profits, Bill could still not afford to hang up his hat.

In May 1911, a train carrying the show to Massachusetts crashed. Scores of animals escaped from the wreckage, the cowboys rounded them up and the show went ahead as planned. But the rest of the season was poor. Bad weather and small audiences were against them. To raise cash, Bill sold Scout's Rest Ranch and the Irma Hotel to Lillie, in effect wiping off his remaining debt for his half share in the show.

The 1912 'final farewell tour' was profitable, but all of Bill's money went down the mineshaft, never to re-surface. The mine was supposed to finance Bill's retirement. He was now approaching his 70s, desperate to put his feet up at the old TE, but the mine's meagre output was insufficient to pay off his debts – so Buffalo Bill kept on shooting glass balls, saving the Deadwood stagecoach and riding to rescue the emigrant settlers in their log cabin. He badly needed a loan to repay creditors knocking on his door.

Assistance – if that is an appropriate word for what was offered – arrived in the form of an unscrupulous businessman and opportunist called Harry Tammen, part-owner of the *Denver Post* newspaper and a small-time circus operation called Sells-Floto. Tammen agreed to loan Bill $20,000 simply to make the old man solvent again. But strings were attached – miles of them, tying Bill down for the rest of his life . . . and even in death.

A statement was issued stating that Buffalo Bill had joined Sells-Floto Circus – which was news to Bill. Lillie demanded to know what was going on and Bill told him to pay no attention to Tammen's claim. The Two Bills carried on touring during the wet winter of 1913, losing money in every town. Half the Indians deserted. An enlarged prostate gland made it uncomfortable for Bill to ride his horse Isham, so he shot glass balls thrown into the air from a buggy pulled around the arena.

The show eventually arrived in Denver, where Tammen was waiting to call in the $20,000 owed by Bill. He did not have the cash and, to make matters worse, another company owned by Tammen printing programmes and tickets for the Two Bills, demanded payment. When neither of the Bills could produce funds, Tammen sent in bailiffs to seize assets for the full amount owed to himself and the printers, effectively closing the show down.

With no money to pay the company or feed the animals, Bill was brought to his knees. His gold mine in Arizona had bled him of his fortune, failing to produce enough gold to cover his debts and a grade of tungsten ore which was too costly to mine. The remaining Indians were forced to sell their costumes in order to raise

The mine's meagre output was insufficient to pay off his debts – so Buffalo Bill kept on shooting glass balls . . .

money to get home. Bill told his musicians to disappear before the sheriff's men snatched their instruments away. An admirer sent Bill $500, which he used to help some of his stranded workers. Lillie filed for bankruptcy, while Bill saw his horses, cattle, wild animals, wagons, buggies, saddles, bridles, props, costumes and equipment put up for auction at knock-down prices. Bill's favourite horse Isham went under the auctioneer's hammer for $150, bought by a friend, who promptly dispatched the animal to the TE ranch as a gift to Bill.

The demise of the Wild West and the sale of its assets broke Bill's heart. He returned to the old TE ill and downcast. Waiting for him was an offer to visit London and appear in music halls for $2,500 a week. The offer was tempting. It would be a chance to get away from Tammen's clutches, return to a city where he had always been welcome and earn some money. He wrote back asking for $5,000 – but there were no takers.

Meanwhile, Bill was dreaming up new moneymaking ideas from the peace and quiet of the old TE. He was aware that 'moving pictures' were taking off in a big way. Large stores were clearing out stock and projecting short films on to sheets hung from walls, charging a few cents admission. They became known as nickelodeons. Films were also shown in between vaudeville and music hall acts and were popular with audiences.

Now that the medium was beginning to capture the public imagination, why not make a series of films about the life and adventures of Buffalo Bill?

As an experiment, Thomas Edison had filmed seven Wild West episodes using his Kinetoscope system when the Wild West appeared in New York in 1894. In 1897, Edison produced a short film called *Buffalo Bill and Escort*, followed by another capturing one of Bill's parades through the city's streets. Now that the medium was beginning to capture the public imagination, why not make a series of films about the life and adventures of Buffalo Bill, with W.F. Cody himself appearing as he had years before in the theatre?

As usual, Bill needed money to get his ideas off the ground and no one was going to loan him anything while he was still in debt to Tammen. So Bill offered Tammen the project, hoping the wily businessman would loosen his grip and help create an environment to generate new money to repay old debts.

With Tammen as a partner, eight short films were made under the collective title *The Indian Wars*, directed by and starring W.F. Cody and produced in association with Essanay, later responsible for producing Charlie Chaplin's first comedy shorts.

Scenes included the famous duel with Yellow Hand and the Battle of Wounded Knee. Real locations were used and the US Army loaned Bill six hundred members of the 12th Cavalry plus General Miles to ensure authenticity. Bill approached film making with the same zest with which he had created the Wild West years before, directing action scenes and crowds from behind a primitive hand-cranked camera as if he had been in the movie business for years. Sadly all copies are now lost, although fragments of Edison's footage featuring Bill, Annie Oakley, Johnnie Baker and assorted Indians survive.

While the films were being edited for nickelodeons, Bill went out into Sells-Floto's tatty sawdust arena and became one of Tammen's circus acts for $100 a day plus a percentage of ticket receipts. Rheumatism and his inflamed prostate made it agony to ride and he often appeared in the ring riding inside a buggy, but he was determined to buy his way back to freedom.

It has been claimed that Bill started drinking heavily again during this period, filling large beer glasses full of whisky, and tipping back as many as three a day. If this is true, it did not prevent him from giving 366 performances in 183 days. He covered nearly 17,000 miles and was in a state of near collapse when he returned to the TE.

The following year was a little better. His health had slightly improved and Lulu began spending time with her husband for the first time in years. They travelled together in the same railway car and appeared like any other elderly couple, chatting and laughing with each other. Lulu also kept the whisky bottle out of Bill's reach.

When Tammen increased admission prices, using old advertising posters listing out-of-date ticket prices to announce the show's arrival, Bill was furious. He was now reduced to appearing in a third-rate circus charging inflated prices, housed in an old tent held down by rotten guy-ropes.

It was time to quit and he told Tammen he was leaving, his debt fully paid. Two loaded pistols lay on the table as he confronted Tammen inside his tent. Bill became so worked up that his hand occasionally reached for one of the guns. Nervously, Tammen agreed to release Bill at the end of the 1916 tour. But he was not yet finished with Buffalo Bill.

Meanwhile, Bill's 'moving pictures' were ready to be screened and the old showman went out on the road again, exchanging the sawdust arena for some of America's first cinemas. As his films rattled through the projector and flickered on to small screens, the old scout gave a live commentary to smart New York audiences about a place which no longer existed, called the 'frontier'. He told them that this was a place where Indians had once hunted huge buffalo herds, convoys of prairie schooners had carried settlers to new lives, where Pony Express riders rushed mail on horseback and stagecoaches bounced passengers down dusty trails between one wooden town and another. Now it was all gone. Cowboys fought Indians only in dime novels, being needed instead to fight Germans in the war now raging in Europe. They sailed across oceans in huge passenger liners, drove Ford motor cars and even used aeroplanes to carry mail between states. The Wild West was history, yesterday's news, and Buffalo Bill part of its passing.

The Wild West was history, yesterday's news, and Buffalo Bill part of its passing.

The audiences politely listened to the old gentleman with the white hair and beard, more interested in his moving pictures than the words he was saying to accompany them. At the end of the evening they politely applauded and then caught motor taxis and electric powered streetcars home to New Rochelle and Park Avenue.

To raise more cash, Bill sold his services in advance to the Miller Brothers and Arlington 101 Ranch Wild West, a show with a loyal following but in poor financial health. For $100 a day and a share of the profits over $2,750, Buffalo Bill was all theirs. Johnnie Baker was also hired to help devise a new show, co-starring cowboys and Indians, sharpshooters

A rare photograph of Bill with his wife Lulu, taken in 1916, the year before his death. (The American Collection)

plus high jumping horses and acrobats. Demonstrations of cavalry charges and field guns were also included to acknowledge the part America was now playing in the European theatre of war.

The old Deadwood stagecoach made a comeback and some of Bill's Indian friends re-joined the company, but business was mixed and the kind of money Bill expected to earn not forthcoming. First it rained non-stop, then there was a heatwave, neither of which was good for business.

There were times when Bill could hardly sit on his horse due to the agony from his ailing prostate. Johnnie Baker was always there to assist, helping him climb into the saddle and watching as the once great showman sat, chin slumped on his chest, eyes closed, waiting for his entrance. But when the curtains opened, Buffalo Bill came alive again, galloping into the arena, waving his hat in the air, shooting glass balls and looking every inch the old-time western hero. Then he rode out and had to be lifted from his horse and taken to a bed to lie down until it was time to shine again for the public's pleasure.

There had been so many 'final appearances' that no one noticed this one – not even Bill.

Buffalo Bill's final appearance before an audience was in Portsmouth, Virginia, in November 1916. There had been so many 'final appearances' that no one noticed this one – not even Bill. He had planned a Christmas break then a return to the 101 Ranch Wild West the following year, and travelled to Wyoming to attend a dinner given in his honour. He arrived so drained and exhausted that Lulu sent for a doctor, who examined him, told him to rest and cut out smoking.

In January he visited a Colorado sanatorium to take a mineral water cure, but collapsed after two days and was transferred to his sister's home in Denver. Bill was suffering from umeric poisoning, which had caused his heart and kidneys to deteriorate. He knew he was going to die. Newspapers carried stories that there was no hope of Buffalo Bill Cody recovering.

On 9 January, Bill was baptised into the Catholic Church by a priest at his bedside. Lulu, his daughter Irma and his sister looked on. Johnnie Baker was racing from New York to Denver by train to be with 'the Colonel' during his last hours.

That night a doctor came to visit Bill, who asked about his chances for survival. Avoiding giving a straight answer, the doctor replied that there was a time when a physician had to commend his patient to a Higher Power.

'How long?' demanded Bill.

'The sand is slipping away . . .', began the doctor.

'How long?' insisted Bill.

'About thirty-six hours, sir.'

Bill called in his brother-in-law who was waiting in the next room. 'The doc says I've got thirty-six hours. Let's play some cards.'

Opposite: William Frederick Cody – stagecoach driver, army scout, buffalo hunter, Indian fighter, cattle rancher, Wild Westerner, businessman, stock company actor, showman extraordinaire and an American legend. This extraordinary photographic study of Buffalo Bill looking back on his amazing life was taken shortly before his death in 1917. (Henry E. Huntington Library and Art Gallery, San Marino, California)

Buffalo Bill Cody died at 12.05 p.m. on 12 January 1917. Johnnie Baker arrived too late to be with the man who had been a father figure to him. Minutes after the doctor had confirmed Bill's heart had stopped beating, news was telegraphed around the world by Western Union. For a couple of days Buffalo Bill knocked news of the Great War raging in Europe from the front pages of the world's newspapers. He had been making headlines for decades. He was doing it again by taking his final bow. Newspapers said that he had crossed the great divide to join other great scouts on the happy hunting grounds.

President Woodrow Wilson led the tributes. Others came from King George V who had ridden in the Deadwood stagecoach as a boy, from army top brass, politicians, civic dignitaries and people from the world of entertainment. Annie

Oakley – 'Little Sure Shot' – now a silver-haired lady living in retirement with Frank Butler in Maryland, wrote a tribute to her old boss in the local newspaper published in the town named after Bill, the *Cody Enterprise*:

> He was the kindest, simplest, most loyal man I ever knew. He was the staunchest friend. He was in fact the personification of those sturdy and loveable qualities that really made the West and they were the final criterion of all men, East and West. Like all really great gentlemen he was not even a fighter by preference. His relations with everyone he came into contact with were the most cordial and trusting of any man I ever knew.
>
> I travelled with him for 17 years – there were thousands of men in the outfit during that time . . . and the whole time we were one great family loyal to him. His word was better than most contracts. Personally, I never had a contract with the show after I started. It would have been superfluous.
>
> He called me 'Missie' almost from the first, a name by which I have been known to my intimate friends ever since.
>
> It may seem strange that after the wonderful success attained, he should have died a poor man. But it isn't a matter of any wonder to those who knew him and worked with him. The same qualities that insured success also insured his ultimate poverty. His generosity and kind hearted attitude towards all comers, his sympathy and his broad understanding of human nature, made it the simplest thing possible to handle men, both in his show and throughout the whole world. By the same token he was totally unable to resist any claim for assistance that came to him, or refuse any mortal in distress. . . . The pity of it was that not only could anyone that wanted a loan or gift get it for the asking, but he never seemed to lose his trust in the nature of all men, and until his dying day he was the easiest mark above ground for every kind of sneak and goldbrick vendor that was mean enough to take advantage of him . . . .
>
> His heart never left the great West. Whenever the day's work was done, he could always be found sitting alone watching the sinking sun, and at every opportunity he took the trail back to his old home.

Bill's coffin was taken to the Capital Rotunda in Denver, where it lay in state for a day. Over 25,000 people filed past lines of soldiers to pay silent last respects to the great scout and showman. Bill's last horse, McKinley, saddled, bridled and with its stirrups reversed, led the funeral procession in which hundreds of army veterans, boy scouts, freemasons, Elks, cowboys and Indians marched to the sound of a drum and fife band.

Bill's favourite songs were sung before the burial service was read over the coffin. But Bill's burial would not take place for another five months – thanks to Harry Tammen.

Bill's burial would not take place for another five months – thanks to Harry Tammen.

There was confusion over where Bill wished to be buried. His Will stated that he wanted his last resting-place to be on top of Cedar Mountain, overlooking Cody, Wyoming, and he bequeathed $10,000 to cover expenses. Others said he wanted to lie in the earth near the old TE ranch. Leading American cemeteries from Arlington to Omaha offered to take the body of Buffalo Bill into their soil. Louder voices stated that his deathbed wish was to be buried on Lookout

Mountain near Denver, where three other states could be seen from the top – Nebraska, Wyoming and Kansas. The loudest voice was Harry Tammen's who secured a place for himself on a committee deciding where Buffalo Bill should finally rest and used the *Denver Post* to launch an appeal for funds to build a suitable tomb for the old scout.

When it was discovered that Bill's $10,000 to cover funeral and burial costs at Cedar Mountain did not exist, Tammen persuaded Lulu and Johnnie Baker to favour Lookout Mountain. And so Denver – and Tammen – won the day. While a grave was hewn out of mountain granite, lined with concrete, and a 'burglar-proof steel grave vault' made by the Champion Chemical Company of Springfield, Ohio, Bill lay on a slab in the coldroom of a Colorado mortuary.

On the morning of 3 June 1917, over three thousand motor cars and hundreds of horse-drawn carriages snaked to the summit of Lookout Mountain. The motorcade included gaudy circus wagons with the Sells-Floto name painted on the side. It took two hours for the public, shuffling past two abreast, to pass the coffin in the heat of the day. A Masonic burial service was read out, a poem recited and a piece of Masonic regalia dropped into the open grave. 'Taps' was sounded on a bugle and an eleven-gun salute fired into the warm afternoon air.

Major John M. Burke, first of the truly great press agents to become a household name, photographed towards the end of his illustrious career with Buffalo Bill's Wild West. (The American Collection)

Major Burke would have approved of the send-off given to his old boss. But he was not there in person, too ill to travel from his Washington retirement lodgings to mastermind the publicity campaign surrounding Bill's final bow from the public arena. America's first and most original public relations man died in Washington three months after Bill's death.

On 13 April 1917, the *Washington Post* reported:

Indian fighter and many years friend of Buffalo Bill (William F. Cody), Major John M. Burke has answered the last call and gone to join his former chief. Major Burke died in his 75th year early yesterday morning at Providence Hospital. He had been ill since Monday with pneumonia. . . . Major Burke returned to Washington about six months ago, and made his home at the residence of Mrs Allison Nailor, 1315 Fifteenth Street Northwest. He had failed ever since the death of Buffalo Bill last January. The Major sent Buffalo Bill numerous telegrams while the latter was on his deathbed and insisted that the wonderful grit of the great Indian scout would pull him through. When the word came that his old friend had passed away, Major Burke was inconsolable and he was missed from accustomed haunts for several days. When he returned, it was noticed that he was lacking in the buoyancy and cheer that has always marked his appearance. From the day Buffalo Bill died, Major Burke began to pine.

The deaths of Colonel William F. Cody and Major John M. Burke signalled the cue for a Last Post to an era. It was time to ring down the red velvet curtain, gather up the sawdust arena, close the show, send the customers home and – as today's filmmakers might say – fade to black, cue closing titles.

POSTSCRIPTS
AND CURTAIN CALL

Bold as a lion, always a hero
Under hot suns or in frost below zero;
Fearless in battle, tender in woe,
Faithful to friend, relentless to foe;
And now near by Denver, on Mount Lookout's crest,
Lies peacefully sleeping, in unbroken rest . . .
Our hero whose word was his bond.

'A young admirer' in *More Adventures*
with Buffalo Bill (1949)

SALSBURY'S POSTHUMOUS POSTSCRIPT – THE LONDON INDIANS GO HOME
– GLASGOW'S 'GHOST DANCE' SHIRT – 'BUFFALO BILL CAME HERE' – BOOKS,
MOVIES AND MUSICALS – LARGE AS LIFE AT DISNEYLAND-PARIS – LANDMARKS

The Beinecke Library at Connecticut's Yale University contains many rare books and manuscripts in its American literature collection, including private letters, personal papers, scrapbooks, photographs and memorabilia once owned by Nate Salsbury. They were given to the library by Salsbury's daughter, Rebecca, who worked untiringly to preserve his achievements – and some documents are startling to read.

The memoirs that Bill's former business partner was planning to write in retirement were given a draft working title of *Sixteen Years in Hell with Buffalo Bill*. On the surface the title sounds like a typical tongue-in-cheek Salsbury reference to his private and professional relationship with Bill, and the memoirs were never completed. But fragments of manuscript, published in *Colorado Magazine* long after both partners were dead, reveal that he was perfectly serious about the sentiments expressed in the title.

Surprisingly, the good-natured Salsbury emerges as a bitter man, regarding Bill as a drunkard, whose only loyalty was to incompetent cronies. His writing also claims full credit for creating the Wild West as a major entertainment. Salsbury knew that when he wrote the following passage, it would not be popular with his readers:

I know that there will be a world of protest to these lines, but that the Wild West
Show was an invention of my own entirely, is proven by the letters in Cody's own

hand which I have preserved as indeed I have preserved every scrap of writing he had ever signed and addressed to me. It is lovely to be thus fortified against protestations and abuse that would surely follow if proof did not exist of what I have stated.

Salsbury adds:

I should never have put this relation of the origin of the Wild West show on paper if there had not been in all the years that have passed, a most determined effort on the part of John Burke and other hero worshippers who have hung on to Cody's coat-tails for their sustenance, to make Cody the originator of the show, for in doing so they can edge in their own feeble claims to being an integral part of the success of the show. The men I speak of were all participants in the failure that followed the first venture by Cody and were retained in the management of the show by me at the request of Cody, who lives in the worship of those who bleed him.

'Burke and Keen and the rest of the Codyites have never forgiven me . . .'

It is just as surprising to read Salsbury's opinions of Major Burke and Wild West Treasurer, Jule Keen:

Burke and Keen and the rest of the Codyites who have followed the show from the day I took hold of it have never forgiven me for taking the reins of management out of their hands where they had been placed by Cody and Carver. They have always resented me because it unseated their hero in the business saddle of the show, which needed someone that could ride it.

Mind you, I do not wish to detract from any merit these gentlemen have shown in their employment, for taking Burke as an instantaneous picture he is the limit. In his particular position of almoner general to the newspapermen of the world, Burke has more personal friends than any man I ever knew. I do not believe there is another man in the world who could have covered as much space in the newspapers of the day as John Burke has done and I do not believe there is another man in the world in his position that would have had the gall to exploit himself at the expense of the show as much as John Burke!

Salsbury writes that Jule Keen,

. . . is honest and able in his department but that lets him out. He has absolutely nothing else to make him of value to any show. I mention these two men because they have been prominent in the affairs of the show, the small fry don't count for much in this summing up.

Strangely for someone who was himself once a headline performer, Salsbury always insisted on remaining in the shadows, allowing Bill to stand in the limelight. He appreciated that Buffalo Bill was the star and the main attraction audiences paid to see. If he had wished to satisfy his actor's ego, Salsbury could have insisted on having a featured part in the Wild West. As an accomplished performer in everything from Shakespeare to vaudeville, he would have been perfectly cast as the show's orator, the only company member on view for the duration of the proceedings.

But Salsbury never demanded a performing part in the Wild West. In July 1887 he told the British newspaper *Topical Times*:

> I have been before the public for the past twenty years as an actor. For the last twelve years I have had the assurance to pose as a star in the combination known as The Salsbury Troubadours – a company which has, and still continues to enjoy, a reputation second to none in attractiveness. Feeling my responsibility in the Wild West as general director, I have discontinued acting for the time being, and probably for ever. From the present outlook, it is likely that the Wild West will command my attention for several years to come.

Salsbury knew both his strengths and weaknesses. Although he had enjoyed success on the American stage, he knew he could never command the same respect in the English theatre.

'I have played every line of business known to the footlights – that is everything from Hamlet down.'

> I have played every line of business known to the footlights – that is everything from Hamlet down. I have played all kinds of dialects and dignified parts – Shylock for example. I played that part a great number of times. But if you were to ask me if you are ever likely to see the Salsbury Troubadours in England, that is a question I cannot reply to. I think this (British) market is already overstocked; and for an American company to come to England, which is the home of tragedy, comedy, burlesque and farce is very much like carrying coals to Newcastle. I question very much whether I could show the English public anything that they have not already seen.

So Salsbury concentrated on doing what he knew better than anyone in America or England – presenting ground-breaking large-scale public spectaculars and taking them to as many people as possible. If he ever felt the public needed reminding about his contribution to the Wild West's success – which was considerable – he could have ordered Major Burke to arrange more interviews with journalists writing for newspapers from New York to Newcastle. But he chose not to. He rarely made comments to newspapermen when the show arrived in town, being too busy organising the business end of a tour to stand still for more than two minutes and be interviewed.

Salsbury's resentment towards Bill during the closing years of his life is therefore hard to understand. Nate Salsbury was always credited as co-presenter of the Wild West. His photograph wearing a black Derby hat appeared on Wild West posters and alongside biographical sketches in show programmes. The 1892 programme for the Wild West's second season at Earls Court clearly states:

> The Amusement Department will be under the personal supervision of this eminent actor, whose successful career is now a matter of American Stage History. . . . The Wild West will be presented in a manner and style commensurate with his well-known managerial ability and artistic judgement. Mr Salsbury long ago invested in the cattle business in Montana, and is now part owner of one of the largest and most valuable ranches in the Northwest. During his repeated visits to the same he became impressed with the scenes and episodes witnessed, and thought of the feasibility

of presenting them as far as practicable to citizens of the East. An interchange of opinions with Col. Cody disclosed a similar intention, so that to the fertile brains of Messrs Cody and Salsbury, we are indebted for the first conjuring up of this novel project.

'Buffalo Bill was a most *difficult person to deal with.'*

Bill continued to credit Salsbury on Wild West publicity material long after his partner had retired, too ill to carry on. Advertisements for the 1903 Olympia season in London state that parts of the show 'are under the direction of Mr Nate Salsbury'. Buffalo Bill's own later accounts of his life with the Wild West were also fulsome in their praise of Salsbury, who received numerous mentions – all of them admiring and generous – about the man he called his 'pard'.

Perhaps Salsbury's bitterness stemmed from a quest for perfection. His papers also include unpublished poems and plays never produced. Was he secretly a frustrated writer and artist, never satisfied with the quality of his own performances? Or was he simply in awe of his star performer's charisma? Perhaps we should give the last words on this matter to Mr Nate Salsbury of New Burn, North Carolina, grandson of Nate Salsbury the showman, who told this author: 'I have concluded that Buffalo Bill was a *most* difficult person to deal with – a person greatly impressed by his own greatness. You and I have seen many such personalities in our lifetime.'

The two Native Americans who died while appearing with Bill at the 1892 Earls Court season finally returned home to South Dakota in 1997.

Long Wolf, the Oglala Sioux Chief who died from pneumonia and Star, 20-month-old daughter of Ghost Dog, killed after falling from a saddlebag in the arena weeks later, were buried together in Brompton cemetery, near Earls Court. They remained in alien territory for 105 years, lost but not forgotten by relations back in the Black Hills of South Dakota.

But they were far from lost to scores of people daily walking dogs, jogging, cycling, roller-blading and skateboarding through the wide, shady avenues separating 60,000 tombs and monuments. They knew where the tall stone cross marking the resting place of the old Chief and the young papoose was located, along with graves of suffragette leader Emmeline Pankhurst, tenor Richard Tauber, cricketer John Wisden and 'Gentleman' John Jackson the bare-knuckle boxer. The resting-place of Long Wolf and Star was well known, recorded and easy to locate, provided you knew where to look and whom to ask.

Their return to South Dakota was the culmination of a six-year campaign which began when Worcestershire housewife, Elizabeth Knight, found a dog-eared book in a local flea market containing a lament on Long Wolf's burial, written by Robert Cunningham Grahame, an adventurer, politician and friend of Buffalo Bill. Grahame's poetic lament stated that the Chief lay neglected in a lone corner of a crowded London cemetery, lost in thick ranks of palefaces, 'waiting for the last war whoop'. Native Americans believe that a spirit cannot rest until a body is brought home to lie in native soil.

Elizabeth Knight visited the grave with a wolf symbol carved on to the cross, the howling image of his namesake still discernible despite the ravages of London's weather. She then began searching for Long Wolf's descendants through an advertisement in the American newspaper *Indian Country Today*. John Black Feather, the old Chief's great-great-grandson living in Tempe, Arizona, saw the advertisement. He said that his mother, Jessie, had been trying to locate her grandfather's resting-place for years. Descendants of Star's family were also found living near Wounded Knee.

It took years to cut through British and American red tape to bring the Native Americans home. The cost was estimated at $15,000 for exhumation expenses and travel. Fund raising took place on both sides of the Atlantic and over 100 people contributed. When money was finally raised, and hundreds of forms and permits applied for, submitted and rubber-stamped by British and American governments and mortuaries in both countries, a small delegation from the Oglala Lakota nation in South Dakota finally arrived in England to bring their ancestors home.

The Cody family still technically owned the cemetery plot containing Long Wolf and Star, and permission was given by Bill's descendants in Wyoming to open up the grave. The Surrey branch of an American funeral company, which offered its services free, carried out the exhumation. Large screens were placed around the plot and a mechanical digger, normally used to remove earth covering burst water pipes, was brought in to dig 13 ft down in a tight space measuring just 7 ft long and 3 ft wide.

John Black Feather, a great grandson of Chief Long Wolf, wearing an eagle-feathered head-dress, leads a procession in London's Brompton cemetery bringing the remains of his ancestor home to his tribal lands in September 1997. (Photograph: Alan Gallop)

Once the remains were located, Long Wolf's descendants gathered around the grave to sing songs: 'Takala kun miye ca/ohitiye waun kun/wana henamala yelo.' ('*My people, take courage/a warrior I have been/Now I am no more.*')

The last remains of Long Wolf and Star – their tribal ornaments still intact – were wrapped in buffalo hides, placed in a single coffin draped in the Sioux flag and the Stars and Stripes and loaded on to a dray-carriage pulled by two black horses. A single drum was sounded by a tribal medicine man as Native American mourners wearing eagle-feathered head-dresses led a procession from the graveside to a church near Earls Court where a farewell service for Long Wolf and Star took place in front of 200 people.

Like everything else connected with Buffalo Bill and his Indians, the occasion was a media circus and Major Burke would have approved of the press turnout that day and the resulting coverage on the evening television news and next day's national newspaper pages in Britain and the United States.

When Long Wolf and Star finally arrived home, their remains were laid in a tepee before entering the ground once more in Wolf Creek Community, the ancestral burial grounds on the open plains of the Pine Ridge Indian Reservation at Wounded Knee. At the gravesides, a medicine man said prayers to the four winds, in which the souls of Long Wolf and Star would travel. They were home at last.

Watched by a large posse of British and American news reporters, photographers and TV camera crews, the coffin containing the remains of Chief Long Wolf and Star Ghost Dog, is loaded on to a dray cart at London's Brompton cemetery before the long journey to their final resting place near Pine Ridge. (Photograph: Alan Gallop)

In the summer of 1999 the remains of Paul Eagle Star were rescued from the 'Boot Hill' section of Brompton cemetery and taken back to his native earth on the plains of South Dakota in a much quieter fashion. There were no reporters or television cameras around when the remains of his coffin were located beneath another, which had been buried on top in the crowded cemetery. This quiet and unpublicised act was carried out and funded by private individuals who managed to avoid the media circus which had surrounded the departure of Long Wolf and Star.

The bloodstained 'Ghost Dance' shirt, supplied to Glasgow's Kelvingrove Museum in 1891 by George Crager, was spotted by an American lawyer of Cherokee descent called John Earl, while on a tour of Scotland in 1992. Earl reported his find to the Wounded Knee Survivors' Association, which campaigns for the rights of Sioux Indians.

Members wrote to the Glasgow museum asking for the shirt to be returned and when the request was refused, the Indians appealed to the city council. The public was asked to make its views known and a public forum held at which a Sioux representative made a strong case for the shirt to be returned, although Glasgow's Lord Provost, Pat Lally, was against it.

The story ends on a happy note, however. Glasgow's 'Ghost Dance' shirt was returned to the South Dakota Historical Society's Cultural Heritage Centre in Pierre, South Dakota in July 1999 at a special ceremony at which Native American chants were sung and a Scottish piper played a lament. The shirt will remain on show until a museum devoted to the cultural life of the plains Indians near Wounded Knee Creek is created – although it will be some years before this is opened.

Buffalo Bill rode off into the sunset over 80 years ago, but he lives on in Britain thanks to memories and recollections passed down from one generation to another. There are plenty of people still around who recall grandparents proudly telling how they saw the great Buffalo Bill perform in their town. Many still possess dog-eared copies of the 100-page souvenir programmes, which sell for hundreds of pounds at collectors' auctions. Others own ageing, sepia coloured postcards showing Bill, wearing fringed buckskins, leather boots, a large hat with a turned-up brim on top of his flowing locks, leaning on his rifle and standing in front of painted scenery at the London studios of society photographers Elliot & Fry in 1892. A similar print is included in the Royal Archives at Windsor Castle (see page 52).

Some can still point to a house he once stayed in, a street he walked down or a piece of land in a gloomy industrial landscape, which for a day or two long ago came alive and was transformed into the rugged frontier of the American Wild West, complete with cowboys and Indians.

Television, films, plays, books, museums, visitor attractions and the Internet continue to keep his name and fame alive. Bill still appears with regularity in the world's newspapers and magazines, and there are times when it seems as if Major Burke's spirit is still pulling the publicity strings.

Bill's death prompted publishers to re-issue old books and produce new ones – fact and fiction – about his adventures. A surge of dime novels about the western hero appeared throughout the 1920s and '30s, making way for illustrated comic book stories in the 1940s.

Buffalo Bill books were still being printed in the 1950s when British company, Aldine (later The Popular Press), produced a new collection of stories every December – 'an ideal Christmas stocking filler for every right-minded boy'. They were full of action-packed stories, drawings and tips about how to survive when your wagon train is attacked by savage Indians – just the thing imaginative post-war British youngsters needed to read during the dark years of rationing and austerity following the Second World War. The stories were worth remembering because readers from Croydon to Carlisle never knew when they might have to skin a grizzly bear, share a peace-pipe with a Sioux Chief, extract water from a cactus or capture a bandit appearing on a 'Wanted' poster.

Readers never knew when they might have to skin a grizzly bear, share a peace-pipe with a Sioux Chief, extract water from a cactus or capture a bandit . . .

The books were edited by Wingrove Willson, who also contributed some stories under his own name and others under pseudonyms such as 'Buck Ingham', 'G. Clabon Glover' and 'Nat Knowlden'. The 1951 edition begins: 'My dear Chums . . . I hope you will find much pleasure in taking the trail again with our trusty friend Buffalo Bill. He is a good companion – as steadfast and true as he is brave and unyielding. That we may all be as worthy of that tribute as was the Great Chief of Scouts, is the sincere wish of your Editor-chum.'

The writing style in Buffalo Bill books and annuals remains much the same from Ned Buntline's *Buffalo Bill, the King of the Border Men* (1869) to Buck Ingham's *The Making of a Man*, appearing in the 1949 British edition of *More Adventures with Buffalo Bill*, in which cowboys confront each other and growl 'draw'; Indians greet scouts and exclaim 'how!' and bandits are reformed by Buffalo Bill and go on to become lawmen, broncobusters and state senators.

Buffalo Bill has never been far away from the cinema. Following his earliest personal appearances for Edison, actors have played the role of William F. Cody in nearly 40 feature films, starting with Art Accord in the Universal Pictures serial *In the Days of Buffalo Bill* (1923) and George Waggner in John Ford's epic *The Iron Horse* (1924) to Tim McCoy in *The Indians are Coming* (1930), Roy Rogers in *Young Buffalo Bill* (1940), Joel McCrea in *Buffalo Bill* (1944), Charlton Heston in *Pony Express* (1953) and Paul Newman in *Buffalo Bill and the Indians – or Sitting Bull's History Lesson* (1976).

Many films are cinema versions of the dime novels, taking Buffalo Bill's life as their basis and then placing his character into fictional situations. Robert Altman's *Buffalo Bill and the Indians* is one of the more interesting. Produced for America's bi-centennial celebrations in 1974, the picture is set at the Wild West's winter camp where Bill (Paul Newman) and Nate Salsbury (Joel Grey) bring in a new crowd-pleaser for the next season in the shape of Chief Sitting Bull (Frank Kaquitts), while Ned Buntline (Burt Lancaster) tells tall tales about Bill's early life in a nearby saloon, waiting for his protégé to give him a royal welcome.

The film is perfectly cast and also includes Geraldine Chaplin as Annie Oakley, Kevin McCarthy as Major Burke and Harvey Keitel as nephew Ed Goodman. The actors and sets wonderfully re-create the look of the Wild West. But the script, loosely based on a Broadway stage play called *Indians* by Arthur Kopit, lets the film down – along with the director's annoying 'trademark' habit of allowing dialogue to overlap. The film attempts to show that Buffalo Bill, portrayed as a drunken womaniser, idolised by his cronies, could never tell where reality ended and fiction began. To Altman's Buffalo Bill, they are one and the same thing, with no dividing line.

The only place in the world where visitors can experience something of what Buffalo Bill's Wild West was like in its hey-day.

Annie Oakley was also immortalised on celluloid, most notably by Barbara Stanwick in *Annie Oakley* (1935) and in a long-running American television series produced in the 1950s and starring Gail Davis as Annie, who has left the Wild West to become a female law enforcer.

Irving Berlin's stage musical, *Annie Get Your Gun*, probably did more to introduce Annie Oakley to new audiences than any other medium since her years with Bill. The show, originally produced in 1946 with Ethel Merman as Annie, ran for three years on Broadway and has since been produced all over the world, including a Tony award-winning revival in New York in 1999. The show was turned into a film starring Betty Hutton (replacing Judy Garland, who was fired) in 1950.

Buffalo Bill lives on in Europe too. He still appears twice-nightly with the Wild West. Thousands cheer as Bill rides in to rescue the Deadwood stagecoach, 'Annie Oakley' shoots at targets, cowboys perform rope tricks, demonstrate riding skills and drive cattle across the empty plains. Indians hunt buffalo, there is a rodeo and even 'Chief Sitting Bull' makes a personal appearance.

Where? The only place in the world where visitors can experience something of what Buffalo Bill's Wild West was like in its hey-day is at Marne-la-Vallée, on the eastern outskirts of the French capital – better known as Disneyland Resort Paris.

Disney never short-changes customers and its re-creation of Buffalo Bill's Wild West is no exception. Using modern-day production techniques to blend the best of the Hollywood western with old-time rodeo skills, it captures the show's original spirit in a huge indoor arena. The performers are all 'real' cowboys and Indians, too.

On arrival, the audience congregates in a large reception area where they can view horses appearing with the show in their stalls. There are original Wild West posters, handbills and photographs on display and an assortment of pistols and rifles in show cases. Some of Frederic Remington's limited edition bronze sculptures of broncobusters decorate a bar, and a cowboy trio entertains the crowd.

As the audience takes its places around the vast arena, they are given cowboy hats.

The show's programme describes the show as 'America with a capital "A", the America that Europeans dream of' which is just what Bill had in mind when he crossed the Atlantic with the Wild West for the first time in 1887.

As the audience takes its places around the vast arena, they are given cowboy hats. They sit down to enjoy a dinner of corn bread, chilli, sausage, chicken and ribs. There is corn on the cob and apple pie, and all the beer or Coca-Cola you can drink. And then it's show time. . . .

An actor, who is also a skilled rider, plays the part of Buffalo Bill, and he certainly looks the part. In no time the arena is full of cowboys and Indians, horses, wagons and an overland stagecoach. As well as watching it, you also smell it, as you wave your cowboy hat in the air and cheer on your favourite rough rider in a relay race.

Yes, it's show business – but it is also highly entertaining, brilliantly staged, re-creating the magic that audiences of all ages and nationalities encountered when they turned out in their millions to see Buffalo Bill travel 'eastward ho' over a century ago.

Most of the sites where Buffalo Bill's Wild West performed on its tours of England, Wales and Scotland have vanished under bulldozers and have become centres of today's consumerism – housing estates, shopping malls, business parks, sports stadiums or motorways.

Earls Court and Olympia still present exhibitions, rock concerts and operas with large casts. Earls Court today looks different from 1887 when the American Exhibition and Buffalo Bill's Wild West were the first attractions presented there. No original buildings are left, but the same private houses, which once backed on to the Wild West arena, remain. The underground railway network brings thousands of people to Earls Court station daily to visit exhibitions, trade shows and lavish entertainment spectacles, just as it did when Victoria was Queen of the British Empire and Buffalo Bill was King of the Border Men.

For many years, Olympia was winter home to Bertram Mills' Circus, and scores of animals once again appeared in its sawdust arena in the 1950s as they had when Bill's horses and cattle took up residence in 1902.

Travellers to America's Midwest have a far better chance of finding places associated with Buffalo Bill's life and times. The Buffalo Bill Historical Center in Cody, Wyoming, is the most complete depository of items related to his life and adventures, a dazzling museum and a tribute to the town's original founder. It includes a firearms museum and another devoted to Native American Indians. The Whitney Gallery of Western Art is also included, along with an extensive research library.

The town of Cody itself is still a thriving community where Bill's spirit lives on in its streets and buildings – especially the Irma Hotel, 'Buffalo Bill's Hotel in the Rockies', named after his youngest daughter and still very much open for business.

The Buffalo Bill Dam, located above the Shoshone River, dates from 1905. Over the years it has helped turn the virtual desert of the Big Horn Basin into one of Wyoming's most fertile farming regions, irrigating 93,000 acres. Bill raised the initial funds for the project, which was finally completed in 1910 after several contractors went bust as bad weather and floods hindered their work.

Scout's Rest Ranch in North Platte, Nebraska, is a popular visitor attraction located near Cody Park, scene of Bill's first Wild West show. Standing in the park is a fine, full-size, bronze statue of Bill in his western clothing. British artist, Bryan Micklelburgh, skilfully created it in 1998 as a gift to the citizens of the United States. Lloyds of London valued the piece at $250,000. Bryan's bronze heads of Buffalo Bill have been exhibited at London's Royal Academy and are much sought after by collectors of western art.

There is little chance that the man responsible for introducing the world to the western will ever be forgotten.

Lookout Mountain, where Bill rests alongside Lulu – who joined him in 1921 – is home to another museum dedicated to Buffalo Bill, and founded by Johnnie Baker. It is situated next door to 'a grave with a view' – and publicity material describes Colonel and Mrs Cody's last resting place as 'overlooking the Great Plains and the Rockies. Feel the breezes from the high peaks of the Continental Divide, smell the Ponderosa Pines . . .'. The museum exhibits an excellent collection of artefacts from Bill's life, western art and firearms. It also presents various 'live' events annually, including a re-creation of Bill's burial ceremony 'concluded by a cannon salute', a lookalike contest, and 'Buffalo Bill Days' when people wear clothing from the old west.

With such a legacy, and so much of Buffalo Bill still in evidence, there is little chance that the man responsible for introducing the world to the western in the closing years of the nineteenth century and early years of the last one will ever be forgotten in the new Millennium.

Boys, what a wonderful life he spent
In daring deeds wherever he went!
Long may his exploits healthily thrill –
Let's take our hats off to Buffalo Bill!

'A young admirer' in
More Adventures with Buffalo Bill (1949

ROUND-UP OF BUFFALO BILL'S BRITISH WILD WEST TOURS 1887–1904

1887–8 'Golden Jubilee' Wild West Season:

Earls Court, London : 9 May–31 October 1887
Aston Lower Grounds, Birmingham : 6–26 November 1887
Manchester Racecourse, Salford : 14 December 1887–30 April 1888
Holderness Road Football Ground, Hull : 5 May 1887

1891–2 London and Regional Wild West Tour:

The season opened in Leeds in June 1891 followed by one- or two-week visits to Liverpool, Manchester, Sheffield, Nottingham, Birmingham, Leicester, Cardiff, Bristol, Portsmouth, Brighton, Croydon, Glasgow and a second engagement at Earls Court, London between May–July 1892 (with a side trip for a one-off private afternoon performance at Windsor Castle on 25 June 1892).

1902–3 'Final Farewell' Tour of England & Wales by 'Buffalo Bill's Wild West & Congress of Rough Riders of the World':

The tour opened on December 26 1902 at The Olympia, London for a 14-week season ending on 4 April 1903. The show then travelled to Manchester for an engagement between 13 April–2 May before moving on to Liverpool between 4 and 23 May. With the exception of a two-week engagement in Birmingham (1–13 June) and a week in Cardiff (6–11 July), the show played mostly one-day engagements (with occasional two- or three-day bookings) in nearly 90 other English and Welsh towns and cities, starting in Warrington on 25 May and ending in Burton-on-Trent on 23 October. Thanks (again) to Major John M. Burke, who commissioned a detailed map of routes covered on the 1902–4 tours, we know that the Wild West travelled a distance of 2,881 miles by rail, plus an additional 269 miles from railway sidings to showgrounds and back again on 'Buffalo Bill Express' trains in 1903.

An A–Z of other towns visited in 1903 is as follows:

Aberdare	Grantham	Plymouth
Abergavenny	Great Yarmouth	Portsmouth
Ashford	Guildford	Ramsgate
Banbury	Halifax	Reading
Bangor	Hastings	Rhyl
Barnstaple	Hereford	Rugby
Bedford	Ipswich	Ruabon
Birkenhead	Keighley	Salisbury
Boston	Kettering	Sheffield
Bournemouth	Kidderminster	Shrewsbury
Bradford	King's Lynn	Southampton
Brighton	Leamington	Southend
Bristol	Leeds	Spalding
Burton	Leicester	Stafford
Bury St Edmunds	Leyton	Swindon
Canterbury	Lincoln	Taunton
Chatham	Llanelli	Tunbridge Wells
Cheltenham	Loughborough	Wakefield
Chesterfield	Lowestoft	Warrington
Colchester	Luton	Watford
Coventry	Maidstone	Wellingborough
Croydon	Margate	Westbury
Derby	Newark	Weston-super-Mare
Dudley	Newton Abbot	Weymouth
Eastbourne	Northampton	Wisbech
Ely	Norwich	Wolverhampton
Exeter	Nottingham	Worcester
Folkestone	Oxford	Yeovil
Gloucester	Peterborough	

1904 'Positively The Last and Final Farewell Tour' of England, Wales & Scotland by 'Buffalo Bill's Wild West & Congress of Rough Riders of the World':

The tour opened in Stoke-on-Trent on April 24 and ran through until 21 October 1904 when the Wild West eventually made its 'final' UK appearance in Stoke-on-Trent – just a few miles away from where the season had originally begun six months earlier. In between, the company played short engagements in 130 other towns and cities, travelling 4,114 miles by rail and a further 441 miles from railway sidings to showgrounds and back again. Following the tour, the Wild West sailed 3,025 miles from Liverpool back to New York – covering around 10,000 miles in seven months.

An A–Z of other places visited by the Wild West in 1904 is as follows:

Aberdeen	Fraserburgh	Pembroke Dock
Aberystwyth	Gainsborough	Penrith
Aldershot	Galashiels	Penzance
Arbroath	Glasgow	Perth
Ashton-under-Lyme	Glossop	Peterhead
Ayr	Great Grimsby	Plymouth
Barnsley	Greenock	Poole
Barrow-in-Furness	Harrogate	Portmadoc
Barry Dock	Hawick	Preston
Berwick-on-Tweed	Hexham	Redhill
Blackburn	High Wycombe	Rochdale
Blackpool	Hitchin	Rotherham
Bodmin	Holyhead	Saltcoats
Bolton	Horsham	Scarborough
Bridgend	Huddersfield	Skipton
Bridgewater	Hull	South Shields
Builth Wells	Huntley	Southampton
Burnley	Ilford	Southport
Bury	Ilkstone	St Albans
Camborne	Inverness	St Helens
Cambridge	Kendal	Stirling
Cardiff	Kilmarnock	Stockport
Carlisle	Kirkaldy	Stockton-on-Tees
Carmarthen	Lancaster	Stourbridge
Caernarvon	Leigh	Stranraer
Castleford	Lewes	Stroud
Chester	Llandudno	Sunderland
Chorley	Llanelli	Taunton
Coatbridge	Macclesfield	Torquay
Crewe	Mansfield	Trowbridge
Darlington	Maryport	Truro
Dolgellau	Middlesbrough	Walsall
Dorchester	Montrose	Wellington
Dumbarton	Motherwell	Wells
Dumfries	Neath	West Hartlepool
Dundee	Newbury	Whitehaven
Dunfermline	Newcastle upon Tyne	Wigan
Durham	North Shields	Wimbledon
Edinburgh	Northwich	Winchester
Elgin	Nuneaton	Windsor
Exmouth	Oldham	Workington
Falkirk	Oswestry	Wrexham
Forfar	Paisley	York

FURTHER READING

A number of books have provided valuable background material on the life of William F. Cody. Many are now out of print and/or difficult to obtain, necessitating much browsing through second-hand bookshelves, which this author regards as pleasure rather than pain. The Internet, however, is a great time saver and a fast way of locating rare books. Many titles listed below were found through bookshops offering 'on line' services via the World Wide Web:

Cody, W.F. *The Life of Buffalo Bill* – originally published in 1879, now available in various editions. This was Bill's first attempt at producing an 'autobiography' and large parts were 'ghost-written' – probably by Colonel Prentiss Ingraham. It ends as Bill's theatrical career is at its height and he prepares to take a new play to England. The Wild West and his conquests of the United States and Europe were still to come. This edition is quite easy to find and has been re-printed many times.

Cody, W.F. *Story of the Wild West and Campfire Chats*, Eastern Publishing Co., Boston, 1889. This is the second 'autobiography' and the hand of Major John M. Burke is very much in evidence. The book includes the birth of the Wild West and its first journey across the Atlantic and triumphant season in London for Queen Victoria's Jubilee in 1887. Some editions of the book include drawings by the great American artist and friend of Buffalo Bill, Frederic Remington. Out of print and difficult to find.

Cody, W.F. *Autobiography of Buffalo Bill*, originally published in New York in 1920, now published on the Internet by The West Film Project (www:pbs. org/weta/thewest). More or less a re-write of the first two books, with extra bits added and others taken away. Thanks to the Internet, the book is available to everyone.

Cody, Helen Wetmore. *Buffalo Bill – Last of the Great Scouts*, originally published by the Duluth Press Publishing Company in 1899 and reprinted by University of Nebraska Press in 1965. Bill's sister idolised her elder brother and refused to hear a bad word about him. Originally produced by the publishing company Bill bought for his sister's husband, it is full of inaccuracies, but was a great success when it first appeared during the great days of the Wild West. A wagonload of books plus an Indian would be positioned next to the ticket office. The Indian would dance and copies of the book would be sold for $1 with a fifty cent admission ticket thrown in for good measure.

The book sold well on both sides of the Atlantic and is easy to find in second-hand bookshops – but don't believe everything you read inside.

Cody, Louisa. *Memories of Buffalo Bill*, D. Appleton & Co., 1919. When Bill died, his wife needed to generate an income and wrote this glowing tale of a blissful life and happy marriage, even though she had publicly attempted to divorce him and drag the name of Buffalo Bill through the mud. It quickly went out of print and, thankfully, remains there.

Foote, Stella Adelyne. *Letters from Buffalo Bill*, Foote Publishing Co., Billings, Montana, 1954. A fascinating insight into Buffalo Bill's personality through good times and bad, told in a series of letters to family and friends. Some letters from Bill's nephew, Ed Goodman, from England to his family back in America in 1887–8 are also included, providing a unique eye-witness account of Buffalo Bill's time in the country. Sadly the book is now out of print, but well worth searching for.

Blackstone, Sarah J. *The Business of Being Buffalo Bill*, Praeger, 1988. More letters to and from Buffalo Bill with an interesting appendix covering the Campo Bonito mine in Arizona and legal agreements with Nate Salsbury and Harry Tammen. The book is still in print at the time of going to press.

Sayers, Isabelle S. *Annie Oakley and Buffalo Bill's Wild West*, Dover Publications Inc., 1981. A well-written and illustrated account of Annie Oakley's life and times with Buffalo Bill. Still available in the United States.

Russell, Don. *The Lives and Legends of Buffalo Bill*, University of Oklahoma Press, 1960. The definitive biography of Buffalo Bill, meticulously researched and beautifully written. Easily available in the United States and well worth reading for its passion for detail.

Walsh, Richard J. and Salsbury, Milton S., *The Making of Buffalo Bill – A Study in Heroics*, A.L. Burt Company/The Crescent Library, New York, 1928. The book was intended to be a collaboration between Walsh and Nate Salsbury's oldest son, Milton, who died before the first chapter was written. As a result, any special insight into the mind of Nate Salsbury, which might have been originally intended, is lacking in the book, which was one of the first of its kind to tell the true story of Buffalo Bill and the man behind the myth. Now out of print.

Croft-Cooke, Rupert and Meadmore, W.S. *Buffalo Bill: The Legend, the Man of Action, the Showman*, Sedgwick and Jackson, London, 1952. The book, which more or less re-introduced the 'real' Buffalo Bill to the world, is little more than a re-telling of Walsh and Salsbury's book, with plenty of important sections missing.

Foreman, Carolyn Thomas. *Indians Abroad*, University of Oklahoma Press, 1943. The story of how Europe became fascinated with Native Americans in the eighteenth and nineteenth centuries and what the Indians themselves thought of the things they heard, saw and experienced. Long out of print.

Wilson, R. L. with Martin, Greg. *Buffalo Bill's Wild West – An American Legend*, Greenhill Books, London, 1998. A lavishly illustrated volume produced to coincide with the Buffalo Bill exhibition at the Royal Armouries in Leeds during the summer of 1998. A superb companion piece to any other book about Buffalo Bill mentioned here, it includes numerous images from the Michael Del Castello Collection of the American West, the Buffalo Bill Historical Centre, Cody, Wyoming, and the Autry Museum of Western Heritage, Los Angeles, California. Still in print and easy to obtain in both the UK and United States.

INDEX

Note to readers: page numbers in *italics* refer to illustrations